Constitutional Review and International Investment Law

Constitutional Review and International Investment Law

Deference or Defiance?

DAVID SCHNEIDERMAN

Great Clarendon Street, Oxford, OX2 6DP,
United Kingdom

Oxford University Press is a department of the University of Oxford.
It furthers the University's objective of excellence in research, scholarship,
and education by publishing worldwide. Oxford is a registered trade mark of
Oxford University Press in the UK and in certain other countries

© David Schneiderman 2024

The moral rights of the author have been asserted

All rights reserved. No part of this publication may be reproduced, stored in
a retrieval system, or transmitted, in any form or by any means, without the
prior permission in writing of Oxford University Press, or as expressly permitted
by law, by licence or under terms agreed with the appropriate reprographics
rights organization. Enquiries concerning reproduction outside the scope of the
above should be sent to the Rights Department, Oxford University Press, at the
address above

You must not circulate this work in any other form
and you must impose this same condition on any acquirer

Public sector information reproduced under Open Government Licence v3.0
(http://www.nationalarchives.gov.uk/doc/open-government-licence/open-government-licence.htm)

Published in the United States of America by Oxford University Press
198 Madison Avenue, New York, NY 10016, United States of America

British Library Cataloguing in Publication Data

Data available

Library of Congress Control Number: 2023948491

ISBN 978–0–19–888556–6

DOI: 10.1093/oso/9780198885566.001.0001

Printed and bound by
CPI Group (UK) Ltd, Croydon, CR0 4YY

Links to third party websites are provided by Oxford in good faith and
for information only. Oxford disclaims any responsibility for the materials
contained in any third party website referenced in this work.

To the Memory of Departed Friends and Mentors

Acknowledgements

One could say this book has been a long time coming. It was prompted by the entering into force of the North American Free Trade Agreement in January 1994. As a scholar of Canadian constitutional law, I was startled to learn in the morning paper that Phillip Morris was threatening to sue the Government of Canada for imposing plain packaging on tobacco products sold in the country. The taking of property rights, among other classical economic rights, were omitted from Canada's constitutional Charter of Rights of 1982 and in the numerous rounds of failed constitutional reform that followed. As I began to study the implications of investment treaty obligations on signatory states, it became clear that not only was constitutional law being conscripted into treaty text but that particular versions of those rights were being transmitted abroad and accepted by states whose own constitutional orders were not perfectly aligned with those international edicts.

I have since then been writing about the constitution-like features of investment law with a view, in part, to alerting comparative constitutional law scholars to the production of what looks like constitutional law at the international level and to the inevitable friction that was due to occur with national constitutional law. I was obliged, on many occasions, to hypothesize about these tensions. Once a body of constitutional jurisprudence began to emerge, I resolved to comparatively evaluate some of these rulings with a view to answering this question: how are courts responding to the diminished policy space accorded to states under investment treaty commitments? This book should be understood as the product of an ongoing inquiry of nearly 30 years.

I began this work while on leave from my home institution, the Faculty of Law at the University of Toronto. I am grateful to the Department of Law at Stockholm University, where I served as Visiting Professor in 2018–2020, and to the Department of Law at Gothenburg University, where I served as Torgny Segerstedt Visiting Professor in 2019–2020, for hosting me as I began this study. I was able to undertake comparative research in various foreign languages, particularly the country case studies found in Part II, with the assistance of students and scholars from various universities around the world. I am grateful to this group for their willingness to respond to my questions and queries: Amos Atzmon, Alberto Cruces Burga, María Camila Camargo, Nir Kremerman, Meir Kuba, Ferdinand Andi Lolo, and Jessica Marpaung. I am indebted to the Social Sciences and Humanities Research Council of Canada for financial support which enabled me to secure their help. I also benefited, in later stages, from the keen editorial eye of Jane Fallis Cooper and bibliographic assistance from Jacob Jones. As comparative constitutional law is always a perilous adventure, I am indebted to the following academic colleagues for reading the chapters that touched upon their areas of expertise: Carlos Bernal, Eleonora Bottini, Sujit Choudhry, Markus Krajewski, Tim Lindsey, Doreen Lustig, Roger Merino, Federico Suarez, and Carlos M. Vásquez. I also benefited from the comments of external reviewers and support throughout from Fay Gibbons and Kathryn Plunkett of Oxford University Press. None of these wonderful people should be held responsible for what follows. I have endeavoured to reduce the book's flaws but, whatever errors remain, they are my own.

Many translations of constitutional rulings not otherwise publicly available in the English language were generated by Google Translate or Deep L and, in one instance, by ChatGPT. Translations of constitutional texts mostly were obtained from the helpful site Constituteproject.org. Parts of Chapter 1 are drawn from 'Investor Rights and the Judicial Denial of the Neoliberal Constitutionalism' which appeared in Simon Archer, Daniel Drache, and Peer Zumbansen (eds), *The Daunting Enterprise of Law: Essays in Honour of Harry W. Arthurs* (McGill–Queen's University Press) at 169–85.

I dedicate this book to the memory of dearly departed friends and mentors whose influence can be felt in many of the pages that follow.

Contents

1. Introduction — 1
   - I. Under Pressure? — 1
   - II. Disciplinary Divides — 4
   - III. The Judicial Branch — 8
   - IV. The Economic Branch — 12
   - V. Hidden Transcripts? — 14
   - VI. The Executive Branch — 16
   - VII. The Book's Outline — 19

PART I

2. Nothing to See Here: Northern North America — 27
   - I. Introduction — 27
   - II. Canada: Standing on Guard — 27
   - III. America: Mending Every Flaw — 39
   - IV. Conclusion — 49

3. Taking the Lead: Europe — 51
   - I. Introduction — 51
   - II. 'In No Way Unconstitutional': France — 54
   - III. 'Lasting Negative Effects'?: Germany — 62
   - IV. Protecting 'Choices Democratically Made': EU — 66
   - V. Of Doubtful Democratic Legitimacy: Germany Again — 75
   - VI. Conclusion — 78

PART II

4. Of Little Constitutional Interest: Peru — 81
   - I. Introduction — 81
   - II. The Bear Creek Dispute — 82
   - III. Investment Law and Policy — 86
   - IV. Constitutional Order — 88
   - V. The Court — 92
   - VI. The Record — 95
   - VII. The Cases — 100
   - VIII. Conclusion — 108

5. Conditionally Constitutional: Colombia — 110
   I. Introduction — 110
   II. The Eco Oro Dispute — 112
   III. Investment Law and Policy — 115
   IV. Constitutional Order — 117
   V. The Court — 121
   VI. The Record — 126
   VII. The Case — 134
   VIII. Conclusion — 141

6. The People's Voice: Indonesia — 143
   I. Introduction — 143
   II. The Churchill Mining Dispute — 144
   III. Investment Law and Policy — 147
   IV. Constitutional Order — 150
   V. The Court — 153
   VI. The Record — 157
   VII. The Case — 159
   VIII. Conclusion — 163

7. Shackling the Future: Israel — 165
   I. Introduction — 165
   II. Stabilizing Investment Commitments — 167
   III. Investment Law and Policy — 170
   IV. Constitutional Order — 171
   V. The Court and the Record — 174
   VI. The Case — 178
   VII. Conclusion — 185

8. Conclusion — 187
   I. First, A Brief Summary — 187
   II. Democracy (Not) Vindicated — 188
   III. (Un)Easy Coexistence — 193
   IV. (Mono)Cultural Dialogue — 196

Bibliography — 203
Index — 241

1
Introduction

I. Under Pressure?

Is it a coincidence that the present revival of interest in comparative constitutional law was accompanied by the rise of international economic law? Both projects, after all, were advanced by a geo-political transformation of global significance. Formerly Soviet-controlled satellite states, and client states elsewhere in the developing world, joined in the political, economic, and constitutional project that had been offered up by leading North Atlantic states for some time. Contemporaneous with the worldwide spread of liberal constitutionalism was the rise of a political project with the aim of having states give up policy space in a wide range of economic subjects that could impede the movement of trade and investment.[1]

To what extent are these two projects compatible? Once fixed within the boundaries of states, it is said that foreign capital is vulnerable to changes in state policy.[2] So as to forestall the diminution in value associated with these changes (labelled 'political risk'),[3] investment treaties enable foreign investors to bring states before international tribunals for treaty violations in order to recoup their losses (widely referred to as the investor–state dispute settlement system or ISDS). These enforceable treaty rights resemble, in many ways, national constitutional constraints that prohibit discrimination and that protect property, contract, and due process rights.[4] If the two projects resemble each other, having, at high levels of generality, elective affinities that are hard to deny, there may be little discord between them.[5] So says the European Commission's Colin Brown, who maintains that 'key substantive investment protection obligations' resemble rights that 'are commonplace in other legal systems'.[6]

This smoothing over of constitutional difference, however, elides salient particularities that are the cumulative product of constitutional tradition, precedent, and text. In such instances, constitutional commitments can rub against Brown's

---

[1] It is, therefore, with good reason that Choudhry asks: is 'legal globalization the counterpart to economic globalization?' in Choudhry (2013) at 45. This is a question that is asked but not answered by him.
[2] The classic formulation of this problem is by Vernon (1971) (the 'obsolescing bargain').
[3] Moran (1998).
[4] As I have argued elsewhere. See Schneiderman (2008) and Schneiderman (2020).
[5] On elective affinities, see Weber (1978) at 1208 (referring to the elective affinity between religious 'sects', premised on exclusivity and voluntariness, and political democracy).
[6] Brown (2018) at 3 (offered as an argument in support of the spread of investment disciplines).

version of international constitutional law. To the extent that states are constitutionally empowered to take measures that diminish investor profitability, investment law's logic dictates that states grant priority to the treaty rights of foreign investors. As Brown maintains, 'it behoves us, particularly at the present time, to uphold' investor protections as, otherwise, 'it means negating the very core of international law'.[7] Insofar as there are tensions between these two legal orders, investment law can, on the one hand, serve to constitutionally diminish state policy capacity.[8] On the other hand, national constitutions enable states to behave in ways that upset international commitments made under investment treaties.

This book is an inquiry into the domestic effects of the legal regime to protect foreign investors on constitutional law.[9] One means of empirically documenting whether there is concord or discord as between investment law and national constitutional law is to study the response of apex courts to these constitutional encounters. Apex courts, it is said, are 'lynchpins supporting or undermining' international legal commitments.[10] Insofar as they police the interface between the international and the national, they take on roles of 'considerable importance'.[11]

Judges have expressed some anxiety about this new legal order usurping national court jurisdiction. Australian Chief Justice French identified a 'tension' between investment arbitration and the 'legitimate functions' of the three branches of government that would have 'general implications for national sovereignty, democratic governance and the rule of law'.[12] Presumably, for this reason, the Council of Chief Justices of Australia wrote to the Commonwealth Attorney-General in November 2014 expressing concern that investment agreements with ISDS could 'call into question the decisions of domestic courts'.[13] The German Magistrates Association (*Deutscher Richterbund*) expressed disapproval of the European Commission proposal for a multilateral investment court, seeing 'no need for the establishment of a special court for investors'. 'It is for Member States of the EU to ensure' the Association wrote, 'access to justice for all and to ensure feasible access for foreign investors, by providing the courts with the relevant resources'.[14] Lower court judges in South Korea were disciplined for expressing opposition to ISDS in the

---

[7] Brown (2018) at 4.
[8] UNCTAD (2015) at 125 ('they limit regulatory space').
[9] It is important to emphasize that this book does not focus on enforcement of arbitration awards by national courts (but for a brief discussion of the US Supreme Court decision in BG Group) nor does it focus on courts as a replacement for investment arbitration. For a discussion of the former, see Rajput (2021) and, for the latter, see Kohler and Potestà (2020). This book also does not take up the vast number of other cases where domestic courts have interpreted investment treaties that raise non-constitutional questions. See, for example, Hamida (2009).
[10] Alter (2018) at 248.
[11] Von Bogandy and Venzke (2014) at 133.
[12] French (2014); French (2015).
[13] Quoted in French (2015) at 3, referring to a letter from the Council of Chief Justices to Attorney-General dated 6 November 2014.
[14] German Magistrates Association (2016).

Korea–US free trade and investment agreement (KORUS–FTA). The agreement, they complained, erodes judicial sovereignty and offends the separation of powers. Senior provincial district court Judge Choi Eun-bae was denied reappointment for posting a message on Facebook critical of the President for signing the agreement.[15] A second district court judge received a six-month suspension for making similar remarks over an internal judicial intranet.[16] Dozens of other Korean judges have expressed similar opinions.[17] Kim describes this judicial reaction as 'extraordinary'—the Korean judiciary 'have traditionally refrained from making comments on politically controversial issues'.[18]

This book offers an empirically minded examination of selected apex court responses to the challenge of shrinking constitutional space due to investment law's 'downward pressure' on states.[19] Instances where national judiciaries have directly confronted the challenge of international economic law, admittedly, are uncommon. Among those rare occasions, Kelsey documented how the Philippine Supreme Court, in upholding a Senate motion to accede to the World Trade Organization (WTO), effectively 'repeal[ed] the nationalist economic principles of the Philippines Constitution'.[20] There simply was no choice but to constitutionally comply with WTO requirements, the Court concluded. The alternative was 'isolation, stagnation, if not economic self-destruction'.[21] Kim described several 'aborted' constitutional challenges to the KORUS–FTA on the grounds that the legislative branch was excluded from the treaty-making process, amounting to a constitutional amendment of the rights to property and equality.[22] The Korean Constitutional Court rejected each of these challenges,[23] preferring to signal a constitutional way forward rather than impeding the advance of international economic law. I have previously detailed a Colombian Constitutional Court ruling addressing the constitutional compatibility of a UK–Colombia bilateral investment treaty.[24] The Court declared the treaty to be inconsistent with the 1991 Constitution's equality and property clauses.[25] The Constitution promptly was amended to remove these offending impediments to the progress of the investment treaty regime.

---

[15] Jeong-pil (2011).
[16] Hee-jin (2012).
[17] Rahn (2011).
[18] Kim (2017) at 463.
[19] Haas (1983) at 30.
[20] See Kelsey (1999) at 548 on *Tañada v. Angara* (1997) Philippines Supreme Court, GR No. 118295 (2 May) at https://lawphil.net/judjuris/juri1997/may1997/gr_118295_1997.html (last accessed 21 June 2021).
[21] Quoted in Kelsey (1999) at 549. I discuss how the *Tañada* ruling (n 20) neutralized national economic principles in the 1987 Philippines Constitution in Schneiderman (2023).
[22] Kim (2017) at 462–3.
[23] They were denied mostly on grounds of standing but, in addition, on the ground that KORUS–FTA could not amount to a de facto constitutional amendment in Kim (2017).
[24] Schneiderman (2000).
[25] C-358/96.

4   INTRODUCTION

It is rare to see, as in the Colombian case, an apex court directly confronting this challenge by issuing a declaration of constitutional invalidity. More often, and as the empirical studies in this book suggest, courts have responded to the diminution of constitutional jurisdiction in more indirect ways. They prefer, for instance, addressing the absence of legislative participation in treaty-making (contra the Korean case) or issuing declarations of conditional constitutionality that require the executive adjust treaty text to ensure constitutional compatibility. On the other hand, courts also have preferred simply to ignore or minimize the significance of that threat. By documenting the range of responses to the challenge posed by international investment law to constitutional law in selected states and regions one learns how constitutional collisions are ignored, elided, or otherwise managed.[26]

II. Disciplinary Divides

This book aims to bridge the divide between two fields: comparative constitutional law and international investment law. I have long maintained that the resurgence, even convergence, in constitutional practice and the rise of legal limits to state action in relation to markets, should be of interest to comparative constitutional scholars.[27] Yet the field of comparative constitutional law has, for the most part, kept a safe distance from these developments. Though a burgeoning and lively field within the legal academy, scholars of comparative constitutional law, with few exceptions, have been uninterested in examining the dampening effects on constitutional law and discourse of the market-preferring ideology—loosely referred to as neoliberalism[28]—that is channelled via international economic law. There are only isolated occurrences of an encounter, for instance, Comella has offered a book-length argument in support of a constitutional right to arbitration, treating the entrenchment rights to investor–state dispute settlement as a beneficial part of that enterprise.[29]

International investment law scholars, by contrast, have shown some interest in comparative public law but they too often embrace a narrow view of the legal systems that are relevant to that enterprise (looking, principally, to powerful capital-exporting ones).[30] A few scholars acknowledge the coincidental rise of comparativism, rights, and constitutional reform that is designed to privilege

---

[26] 'Regime collision' is a concept familiar to systems–theoretical approaches to reflexive constitutionalism (see Fischer-Lescano and Teubner [2004]). This book, however, is not meant to be a contribution to that body of scholarship, though valuable insights can be gained from it (see Schneiderman [2011] and Schneiderman [2013a] c. 2).
[27] For example, Schneiderman (2010) and Schneiderman (2020).
[28] On neoliberalism as a 'messy hybrid' see Peck (2010) at 7.
[29] Comella (2021).
[30] This approach, which reproduces methods associated with nineteenth-century understandings of civilized justice, is analysed in Schneiderman (2022), c. 3.

already powerful political and economic interests.[31] Such works typically focus upon how bills of rights entrench elite power or constitutionalize a version of the limited state. That research agenda has not been directed at how international economic disciplines line up with the preservation of elite hegemony at national levels.[32] There has been more interest in this connection precipitated, in part, by European Court of Justice (CJEU) rulings in addition to courts in Latin America. For instance, an edited volume explores the interaction between constitutional and investment law from divergent viewpoints and not in any systematic fashion.[33] Others have commented on selected apex court rulings mostly with a view to smoothing over disagreement between courts and the regime to protect foreign investors.[34] I discuss a number of these proposals in the Conclusion. While they all are valuable contributions, it remains the case that investigations of the relationship between comparative constitutional law and investment law are scarce.

The divide between the comparativists and internationalists may have something to do with their styles of scholarship. Internationalists are preoccupied with erecting rules and institutions that not only bridge but supersede differences between states.[35] This is associated with 'convergence'[36] or a 'universalism' that calls upon courts to 'pay no heed to national legal particularities'.[37] Those who ascribe to international law the values and structure associated with a constitution reinforce this message: international constitutional law generates modes of governance that cannot be resisted.[38] Yet this is not so easily achieved as few states mandate the supremacy of international law over domestic constitutional law.[39]

Comparativists, by contrast, are more interested in legal difference, often the product of transplants and under the influence of dominant legal traditions.[40] In the comparative constitutional context, this approach has been labelled as 'genealogical'[41] or characterized as 'resistance,' a 'particular kind of nationalistic, expressive use of constitutionalism'.[42] Knop recommends that internationalists consider

---

[31] For example, Hirschl (2004) at 11; Hirschl (2014) at 97; Ginsburg (2003) at 25.
[32] A recent edited collection addresses how constitutional provisions constrain economic policy during times of 'severe financial crisis'. This collection is not focused upon the international law–comparative constitutional law interface generally but concentrates mostly on Europe. See Ginsburg, Rosen, and Vanberg (2019).
[33] Schill and Tams (2022). I discuss one of the chapters in this volume, by Prieto Muñoz (2022), in more detail in the Conclusion.
[34] For example, Prieto Muñoz (2022), Witte (2018), Fandiño-Bravo (2015), Titi (2020).
[35] Kennedy (1997) at 552.
[36] Jackson (2010) at 8.
[37] Choudhry (1999) at 833.
[38] Kennedy (2009).
[39] Peters (2009) at 184.
[40] Kennedy (1997) at 583. In this way, Kennedy ascribes to comparativists an indifference toward politics and government that they share with private international lawyers.
[41] Choudhry (1999) at 838–9.
[42] Jackson (2010) at 8. Riles (1999) at 229 describes comparativists as sharing, among other things, a 'passion for looking beyond [and] an empathy for differences but also for similarities' (emphasis in original omitted).

leaning in a similar direction.[43] Rather than envisaging international law as a mode of governance to be slavishly followed, she suggests that we understand the incorporation of international norms within domestic legal systems as reflecting differing national perspectives to the problems posed by international law.[44] This heterogeneity in approaches to incorporating international law is described, in comparative constitutional law terms, as 'dialogical'[45] or a stance of 'engagement' which is 'open to the possibilities of both harmony or dissonance between national self-understandings and transnational norms'.[46] Comparative jurisprudence serves, in this way, as an 'interpretive foil' for the justification of difference.[47]

Brought into the foreground of this encounter is the judicial role in the production of international political economy (IPE).[48] International political economists are interested in macrostructures that govern the global economy but eliminate much of the romance associated with internationalist scholarship.[49] American-based IPE scholars, instead, emphasize the formation of regimes[50]—a bundle of rules and institutions, sometimes legally binding[51]—as the means by which international cooperation can be achieved in discrete policy areas.[52] Neither is power entirely dropped out of the picture.[53] Outsize influence may have been exercised by powerful state actors in the regime's set-up.[54] Regimes may have been 'imposed' or 'negotiated' (and elements of both may be present).[55] Regime maintenance, in a world without a single hegemon, requires that 'costs' be shared more broadly among state participants—even among a coalition or bloc[56]—making

[43] International law, Knop complains, is understood by its practitioners as having 'meaning, but no culture', while its critics claim that is has 'culture, but no meaning' in (2000) at 528.
[44] Knop (2000) at 531.
[45] Choudhry (1999) at 835–8.
[46] Jackson (2010) at 9.
[47] Choudhry (2013) at 63–4. Somewhat similarly, see Kuo (2021).
[48] In Schneiderman (2013b) I examine how the British school of international political economy can be recruited to aid in this task.
[49] Likely due to the ongoing influence of the realist school of international relations. See Keohane and Nye (2011) at 264.
[50] I have earlier characterized the web of investment treaties as comprising a regime that renders commitments legally binding and behaviour more predictable in Schneiderman (2008) at 26–7. See also Salacuse (2010) and Ratner (2020) at 13–15. Bonnitcha, Poulsen, and Waibel (2017) at 7 prefer to describe the investment treaty regime as part of a 'regime complex' comprised of 'partially overlapping institutions governing international investment'.
[51] See the oft-cited definition in Krasner (1983) at 2 ('principles, norms, rules, and decision-making procedures'). See also Keohane (1984) at 59 and discussion in Young (1999) at 2–3.
[52] Keohane (1984) at 51 distinguishes cooperation from 'harmony', where state behaviour is automatically inclined towards others, rendering cooperation 'unnecessary'.
[53] Though great power influence often is treated as benign, hence, the treatment of world trading and finance regimes as 'public goods'. See Kindleberger (2000) and Leaver (1994) at 136–8.
[54] Keohane (1983) at 146. Keohane prefers to describe such arrangements as 'voluntary' though he maintains that this does not imply 'equality of situation or outcome' in the regime's design or output. According to Haas (1983) at 31, 'states with the strongest capabilities in a given issue-area tend to dictate the form of regime.' On the influence of power and preferences of capital exporting states on BITs, see Allee and Peinhardt (2014).
[55] Young (1983) at 99–100. Bringing to mind Gramsci's conception of hegemony as evincing both coercion and consent in Gramsci (1971) at 168.
[56] Haas (1983) at 46.

breakdown of the regime less likely to occur.[57] Regime resilience can be explained by numerous factors,[58] including the desire, on the part of capital-importing states, to attract new inward investment by making credible commitments, fear of capital flight should these states exit from the regime, even a desire to limit 'domestic freedom of action'.[59] As competition between states for capital intensifies,[60] it correspondingly weakens their ability to deliver on national policy objectives.[61] Control-oriented regimes that are legalized—having an ability to legally enforce binding constraints—diminish state capacity even further.[62] Domestic effects (sub-systemic levels that encompass courts) are less of a preoccupation for regime theorists than state behaviour at the level of the international system.[63] One object of this book is to consider the extent to which apex courts are implicated in regime maintenance, by either accommodating or resisting investment law regime's disciplines.[64]

Have courts acquiesced to global economic influence or exhibited a willingness to push back—putting 'upward pressure' on the regime[65]—in the name of constitutional law? Until recently, Benvenisti observes, national courts were not interested in engaging with international law in the context of domestic legal adjudication. National court judges, he reports, were 'apprehensive,' expressing a reluctance extending even to 'matters of international trade and economic cooperation'.[66] The policy of benign neglect, he argues, has since been replaced with a more 'strategic' response that is intended to vindicate both democracy as well as judicial autonomy.[67] The hope, Benvenisti and Downs write, is that engagements between the local and the international exhibit 'greater mutual respect'—giving rise to a workable division of labour between domestic courts and international adjudicators.[68] When national courts defer or exhibit respect for international courts, what

---

[57] Lipson (1983) at 236. This helps to explain, Lipson suggests, duration of the GATT. Also see discussion in Cohen (2008) at 103.
[58] Keohane (1984) at 89–95 prefers to rely upon rational choice explanations, such as reducing transaction costs and asymmetries of information.
[59] Guzman (1998), and Elkins, Guzman, and Simmons (2006) (on credible commitments); Danzman (2019) (summarizing evidence on attracting FDI); and Kahler (2001) at 286 (on freedom of action). On the distinction between capital-importing and capital-exporting states, see discussion infra, n. 88.
[60] Streeck (2017) at 87. They have become the 'suitors' of transnational capital, write Stopford and Strange (1991) at 56. This is what Sassen (2002) at 232 likens to 'state work'.
[61] Stopford and Strange (1991) at 215.
[62] Keohane (1983) at 167.
[63] Keohane and Nye (2011) at 271 (due to their interest in 'parsimony'). What happens when 'tightly binding agreements' do not allow states an ability to exercise policy capacity that is expected of them? See Frieden and Martin (2003) at 125 who include courts among those domestic institutions that can be expected to respond to regime constraints.
[64] Kratochwil and Ruggie (1986) at 772.
[65] Haas (1983) at 30.
[66] Benvenisti (1993) at 182.
[67] They can achieve this end, Benvenisti argues, only by seeking out judicial allies in other national courts in order to forge 'a coordinated, cross-boundary judicial resistance to the forces of globalization' [(2008) at 244]. On the rise of judicial networks, see Slaughter (2003) at 193.
[68] Benvenisti and Downs (2017) at 164.

emerges, Alter claims, is a 'national culture of constitutional obedience to international law'.[69] The extent to which there is a shift in judicial attitudes in the direction of fealty to the international is a question that this book, in part, aims to interrogate.

III. The Judicial Branch

How might we theorize the judicial role in the structuration of international investment law? Do judicial elites behave as do other national political and economic elites? Should we subsume judicial behaviour under national strategies to make states more economically successful in global markets?[70] Or will judges prioritize values associated with the national legal culture in which they are embedded even if they do not line up with international economic ones?

Consider how Duncan Kennedy and Upendra Baxi each identify competing ideal types that accommodate or resist these tendencies. Kennedy identifies a 'third globalization' of legal thought, the period in which international business elites have successfully conjoined classic property rights (associated with nineteenth-century vested rights doctrine) with minoritarian identity rights. These latter rights are equivalent to those barring discrimination historically suffered by minorities at the hands of legislative majorities.[71] Judiciaries are receptive to these sorts of claims by economic elites, though their response can vary. In so far as judicial solicitude is the more common response to claims of corporate suffering, it generates suspicion that there remains an alliance between the judicial branch and political and economic interests.[72]

Constitutional courts in the Global South, Kennedy admits, will be expected to 'mediate' between demands for societal protection—measures that protect campesinos, the urban poor, and even local business interests—and legal disciplines produced by international law, often authored by Global North actors. Sometimes courts nullify societal protections running afoul of international rules and, at other times, 'soften' the impact of neoliberal disciplines.[73] Mediation, for Kennedy, means 'that neither side gets everything it wants'. The advantage gained by judicialization is that economic elites get to relocate societal conflict from the

---

[69] Alter (2018) at 244.
[70] Cox describes 'domestic-oriented agencies of the state' which serve 'as transmission belts from world-economy trends and decision making into the domestic economy as agencies to promote the carrying out of tasks they had no part in deciding' in (1991) at 193. Later, in Cox (2002) at 33, he characterized the transmission belt metaphor as 'misleading' as it minimized the agency available to state actors even under the highly constrained conditions of global competition.
[71] Kennedy (2006) at 67. I associate the idea of a new 'juridical subject' as originating with Foucault (2008) at 295 in Schneiderman (2022) at 139–40.
[72] Kennedy (2020) at 100.
[73] Kennedy (2006) at 69.

arenas of 'pure politics' to ones that, traditionally, have looked with disfavour upon social protection.[74] Legal fora seemingly are depoliticized ones—objective legal expertise is expected to preside over these disputes.[75] Yet legal outcomes are not entirely indeterminate. Instead, Kennedy describes legal materials as 'consciously manipulate[d]' to produce 'ideologically predetermined' outcomes.[76] The judiciary turn out to be unreliable allies in the cause of defying international economic law's edicts.

Baxi offers a contrasting account of judges on apex courts. Drawing upon the Indian experience, he expects more opportunity for judges to behave as activists for the cause of the social. In this guise, courts behave as 'platform[s] of resistance to neo-colonial practices of power'.[77] Courts can serve on behalf of the '*multitudes* against the dominant and hegemonic *miniscule*, or virtual oligarchy'[78] who have 'harvested' the discourse of human rights on their own behalf.[79] Yet Baxi well knows that courts are under pressure to confer privileges to traders and investors. Baxi acknowledges that the legal disciplines of international economic law 'generate powerful conceptions of economic rationalism,' that 'facilitate the "structural adjustment" of judicial review and activism'.[80] This is compounded by the influence of Global North 'interpretive communities' who promote a modest role for the judiciary which many in the Global South seek to emulate.[81] But judicial modesty, if more suitable for judicial branches in the Global North, are more 'problematic' in the Global South, where the judiciary regard themselves as 'equal partners' to the political branches. They are 'even at times by default the sole authors in the development of a constitutional ethos and culture'.[82]

Baxi exhorts us to understand judicial decision-making as politics by other means, indistinguishable from legislation.[83] The only question is: what kind of politics will prevail—one that is critical-aspirational or one that is legitimating of hegemonic power relations? Too many judges in the Global South, Baxi complains, treat judicial activism as the 'deviant case' rather than serving to secure social justice for the poor and oppressed.[84] Pressures associated with international economic law make it even less likely that judicial outcomes will offer counter-hegemonic solutions that 'attempt to redress the people's miseries'.[85] They are more

---

[74] Kennedy (2020) at 97, Kennedy (2006) at 70.
[75] Kennedy (2006) at 70.
[76] Kennedy (2020) at 111.
[77] Baxi (2000) at 157.
[78] Baxi (2003) at 583.
[79] Baxi (2006) at 258ff labels these 'trade-related market-friendly human rights'.
[80] Baxi (2003) at 568. See also his discussion of what Justice Krishna Iyer termed 'imperial legal culture' in Baxi (2007).
[81] Baxi (2000) at 166.
[82] Baxi (2000) at 167.
[83] Baxi (1985) at 235.
[84] Baxi (2000) at 168.
[85] Baxi (1980) at 247.

likely, instead, to accept that 'tender solicitude' is owed to powerful economic interests.[86] It is apex courts that can offer the 'most formidable challenge' to forms of legal hegemony—serving as 'modest sites of resistance to global economic constitutionalism'.[87] The question is whether constitutional judges are capable of mounting this sort of defiance.

The empirical studies collected here—both regional and country case studies—reveal a range of judicial responses to the threat of shrinking constitutional space among capital exporting and capital importing states.[88] They conveniently can be placed along a continuum from 'deference' to 'defiance,' and further distinguished between 'hard' and 'soft' approaches.[89] Courts exhibit a hard deference to regime demands when they disavow any encroachment on constitutional space or, when acknowledging intrusion, insist that national law yield to the international. These two approaches, dominant (but not exclusively so) in capital-exporting states and regions, are akin to the convergence account in comparative constitutional law. Moving along the continuum, in the direction of soft deference,[90] are instances where apex courts accede to the diminution of constitutional space by adopting a pragmatic approach, a stance that is more common to courts situated in capital-importing states. Judges there undertake a reflexive accounting of the costs and benefits of adapting to the international legal field, resembling a version of the genealogical account in comparative constitutional law. There is, moving further along, evidence of what can be called soft defiance: not fully a rejection of international or foreign influences but more of a strategic rebuff. At the farthest end is the stance of hard defiance, where an apex court outright rejects restrictions imposed by investment law on host constitutional space. Courts serve, in these instances, as judicial avatars for the social and betray international legal edicts. Not one of the apex court case studies taken up here reveal this last sort of disposition (see Figure 1.1).

Rarely have courts exhibited hard defiance. The Colombian Constitutional Court ruling of 1996, mentioned above, offers one such instance.[91] The Ecuadorian Constitutional Court, for the most part, embraced hard defiance in a series of constitutional challenges to investment treaties to which Ecuador was a party. Article

---

[86] Baxi (2003) at 568.
[87] Baxi (2005) at 552.
[88] I will rely upon the distinction between capital-exporting and capital-importing states, rather than other binaries such as developed vs. developing states or Global North vs. Global South states. The distinction, admittedly, has been breaking down. UNCTAD, as early as 2009, identified how 'some emerging economies increasingly see themselves as capital exporters as well as capital importers' while 'a few developed countries, notably Canada and the United States ... have begun to regard themselves as capital importers *and* capital exporters'. See UNCTAD (2009) at 37–8. Lines are less blurred if we define 'capital-importing' states as those whose inward stocks of FDI typically exceed outward stocks of FDI. Compare with Van Harten (2008) at 106, fn. 1.
[89] Zürn's typologies range from 'faithfulness' at one end to 'betrayal' at the other. He further distinguishes, as I do here, between 'hard' and 'soft' versions in Zürn (1993) at 297.
[90] The term 'softness' is the one Zürn (1993) at 297 uses for a state foreign policy likely to participate in regime formation.
[91] C-358/96.

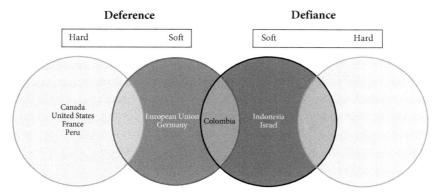

Figure 1.1 Range of Judicial Responses

422 of the 2008 Constitution was meant to put a halt to ISDS by declaring that no jurisdiction would be ceded to international arbitration concerning commercial and contractual disputes.[92] These rulings are less instructive, however, as the Ecuadorian Court was grappling with interpretation of a constitutional directive barring international arbitration rather than investment law's shrinking of state policy space.[93] It is because of this constitutional bar that ISDS was deemed incompatible with the Constitution.[94] The Court has changed course since then, following the lead of newer Presidents who have re-engaged with ISDS.[95]

In regime theory terms, there has been less discord and more cooperation exhibited by apex courts. By playing along with rules laid down, the investment law regime has, for the most part, promoted international 'cooperation' while dampening host state policy space that is otherwise constitutionally available.[96] There has been, in sum, much less discord.[97]

---

[92] The first clause of Article 422 provides: 'Treaties or international instruments where the Ecuadorian State yields its sovereign jurisdiction to international arbitration entities in disputes involving contracts or trade between the State and natural persons or legal entities cannot be entered into.' The one exception, in the second clause, concerns disputes between Latin American states which would be resolved before regional tribunals. The original intention of the Constituent Assembly, Espinosa (2020) at 366–7 explains, was 'crystal clear' though the wording used was 'defective', giving rise to 'more limited scope of application than initially thought', writes Fach Gómez (2012) at 455.

[93] The Court avoided testing the substance of treaties (but for the BIT with Germany, examining MFN and retroactive application) against constitutional text. See Espinosa (2020) at 2661. The rulings were variable both in their conclusions and in the quality of their reasons, but all found the BITs to be constitutionally incompatible. See Espinosa (2020) and Fach Gómez (2012). The commission charged by then President Correa to evaluate constitutional compatibility interrogated the content of BITs more closely. See http://caitisa.org/index.php/home/enlaces-de-interes (last accessed 7 March 2023).

[94] Fandiño-Bravo (2015) at 713.

[95] Prieto Muñoz (2022) at 177–8. I discuss this shift in Ecuadorian investment policy after the departure of President Correa who ushered in the 2008 Constitution in Schneiderman (2013a), c. 5.

[96] Keohane (1984) at 51. Cooperation is distinguished from 'harmony', where actors automatically adjust behaviour to align with the goals of others. Harmony is an 'idealized', 'unreal', and 'rare' in international affairs, claims Keohane (1984) at 51–2.

[97] Keohane (1984) at 52–3 and Zurn (1993) at 297.

Among capital-exporting states (discussed in Part I), the studies reveal convergence in the direction of neglecting, even erasing, the impact of international investment law on domestic policy space. This suggests that there is a common judicial response, within apex courts of dominant and powerful states, that favours the maintenance of international investment law's constraints. Among capital-importing states (discussed in Part II), there is a greater range of responses.[98] There is a paucity of evidence, however, that courts are coordinating in order to resist limits that international legal disciplines set upon national constitutional spaces. What is revealed, instead, are a variety of outcomes that redirect concerns away from international law to internal constitutional demands, with a focus upon executive prerogatives and procedural defects in the interests of defending democratic values. There is, I surmise, often something else going on than is admitted by the public transcripts of apex courts.

IV. The Economic Branch

Foreign investment law was borne out of relations of domination and subordination. This is not to say that the principles of equality and reciprocity between states do not also provide structural supports for the regime. Rather, it is to say that the regime's success has been predicated upon superior economic power conjoined with narratives about paths to economic success.[99] Weber relatedly describes two ideal types of domination: one, powered by market influence and, the other, by virtue of authority.[100] Elements of both ideal types have contributed to the spread of investment law.

The economic power of capital-exporting states, aided by legal advisors and allied international organizations, helped to construct the regime at its origins. Poulsen documents how developing states were persuaded to sign on to investment treaties on the basis that it would have the effect of attracting new foreign investment. Yet there was little or no evidence to support this proposition.[101] Aaron Broches, Executive Director of the IBRD, and lead lawyer in driving the process towards ratification of the Convention on the Settlement of Investment Disputes Between States and Nationals of other States (1966), left developing countries with 'the lingering impression of additional foreign investment', St. John reports.[102] It is

---

[98] It is undeniable that 'positions on ISDS do not correspond neatly to a capital-importing versus capital-exporting dichotomy'. See Calvert and Tienhaara (2022) at 2 and discussion in supra, n. 87.
[99] Strange includes, in her definition of 'structural power,' control over production and 'knowledge, beliefs, and ideas' in (1988) at 26.
[100] Weber (1978) at 943.
[101] Poulsen (2015). See, for example, discussion of the British Foreign Office policy at 67–8.
[102] However, Broches 'rarely made direct claims' that additional inward investment would be forthcoming, observes St. John (2018) at 218.

this promise of wealth-creating foreign investment that helps to explain the spread of the investment treaty regime. Any correlation between signing investment treaties and attracting new inward investment, however, remains tenuous[103]—the regime appears to 'rest upon promise, not on performance.'[104]

The content of investment treaties is driven by developed country models, often offered to developing states on a take-it-or-leave-it basis. Capital-exporting state supremacy is confirmed by content analysis of investment treaties. Data compiled by Alschner and Skougaerskiy suggests that while 'developed countries successfully align the outcome of negotiations with their treaty design preferences ... developing countries seem to have little say over the content of the treaties they sign and are therefore exposed to a more diverse array of legal commitments'.[105] As treaty text evolves, and more legal precision is attained, report Manger and Peinhardt, reforms are 'driven primarily by capital-exporting states' who 'change the content of treaties to reduce ambiguity in order to avoid outcomes that contradict their interests'.[106] Power and politics, conclude Allee and Peinhardt, 'is alive and well' in treaty design, reflecting 'deliberate strategies on the part of powerful states'.[107] It is beyond dispute that capital-exporting countries have had a firm grasp of the pen during investment treaty negotiations.

It is not only superior economic power that has enabled powerful states to dominate the content of investment treaty law. Their presumed superior knowledge about securing paths to economic success—their seeming competence and authority in these affairs—also plays a role. Economic growth is assumed to proceed up the same ladder of 'success' as had economically powerful states, about which these states have intimate knowledge and experience. There is only a single path to economic prosperity, developing states are told, and any 'normal' state will follow in those same footsteps.[108] Yet we know that such paths to development largely are mythical ones. No developed country adhered to anything like investment law's strictures in the past, rather, they repeatedly behaved in ways that would contravene those strictures today.[109] Nevertheless, capital-importing states are told that powerful capital-exporting states know better—they are well suited to dictate investment law's content. Keene associates this mission with the lingering effects of the eighteenth- and nineteenth-century discourse of 'civilization'. 'Advanced' western civilization purports to know better how the world should be organized.[110]

---

[103] For example, Bellak (2015).
[104] Moore (1966) at 506.
[105] Alschner and Skougaerskiy (2016) at 574.
[106] Manger and Peinhardt (2017) at 921.
[107] Allee and Peinhardt (2014) at 82.
[108] Normal in its two senses as identified by Hacking (1990) at 168: as the 'existing average' and as the 'figure of perfection to which we may progress'.
[109] Chang (2002).
[110] Keene (2002) at 9. Keene identifies two conflicting normative principles at work in international society: the first premised on the equality of states and, the second, on the spread of civilization in (2002) at 143–4.

This claim to superior knowledge, precipitating a 'duty to obey', now takes shape via a legally binding regime. Economic power is transformed into formally regulated relationships with the ability to command compliance, lending an air of objectivity to the enterprise.[111] The legal commands undertaken by signatory states are obediently followed to such a 'socially relevant degree',[112] investors can now bank on regulatory stability or a sum of damages if their expectations are upset.

V. Hidden Transcripts?

The institutionalized power of capital-exporting states has implications for the room to manoeuvre available to legal elites, principally the judicial branch in capital-importing states. If Baxi has grounds to be hopeful about constitutional courts serving as avatars for the subaltern, judges may feel inhibited in what they can say in public—other opinions remain hidden from public view. To better understand what may be going on underneath surface appearances, I turn to James Scott who distinguishes between the 'public' and 'hidden' transcripts of those subordinated by dominant authority. He offers a qualitative account of how the protagonists in such relationships are not entirely forthcoming when they say things in public, unlike what they may say in private.[113] These 'hidden transcripts' are a form of 'fugitive political conduct' in the context of particular power relations. The public transcript will conform to how the dominant 'would wish to have things appear'.[114] The public version, he writes, is a 'self-portrait of dominant elites as they would have themselves seen'.[115] 'It is designed to be impressive', Scott adds, 'to affirm and naturalize the power of dominant elites, and to conceal and euphemize the dirty linen of their rule.'[116] Private transcripts, in contrast, are the 'offstage responses and rejoinders' to what is offered in public.[117] It gives expression to the acrimony that is not acceptable amongst polite company.

Scott draws these insights from studies of slavery, caste, and serfdom. I do not mean to say, of course, that judges on apex courts experience these forms of subjugation.[118] Rather, it is to suggest that the public reasoning of apex courts, particularly those engaging in soft defiance, may be disguising their disapproval in publicly available transcripts. Why, it can reasonably be asked, would apex courts

---

[111] As 'if the ruled had made the content of the command the maxim of their conduct for its very own sake' in Weber (1978) at 946.
[112] Weber (1978) at 948.
[113] Scott (1985) at 286 ('The fact is that power-laden situations are nearly always inauthentic: the exercise of power nearly always drives a portion of the full transcript underground.').
[114] Scott (1990) at 4.
[115] Scott (1990) at 18 (emphasis in original omitted).
[116] Scott (1990) at 18. Scott maintains that the powerful in such relationships 'also develop a hidden transcript representing the practices and claims of their rule that cannot be openly avowed' (at xii).
[117] Scott (1990) at 111.
[118] Scott (1990) at x.

be reluctant to say what they mean—why exhibit such inhibition? Scott insists that hidden transcripts can rise to the public surface when two conditions are satisfied: first, when announced in a sequestered, safe site that the dominant cannot reach and, second, 'when the sequestered milieu is composed entirely of close confidants who share similar experiences of domination'.[119] Are not apex courts safe sites out of the reach of the dominant, composed of judges who are all similarly situated in terms of their subordination to powerful interests, whether they be public or private? Moreover, their independence and security of tenure should enable them to say in public what they mean in private.

We know, however, that, even in situations of non-domination, judges often act strategically. If the 'attitudinal' model of judicial behaviour aims to explain legal outcomes with reference to judicial preferences,[120] we know that judges are not unconstrained actors who simply channel their ideological preferences or those of their appointing authority. The 'strategic' model of judicial behaviour instead understands judges as rational actors who pursue strategies in order to attain their preferred outcomes, but that these are constrained by their institutional interdependence.[121] While fidelity to law matters, the response that judges elicit from the institutional environment within which they operate better explains judicial outcomes.[122] Environment, Murphy adds, encompasses 'not only widely shared societal values' that can constrain judicial choice, but 'the specific political context' which can serve as an impediment to the realization of judicial objectives.[123]

If we combine the strategic account of judicial decision-making with the idea of hidden transcripts, we can hypothesize that apex courts that move in the direction of softness—either deference or defiance—may not be vindicating constitutional norms pure and simple but moderating their response to the diminution of constitutional space in terms that will be familiar (maybe even welcome) to an external audience composed of lawyers, judges, scholars, and officials within foreign affairs bureaus housed in capital-exporting states. For instance, when apex courts issue reasons that reinforce the separation of powers, they may be reaching for reasons more readily acceptable to its diverse audience, including those who exert pressure on capital-importing states to adhere to the investment rules regime.

Judicial reasons that rely on constitutional norms, to be sure, resonate as genuine rather than as strategic.[124] But in circumstances where courts are aware of the

---

[119] Scott (1990) at 120.
[120] See Segal and Spaeth (1993) at 32–3.
[121] Epstein and Knight (1998) at 12; Epstein and Knight (2000) at 626. Justices, they write, 'are strategic actors who realize that their ability to achieve their goals depends on a consideration of the preferences of other actors, the choices they expect others to make, and the institutional context in which they act' in Epstein and Knight (1998) at 10.
[122] Murphy (1964) at 199. An institutionalist approach looks to the constraining influence of institutional norms and path dependence to explain judicial behaviour. See Smith (2008) and Maveety (2002) at 28–9.
[123] Murphy (1964) at 32–3.
[124] On the difficulty of discerning between the two, see Schneiderman (2018a).

dampening effects of investment law on constitutional space, they may prefer to issue restrained reasons that conceal the hidden transcript of defiance. Conversely, for apex courts that make their home in capital-exporting states—the principal authors and promoters of the investment law regime—it is in the interests of their principal audience that those protections persist, and are even enlarged, for home state investors. Here too apex courts are behaving strategically. They may even prefer to 'conceal' or 'euphemize,' in their public transcripts, 'the dirty linen' of rule by their home states.[125] In such circumstances, the policy preferences of the political branches align neatly with the judicial branch. This may be because apex courts are agnostic about these questions and simply wish to get out of the way of the political branches in so far as it concerns the conduct of foreign affairs. Alternatively, courts may find that the objective of protecting home state investors abroad to be roughly in alignment with constitutional values they espouse in their daily work and may even align with their own personal policy preferences. Whatever the case, it may be that apex courts that are deferential to investment treaty edicts are not telling us the whole story.

Nor does it appear to be the case that courts in long-standing democracies are more likely to disfavour encroachments by international law. The studies herein suggest otherwise: that power and political economy play a role in how apex courts respond to the threat of shrinking constitutional space. That is, these courts are behaving strategically, responding to the political, economic, and legal environments in which they operate.

VI. The Executive Branch

While all branches of government—executive, legislative, and judicial—typically participate in treaty-making and implementation, it is the executive branches within national states that are the principal authors of international legal regimes. The executive is the external face of national sovereignty, conducting foreign affairs, determining the conditions giving rise to war and to the making of peace. External partners are not expected to have to navigate internal political conditions in order to conduct foreign relations (though many states have staff within embassies and consulates to perform such political intelligence-gathering functions). Indeed, the Vienna Convention on the Law of Treaties (VCLT) is premised upon this principle—the internal organization of states do not stand in the way of treaties giving rise to international responsibility.[126]

If the practice of executive dominance emerges out of post-Westphalian interstate diplomacy, the principle is traceable back to Locke's *Second Treatise*, a tract

---

[125] Scott (1990) at 18.
[126] 1155 UNTS 331, Art. 26.

that arises out of tensions between the exercise of monarchical prerogatives and the English Parliament. While distinguishing between three intersecting powers (executive, legislative, and judicial), Locke separates out what he calls the 'federative' power—the power to wage war and make peace—from executive and legislative power. As it concerns relations lying beyond the borders of the commonwealth, he likens this power to one available to all in the state of nature. Generalizing from the English case, Locke acknowledges that this power typically will be vested in one person with the sole discretion to determine its use. Federative power concerns affairs that are 'much less capable to be directed by antecedent, standing, positive Laws... and so must necessarily be left to the Prudence and Wisdom of those hands it is in, to be managed for the public good'. As a practical matter, federative and executive powers will be placed in the same hands and so Locke proceeds to treat them as united in the body of the executive.[127] Executive power continues to exhibit, however, characteristics of natural power, for it 'remains [available] wherever [routine] political power is ineffective'.[128] The prerogative power over foreign affairs is lodged in the executive branch precisely to be able to credibly and efficiently react to threats of war and overtures of peace, in addition to economic relations.

Constitutional texts are far more transparent about the division of labour in treaty-making than in Locke's time. Rules for treaty formation, writes Ginsburg, are 'part of the constitutional core'—some 90 per cent of constitutions provide detailed rules about treaty formation and adoption.[129] Approximately 77 per cent (149 of 192) require legislative ratification for some treaties.[130] These are trendlines that rose dramatically in the latter half of the twentieth century.[131] Treaties commonly mentioned in constitutional texts are those implicating 'national sovereignty' or requiring change to domestic laws. Less common are references to trade and human rights treaties.[132] Legislative participation in treaty ratification is part of what McLachlan describes as an 'unprecedented' insertion of legislative participation (his study concerns Parliamentary democracies) such that it is not appropriate to talk of a separation but a 'distribution of powers'.[133]

All of which suggests that the traditional monist–dualist divide is less salient than it once was. That is, the divide between constitutional regimes where treaties have direct effect (monist) and those that require legislative approval in some manner and form prior to ratification (dualist) is breaking down. In monist

---

[127] Locke (1964) at ¶145, ¶132, ¶152, ¶147, ¶148.
[128] Mansfield Jr (1989) at 199 and Dunn (1969) at 150.
[129] Ginsburg (2019) at 67.
[130] Martinez (2019) at 104.
[131] Verdier and Versteeg (2018) at 215.
[132] Martinez (2019) at 105. Exceptional in this regard is Ecuador's new constitutional reference to treaties that 'bind the State's economic policy... to conditions of international financial institutions or transnational companies', requiring legislative ratification. See Constitution of Ecuador Art. 419 (5), (8) and Martinez (2019) at 105.
[133] McLachlan (2014) at 150.

systems, Verdier and Vertseeg observe, legislative approval typically is required and so plays a 'central role in the treaty-making process'.[134] Most constitutional regimes combine features of both monist and dualist traditions.[135] This is borne out in the case studies that follow.

The proliferation of trade and investment treaties would seem to reinforce this development. These treaties, after all, are intended to significantly impede state capacity. If economic policy is one of the more important tools available to states to guide wealth generation and distribution, the toolkit is emptied somewhat by international economic law. In these circumstances, executive consent to strategies of self-limitation is problematic from a democratic angle. Resiling from policy space, however, is precisely what the investment treaty regime aims to secure.[136] There is little tolerance for democratic experimentation nor are states entitled to reverse course without the payment of compensation.[137] The regime is intended to warrant to foreign investors that their interests will be vindicated in the case of policy uncertainty or reversal that results in the diminution of investment value. Given the significant distrust in democracy exhibited by the regime and its principal actors, legislative participation is a two-edged sword: democratization can bring more legitimacy to the international commitments or, alternatively, imperil their future. It is this latter perspective that animates public choice accounts addressing national legislative participation in treaty-making. Cope and Movassagh argue, for instance, that legislatures have 'little motive to harmonize' laws or interpretations with international law. Their constituencies are local, not international. Legislatures are less likely to serve as 'faithful agents of the international legal order' than executive branch officials, who are more isolated from public opinion and better positioned to think in more cosmopolitan ways.[138]

Could the same also be said of the judicial, as of the executive, branch? Conant hypothesizes that courts will prefer to 'prioritize' their own domestic law and lawmaking institutions over international ones.[139] Cope and Movassagh, conversely, liken judges to executives as they are both 'more insulated' from domestic political pressures. Judges are 'politically freer' they write, and are more likely to 'align their interpretations with prevailing or emerging international law norms'.[140] Benvenisti and Downs argue contrariwise, that executives pursue national interests at odds with international legal norms and that national courts have been too deferential to their executive branches.[141] But this is changing with the rise of judicial networks

---

[134] Verdier and Versteeg (2018) at 217.
[135] Verdier and Versteeg (2018) at 211.
[136] UNCTAD (2018) at 163 (having 'the potential to constrain investment-related industrial policy'), and UNCTAD (2015) at 125.
[137] Schneiderman (2018).
[138] Cope and Movassagh (2018) at 274 and 277.
[139] Conant (2018) at 16.
[140] Cope and Movassagh (2018) at 277–8.
[141] Benvenisti and Downs (2009) at 69–70; Benvenisti (1993).

and the steady exchange of court rulings in cyberspace. We are now seeing, they argue, more judicial 'cooperation' and 'collaboration,' rendering the international system more 'coherent.'[142] 'Collaboration' they write, 'is essential if global governance is to flourish.'[143] I return to this prescriptive account in the Conclusion. It only remains to now describe the book's contents.

VII. The Book's Outline

This book provides an empirical and qualitative evaluation of apex courts that operate in various locales. It is divided into two parts. Part I summarizes the jurisprudence of selected capital-exporting states and regions.[144] The two chapters examine investment law's reach into constitutional domains and discusses representative, mostly recent, cases in each. In Chapter 2, the response of high courts to the threat of diminished jurisdictional space in Northern North America (Canada and the US) are canvassed. Reasons offered by the Supreme Court of Canada, rejecting a constitutional challenge to the North American Free Trade Agreement (NAFTA) are scrutinized in addition to an Indigenous community's challenge to a Canada–China agreement. Canadian courts, we learn, are not that interested in interrogating constitutional dissonance. Because international law is not part of Canadian constitutional law, no constitutional conflict arises. Turning to the United States, there has been no judicial pronouncement on investment treaty conformity with the Constitution. Instead, two rulings are considered, the first concerning the constitutionality of congressional–executive agreements that confer fast-track authority on the executive branch to negotiate trade and investment agreements. In the second case, the effect of an investment treaty reward on host state jurisdiction outside of the United States (in this instance, an award of damages against Argentina) is examined. We learn that US courts largely seek to avoid interfering in these disputes. In the case of investment arbitration, a majority of the Supreme Court concluded that deference was appropriate in investment disputes, just as the Court defers to adjudicators in labour arbitration. These cases remain instructive as they reveal a predilection, as do Canadian courts, to steer clear of the processes facilitating global economic integration.

The second chapter in Part I examines a series of European rulings on the consistency of the investment chapter contained in the Canada–European Comprehensive Economic and Trade Agreement (CETA) with national and regional constitutional instruments. We review, first, a French Constitutional Council ruling, several

---

[142] Benvenisti and Downs (2009) at 61; Benvenisti (2008) at 268.
[143] Benvenisti and Downs (2009) at 69.
[144] On the distinction between capital-exporting and capital-importing states, see discussion in supra, n. 87.

German Constitutional Court rulings, and the response of the European Court of Justice addressing CETA's compliance with the European legal order. All of these courts adopt similar strategies of avoidance, resulting in either hard or soft deference. Deploying somewhat analogous interpretive techniques, they mostly find consistency between the latest version of investment protections found in CETA with constitutional commitments taken up in France, Germany, and Europe. Both the German and European courts, however, display an interest in policing implementation of CETA's investment chapter in the future. The likelihood of that kind of oversight appears slight.

Part II represent the book's core ambition. The constitutional jurisprudence of four apex courts is scrutinized in countries that are principally capital-importing states.[145] This Part aims to reveal how selected high courts are responding to the changing landscape of constitutionalism, where the exigencies of economic globalization are driving towards convergence even as constitutional fundamentals are meant to reflect national legal and constitutional cultures. These detailed case studies address the threat of shrinking jurisdictional space by virtue of international investment law (in the cases of Peru, Colombia, and Indonesia) or investment policy commitments that serve similar binding functions (in the case of Israel). These four case studies, each of which culminates in a recent constitutional ruling, are not offered up as a comprehensive survey of judicial engagement with investment treaty constraints. They are offered, instead, as salient examples of the types of encounters that, increasingly, are the subject of constitutional litigation.

The chapters adopt roughly similar templates. First, an investment dispute is summarized so as to illustrate how investment treaty law and arbitration shrinks host state policy space. It also provides context for the particular constitutional ruling taken up at the end of each chapter. The state's investment treaty policy record is subsequently addressed, followed by a summary of key articles of the country's constitution. Next, the main features and jurisdiction of the apex court are identified together with the court's record as regards its relationship with the political branches. Of importance is whether the court has displayed independence from the political branches, in particular, the executive branch. Each chapter summarizes the judicial record as it pertains to accommodating or resisting plans to liberalize the economy, schemes that typically align with investment treaty design. Finally, each chapter culminates with a deep dive into a recent constitutional ruling that tests investment treaty law (or its equivalent) against constitutional law. Exhibited in these rulings are a range of responses, from hard deference to soft defiance.

A few words are warranted to explain why in-depth country studies are undertaken in Part II. What is the rationale for examining constitutional text, practice,

---

[145] Following the methodological point in supra, n. 88, these are states whose inward stock of FDI typically exceeded their outward stock.

inter-branch relations, in addition to the judicial record, in order to gauge an apex court's response to the challenge of shrinking constitutional space? Experience both teaching and writing about comparative constitutional law has caused me some unease. Too often, scholarship attracts only surface analyses. One will not learn how a particular case or doctrine fits into a larger pattern of history, text, practice, and judicial interpretation, features that I associate with constitutional culture.[146] Context, in other words, is largely left out of the picture.[147] The method adopted here aims to understand differing constitutional orders with reference to these legal, institutional, and political–economic considerations—the contexts of meaning in which constitutional understandings are produced—which often are elided.[148] It is a method I have chosen to adopt in my own teaching and scholarship, and one that is meant to be on display in this work. I now turn to a summary of each of these country studies.

In the case of Peru, we learn that the executive branch has made signing comprehensive free trade and investment agreements a priority. It has also expected the legislative branch to fall into lock step with its priorities. In a series of constitutional challenges, the Peruvian Constitutional Court at first adopted an avoidance strategy. These disputes were not yet ripe for constitutional challenge as treaties had not yet been ratified by the other state party. The constitutionality of the Peru–China Free Trade Agreement, however, was ripe for resolution and so was squarely before the Court. The chapter reveals, consistent with other empirical research, that the Constitutional Court will avoid direct confrontations with the Executive branch. By deeming many of the questions asked—those having to do with state sovereignty, discrimination, and promotion of the general welfare—to be unsuitable for judicial determination, the Court preferred to endorse constitutional compatibility over running afoul of executive branch priorities. As was seen in some of the country studies in Part I, the Peruvian Constitutional Court generates another example of hard deference.

The Colombian Constitutional Court has a lengthy record of evaluating investment treaties for their constitutional compliance. The Court has shown as much interest as disinterest in closely scrutinizing these texts. After constitutional amendments were precipitated by the Court's ruling that a Colombia–UK Bilateral Investment Treaty (BIT) was unconstitutional,[149] the Court has consistently been deferential to the political branches. The Court's decision in C-252/19, concerning the constitutionality of a Colombia–France BIT, exhibited less deference but

---

[146] For an illustration of how I have worked the idea of constitutional culture into my own work, see Schneiderman (2015).
[147] A problem that Law (2022), in part, aims to solve.
[148] I am guided by what Weber (1978) at 8–9 calls 'the rational understanding of motivation, which consists in placing the act in an intelligible and more inclusive context of meaning ... for a science which is concerned with the subjective meaning of action, explanation requires a grasp of the complex of meaning in which an actual course of understandable action thus interpreted belongs'.
[149] Discussed above in text associated with nn. 24–5.

adopted a pragmatic posture. This is because the Court took seriously the question of constitutional conformity, insisting that the Executive renegotiate the terms of the treaty. But rather than undoing the investment treaty regime, the Court issued a series of conditional rulings that remedied constitutional defects so that the revised treaty text looked more like attenuated investment treaty rights being promoted by other capital-exporting states. The effect of the ruling was to trim some of the treaty's excesses so that it was more in conformity, not only with the Constitution, but with investment treaty trendlines exhibited in newer treaties like CETA's investment chapter. As the ruling in no way threatens the future of the Colombia's investment treaty policy it exhibits only soft defiance to international prerogatives.

Indonesia had a very active investment treaty programme until it was dragged, as respondent state, into a number of controversial investment disputes. Disputes were characterized as frivolous and state losses as illegitimate, precipitating a rethink of Indonesia's commitment to the investment treaty regime. While the Constitutional Court has not had an opportunity to weigh in on the compatibility of investment law with the Indonesian Constitution, it has not been shy in thwarting plans intended to liberalize the economy, reinforcing commitments to economic democracy contained in the Indonesian Constitution. The Court had an opportunity to indirectly weigh into the investment treaty debate by reviewing the Treaty Law of 2007, signed and ratified by the President and without legislative scrutiny or consent. This was the common practice in Indonesian foreign relations law. In their ruling, the Court stepped in to mandate the participation of the legislative branch in ratifying trade and investment agreements. Such treaties had 'a fundamental impact on the people' that was 'linked to the state's financial burden,' the Court ruled, which engaged the constitutional interest of the legislature. While this outcome did not have the direct effect of frustrating the executive's investment treaty policy, it could impede its future progress. For this reason, I characterize the ruling as exhibiting soft defiance to the regime's strictures.

The Israeli case is different from most of the others discussed in this book. The case under examination concerned a challenge to commitments, made by the government of then Prime Minister Netanyahu, to refrain from making regulatory changes to the gas industry for a period of 10 years in exchange for the development of four natural gas fields in the Mediterranean Sea by Houston-based Noble Energy. The litigation before the High Court of Justice concerned commitments made pursuant to contract, not yet the subject of an investment dispute, triggering review under Israel's common law constitution rather than under Israel's Basic Laws. At issue in the legal proceedings, however, were elements ordinarily associated with investment treaty law. Investment treaties may include 'stabilization' clauses, such as the one found in the gas contract, while other contractual commitments may receive protection via an 'umbrella' clause. The extent to which regulatory environments can be said to be 'frozen' is also a live issue in the interpretation of the fair and equitable treatment standard of treatment and its legitimate expectations doctrine.[150] The High Court maintained that the executive could not bind future legislatures to this sort of commitment. Even though a potential investor-state dispute was looming in the shadows, the ruling rubs against investment law trendlines: though interpretation will vary, no tribunal has found such clauses to be invalid or unenforceable.[151] The Court's ruling exhibits soft defiance because it was not inhibited from concluding that such measures contradicted the sovereign powers of 'well developed' states.

Having concluded the descriptive and empirical parts of the book, the conclusion takes a more critical turn. Theorists working at the interface of the local and the global have been preoccupied with the disconnect between the authors and addressees of law. Law-making institutions are increasingly incongruent with those who are subject to law production, unsettling the democratic foundations for self-government. By interrogating recent scholarship aiming to bridge this gap, we learn that many of their prescriptions aim to smooth over conflict and exonerate the judicial branches of responsibility for yielding to the power of international investment law. There is an expectation of some reciprocity: investment tribunals, for instance, will be expected to issue reasons attentive to local constitutional conditions. The centre of gravity of these proposals, however, is upon apex courts—the guardians of national constitutional law—succumbing to the regime of investment law, irrespective of constitutional texts and contexts.

We can conclude, in light of the case studies and review of the scholarship, that the regime for the protection of foreign investors remains resilient insofar as enforcement of constitutional commitments by high courts will not force the regime's imminent collapse. Rather, it is more likely that ISDS will recede into the background—becoming less constitutionally and politically salient—until the such time as the regime's disciplines prove, again, to be untenable from a constitutional and democratic point of view.[152] It is doubtful that courts in capital-exporting states will be interested in arguments that have the effect of unravelling this legal order without this sort of impetus. As for courts in capital-importing states, whether they will have the courage to undertake an assault on the regime's ramparts remains an open question. It might be that, to the extent the regime can be likened to disciplines imposed by metropolitan authorities on subordinate states under imperialism and colonialism, indefensible analogies will help to loosen the ties that bind.[153]

---

[150] Generally, Dolzer and Schreuer (2012) at 81–4.
[151] Dolzer and Schreuer (2012) at 83.
[152] For a discussion of the regime's ongoing legitimacy problems, see Schneiderman (2017b).
[153] For more on these linkages, see Schneiderman (2022).

PART I

2
Nothing to See Here
Northern North America

I. Introduction

Despite the muscular constitutional constraints that exist in the developed states of North America—in both Canada and the United States (US)—they have not served as impediments to participating, even leading the charge, in the spread of investment disciplines worldwide. Both states are good candidates to illustrate how constitutional law serves not to obstruct the widening embrace of investment law. In the case of the US, this is facilitated by ensuring that investment law mirrors US constitutional strictures. In the case of Canada, to which I turn first, this is achieved by eliding the impact investment disciplines can have on constitutional law. Both examples reveal the degree to which courts in capital exporting countries prefer to smooth the path for the movement of capital across borders unimpeded by constitutional particulars.

II. Canada: Standing on Guard

At its origins in 1867,[1] the Canadian Parliament was granted all powers 'necessary and proper' to implement obligations that were adopted by the mother country, Great Britain, on behalf of its empire.[2] In other words, Great Britain had authority to engage in treaty formation, while Canada's federal government had the power to implement those commitments irrespective of whether they fell within national (federal) or sub-national (provincial) jurisdiction.[3]

---

[1] The heading in this part is adapted from Canada's national anthem. Lyrics at https://www.canada.ca/content/dam/ircc/migration/ircc/english/celebrate/pdf/national_anthem_e.pdf (last accessed 10 March 2023).

[2] Section 132 of the 1867 Constitution provides: 'The Parliament and Government of Canada shall have all Powers necessary or proper for performing the Obligations of Canada or of any Province thereof, as Part of the British Empire, towards Foreign Countries, arising under Treaties between the Empire and such Foreign Countries.' That the phrase 'necessary and proper' mimics the last clause of Art. 1, s. 8 of the US Constitution has not been noticed by most Canadian commentators. It is hard to believe this was not deliberate copying. For an extensive early treatment of this authority, as compared to the US, see Smith (1923) at c. VI.

[3] This is anomalous, in a state organized on federal principles. It reflects continuity over Canada's external affairs held by Great Britain, pre-Confederation.

Centralization of treaty implementation in the federal government likely was desired early to avoid the embarrassment of a British colony behaving inconsistently with international commitments, giving rise to treaty violations.[4] It was not the case, however, that Canada did not participate in international affairs in the late nineteenth century. Shortly after 1867, Canada began insisting on representation in treaty negotiation and slowly began to assume functions formerly exercised by the British Crown on its behalf.[5]

The hoped-for unity of the British Empire would slowly crumble, however, particularly after Canada suffered great losses during the First World War.[6] By this time, Canadian representatives signed onto international treaties on Canada's own behalf. If the Judicial Committee of the Privy Council could, in 1932, recognize the federal government's authority to implement an aviation treaty (the Regulation of Aerial Navigation Convention of 1919),[7] by 1937, this power was denied the federal government in the case of conventions adopted by the International Labour Organization of the League of Nations, pursuant to the Treaty of Versailles at negotiations where Canada was independently represented.[8] The unilateral power to implement imperial treaty obligations was now defunct. Though inheriting the prerogative to form international obligations, judicial authority now demanded that the federal government could only implement those obligations that fell within its jurisdictional ambit. Otherwise, the provinces were expected to implement treaty obligations falling within their constitutional jurisdiction that Canada took up at the international level.

Canadian federalism continues to operate on the dualist premise that international affairs remain within executive prerogative and that treaty implementation may require that both levels of government take steps to fulfill those obligations. That constitutional understanding has been adjusted to meet the demands of successive Quebec governments that have insisted on participation in international affairs when the province's interests are at stake.[9] Other provinces also have, on occasion, been consulted or invited to participate in international treaty making. In the case of the free trade and investment agreement between Canada and the European Union (CETA), Europe insisted upon provincial consultations seeing as

---

[4] The object, as Cyr (2009) at 221 suggests, was to ensure that the imperial government was not 'held in violation of international obligations'.

[5] See Edward Porritt, *The Fiscal and Diplomatic Freedom of the British Overseas Dominions* (Oxford: Clarendon Press, 1992) 193, 195.

[6] Soward (1958) at 130.

[7] In *re the Regulation and Control of Aeronautics in Canada* [1932] Appeal Cases 54 at 63 (Aeronautics Reference).

[8] *A.G. Canada v. A.G. Ontario* [1937] Appeal Cases 326 at 343 (Labour Conventions Reference).

[9] See, for example, Quebec Premier Daniel Johnson (1968) at 72–3, calling for jurisdiction over foreign policy in areas of provincial interest. On this doctrine, associated with academic and civil servant Paul Gerin-Lajoie, see discussion in Cyr (2009) at 15ff.

provincial compliance with trade and investment commitments otherwise might not be fully respected.[10]

But for the most part the executive branch of the Canadian federal government, under the control of the Prime Minister's office, calls the shots when it comes to investment treaty commitments. And provinces are expected to abide by these commitments, irrespective of the diminution of policy space that ensues. This was made plain by the provinces of Ontario and New Brunswick both abandoning policies that were alleged to give rise to violations of the investment chapter in the North American Free Trade Agreement (NAFTA). Both provincial governments contemplated disrupting private car insurance markets by mandating government-run no-fault automobile insurance. In each instance, the province backed down from their own proposals. This was done even after a successful election campaign was won in New Brunswick on the very issue.[11] Both provinces yielded without ever pointing the finger specifically at NAFTA's constraints. Little else, however, explains these setbacks other than claims for massive compensation that would have been owed to the private insurance industry due to these initiatives. Nevertheless, Canada has been actively pursuing investment treaty partners ever since NAFTA came into force in 1994. Canada has 42 foreign investment protection agreements (FIPAs) presently in force coupled with 20 trade agreements that include investment chapters.

Justices of the Supreme Court of Canada, too, have revealed themselves to be interested in smoothing the path to greater economic integration with the rest of the world. In Hunt (1993),[12] the Supreme Court constitutionalized rules for the recognition of extra-provincial legal proceedings, analogous to the US Constitution's 'full faith and credit' clause.[13] At issue was a Quebec 'blocking statute' that prohibited the removal of documents from within Quebec required in any legal proceedings taking place outside of the province. The Court found the Quebec law as beyond the power of the provincial legislature and, therefore, 'constitutionally inapplicable'.[14]

The Court relied on numerous textual footholds, but none specifically empowered the Court to produce this outcome.[15] There was, instead, an economic imperative that drove the justices to their conclusion. The legislation, Justice La

---

[10] European negotiators must have known that governments change hands and that consultation with one sub-national government does not bind successor administrations. On the disparate reservations negotiated by different provincial governments in CETA, see Shrybman (2012).

[11] Premier Bernard Lord's Conservative party secured that election victory, in part, by promising no-fault insurance in response to escalating car insurance rates causing economic hardship to citizens of New Brunswick.

[12] Hunt (1993) and see discussion in Bakan, Ryder, Schneiderman, and Young (1995).

[13] US Constitution, Art. IV, s.1.

[14] Hunt (1993) at 324.

[15] Invoked were the intentions of the framers in 1867, the fact of economic mobility rights in the Charter, the Canadian economic union reflected in s. 121, and the unitary structure of the Canadian court system.

Forest wrote, 'discourages international commerce and ... [the] conduct of litigation'.[16] This would increase litigation costs and undermine the unity of the 'Canadian marketplace'.[17] Building on themes outlined in an earlier ruling, it was clear that '[a]ccommodating the flow of wealth, skills and people across state lines has now become imperative'.[18] Constitutional text in *Hunt* was no impediment to constructing a new constitutional rule to accommodate international economic exigencies.

The Supreme Court has not expressly weighed in on the conformity of investment treaty law with constitutional law. The Court only refused leave to appeal in the case to which we now turn. The lower court proceedings reveal a judicial reluctance, however, to temper Canadian investment treaty policy in light of the Canadian constitution. The Canadian judiciary, it would seem, lacks the 'constitutional courage'[19] to admit that external legal regimes can have the effect of significantly transforming domestic constitutional commitments. I turn first to decisions of Ontario courts launched by a group of NGOs, together with a Canadian trade union,[20] challenging the consistency NAFTA's investment chapter with Canada's constitution.[21] I then turn to rulings by the Federal Court of Canada responding to a constitutional challenge to the Canada–China Foreign Investment Protection Agreement that was initiated by the Hupacasath First Nation.

It turns out, according to these Canadian judges, that investor rights have little connection with constitutionalism. It is important to underscore that, in contrast to US understandings, no great Canadian values are being projected abroad by investment treaty commitments. Instead, Canada is channelling the desires of powerful economic actors, mostly those in the Canadian mining sector, who are seeking to secure the success of investment law disciplines but on a global scale.[22]

(i) *CUPW v. Canada*

The first piece of constitutional litigation under consideration appears to have been a collateral attack on a pending NAFTA dispute initiated by the private courier service, United Parcel Service (UPS), against the Canadian Government. Claiming a denial of national treatment (or discrimination on grounds of nationality), among

---

[16] Hunt (1993) at 327.
[17] Hunt (1993) at 330.
[18] *Morguard Investments Ltd. v. De Savoye (1990)* 76 DLR (4th) 256 (SCC) at 270.
[19] Arthurs (2003) at 4.
[20] They were the Council of Canadians (CoC), the Canadian Union of Postal Workers (CUPW), and the Charter Committee on Poverty Issues (CCPI).
[21] A constitutional challenge to CETA was launched in Federal Court of Canada in October 2016 but discontinued in June 2017. See *The Honourable Paul Helleyer, P.C. et al v. Justin Trudeau et al*, Court File No. T-1789-16. The plaintiff's name is wrongly spelled—it is Hellyer.
[22] Mertins-Kirkwood (2022).

other things, UPS was challenging the ability of wholly government-owned Canada Post to subsidize its own courier delivery service. As has often been the case, the Canadian Union of Postal Workers (CUPW) was denied standing to make written or any other submissions at the hearing.[23] A constitutional challenge would provide an alternative venue for CUPW, together with likeminded allies, to have their day in Court, albeit, in an entirely different venue addressing entirely different legal questions.[24]

Two levels of court addressed the constitutional questions: the Ontario Superior Court of Justice and the Ontario Court of Appeal. Leave to appeal to the Supreme Court of Canada was denied. All of the judges declined to scrutinize NAFTA for failing to live up to constitutional standards embodied in the 1867 and 1982 Constitution Acts. The argument made by the applicants was that NAFTA's investment chapter ran afoul of the Canadian constitution in two principal respects. First, NAFTA unconstitutionally transferred jurisdiction ordinarily within the purview of Canadian superior courts (s. 96) to private tribunals and, second, NAFTA violated the Charter of Rights and Freedoms[25] by enabling NAFTA to impugn laws and regulations that promote human health, security, or working conditions—protections that work to the advantage of equality-seeking groups. There also were ancillary arguments about unwritten constitutional principles—that NAFTA offended the rule of law and constitutionalism—and the right to a fair hearing (section 2[e] of the Canadian Bill of Rights) that are not addressed here.

The first argument made was the strongest in what was, otherwise, not a very strong case. It concerned the arcane question of the jurisdiction of superior courts in Canada in 1867. Much of the established jurisprudence in the field concerned provinces establishing inferior courts and tribunals that eroded the original jurisdiction of superior federal courts. The argument cleverly asked if NAFTA investment tribunals were performing functions 'identical or analogous' to those performed by Canadian courts.[26] Professor Andree Lajoie, in her affidavit sworn in support of the application, concluded that 'exclusive and inherent jurisdiction' to determine the legality and wrongfulness of government action, including exclusive authority to decide matters concerning expropriation, fell within the jurisdiction of s. 96 Canadian superior courts at the Constitution's origins in 1867.[27]

---

[23] ICSID rules have since been modified to enable written, but not oral, submissions easier for intervenors to submit, even if one of the parties to the arbitration is opposed. See ICSID Arbitration Rule 67 (2022).
[24] UPS subsequently lost the dispute. See *United Parcel Service of America Inc. v. Canada*, (Award and separate opinion) Ad hoc—UNCITRAL Arbitration Rules (24 May 2007).
[25] By depriving Canadians of life, liberty, and security of the person, not in accordance with the principles of fundamental justice (s. 7) and offending equality rights (s. 15).
[26] See *Re Residential Tenancies Act* [1981] 1 SCR 714.
[27] See Lajoie (2003) at para. 10. Additional affidavits, from Professor of Law M. Sornarajah of National University of Singapore and Professor of Political Economy Stephen Clarkson of the University of Toronto described NAFTA's regime of foreign investment protection, highlighting its radical departure from past international practice and constitution-like features. All of these affidavits are available at

Justice Pepall's ruling in the first instance rejected the s. 96 claim. In Canada's constitutional system, treaties are executed by the executive branch and implemented by the legislature with the requisite authority. For this reason, NAFTA, she concluded, is 'not part of Canada's domestic law' and so did not attract the application of s. 96.[28] Nor could it be said that s. 96 jurisdiction had been transferred to NAFTA investment tribunals. 'International law and domestic law are distinct legal systems that operate in different spheres', she declared.[29] The crux of the problem is that Justice Pepall did not want to tie the hands of the executive should it choose to enter binding treaty commitments. If she 'were to accede to the Applicant's submissions', she confessed, 'Canada would be constrained by its domestic laws from entering into an international agreement'.[30] That simply was intolerable for this Justice of the Ontario Superior Court.

What about arguments made under the Charter of Rights and Freedoms? Here again, the judge would not proceed down the path suggested by the applicants. There only were a few NAFTA claims against Canada on the record, which she considered 'inadequate' to render a decision of the sort requested.[31] The applicants, she claimed, failed to show how Charter rights 'were infringed in any of the tribunal decisions' or that they 'affected' any Charter rights.[32] NAFTA tribunals, Justice Pepall noted, have 'no authority to change' Canadian law nor does investment arbitration 'affect or determine the rights of Canadians'.[33] Her decision elided entirely the ways in which investment treaty law and arbitration can have the effect of constraining state capacity, which is precisely its intended effect.[34]

On appeal, Justice Goudge, writing for a unanimous Ontario Court of Appeal, affirmed the application judge's ruling. NAFTA's investor–state arbitration process is not, he held, incorporated into Canadian domestic law, only the ultimate 'decision' that a tribunal may issue.[35] Nor are NAFTA tribunals analogous to superior courts mentioned in s. 96 of the 1867 Constitution. 'We have been shown nothing', Justice Goudge declared, 'that suggests that there were any domestic causes of action known to superior courts at the time of Confederation that could be said to be broadly analogous to these international obligations', such as those that afford

---

http://www.international.gc.ca/trade-agreements-accords-commerciaux/topics-domaines/disp-diff/cupw.aspx?lang=eng (last accessed 16 October 2022).

[28] Council of Canadians (2005) at para. 37.
[29] Council of Canadians (2005) at para. 41. This resembles Justice Butler's opinion in *Costello v. Ireland* [2022] IEHC 600 at para. 90 regarding the compatibility of the EU–Canada investment chapter in CETA with the Irish Constitution. He accepted that 'CETA creates rights and obligations as a matter of international law but does not form part of or have direct effect in our domestic legal system'.
[30] Council of Canadians (2005) at para. 43.
[31] Council of Canadians (2005) at para. 63.
[32] Council of Canadians (2005) at para. 64.
[33] Council of Canadians (2005) at para. 65.
[34] UNCTAD (2015) at 125.
[35] Council of Canadians (2006) at para. 25.

national treatment to foreign investors.[36] It probably is correct to say that under national law at that time, legislatures could discriminate against foreign owned wealth with impunity. There was one 'arguable exception,' Justice Goudge admitted, and that concerned expropriation. Even here, however, the NAFTA scheme was 'animated' by different principles. It was not 'designed to regulate the government taking of domestic private property' but to facilitate private investment flows. This was a sufficient distinction to characterize as 'novel' the jurisdiction of NAFTA tribunals from superior court jurisdiction.[37] The Charter of Rights argument was swiftly dispatched in a single paragraph: it concerned 'mere speculation of harm' and so was 'premature'.[38] It is notable that an otherwise sophisticated judiciary would conclude that investment law strictures, concerning indirect expropriation or regulatory takings for instance, do not regulate state behaviour but merely promote private investment flows. It elevates to a first order effect that which is only a second order, aspirational, effect.[39]

Much is clarified by the argument of the Charter Committee on Poverty Issues (CCPI) that was filed subsequent to the Ontario Court of Appeal decision. It was this group that had carriage of the application for leave to appeal to the Supreme Court of Canada. The CCPI chose to abandon the s. 96 argument while refusing to yield ground on the Charter argument which, the group believed, was more persuasive. The CCPI argued that the courts below had misconceived the Charter argument. The claim was not that NAFTA tribunals should be expected to apply the law of the Charter, but that executive action should be expected to comply with the Charter. Treaties, in other words, should be expected to conform to the Charter's constitutional commitment to human rights.[40] The CCPI was asking the Supreme Court of Canada to do no more than the German Constitutional Court has done as regards delegation of authority to the European Union in its Solange rulings.[41] Canadian courts should be expected to strictly scrutinize executive treaty-making to ensure constitutional conformity. The object was to domesticate, and thereby discipline, international investment law by reason of Canada's own constitutional commitments.

Canadian courts, however, have exhibited little eagerness in supervising exercises of executive branch authority. Even if subject to review under the Charter of Rights and Freedoms, judges seem hesitant to trench too far into the domain of prerogative power over foreign affairs.[42] Yet the lower court judges in this case

---
[36] Council of Canadians (2006) at para. 39.
[37] Council of Canadians (2006) at para. 40.
[38] Council of Canadians (2006) at para. 59.
[39] As revealed by the empirical evidence revealing an ambiguous relationship between signing investment treaties and attracting new inward investment. See the summary in Danzman (2019).
[40] Porter (2007) at para. 26.
[41] See Solange I (1974) BVerfGE 37, 271 (German Constitutional Court) and Solange II (1986) BVerfGE 73, 378 (German Constitutional Court) at para. 30.
[42] The Supreme Court of Canada early on declared that the executive branch is subject to the Charter's disciplines and has on occasion issued remedies directing the executive to take certain action,

did not speak in terms of the separation of powers. They were not so preoccupied with conserving executive discretion as with steering clear of a legal field viewed as novel and alien. They were lent a hand in this endeavour by the evidence of the late James Crawford, then Whewell Professor of International Law at the University of Cambridge and investment arbitrator. Crawford swore an affidavit on behalf of the Government of Canada that was meant to join issue with points made by Professor M. Sornarajah, then C.J. Koh Professor at the Faculty of Law of the National University of Singapore.[43]

Professor Crawford opined that NAFTA and other investment treaties do not deprive states of 'their regulatory powers over the economy and the environment'.[44] Should a government run afoul of treaty strictures, such as the one concerning indirect expropriations (regulatory takings), it can adopt this measure so long as, among other things, compensation is provided to an investor. By way of example, Crawford took up the claim of the Virginia-based Metalclad Corporation against Mexico.[45] Metalclad had claimed that Mexico expropriated its investment by impeding the opening of a hazardous waste facility site formerly shut down for leeching chemicals into the local water supply. The municipality refused to grant the requisite construction permit while the Governor issued an ecological decree barring development that threatened a rare species of cactus in the vicinity of the site. No government action was forestalled in this case, Crawford maintained. 'It is not true that Mexico's concerns were ultimately overridden', he maintained.[46] Instead, Mexico got what it wanted and the investor was compensated for its losses. For this reason, Professor Crawford characterized as 'overstated, if not greatly misconceived' the argument that NAFTA is part of a 'new international constitutional order'.[47] Like the fifth and fourteenth amendments to the US Constitution, takings are not outright banned but only require the provision of 'just compensation'.[48]

The 'applicable law' provision in investment treaties, Professor Crawford maintained, served to underscore the autonomy of these distinct systems. Investment tribunals under NAFTA apply treaty and international law, not the internal law of national states.[49] 'In fact,' Professor Crawford added in a footnote, 'NAFTA tribunals have resisted the application of US constitutional principles in favour of

---

but there remains reluctance to tread on that branch's toes. Compare *Khadr v. Canada (Prime Minister)* [2010] 1 SCR 44 with *Burns v. United States* [2001] 1 SCR 283.

[43] Sornarajah is one of the world's foremost critics of investment arbitration and offered expert evidence in support of the applicants' legal arguments. I reluctantly was drawn into this war of affidavits. What follows draws on some of the points made in my sworn affidavit in response to Crawford's in Schneiderman (2004).
[44] Crawford (2004) at para. 33.
[45] Metalclad (2001). See discussion of this dispute in Schneiderman (2008) at 82–6.
[46] Crawford (2004) at para. 32.
[47] Crawford (2004) at para. 40 (quoting Sornarajah).
[48] See the discussion in Dana and Merrill (2002) at 163–4.
[49] Crawford (2004) at para. 5.

formulations based on customary international law'.[50] Yet, tribunals have repeatedly had recourse to the American Law Institute's *Third Restatement of the Foreign Relations Law of the United States*, which mirrors US constitutional practice, to fill in the meaning of investment law's takings rule.[51]

Professor Crawford claimed that there 'is no evidence that [NAFTA] Chapter Eleven awards are constituting, so to speak, a clog on the equity of legislative action in the public interest'.[52] Yet, the record reveals that NAFTA's takings rule may have deterred the House of Commons from mandating the plain packaging of cigarettes sold in Canada, in 1994, after lawyers for big American tobacco threatened to sue under NAFTA for hundreds of millions of dollars.[53] As mentioned above, there likely was a similar chilling effect that deterred the Premier of New Brunswick, Bernard Lord, from adopting a public auto insurance scheme despite the recommendation of an all-party committee of the legislature to so proceed.[54] Van Harten and Scott have documented, in semi-structured interviews with government officials from the province of Ontario, that lawyers from the trade ministry have intervened in environmental policy decision-making, relying upon investment treaty commitments, to protect business interests.[55] There likely are other such instances not yet well documented in Canada and elsewhere in the world. Regulatory chill, in other words, is not a non-trivial phenomenon.[56]

Having dispensed with all this evidence in desultory fashion, these courts abandoned any role in supervising Canadian agency in both spreading investment law disciplines and internalizing them within its constitutional order. Canadian courts evinced a little more interest in the impact of investment treaty law on constitutionally recognized Aboriginal rights, but not much more.

---

[50] Crawford (2004) at para. 44, fn. 46.
[51] For example, *Pope & Talbot Inc v. Canada*, Interim (2000) Award, Ad hoc—UNCITRAL Arbitration Rules (26 June), referring to American Law Institute (1987) at para. 712, comment (g). In the next section I discuss the influence of US constitutional law.
[52] Crawford (2004) at para. 34.
[53] See Schneiderman (1996) at 120–9 concerning the abandonment of Canadian tobacco plain packaging proposals. Bonnitcha (2014) at 125 claims that '[o]pposition by foreign investors does not appear to have been significant in that decision'. This is too blithe a conclusion. The controversy erupted into the national spotlight once US-based tobacco multinationals objected to the scheme. Bonnitcha cannot know what was 'significant' in the decision to abandon the scheme as it remains cloaked in cabinet secrecy.
[54] See Shrybman and Sinclair (2001).
[55] Van Harten and Scott (2016) at 108. I have argued that the Government of Canada abandoned a proposal to mandate plain packaging of tobacco products in Schneiderman (2008). The finding by Coté (2016) at 14, that there are low levels of awareness among Canadian regulators, is consistent with the story I tell about the Canadian plain packaging proposal. It was abandoned by the executive branch only after a parliamentary committee recommended the government proceed with its proposal (in Schneiderman [2008] at 127–8). See Moehlecke (2020) on the real but limited impact of ISDS on chilling policy space.
[56] See Hill (2015) quoting lawyer and arbitrator Toby Landau ('Regulatory chill, so-called, in my opinion definitely exists'). Also see Landau (2018) and Maffett, Milone and Rao (2023).

(ii) *Hupacasath First Nation v. Canada*

A similarly futile attempt at halting the spread of investment treaty disciplines via Canadian constitutional commitments was sought by the Hupacasath First Nation. On this occasion, the 'duty to consult' was invoked, a constitutional obligation to accommodate Aboriginal interests when government action is likely to harm an unresolved Aboriginal rights claim. The constitutional duty to consult arises 'as a prelude to a potential infringement' of Aboriginal or treaty rights, in addition to Aboriginal title, and before a court has made a final determination about those rights.[57] The Hupacasath sought to enjoin the Government of Canada's ability to enter into a foreign investor protection agreement with the People's Republic of China without first consulting with and addressing the pending Aboriginal rights claim under s. 35 of the Constitution made by the Hupacasath.[58]

The Hucapasath First Nation argued, among other things, that obligations owed to Chinese investors arising under a Foreign Investment Protection Agreement (FIPA)would limit the 'reasonable accommodation' available to Aboriginal claimants in cases where there has been a breach of the duty to consult. This is because it is foreseeable that governments would wish to take into account the concerns of disgruntled foreign investors when fashioning measures to fulfill the constitutional duty to consult. What is deemed reasonable, in other words, would be influenced by investment law constraints. Canada likely would prefer not to antagonize too greatly the interests of foreign investors. Moreover, Canadian courts might very well condone this sort of solicitude towards foreign investors. The Justices of the Supreme Court of Canada had previously indicated that they do not want to construct an edifice of constitutional rights that acts as a bar to the efficient economic exploitation of natural resources that lie within First Nations lands. They have been inclined to treat less favourably Aboriginal constitutional claims that impede the non-constitutional interests of resource developers in areas such as 'agriculture, forestry, mining, and hydroelectric power'.[59] The odds were not so great, then, that the Hucapasath would receive a sympathetic hearing from the Canadian judiciary.

Christopher Thomas, a prominent Canadian investment lawyer and arbitrator, tendered an expert opinion on behalf of the government in reply to the expert opinion supplied by Professor Gus Van Harten of Osgoode Hall Law School. Thomas opined that the Canada–China FIPA 'does not purport to change the allocation or distribution of government powers' and that the 'totality of powers of

---

[57] Lawrence and Macklem (2000) at 255. For judicial exposition, see *Haida Nation v. B.C. (Minister of Forests)* [2004] 3 SCR 511 and *Tsilhqot'in Nation v. B.C.* [2014] 2 SCR 257. That duty to consult now runs throughout all phases of Aboriginal and Canadian state relations.

[58] Much of this story is told in Van Harten (2015), Part III. Former Assembly of First Nations Grand Chief Ovide Mercredi made this same argument in response to the proposed Multilateral Agreement on Investment (MAI) in the late 1990s. See Mercredi (1998) at 69.

[59] See *Delgamuukw v. British Columbia* [1997] 3 SCR 1010 at para. 165. But see qualifications issued by the Supreme Court in *Tsilhqot'in Nation v. British Columbia* [2014] 2 SCR 257.

the Canadian State ... made under or pursuant to the Constitution Act, remains unchanged'.[60] The treaty, he declares, has no '*supra*-national effect'—it 'does not supplant Canadian law, which remain fully in effect'.[61] Instead the treaty operates as do all other investment treaty commitments Canada has entered into, including NAFTA's investment chapter. The treaties, moreover, are unlikely to give rise to a limitation on Aboriginal rights. Though 'one cannot categorically rule out the possibility of a claim in the future ... the NAFTA experience does not suggest a substantial probability of a spate of claims based on measures based on aboriginal rights or interests'.[62] Thomas' opinion is carefully framed—the Canada–China FIPA does not 'purport' to limit governmental power; it operates in the same way as do other international treaties; and the law is continually evolving and improving.

Chief Justice of the Federal Court of Canada, Paul Crampton, dismissed the Hupacasath application. He accepted the government's submission that the alleged adverse impact of the Canada–China FIPA on the Hupacasath was 'speculative, remote and non-appreciable'.[63] There was no evidence before him of actual or prospective Chinese investment in lands on or near those claimed by Hupacasath.[64] There was no scenario the Justice could contemplate in which the Hucapasath would run afoul of investment treaty obligations or in which an investment tribunal would not fully take their interests into account into its deliberations.[65] When asked to reach the same conclusion as had Ontario courts in the CUPW case regarding the constitutional insignificance of investment treaty arbitration, Chief Justice Crampton would not rule out the possibility that investment law 'may trigger' the constitutional duty to consult. This was because of the lower evidentiary requirement to trigger the duty: a non-speculative and appreciable impact on an unresolved but pending Aboriginal right.[66]

Nevertheless, on every other substantive question, the judge preferred Thomas' evidence. He accepted Thomas' opinion that the minimum standard of treatment under international law is a 'very low procedural "baseline"'.[67] Though this may be Canada's desired interpretation, few tribunals have followed suit. The Glamis Gold tribunal's award, for instance, which Thomas relied upon throughout, treated NAFTA's international minimum standard as having evolved beyond the minimum baseline to include the modern doctrine of legitimate expectations.[68] The

---

[60] Thomas (2013) at para. 22.
[61] Thomas (2013) at paras. 23 (emphasis in original), 24.
[62] Thomas (2013) at para. 30.
[63] Hupacasath First Nation (2013) at para. 59.
[64] Hupacasath First Nation (2013) at para 133(e).
[65] The decision in *Glamis Gold Ltd. v. United States* (2009) Award, Ad hoc—UNCITRAL Arbitration Rules (8 June) was offered by Thomas as an exemplar of how 'societal' (in that case, Aboriginal) interests are 'taken into consideration' by investment tribunals. See Thomas (2013) at paras. 31, 199–204.
[66] Hupacasath First Nation (2013) at para. 68.
[67] Hupacasath First Nation (2013) at para. 95.
[68] Glamis Gold, supra n. 65 at paras. 619, 621. See also *Mondev International Ltd. v. United States* (2002) Award, ICSID Case No ARB(AF)/99/2 (11 October). On the doctrine of legitimate expectations, see Ostřanský (2018).

expert opinion obfuscates this and similar developments within investment treaty arbitration.

Weighing in on the effect of investment disciplines on available policy space, Chief Justice Crampton declared that there is 'no evidence that any sub-national governments in Canada have been fettered or "chilled" by NAFTA or the 24 FIPAs in force, from regulation in the public interest'.[69] Professor Van Harten did not speak precisely to regulatory chill in his affidavit but instead emphasized the vast array of policy areas within federal, provincial, and Aboriginal law-making authority that fall within investment treaty strictures. I have already mentioned a couple of episodes in which regulatory chill likely played a role in impeding the development of Canadian law. The hasty dismissal of this aspect of the claim seems crude—investment treaties are meant, after all, to hamper policy space.

The Federal Court of Appeal dismissed an appeal by the Hupacasath. Deference was owed to findings of fact made by the lower court judge and, in any event, declared Justice Stratas for the Court, 'I would have made the same factual findings'.[70] There was no causal link, Stratas J. concluded, between the claimed adverse impact on Hupacasath Aboriginal rights and signing of the Canada–China FIPA. This was entirely 'speculative' having resort only to 'assumptions, conjectures and guesswork'.[71] According to this logic, wrote Justice Stratas, virtually any government action would trigger the duty to consult.[72] This, he implied, would be intolerable.

The Federal Court of Appeal, it appears, would not have departed from an important finding made by Chief Justice Crampton. Justice Stratas accepted the government's claim that, as Professor Van Harten was an outspoken critic of the Canada–China FIPA, his expert evidence was to be discounted.[73] In an extraordinary exhibition of disdain, the Chief Justice characterized Van Harten's evidence as 'baldly stated and unsubstantiated'. Instead, the judge preferred Thomas' evidence, which he described as 'more neutral, factually rigorous and persuasive'.[74] This is despite the fact that Van Harten has authored numerous important books on the subject, including a sophisticated empirical study of outcomes in investment arbitration.[75] Van Harten, moreover, indicated to the Court that he has a 'policy of not taking paid work as a counsel, arbitrator, or expert in investment treaty arbitration' and has, over the years, declined invitations to so act.[76] Thomas,

---

[69] Hupacasath First Nation (2013) at para. 133(d).
[70] Hupacasath First Nation (2015) at paras. 77, 78.
[71] Hupacasath First Nation (2015) at para. 118.
[72] The Supreme Court of Canada, sometime later, shielded the production of legislation in Parliament from the constitutional duty to consult in *Mikisew Cree First Nation v. Canada* [2018] 2 SCR 765. The Court has not ruled on the duty to consult in the course of treaty-making, however. The Court has affirmed that the Charter of Rights and Freedoms applies to cabinet decisions, including the royal prerogative over defence in *Operation Dismantle v. The Queen* [1985] 1 SCR 441. See infra n. 42.
[73] Canada (2013) at para. 154.
[74] Hupacasath First Nation (2013) at paras. 38, 43.
[75] Van Harten (2007) and Van Harten (2013a).
[76] Van Harten (2013b) at para. 22.

by contrast, makes no secret of the fact that he earns a living as member of the club of investment lawyers and arbitrators.[77] The judge preferred the evidence of a lawyer who has an interest in the maintenance and spread of the legal regime to protect foreign investors and, indirectly, an interest in the government's success in this case. A self-interested private lawyer's evidence was preferred over that of an engaged academic who, almost single-handedly, raised the public profile of the Canada–China FIPA.[78]

To conclude, Canadian courts have chosen not to impede, or even slow down, Canada's investment treaty programme. Yet no particular Canadian constitutional values are being promoted. Instead, as we learn in the next part, it is a version of US constitutional property, contract, and due process rights that are being elevated to the international plane. This underscores the degree to which a semi-peripheral state such as Canada, even if a member of the clubs populated by powerful capital exporting states (for instance, the G-7 and the OECD), is largely following edicts laid down elsewhere. Foreign policy ideas are hatched in another place, sometimes in the US and at other times Europe, which are then adopted as Canada's own.[79]

III. America: Mending Every Flaw

New historiography suggests that the 1787 American Constitution was devised to ensure the reception of the United States into the international community of nations.[80] Under its first Constitution, the Articles of Confederation, the US was considered an unreliable treaty partner. A new constitutional project was framed to 'earn a favorable reception abroad and facilitate the new nation's integration into the Atlantic world of commerce and civilization'.[81] This second constitution would grant to the federal government the capacity to live up to international obligations. Treaty-making power would therefore be centralized in the new national government. The President was entitled to bring treaties for signature to the US Senate which, after a two-thirds vote of those present (Art. II, s. 2, c. 2), would become supreme law akin to other federal law, according to the Constitution's supremacy clause (Art. VI, cl. 2).[82] The House of Representatives would be shut out entirely of

---

[77] Thomas derives substantial revenue from this work, having been involved in some 68 arbitrations, 47 as arbitrator. For a list see https://www.italaw.com/arbitrators/j-christopher-thomas (last accessed 18 October 2022) and http://investmentarbitrationdatabase.com/arbitrators/j-christopher-thomas (last accessed 18 October 2022).
[78] See the book-length critique of the Canada–China FIPA in Van Harten (2015).
[79] Clarkson and Mildenberger (2011) at 186.
[80] The heading for this section is adapted from 'America the Beautiful' ('God mend thine every flaw') lyrics at https://www.classical-music.com/features/articles/america-the-beautiful-lyrics/ (last accessed 21 October 2022).
[81] Golove and Hulsebosch ()2010 at 936.
[82] *Missouri v. Holland* (1920) 252 US 416. Congress, via Article 1, section 8, has authority to implement non-self-executing treaties. See discussion in *Made in the USA Foundation* (1999) at 1317ff (Congressional power is, at least, concurrent with the treaty making power at 1320).

this lawmaking process.[83] States also would be prohibited from entering into 'any treaty, Alliance or Confederation' (Art. 1, s. 10, cl. 1). It was said that depriving the House of Representatives and states from participating in the production of binding international law would insulate 'compliance with international legal obligations from [the influence of] direct popular control'.[84] Only in the case of 'non-self-executing' treaties—a very narrow category into which few treaties will fall[85]—was Congress expected to pass a law to implement treaty commitments, involving both chambers.[86] Otherwise, participation by the House would take place only after international obligations had properly been adopted by Article II processes.

This treaty practice was contested early in the life of the republic, much of the resistance prompted by the 1794 Jay Treaty between Great Britain and United States. The Jay Treaty aimed to provide a set of mechanisms for resolving outstanding disputes following the American Revolution. Article VI of the treaty included a mechanism for the settlement of debts owed to British creditors by US citizens that had been barred by state legislation. A Commission constituting five persons were to be appointed (two by the US and two by Great Britain, the fifth by the unanimous vote of the other four) with authority to take into account 'all claims ... according to the merits of the several cases, due regard being had to all the circumstances thereof, and as justice and equity shall appear to them to require'.[87] The Commission quickly was inundated with claims totaling US$25 million, significantly exceeding the sum set aside by Congress (US$300,000) and prolonging the life of the Commission well beyond its 18-month mandate. As it turns out, the Commission's life was short-lived for other reasons, having to do with the extreme unpopularity of the Jay Treaty and encompassing claims made by British citizens charged with high treason during the revolutionary period.[88] Ultimately, the US settled all claims by payment of a lump sum of US$2.664 million to the Secretary of the Treasury in London.[89]

Treaty practice has evolved significantly since then. So much so that no longer does the Senate, together with the President, exclusively control treaty-making. Congressional–Executive Agreements allow both chambers of Congress to participate in the production of international obligations. '[N]early everything done through the Treaty Clause,' Hathaway writes, 'can and should be done through congressional-executive agreements approved by both Houses of Congress.'[90] The

[83] Golove and Hulsebosch (2010) at 996. This gave rise to 'ferocious' debates in the early republic over the role of the House (ibid. at 1018).
[84] Golove and Hulsebosch (2010) at 1054.
[85] Vázquez (1995) at 716.
[86] See American Law Institute (2018), Pt. III, s. 310. Self-Executing and Non-Self-Executing Treaty Provisions, Reporter's Notes 1–14.
[87] Moore (1898) at 276–7.
[88] Moore (1898) at 289.
[89] Moore (1898) at 298.
[90] Hathaway (2008) at 1241.

doctrine of 'interchangeability'[91]—Congressional–Executive agreements being interchangeable with Article II processes—now controls treaty-making's dominant form.[92] Congress can involve itself either before or after a treaty has been negotiated.

Of particular interest is the process by which prior authorization to negotiate is granted to the executive branch by Congress. Once negotiated by the executive, the treaty is returned to Congress for an up-or-down vote with no opportunity for amendment or filibuster.[93] This 'fast track process,' inaugurated under the Trade Act of 1974, grants to both Houses input into treaty negotiations and enables them to hold the executive fast to these precommitments. According to Ackerman and Golove, the process grants to 'both Senators and Representatives … many opportunities to voice their concerns and threaten the executive with the prospect of ultimate defeat should their advice be ignored'.[94] The preponderance of trade and investment treaties have been authorized using this procedure since the 1980s.[95]

The constitutionality of this practice is doubted by Tribe. The text specifies that a two-thirds majority vote is required in the Senate to advise and consent to treaties, not a simple majority vote in both Houses of Congress. The Constitution expressly bars states from entering any 'treaty' or 'Agreement or Compact with another State, or with a foreign Power' (Art. 1, s. 10, cl. 1 & 3). These textual commitments generate 'powerful evidence' that congressional–executive agreements are not interchangeable with treaties even as agreements have 'found a settled place' in constitutional practice.[96]

Some international lawyers point to the antecedent roots of investment law in the British–US experience under the Jay Treaty.[97] Barton Legum argues that the framers of the US Constitution contemplated arbitral mechanisms for the resolution of disputes between individuals and foreign states. Legum even claims that there is 'significant overlap in both subject matter and procedure' between the Jay Treaty Commission and NAFTA's investment chapter. The novelty, therefore, of investor–state dispute settlement (ISDS) has been 'overstated'.[98] Investment treaty dispute resolution processes depart significantly from the 1794 Jay Treaty, however. As Schwarzenberger notes, the claims under Article VI 'had only an indirect connection with international law'. These private debts more appropriately were the subject of municipal law, but remedies had been foreclosed through retributive

---

[91] McDougal and Lans (1945) at 290, Hathaway (2008) at 1243, and Ackerman and Golove (1995) at 861ff.
[92] Hathaway (2008) at 1260.
[93] Hathaway (2008) at 1304.
[94] Ackerman and Golove (1995) at 906.
[95] Hathaway (2008) at 1305.
[96] Tribe (2000) at 655–6.
[97] 'While bilateral investment treaties and ICSID are relatively recent developments, international arbitration addressing similar subjects has existed for centuries' in Legum (2001).
[98] Legum (2002) at 531.

state legislation. In which case, all that the Treaty did was reflect municipal law remedies while adding the 'overriding criteria' of 'justice and equity'.[99] What the treaty did, in other words, was to mimic results that would have been forthcoming under US private law if states had not blocked access to courts. By contrast, investment treaties seek to avert municipal law and the application of local law in circumstances where remedies before local courts are not foreclosed.[100]

Legum insists, nevertheless, that the subject matter of these disputes is the same—that there is 'significant overlap'.[101] This hardly appears to be the case. The scope of covered investments in investment treaties is far broader than anything contemplated in the Jay Treaty Commission. There is also a vastly broader range of protections available to foreign investors than under the Jay Treaty that include regulatory takings and the capacious fair and equitable treatment standard of protection. The object of modern investment law is to tame state regulatory activity far into the future, unlike this eighteenth-century special commission which was only retrospective in scope.[102] If the goal is not to roll back the regulatory state it is, at least, to ensure that the state does not disrupt investor expectations. In this way, the historical parallel is correct but draws on the wrong model. Here, the more appropriate analogue are eighteenth-century conceptions of limited government. This, according to McGinnis and Movsavian, better represents the aims of modern international economic law: to constrain governments from serving the interests of what Madison called 'factions': well-organized groups that extract rents and concessions so as to impede the disinterested pursuit of the public good.[103]

It is instructive, therefore, to look elsewhere in US history for sources. Vandevelde claims that the origins of bilateral investment treaties can be found in US Friendship, Commerce and Navigation (FCN) Treaties signed after the Second World War. Vandevelde reveals that the US intention in signing FCNs was to internationalize US constitutional law.[104] The State Department would not 'recommend a treaty provision which would go beyond' US constitutional principles. The intention was to not grant to foreign investors treatment 'more favorable' than that available to US citizens.[105] Standards analogous to those in the Bill of Rights were considered suitable for other countries to adopt.

---

[99] Schwarzenberger (1986) at 34.
[100] Only claims based upon a 'denial of justice' aim to address circumstances where local remedies are foreclosed to an investor.
[101] Legum (2001).
[102] Acknowledged by Legum in (2002) at 536.
[103] McGinnis and Movsevian (2000) at 515. See Hamilton, Madison, and Jay (1961) at 77–8 and Wood (2021) at 89.
[104] Vandevelde (2017) at, for example, 23, 26, and 379.
[105] Vandevelde (2017) at 287. Vandevelde admits that 'the treaties did, in some ways, go beyond these constitutional protections' by, for instance, incorporating certain rights 'under customary international law and providing limited protection against exchange controls' which were less robust than US law. But, he insists, any substantive protections 'essentially replicated the treatment that foreign investors already received under existing U.S. law and policy' (at 385).

The successor instruments to FCNs largely have accomplished this goal with accompanying enforcement mechanisms, namely, ISDS.[106] Investment treaties include rights associated with US constitutional law include non-discrimination rights (national treatment). Broadly speaking, foreign investors cannot be treated differently from national economic actors. The office of the United States Trade Representative (USTR) likens this standard to 'guarantees set out in the Equal Protection Clause of the US Constitution'.[107] Prohibitions against nationalization and expropriation, or measures tantamount thereto, directly invite parallels between investment law and US constitutional law. The USTR declares that 'the protection against uncompensated expropriations is drawn from US Supreme Court cases that interpret the takings clause of the U.S. Constitution'.[108] It has long been the desire of the United States, and other capital-exporting states, to elevate to the plane of the international protections of property that are constitution-like. The widespread adoption of treaty annexes to expropriation clauses that incorporate US Supreme Court doctrine regarding regulatory takings under the fifth and fourteenth amendments bespeaks of this success. Criteria are adopted to aid in determining whether an indirect expropriation (or in US parlance, a regulatory taking) has occurred. This requires 'a case-by-case, fact-based inquiry' that considers, among other factors, the 'economic impact' of the measure, the extent to which it interfered with 'distinct, reasonable investment-backed expectations' and the 'character of the government action'. This mirrors the multi-factor analysis for regulatory takings articulated by the US Supreme Court in *Penn Central*.[109] It is astonishing how rapidly this practice, promoted by a change in US treaty practice, has been widely embraced, even for states that do not have constitutional property rights (such as Canada). Or consider standards that ensure investors receive the 'minimum standard of treatment' (MST) required by international law in addition to 'fair and equitable treatment' (FET). Treated as virtually synonymous, they have been interpreted in ways analogous to a nineteenth-century due process clause or a clause that guarantees the enforceability of contracts.[110]

Confidence that American constitutional law determined the content of international law was made plain in the 2002 debate over granting President George W. Bush 'fast-track' authority to conclude negotiations with Chile, Singapore, Morocco, and others. The legislative authorization, in the Trade Promotion

---

[106] This and the following paragraph draw upon Schneiderman (2018a).

[107] USTR (2015a). The international standard goes much further than equal protection doctrine. In the US, run-of-the-mill regulation of the marketplace attracts, under that doctrine, only rationality review—the lowest standard of constitutional scrutiny available. Not only is the international standard of national treatment more intrusive and less deferential, but the standard also encompasses both direct and indirect (or adverse impact) discrimination. Equal protection doctrine in the US is more timid, by contrast, encompassing only direct discrimination.

[108] USTR (2015a).

[109] *Penn Central Transportation Co v. New York City* (1977) 438 US 104 at 124.

[110] See, for example, *Dartmouth College v. Woodward* (1819) 17 U.S. (4 Wheat.) 518 and discussion in Schneiderman (2016).

Authority Act of 2002, resulted in the executive branch being directed to ensure that foreign investors are accorded 'no greater rights' than US investors in the US. A similar confidence that investment law channels US constitutional law was exhibited in 2015 when President Obama sought trade promotion authority for Transatlantic Trade and Investment Partnership (TTIP) and Trans-Pacific Partnership (TPP). According to USTR, '*[t]hese investment rules mirror rights and protections in the United States and are designed to provide no greater substantive rights to foreign investors than are afforded under the Constitution and U.S. law*'.[111] It is precisely for this reason, the USTR explained, that the United States 'has won every one of the handful of cases that have been brought against it and has never paid a penny in damages or to settle a case'.[112] This impressive record could be preserved, President Obama declared at the outset of the 2015 debates, so long as they 'make sure that America writes the rules of the global economy'. 'America should call the shots,' Obama declared.[113]

It was jarring, then, to hear Presidential candidate Donald Trump characterize the North America Free Trade Agreement (NAFTA) as a disaster for the United States during his successful 2017 election campaign run. Renegotiation, if not cancellation, of NAFTA loomed on the horizon.[114] As Trump never specifically addressed NAFTA's investment chapter on the campaign trail, it was unclear what the US position would be entering into renegotiations. If past Republican (and even Democratic) policy were any guide, Trump would have been expected to insist that a successor treaty include rights that are touted as mirroring those found in the US Constitution.

This appeared to be the case on the eve of renegotiations.[115] In July 2017, United States Trade Representative (USTR) Robert Lighthizer indicated that the US would be seeking to strengthen NAFTA's investment chapter by securing 'important rights consistent with U.S. legal principles and practice, while ensuring that NAFTA country investors in the United States are not accorded greater substantive rights than domestic investors'.[116] These USTR objectives were expanded upon in November 2017, indicating that US negotiators would seek to include procedures that more efficiently resolved disputes, ensured open and accessible dispute

---

[111] USTR (2015b) (emphasis in original).
[112] USTR (2015b).
[113] Obama (2016).
[114] Trump planned to pull out of NAFTA a couple of months after taking office but balked. 'I was all set to terminate,' he admitted at the time, 'I looked forward to terminating it. I was going to do it' quoted in Baker and Glasser (2022) at 75.
[115] Negotiations commenced on 16 August 2017 in in Washington D.C., with the second round in Mexico City (1–5 September 2017), the third round in Ottawa (23–27 September 2017), fourth in Washington D.C. (11–15 October 2017), and then a fifth round in Mexico City (17–21 November 2017). The next four paragraphs draw upon Schneiderman (2018b).
[116] USTR, 'Summary of Objectives for the NAFTA Renegotiation' (17 July 2017) at 9, at https://ustr.gov/sites/default/files/files/Press/Releases/NAFTAObjectives.pdf (last accessed 23 February 2018).

settlement, and enabled the submission of amicus briefs.[117] It was also a stated objective to '[p]rovide meaningful procedures for resolving investment disputes, while ensuring the protection of U.S. sovereignty and the maintenance of strong U.S. domestic industries'.[118] By October 2017, however, that position appeared to have evaporated. The US presented to its negotiating partners a vague proposal that ISDS only be available when state parties 'opt in' to NAFTA's investment chapter. In testimony before a Canadian House of Commons Committee, Deputy Minister Steve Verheul of Global Affairs Canada revealed that '[a]t the table, the U.S. promptly said they would opt out' of ISDS.[119]

The rationale for this policy change appears to have been addressed in Lighthizer's statement at the conclusion of the fourth round of NAFTA renegotiations: it was to discourage US investment from being sent abroad and, instead, to keep it in the US. Lighthizer declared that 'it is unreasonable to expect that the United States will continue to encourage and guarantee U.S. companies to invest in Mexico and Canada primarily for export to the United States'.[120] If US investment policy previously championed the movement of capital across borders, it was now about discouraging investment abroad by not providing what Lighthizer described as a form of 'political risk insurance paid for by the United States government'. Firms should be expected to calculate their own risks according to market disciplines and without a 'thumb on the scale', Lighthizer announced. An ISDS opt-in would have the advantage, he acknowledged, of getting the US labour movement to buy in to a revised NAFTA.[121] Remarkably, Lighthizer was channeling an argument advanced by critics of the regime that ISDS privatizes profit but socializes risk.

The Mexico–US–Canada Agreement (MUSCA) eliminates ISDS as between Canada and the US (after a three-year phase out) but retains access to ISDS for investors in Mexico on more limited grounds, having mostly to do with national treatment, MFN, direct expropriation, performance requirements, and covered government contracts in five sectors. There is also an obligation that investors exhaust local remedies for a period of 30 months. The executive branch subsequently

---

[117] These negotiating objectives are drawn from the Bipartisan Congressional Trade Priorities and Accountability Act of 2015, H.R. 2146 (114th), s. 102(b)(4)(H).
[118] USTR 'Summary of Objectives for the NAFTA Renegotiation' (November 2017) at 8–9, at https://ustr.gov/sites/default/files/files/Press/Releases/Nov%20Objectives%20Update.pdf (last accessed 23 February 2018).
[119] Canada, Standing Committee on International Trade, 'Evidence,' Meeting No. 92, 42nd Parl., 1st Sess. (4 December 2017) at https://www.ourcommons.ca/DocumentViewer/en/42-1/CIIT/meeting-92/evidence (last accessed 23 February 2018). 'I was all in on killing ISDS in NAFTA' acknowledges Lighthizer in (2023) at 226.
[120] USTR, 'Closing Statement of USTR Robert Lighthizer at the Fourth Round of NAFTA Renegotiations' (October 2017) at https://ustr.gov/about-us/policy-offices/press-office/press-releases/2017/october/closing-statement-ustr-robert (last accessed 23 February 2018).
[121] Leonard (2017). In his memoir as USTR, Lighthizer (2023) at 226 describes ISDS as 'free political risk insurance for companies who wished to offshore American jobs to countries with weak rule of law'. n

secured approval in the US Congress.[122] It remains to be seen if these policy developments reflect long-term trends in the US or if MUSCA is just an aberration.

We appear to be some distance removed from a discussion of US judicial responses to investment law strictures. The object of the discussion so far has been to argue that US executive and legislative branches treat investment treaty law as advancing protections under US constitutional law. The deviation from this path by the Trump administration was prompted not by a rejection of the project of promoting US constitutional practice but to encourage investment at home rather than abroad. Given the limited role investment treaties play in determining where foreign investments are made, however, this strategy likely will not have much of an effect. In its assessment of the impact of limiting or eliminating access to ISDS for US investors under MUSCA, and extrapolating from data that showed a positive correlation between investor protections and attracting new foreign direct investment, the US International Trade Commission concluded that it would have only a 'limited economy-wide effect on the United States'.[123]

Turning, finally, to judicial engagement with investment law, we learn that the US judiciary is, so far, content to leave intact investment law's disciplines. In neither of the two instances discussed below have the courts directly addressed the degree to which investment law is compliant with US constitutional law. What we do learn, however, is that the judiciary do not wish to obstruct the global spread of what successive executive branches have associated with US constitutional values. In the cases next discussed, US courts have exhibited disinterest in policing the potential constraints on policy options that are available to governments both at home (in the US) and abroad (in Argentina).

(i) *Made in the USA Foundation v. United States*

The US Supreme Court has yet to weigh in on how well America has achieved its ambition of calling the shots. There has been no judicial pronouncement on investment treaty conformity with the US Constitution. Lower federal courts have, instead, considered the constitutionality of congressional–executive agreements with Article II's Treaty Clause. The fast-track process, by which Congress authorized the executive to negotiate NAFTA with Mexico and Canada, was challenged by a number of individual and institutional plaintiffs, including the United Steel Workers of America. At the US District Court, Judge Propst agreed that the institutional plaintiffs satisfied the stringent criteria for standing to constitutionally challenge NAFTA, but not the individual plaintiffs.[124] Having overcome this initial

---

[122] Tucker (2020) at 5–6.
[123] US (2019) at 202.
[124] An 'injury in fact,' 'fairly traceable' to the defendant, and redressable by a favourable decision. See *Made in USA Foundation* (1999) at 1230 and *Lujan v. Defenders of Wildlife* (1992) 504 US 555 at 560–1.

jurisdictional hurdle, the plaintiffs then had to satisfy the Court that the question it was being asked was not a 'political question'. This doctrine is traceable to the ruling in *Marbury v. Madison* where Chief Justice Marshall distinguished between legal questions, warranting a remedy from the court, and political questions which foreclosed a judicial remedy.[125] A later voting rights case, *Baker v. Carr*, enumerated criteria courts should consider in determining whether a case or controversy raises a political question.[126] Among the many criteria, the Court in *Made in the USA* was interested in whether there was a demonstrable textual commitment of this question to another branch of government, whether there was a judicially manageable standard with which to answer the question, in addition to a number of prudential considerations.[127]

It appeared to Judge Propst that even if several indicators pointed in the direction of a political question, this was a legal question, hence, a justiciable one. Moving on to the question of whether NAFTA was constitutionally compliant, Judge Propst observed that there was no judicially manageable standard with which to distinguish 'treaties' mentioned in Article II, requiring two-thirds Senate approval, from commercial agreements requiring the participation of the whole of Congress. Not only was there no workable definition suggested by text or by practice, there also was no indication that the treaty clause was the exclusive means by which international agreements could be carried out. As there was no definitive answer to this question, the judge was inclined to treat congressional authority as 'concurrent' with the executive branch treaty power.[128] In which case, congressional–executive agreements—the process by which NAFTA was negotiated and then approved—are 'done in a constitutional manner'.[129]

On appeal, the Court of Appeals for the Eleventh District vacated the lower court decision, concluding that the question before the court was a nonjusticiable political one. In the opinion of Judge Fletcher, the plaintiffs had the requisite standing but had not presented 'the type of question that can be properly addressed by the judiciary'.[130] Though the judiciary would have a duty to 'invalidate international agreements which violate the express terms of the Constitution', the 'clear assignment of authority to the political branches' to conclude 'commercial agreements' counseled against judicial oversight of this quintessential political function.[131] Moreover, there was no judicially manageable standard with which a court could

---

[125] *Marbury v. Madison* 5 U.S. (1 Cranch) 137 (1803).
[126] *Baker v. Carr*, 369 US 186 at 217 (1962). Judge Propst reduced these to three. See Made in USA Foundation (1999) at 1254, drawing upon *Goldwater v. Carter*, 444 US 996 at 998 (1979).
[127] Such as the need for federal uniformity, potential adverse effects on the economy or foreign relations, the reliance interest of businesses, and the need to respect other branches of government. See Made in USA Foundation (1999) at 1266.
[128] Made in USA Foundation (1999) at 1320.
[129] Made in USA Foundation (1999) at 1323.
[130] Made in USA Foundation (2001) at 1311.
[131] Made in USA Foundation (2001) at 1313.

resolve this constitutional dispute. The plaintiffs supplied no 'analytical framework' but only 'nebulous argument[s]' based upon whether the agreement was 'major', 'significant', or impinged on 'sovereignty'.[132] Indeed, Judge Fletcher wrote, 'in an increasingly global economy, simple bilateral tariff arrangements ... may be said to significantly impinge on sovereignty'.[133] Business firms also have structured their affairs 'in reliance' of trade and investment protections, militating against judicial meddling. Any such intrusion into foreign economic affairs 'likely would have a destabilizing effect on governmental relations and economic activity across the North American continent'.[134]

The Court of Appeals declined to issue any ruling regarding the constitutionality of congressional–executive agreements. By settling the problem with reference to political questions doctrine, the Court simply deferred to settled constitutional practice.[135] The Court would not stand in the way of the political branches proceeding to bind other states to commitments that serve US interests. Even if those commitments do not line up so well with constitutional commitments elsewhere, as we learn in the next case under discussion.

(ii) *BG Group v. Argentina*

A majority of the United States Supreme Court disregarded such dampening effects on constitutional space when undertaking judicial review of the tribunal decision in *BG Group v. Argentina*.[136] At issue before the Court were not the effects of BIT commitments on a foreign state but review of an investment tribunal's decision to accept jurisdiction despite the treaty's local litigation requirement. As arbitrators have authority to determine a tribunal's competence, the panel permitted the investor to proceed immediately to arbitration regardless of the Argentine–UK BIT requirement that the claimant first seek a remedy in local Argentinian courts for an eighteen-month period.[137] The Court of Appeals for the District of Columbia unanimously vacated the award.[138] The Supreme Court ruled otherwise, holding that the tribunal had not exceeded its jurisdiction.

The investment tribunal warranted deference, wrote Justice Breyer for the majority, because '[i]nternational arbitrators are more likely familiar than are judges with the expectations of foreign investors and recipient nations regarding operation of the provision'.[139] In so doing, the majority likened investment arbitration

---

[132] Made in USA Foundation (2001) at 1315, also fn. 33.
[133] Made in USA Foundation (2001) at 1315, fn. 33.
[134] Made in USA Foundation (2001) at 1317.
[135] As Tribe (2000) at 656 acknowledges.
[136] BG Group (2014).
[137] BG Group (2007).
[138] Argentina (2012).
[139] BG Group (2014) at 14.

to private commercial arbitration. The Court's solicitude towards commercial arbitration is informed, in turn, by its deference towards labour arbitration outcomes. Only 'wild deviations from the contract' or 'no contract to arbitrate in the first place' warrant judicial interference in labour disputes the Court has held.[140] As labour arbitration is the 'paradigm of private justice'[141]—a system of 'private law,' according to the Court—significant deference is appropriate.[142] The unusual influence of labour arbitration on BG Group is made plain in Justice Breyer's subsequent book on the role of global and comparative legal developments on the Supreme Court's work. Breyer favourably compares the Court's approach to investment arbitration to the review of labour arbitration awards under US law.[143] How labour arbitration can be likened to this contentious sub-field of public international law is never well explained.

Equating judicial review of labour disputes with determinations of state regulatory capacity in a wide array of policy fields looks like a category mistake.[144] Justice Roberts in dissent, with Justice Kennedy, took a different view: the BIT's local litigation requirement was a condition precedent to an agreement to submit a claim to arbitration. There could be no jurisdiction—no acceptance of the unilateral offer to consent to arbitration—until this condition was satisfied.[145] Justice Roberts had a better sense of the stakes involved. 'It is no trifling matter,' he declared, 'for a sovereign nation to subject itself to suit by private parties: we do not presume that any country—including our own—takes that step lightly.'

That the stakes are quite high is revealed by the fact, as mentioned, that former President Obama, together with the United States Trade Representative (USTR), trumpeted parallels between investment treaty protections and rights available to citizens under the US Constitution when seeking Congressional authorization to complete the TPP (from which the US withdrew). Given the breadth of investment treaty protections, they turn out even to exceed safeguards available to US citizens in the Bill of Rights.[146] The majority of the Court seemed curiously disinterested in such linkages.

IV. Conclusion

The cases coming out of Northern North America reveal a judicial predilection to steer clear of the processes facilitating global economic integration. In the case of

---

[140] BG Group (2014) at 6–7; for example, United Steelworkers (1960).
[141] Getman (1988).
[142] United Steelworkers (1960).
[143] Breyer (2015) at 179–92. Franck (1968) at 187 also likens international conflicts to labour disputes where one or more 'neutrals' will have the power to 'initiate proposals and break deadlocks.'
[144] Roberts and Trahanas (2014) at 754 (2014) ('This approach makes no sense').
[145] BG Group (2014) at 2 (per Roberts C.J.).
[146] See Schneiderman (2018a).

Canada, courts exhibit a desire to retreat in the face of exercises of the prerogative over foreign affairs exercised by the executive branch. International law is, therefore, considered a system separate and apart from Canada's own constitutional order. The constitutionally mandated duty to consult Aboriginal peoples is not engaged when international treaties, to which Canada is a signatory, are intended to grant to foreign investors the ability to exploit lands upon which Aboriginal peoples claim rights and title. The judicial performance turns out to be highly formalistic, even as the Supreme Court of Canada touts contextualized analysis in its Charter of Rights cases. This is not the preferred technique when constitutional questions concern Canada's participation in international economic affairs. The same holds true for US courts, though the cases under discussion in this chapter offer only indirect support for the regime. In cases concerning the constitutionality of congressional–executive agreements and enforcement of an arbitral award against Argentina, US courts exhibit an inclination to defer and a disinclination to impede the progress of international economic affairs.

What Northern North American courts exhibit is an observable tendency, common to courts situated in capital-exporting states, to prefer economic integration over constitutional objection. It is undeniable that Canada and the US also wish to attract greater FDI inflows. Indeed, investment policy under President Trump was fashioned precisely to achieve this end. In both countries, however, FDI outflows typically outpace FDI inflows. As a consequence, investors having their homes in either Canada or the US will wish to preserve the privileges they have secured under the investment treaty regime. This preliminary assessment appears to be that courts located in states that have successfully promoted investment law strictures abroad will choose not to find the international regime to protect foreign investors constitutionally incompatible. In fact, they seem to be eager to get out of the way.

3
Taking the Lead
Europe

I. Introduction

Europe is experiencing something of an identity crisis over investment law treaty strictures. Numerous states have withdrawn from the 1994 European Energy Charter Treaty (ECT), part of the European Union (EU) legal apparatus. The treaty entitles European investors in the energy sector to sue member states for compensation should they violate investment treaty standards of protection.[1] The ECT is said to be standing in the way of transitioning away from harmful fossil fuels that contribute to the climate crisis and towards green energy solutions.[2] Withdrawals are mounting even after attempts at 'modernizing' the ECT.[3] According to the non-paper of the European Commission (EC), even an 'improved' ECT cannot fall into line with EU policy objectives to 'decarbonise its energy mix and achieve climate neutrality by 2050'.[4]

These developments stand in tension with the fact that EU member states have been among the most active proponents of the investment rules regime, perhaps more supportive of the regime than any other region in the world. After the fall of European empires, international treaty making emerged as the preferred legal device with which to secure European investment abroad.[5] Treaties tied the hands of peripheral states in those domains where metropolitan powers had a stake, principally in economic realms. This technique, associated with 'informal empire', allowed metropolitan authorities to tolerate self-rule but via 'informal means'. Such methods could induce newly decolonized governments to 'open their resources, labour and markets'.[6] The Netherlands was the first state to negotiate an investment

---

[1] At the time of writing, Italy, Poland, Spain, France, the Netherlands, Slovenia, and Germany have withdrawn or indicated they will withdraw.
[2] Brauch (2021).
[3] According to Brauch (2022), the reforms merely ' "reaffirm[ed] commitments" to the international climate change regime and to other avenues for cooperation on climate, energy, trade, and investment' without requiring anything more.
[4] European Commission (2023) at 2–3. Non-papers aim to guide 'discussion with Member States on the possible options' available to them (at 1).
[5] See Anghie (2004) at 224 (the facts 'suggest, perhaps, the colonial origins of foreign investment law as an academic discipline') and Sornarajah (2019) at 194 (the 'vigour with which colonial structures continued ... is a story that needs to be told').
[6] Tully (2008b) at 260.

treaty with Investor–State Dispute Settlement (ISDS), while the UK and France followed suit, all adopting similar techniques to protect investments abroad.[7] At present, the EU is promoting a new model for dispute resolution—an investment court with an appellate body—that is being included in new bilateral trade and investment agreements and remains a priority item at the international negotiating table. Arbitrator Charles N. Brower, disgruntled about departures from the arbitral status quo, describes the European innovation of an investment court as an 'invasive species' that has 'slithered into the realm of international arbitration'.[8]

The principle of reciprocity in investment treaty law—which confers rights even on investors from non-European states to sue European ones—has given rise to some interesting legal questions, including constitutional ones. It has the effect of testing investment treaty law against national constitutional law and Europe's legal order, including its constitutional features.[9] Both levels of constitutional engagement, national and regional, will be examined in this chapter. As in the case of Northern North America, we will learn that judges are not interested in threatening the investment treaty regime. Instead, courts are complicit in its construction and maintenance, eliding constitutional conflict by engaging in either hard (denying any encroachment on constitutional space) or soft (acknowledging encroachment but interpreting conflict away) deference.

It comes as little surprise that courts, situated in global capitals at the centre of the spread of economic liberalism, will defer to external economic choices that are promoted by their political branches. Europeans, after all, act as a single economic unit that treats the world as its market.[10] But Europe has also tried to convey a more developmentally friendly visage. For instance, the 1975 Lomé Convention unilaterally granted preferential access to poorer African, Caribbean, and Pacific countries on a non-reciprocal basis. This policy was abandoned in 2000, under pressure from World Trade Organization (WTO) member countries.[11] Non-reciprocal trade preferences were jettisoned in favour of negotiating 'Economic Partnership Agreements' (EPAs) that expanded the scope of investor protections.[12]

---

[7] The first investment treaty with ISDS was that between Netherlands and Indonesia in 1959 in Vandevelde (2010) at 431.
[8] Brower (2021) at xix.
[9] The CJEU describes the EU as possessing a unique 'constitutional framework' in *Moldova v. Komstroy*, CJEU Case C-741/19 (2 September 2021) at para. 44. Von Bogdandy (2010) at 21–2 describes the EU's founding principles as exhibiting a constitutional character and Zuleeg (2010) at 765 characterizes the EU constitution, if incomplete, as a 'fact'.
[10] Foucault (2008) at 54.
[11] It was replaced by the Cotonu Agreement. Stevens (2007) at 223.
[12] By conferring pre-establishment rights (prohibiting, for instance, foreign investment screening), prohibiting capital controls (which could interfere with the repatriation of profits by transnational corporations to shareholders in their home states), and mandating most-favoured nation treatment (which ensures Europeans receive the best treatment available to other foreign investors in CARIFORUM countries). See Van Harten (2008).

Upon the accession of the 2009 Lisbon Treaty, the European Union was authorized to enter into international agreements on behalf of other member states in order to reduce restrictions to the movement of foreign direct investment. This new power granted exclusive competence to the EU to implement a common commercial policy relating to foreign direct investment but, as declared in a subsequent Court of Justice of the European Union (CJEU) opinion concerning an EU–Singapore FTA (free trade agreement), not non-direct (or portfolio)[13] investment.[14] The Lisbon Treaty entitled the European Commission to insist that, moving forward, EU investors 'abroad enjoy a level playing field, which assures both uniform and optimal conditions for investment through the progressive abolition of restrictions on investment'.[15] This entailed maintaining all of the 'best available standards' of protection together with 'binding commitments' represented by an ISDS mechanism. The European Council embraced the Commission's plan of action, agreeing that EU policy 'should increase the current level of protection and legal security for the European investor abroad'.[16] This signalled a diminution in any single member's influence in investment law and policy at the European level. National laws would serve only as a 'source of inspiration' for 'identifying best practices'.[17]

With this new authority in hand, Europe has signed a small number of free trade and investment agreements, among them the Canada–EU Comprehensive Economic Trade Agreement (CETA). In these agreements, the EU purports to correct inequities engendered by ISDS by enshrining a new investment court, remedying some of the defects of party-appointed investment arbitration, narrowing standards of protection for foreign investors, and establishing a committee system to shape future interpretation of the agreement. CETA, characterized as 'state of the art', is influencing developments elsewhere. Whether European proposals amount to a 'fix' of the regime's deficiencies that require correction remains to be seen.[18] The object of this part is not to weigh in on the EU's reform proposals but to evaluate a sequence of legal disputes, brought before each of the French Constitutional Council and the German Federal Constitutional Court, in addition to the CJEU,

---

[13] Portfolio investments typically do not concern ownership or control of an enterprise but only an economic interest such as ownership of shares. See McLachlan, Weinigar, and Shore (2017) at 258 and notes 18–20, infra. Sklair (2002) at 121 describes portfolio investment as the proto-typical form of foreign investment early in the twentieth century.

[14] In Art. 207(1) of the Treaty on the Functioning of the European Union (TFEU) ('The common commercial policy shall be based on uniform principles, particularly with regard to ... foreign direct investment ...). CJEU Opinion 2/15, paras. 82 and 238 on the EU–Singapore FTA (discussed further below), clarified that FDI fell within the exclusive competence of the EU, but that member states had jurisdiction over portfolio investment ('non-direct foreign investment') and dispute settlement mechanisms. Such mixed agreements would require the approval of both the EU and individual member states. For a complaint that splitting competence was an academic exercise see Brown (2021) at 74.

[15] European Commission (2010) at 6, 4.
[16] European Council (2010) at para. 9. This history is outlined in Brown (2021).
[17] Dimopoulos (2019) at 452.
[18] On the EU proposal for an investment court, see Krajewski and Hoffman (2017).

which assess the compliance of CETA with these national and regional constitutional norms. I turn first to a discussion of the French case.

II. 'In No Way Unconstitutional': France

The *Conseil Constitutionnel* (the 'Constitutional Council') is not a typical apex court but a specialized constitutional court with limited jurisdiction. At its origins in 1956, the Council was designed to shield the executive branch from parliamentary incursion—it was to serve as a 'watchdog on behalf of executive supremacy'.[19] The court was initially empowered only to conduct abstract review upon constitutional referrals from four officials: the President, Prime Minister, and either of the speakers of the National Assembly or Senate. A constitutional amendment in 1974 extended referral authority to a minimum of sixty members of either House in the French Parliament.[20] The same privilege of referral was extended to cases where 'an international undertaking contains a clause contrary to the Constitution' (in Art. 54C). In instances of conflict, an international treaty may only be given effect after amendment to the Constitution.

After a pivotal 1971 decision, reading in freedom of association into the 1956 Constitution (relying upon fleeting references to the 1946 Constitutional Preamble of the Fourth Republic and the 1789 Declaration of the Rights of Man),[21] the Council increasingly has assumed the power to exercise judicial review under an implied bill of rights. This jurisdiction was consolidated when, in 2008, the Court was authorized to undertake concrete review, upon referral by either the *Cour de Cassation* or the *Conseil d'Etat*, in actions initiated by individuals ('QPC').[22] This new process has generated hundreds of Council decisions.[23] Conjoined with the force of European human rights law, the Constitutional Council has been 'transformed beyond recognition',[24] coming 'as close as possible to a constitutional court'.[25]

---

[19] Hayward quoted in Stone Sweet (1991) at 47, also at 61.
[20] Art. 61[1] C. See Dyevre (2017) at 326.
[21] Decision no. 71-44 DC of 17 July 1971 at https://www.conseil-constitutionnel.fr/en/decision/1971/7144DC.htm (last accessed 2 September 2020). These include the 'Fundamental Principles Recognized by the Laws of the Republic' (hereinafter 'FPRLR') described in the Preamble to the 1946 Constitution, and upon which the Council relied as the source for freedom of association (at para. 2). See text in Finer (1979) at 275 and discussion in Lasser (2008) at 83 and c. 3, generally. This was not something the framers in 1946 intended to do. It was likened to an 'academic preface' by Jacques Bardoux, quoted in Stone Sweet (1991) at 42.
[22] This is the 'question prioritaire de constitutionalité' (or QPC). See Dyevre (2017) at 328 and Boyron (2013) at 154–5.
[23] Dyevre (2017) at 328.
[24] Boyron (2013) at 173.
[25] Bell, Boyron, and Whittaker (2008) at 158. See the description of this 'truly major and extremely recent transformation' and accompanying European pressures in Lasser (2008) at 68 and c. 3.

It was a petition by 110 members of Parliament, under the Article 54C, that triggered review of CETA by the Constitutional Council. Previously, the Council had ruled upon 14 such referrals, nine of them concerning European-wide treaties. These referrals resulted in seven findings of constitutional validity and six decisions resulting in constitutional amendment.[26] No constitutional problems, however, arose in the case of CETA. As a consequence of the CJEU opinion regarding the EU–Singapore FTA,[27] we learned that CETA qualifies as a mixed agreement. It combines exclusive EU competence over trade and direct investment with member state competence over non-direct investment and dispute settlement. This meant that most parts of the agreement could be provisionally applied but that member state approval was required for certain types of investment and dispute settlement, such as an investment court.[28]

The Constitutional Council's jurisdiction, therefore, was confined to matters shared with the EU or exclusively within national competence.[29] Yet the Council took the opportunity to ask and answer, in a single short paragraph, whether the bulk of the agreement, mostly within EU competence, called into question 'a rule or principal inherent to the constitutional identity of France'.[30] What does this refer to? Constitutional identity is considered a 'fuzzy concept' whose substantive content has yet to be specified by the Council.[31] Asking the question raises the possibility that French constitutional identity will serve as a 'counter-limit' to the primacy of EU law.[32] Such consequences were mitigated, however, by scrutinizing this part of CETA using a lower constitutional threshold, one preoccupied only with 'blatant breaches of France's constitutional identity'.[33] The finding that no conflict exists suggests, first, that constitutional identity 'remains narrowly construed'[34] and signals, second, that the Council will continue to defer to the CJEU, which has the authority to evaluate CETA's conformity with EU law.[35]

---

[26] Cadilhac and Rapoport (2018) at 813–14. On the judicial record, see Vranes (2013).
[27] CJEU Opinion 2/15.
[28] European Council Decision 2017/38 at https://eur-lex.europa.eu/legal-content/EN/TXT/PDF/?uri=CELEX:32017D0038&from=EN (last accessed 28 August 2020).
[29] Decision no. 2017-749 DC of 31 July 2017 at https://www.conseil-constitutionnel.fr/en/decision/2017/2017749DC.htm (last accessed 8 February 2023) at para. 17.
[30] Decision no. 2017-749 DC of 31 at para. 14.
[31] Millet (2019) at 147 describes its content as seeking to 'safeguard paramount national values or domestic rights', referring to the 'overarching republican principle of equality' at 151, 148. This content is identified in Decision no. 2006-540 DC of 27 July 2006. Fromage and de Witte (2021) at 417 describe its content as 'characteristics that distinguish France from other major European states'.
[32] Magnon (2018) at 178, 193, and Cuendet (2022) at 137.
[33] Millet (2019) at 146.
[34] Larik (2017) at 776.
[35] Millet (2019) at 146. Nevertheless, argue Fabbrini and Sajó (2019) at 458, constitutional identity 'as applied by a growing number of constitutional courts and governments represents a real and present danger to the process of European integration as the doctrine is drenched with neo-sovereigntist features and is contrary to the rule of law'. By contrast, Millet (2020) at 151 claims that the Constitutional Council's approach is 'rather harmless for EU integration'.

Turning to the main question of CETA's compliance with the French Constitution, three principal grounds for constitutional inconsistency preoccupied the Council. First, it was claimed that the 'essential conditions for the exercise of national sovereignty' were negatively affected by CETA. This ground, nowhere found in the text of the constitution, refers to a number of key areas in which national jurisdiction must be preserved: 'justice, taxation, monetary policy, border control, defence and national security'.[36] This is the same ground upon which the Council previously scrutinized, from 1992 to 2004, the constitutional compatibility of EU treaties.[37] The Council characterized CETA as not 'obstructing any measure that the States may take in regard to control over foreign investments'.[38] The 'court'—which is how the Council characterized the tribunal of first instance under CETA's dispute settlement mechanism—will not have 'any powers of interpretation or nullification' of decisions taken by the EU or member states'.[39] Rather, it will only have the power to award damages. In short, instead of saying what the law is, an investment court would only be entitled to say what the price is.[40]

By reciting CETA's provisions governing dispute settlement under the investment court model, the Council was sufficiently assuaged to conclude that CETA's investment chapter 'in no way infringe[d] on these [essential] conditions'.[41] While a CETA court could not 'nullify' EU or member state laws, regulation, or policy, an investment court certainly could interpret them. National laws, after all, help to determine not only whether an investment is legally made but whether the state has acted in accordance with its own laws. This invariably requires interpretation.[42] Yet the Council seemed unaware of this fact.

The second principal ground of complaint was the question of 'equality', derived from the preamble of the 1958 Constitution which incorporates both the 1946 Constitution as well as the 1789 Declaration of the Rights of Man.[43] Equality forms part of the 'constitutionality block' of the French Constitution.[44] Whereas

---

[36] Boyron (2013) at 221. Also Robert-Cuendet (2022) at 130–1 who describes the criteria as 'soft and flexible'.
[37] Millet (2019) at 138.
[38] Decision no. 2017-749 DC of 31 at para. 22.
[39] Decision no. 2017-749 DC of 31 at para. 23.
[40] Paraphrasing Michel Rocard in Stone Sweet (2000) at 68, referring to the Constitutional Council decision in Decision 81-32 DC (1982).
[41] Decision no. 2017-749 DC of 31 para. 29.
[42] Douglas (2009) at 69–70 warns that it is fallacious to treat municipal laws as 'facts' as investment treaty claims are grounded in the municipal laws of the host state. These claims are, in part, disputes about 'legal entitlements' accorded under municipal law.
[43] The 1958 preamble, as amended, provides: 'The French people solemnly proclaim their attachment to the Rights of Man and the principles of national sovereignty as defined by the Declaration of 1789, confirmed and complemented by the Preamble to the Constitution of 1946, and to the rights and duties as defined in the Charter for the Environment of 2004.' All of the relevant constitutional provisions, along with relevant precedent, are compiled in 'Décision no. 2017-749 DC Dossier Documentaire' at https://www.conseil-constitutionnel.fr/sites/default/files/as/root/bank_mm/decisions/2017749dc/2017749dc_doc.pdf (last accessed 2 September 2020).
[44] Boyron (2013) at 39, Millet (2019) at 139, and Beranger (2019) at 109. The block includes 17 articles in the 1789 Declaration, 14 principles enumerated in the 1946 Preamble, unwritten principles

previously the Council relied upon 'Fundamental Principles Recognized by the Laws of the Republic' (FPRLR) described in the Preamble to the 1946 Constitution, serving a 'catch-all' role,[45] this has been supplanted by the principle of equality.[46] It is the uber 'overarching republican principle' inhabiting a central place in French constitutional identity, writes Millet.[47] If the Council has taken a mostly formalistic approach to equality analysis in the past, it adopts a more functionalist one in the CETA decision. Though equality requires that the law 'must be the same for all', departures from equality are permitted when regulating 'different situations in different ways' or when in the pursuit of the 'public interest'. In either case, departures from the equality norm are permitted where 'the resulting difference in treatment is directly related to the subject matter of the law providing for such different treatment'.[48] Was it the case that granting to Canadian foreign investors in France special rights, adjudicated before a special court, consistent with equality? Denying these same special rights to French nationals was not a denial of equality, the Council concluded.[49] The 'objective of the general interest' in attracting 'Canadian investors in France' 'is directly in line with the purpose of the agreement', they declared.[50]

The Council was also comforted by the Joint Interpretative Instrument issued by Canada and the EU when confronted by a recalcitrant region in Belgium (Wallonia) standing in the way of CETA's adoption by the European Parliament. The instrument clearly was intended to quiet complaints, increasingly vocal, about the scope of CETA's impact on regulatory capacity. In their joint statement, the parties declared that 'CETA will not result in foreign investors being treated more favourably than domestic investors'.[51] The object of this declaration was to reassure

referred to in the 1946 Preamble (the 'general principles of law recognized by the republic'), and the 2005 Charter for the Environment.

[45] Dyevre (2017) at 325. The 1946 preamble reaffirms the 1789 Declaration which, in Art. 6, declares that 'all citizens are equal in its [the law's] eyes' in Finer (1979) at 270, 281.
[46] Favoureu (1992).
[47] Millet (2020) at 148.
[48] Decision no. 2017-749 DC of 3 at para. 35. This functional approach to equality analysis—distinctions are permissible so long as they further the underlying purpose of the law—was initially adopted by a minority of the Supreme Court of Canada and subsequently rejected in favour of a more contextual and substantive equality analysis. For example, see Justice Gonthier in *Miron v. Trudel* [1995] 2 SCR 418 at para. 54. Consideration of relevance 'instantiates a [return to the] similarly situated, formal equality model' complain Koshan and Watson Hamilton (2011) at 59.
[49] For a similarly deferential illustration see Decision No. 2022-1003 QPC of 8 July 2022. The law provides support for medically assisted procreation to any couple or unmarried woman. The scheme denied benefits to transgender men, either singly or in couples. The Constitutional Council held that the differential treatment was 'directly related to the purpose of the law establishing it' and so dismissed the complaint (at para. 6).
[50] Decision no. 2017-749 DC of 3 at para. 39. See also the conclusion of Attorney General Bot in 'Opinion of Advocate General Bot' (29 January 2019) at para. 209. Robert-Cuendet (2022) at 143 observes that Canadian investors have not insisted upon special investor protections in the past and that CETA 'will certainly not increase the flow of Canadian capital in the future'.
[51] Section 6(a) of the CETA's Joint Interpretative Instrument. Its purpose is described in the preamble (s. 1[e]) as providing 'a clear and unambiguous statement of what Canada and the European Union and its Member States agreed in a number of CETA provisions that have been the object of public debate and concerns and provides an agreed interpretation thereof. This includes, in particular, the impact of

Europeans (Canadians less so) that CETA did not entitle Canadian investors to rights greater than those available to the citizens of European nation states. This 'no greater rights' claim has not been an entirely successful one.[52] The ambit of protection available under investment treaties, despite the Council's conclusion, typically exceed constitutional protections available under numerous European national rights regimes.[53] Legitimate expectations, for instance, are not independently protected in French law.[54] As Robert-Cuendet remarks, it is regrettable that the Council did not undertake a more detailed comparison.[55]

The third ground of complaint was that CETA establishes national legal standards, usurping the state's 'capacity to legislate and govern'.[56] Once ratified, according to Constitution Art. 55, the international treaty would rank in superiority to national law.[57] The Council was reassured that there was no loss of policy capacity. This was because both CETA and the Joint Interpretive Instrument preserve the 'right to regulate' in the pursuit of 'legitimate' public policy objectives.[58] The Council did not acknowledge, however, that these clauses provide few constraints on how investment tribunals evaluate what is a legitimate or non-legitimate use of public policy.[59] Instead, the Council emphasized the supervisory role that would be played by a joint Canada–EU committee, having the power to issue interpretive directives to tribunals after the fact.[60] This interpretive authority, by contrast, is of ongoing concern to the German Constitutional Court, as we learn below.

A fourth principal constitutional objection concerned the absence of any mention of the precautionary principle in CETA's text – that measures for harm prevention be taken even in the face of scientific uncertainty. As there was no stated obligation to respect the principle, incorporated into the Constitution of France via Article 5 of the Environmental Charter of 2005 and forming part of the constitutionality block, it was claimed that CETA was constitutionally flawed. After reciting numerous passages in the agreement devoted to such things as sustainable development, the Council could find no constitutional defect—CETA's provisions

---

CETA on the ability of governments to regulate in the public interest, as well as the provisions on investment protection and dispute resolution, and on sustainable development, labour rights and environmental protection.'

[52] As argued elsewhere. See, for example, Schneiderman (2018).
[53] See Kleinheisterkamp (2015) and Poulsen, Bonnitchal, and Yackee (2015) at 173–4.
[54] Robert-Cuendet (2022) at 143.
[55] Robert-Cuendet (2022) at 141.
[56] Decision no. 2017-749 DC of 3 at para. 45.
[57] Decision no. 2017-749 DC of 3 at para. 44.
[58] Decision no. 2017-749 DC of 3 at para. 45. Referring to CETA Art. 8.9.1 and Section 2 of the Joint Interpretative Instrument on the CETA Between Canada and the European Union and its Member States.
[59] There is little such guidance in CETA despite the Joint Interpretative Instrument's declaration that CETA 'provides clear guidance to dispute resolution Tribunals on how these [clearly defined] standards should be applied' (s. 6 [c]).
[60] Decision no. 2017-749 DC of 3 at paras. 48–51.

cumulatively 'guarantee respect for the principle of precaution'.[61] Moreover, when issuing binding interpretive rulings via the joint panel, EU members would be obliged to follow a legal commitment to respect the precautionary principle in Article 191 of the EU Treaty.[62]

The Council's conclusion on the precautionary principle seems disconnected from 25 plus years of investment arbitration experience.[63] The *Clayton v. Canada* dispute is instructive in this regard.[64] An investment tribunal concluded that Canada violated NAFTA's standard of national treatment by subjecting a US investor's proposal to public scrutiny under the auspices of an independent environmental review panel. Other investments had been granted approval through more expeditious processes and had not been subject to the intensive spotlight of public hearings. Yet, the precautionary principle was at the centre of the environmental review panel's conclusion that the investor's proposal be rejected. The principle, after all, places the onus on those seeking to disrupt the environment to show that 'significant environmental effects can be avoided'.[65] The investor had failed to do so in numerous instances in the process. The environmental review panel preferred to 'err on the side of caution, especially where there is a large degree of uncertainty or high risk'.[66] This, however, rendered the Government liable for damages.[67] It is noteworthy that the panel purported to be interpreting Canadian environmental law as laid down in the applicable statute. It did not presume to be lowering Canadian legal standards.

The Council appeared not very drawn to these, or associated,[68] constitutional complaints. What is noteworthy is the way in which the Council's ruling made little

[61] Decision no. 2017-749 DC of 3 at para. 60. On the principle in investment arbitration, see infra nn. 63–64 in addition to Chapter 5, fn. 26.
[62] Decision no. 2017-749 DC of 3 para. 57.
[63] See Létourneau Tremblay (2022) at 938 (reliance on the precautionary principle 'is not very common' in investor-state arbitration).
[64] For more on the precautionary principle in investment arbitration, see discussion in Chapter 5 on *Eco Oro v. Colombia*, Decision on Jurisdiction, Liability and Directions on Quantum, ICSID Case No. ARB/16/41 (9 September 2021). While the precautionary principle was relied upon by the tribunal to deny the investor's expropriation claim, at para. 683, it was not sufficiently persuasive, on the same facts, to dissuade the tribunal from finding a violation of the treaty's fair and equitable treatment requirement, at para. 811. Also consider *Ethyl v. Canada*, Award on Jurisdiction, UNCITRAL (24 June 1998) concerning a ban on the gasoline additive MMT. Though never decided on the merits, the claim resulted in Canada paying out damages for having sought to ban transborder movement of substance. The scientific evidence suggested that MMT could cause adverse effects to human health. Canada did not ban the additive on health grounds, however, and so settled the claim on the assumption that it could not take the measure without unequivocal scientific evidence to back it up. See discussion of the dispute and the scientific evidence in Schneiderman (2008) at 130–4.
[65] Joint Review Panel Report in Canada (2015) at 20.
[66] Joint Review Panel Report in Canada (2015) at 92.
[67] *Clayton v. Canada*, Award on Jurisdiction and Liability, Permanent Court of Arbitration (PCA) Case No. 2009-04 (17 March 2015) at para. 724. The amount awarded, however, was at the low end: US$7 million. See *Clayton v. Canada*, Award on Damages, Permanent Court of Arbitration (PCA) Case No. 2009-04 (10 January 2019).
[68] Yet another objection had to do with the independence and impartiality of the CETA tribunal of first instance and its appellate body. With little in the way of analysis and, instead, reciting principal parts of the CETA text, the Council concluded there was no infringement of the principles of

effort to justify its constitutional conclusions. The principal focus was upon the relevant text of CETA and the Joint Interpretive Instrument. Nearly one-half of the CETA text is recited as a response to the constitutional complaints.[69] This 'anti-deliberative' and 'question-begging' approach is a common feature of the Council's historic mode of constitutional decision-making.[70] According to Dyevre, the Council is known for 'hiding the choices made behind a smokescreen of cryptic legalese' whose opinions 'remain somewhat more of an exercise in judicial obfuscation than in judicial candour'.[71] Though Dyevre insists that recent opinions are more 'reader friendly',[72] this is not what we see in the CETA opinion. Instead, Cadilhac and Rapoport observe that 'some extracts are unclear, incomplete, if not questionable, and give the impression that the *Conseil constitutionnel* is not totally at ease with its ruling'.[73] The opinion reveals an 'argumentative poverty', confirms Magnon.[74] The ruling would have benefited 'from greater clarity', adds Larik, as the Council refrained from 'deep scrutiny' of the constitutional claims.[75]

An explanation is suggested by Lasser's work on the *Cour de Cassation* (France's apex private law court), who identifies bifurcation between the Council's rulings and the hidden legal work that is ongoing behind the scenes among advocates generals, reporting judges, and academics.[76] He finds a 'softer' version of this bifurcated style at work in the European Court of Justice, having the distinction of being more public. The behind-the-scenes work there is published after all.[77] In a subsequent volume Lasser assimilates the *Conseil constitutionnel* and *Conseil d'État* (the apex administrative court) into this French judicial decision-making model but without further discussion.[78] A former judge, however, confirms that there is much going on behind the scenes at the Constitutional Council. Schnapper reports that 'pragmatism is inevitable'—that *conciliation* or 'balancing' is required for what is inescapably a decision of a 'political nature'. It is political 'in the noble sense of the term', she writes, requiring a 'choice between values inscribed' in the constitutionality block against other values that are 'deemed equally respectable and

---

independence and impartiality (para. 34). A number of other constitutional complaints concerned such things as uncertainty of provisional application and the prolonged period of enforcement of investor rights after termination (20 years) discussed in Larik (2017) at 768–9 and Cadilhac and Rapoport (2018) at 826–8.

[69] Magnon (2018) at 179.
[70] Dyevre (2017) at 342, 345.
[71] Dyevre (2017) at 347. They are 'remarkably laconic' adds Baranger (2019) at 107, 108, and 'formalist to the extreme'.
[72] Dyevre (2017) at 348.
[73] Cadilhac and Rapoport (2018) at 816.
[74] Magnon (2018) at 179.
[75] Larik (2017) at 760, 769.
[76] Lasser (2004) at 60–1.
[77] Lasser (2004) at 236–7.
[78] Lasser (2008) at 49.

legitimate'.[79] As a consequence, decisions 'that may be deemed ambiguous, subtle or open to criticism by doctrine are often the result of compromises between points of view that were initially clearly opposed'.[80] Schnapper's sociological account of decision-making at the Council appears to coincide with what Lasser describes occurring elsewhere in 'multiple', 'overlapping', and 'competitive' French judicial institutions.[81] Brevity may be as much a product of French constitutional culture as it is the consequence of slender agreement over constitutional essentials.[82]

Commentators nevertheless seem content with the Council's conclusions.[83] The Council has 'convincingly explained', writes Larik, why the investment court system, though providing an additional choice of legal remedy, 'only amounts to a limited difference in treatment which can be justified' by 'attracting' Canadian investors in France and vice versa.[84] Moreover 'clarification' of the right to regulate, particularly in the Joint Interpretive Instrument, helped the Council find that 'CETA does not undo domestic legislative and regulatory powers'.[85] Cadilhac and Rapoport conclude that the Council was correct that CETA does not offend the 'essential conditions for exercising national sovereignty'. It 'seems difficult to pretend', they write, 'that trade and investment issues constitute domains of national sovereignty'.[86] From this angle, national laws have nothing to contribute to foreign economic policy, matters over which citizens will argue, debate, organize, and struggle. On the equality question, the Council's decision is 'undisputable'. The derogation from the principle of equality is justified, they write, because it satisfies the public interest test by attracting Canadian investors to France. For Magnon, the equality complaint was 'close to absurd' and the Council's decision in perfect alignment with the purpose of the treaty.[87] Yet there is no evidence offered, either by the Council or these commentators, to support the proposition that these agreements have such effects.[88] European legal remedies will continue to serve as a backstop, ensuring there is no departure from EU primary law.[89] In this respect, the expectation is that EU institutions will continue to supervise enforcement of CETA by

---

[79] Schnapper (2010) at 234, 238.
[80] Schnapper (2010) at 298. The 'final decision', she writes, 'is a compromise between various positions, that of the rapporteur, that of the other advisers, that of the president, normally more concerned with the political effect, that of the secretary general and members of the legal service' who prefer to stick to 'a strictly legal point of view' (at 274).
[81] Lasser (2008) at 88.
[82] Latour (2010) at 222 describes this moment, in the Conseil d'État, as the 'wrath of sovereignty: they decide the issue'.
[83] There were few such comments. Robert-Cuendet (2022) at 147 observes that the decision 'went almost unnoticed'.
[84] Larik (2017) at 771. These passages in the Council's ruling are endorsed by the Institute of International Law 2019 'Resolution on the Equality of Parties Before International Investment Tribunals' in McLachlan (2022) at 50–1.
[85] Larik (2017) at 773.
[86] Cadilhac and Rapoport (2018) at 828.
[87] Magnon (2018) at 185.
[88] See Riffel (2020) at 216–21 for an argument that this differential treatment, as between national and foreign investors in the host state, is justifiable.
[89] Cadilhac and Rapoport (2018) at 831.

investment tribunals. As I suggest below, this looks mostly like a deliberate turning away in order to avoid impeding investment law's progress.

III. 'Lasting Negative Effects'?: Germany

Germany has aggressively been pursuing investment treaty partners while German investors have tenaciously pursued investment claims.[90] Germany, in short, has been entangled in investment treaty law ever since its first treaty with Pakistan in 1959.[91] German public opinion began to shift only after news that a Swedish investor, Vattenfall, had initiated an investment dispute against Germany in 2012 as a consequence of its phasing out nuclear energy production.[92] This, Vattenfall claimed, amounted to an expropriation in violation of the ECT. Meanwhile, the EU was in the midst of negotiations to complete a comprehensive trade and investment agreement with Canada (CETA) and was set to begin a round of negotiations for an agreement with the United States (TTIP). These negotiations prompted robust debate in political and media circles within Germany. Bungenberg reports that law professors, including a former constitutional court judge, vigorously opposed both agreements.[93] The Green Party, together with some left-leaning members of the Social Democratic Party of Germany (SPD)—the SPD was initially supportive of TTIP—led opposition in the German Federal Parliament (the Bundestag).[94] By articulating concerns about shrinking policy space, chilling effects, and potentially large compensation awards, the SPD threatened ratification of future investment agreements with ISDS. The German Federal Constitutional Court (*Bundesverfassungsgerichts*), however, has not seen fit to impede the spread of investment law disciplines—despite the muscular supervisory authority the Court exercises over many aspects of German state and society.

Arising out of the ashes of Nazism, the Court began its work in trepidatious fashion. Enforcement of fundamental human rights in the German Basic Law, for instance, was slow to take off.[95] The Court's First Abortion decision of 1975 was a turning point, however.[96] The majority justices imposed an obligation on the

[90] Bungenberg (2017) at 261, 268.
[91] On the origins of this first treaty, see Venzke and Günther (2022).
[92] I have benefited from the account of the Energy Charter Treaty and German Constitutional Court proceedings in Choudhry (2022).
[93] Bungenberg (2017) at 273, complains that these interlocutors 'had worked little' on these issues. Allegations that critics are misinformed or inexperienced in the issues is a common complaint lodged by supporters of the regime. It is as if the doctrinal intricacies of investment law required training that is unavailable to critics. They are, in other words, not part of the system. See discussion in Schneiderman (2016).
[94] Chan and Crawford (2017) at 692, 698. The SPD leader, Sigmar Gabriel, served as Economics Minister and Deputy Chancellor in the coalition government.
[95] Hailbronner (2017) at 53.
[96] German Federal Constitutional Court BVerfGE 39, 1 (25 February 1075).

political branches to take steps to protect an unborn foetus even though a pregnant woman's negative liberty was the only enumerated right at issue.[97] Positive obligations imposed by 'protective duties' continue to be a remedial tool available to the Court. The Court's innovative doctrine of indirect application (horizontal effect) of German constitutional law to private relations is now well established.[98] Hailbronner characterizes the Court's interpretive approach as a 'maximalist' one, elaborating on the meaning of abstract constitutional norms in a highly decontextualized fashion.[99] This has aided the Court in fashioning a robust jurisprudence with worldwide influence.

This insistence on symmetry between the rigours of the Basic Law and public and private action has implications in the field of foreign relations. The Court has not shied away from subjecting foreign policy decisions to judicial scrutiny. This lack of inhibition is made manifest in a series of rulings on the compatibility of EU law with the Basic Law. In its famous Maastricht decision, the Court insisted that it would be continually seized of supervisory jurisdiction over EU law and policy to ensure compatibility with Germany's constitution.[100] More controversially, the Court has characterized European Central Bank directives as being ultra vires of the Union and contrary to the constitution.[101] Nevertheless, Hailbronner reminds us, '[s]trategic considerations and, sometimes political pressure ... force the Court to backpedal, leaving it to dodge questions entirely or take refuge in gestures of deference not backed up by any more coherent doctrine'.[102] The Court's first CETA decision could be characterized as exhibiting just this sort of behaviour.

This first ruling was prompted by a petition from 165,000 citizens together with political parties in the German Parliament seeking to block German representatives at the European Council from consenting to the provisional application of CETA to Germany.[103] Blocking consent via a preliminary injunction would have had the practical effect of scuttling the deal, at least in the interim. The challenge focussed principally, but not exclusively, on CETA's investment chapter (Chapter Eight) and its mechanism for dispute resolution, namely, a new investment court with a tribunal, at first instance, and an appellate body to review awards.[104] Several constitutional arguments were made by the petitioners, among them that

---

[97] Hailbronner (2017) at 105 suggests that the first abortion decision is 'no longer entirely representative'.
[98] Hailbronner (2017) at 106, 107. See also Alexy (2002) at 354–5.
[99] Hailbronner (2017) at 115.
[100] 2 BvR 2134/92, 2 BvR 2159/92 (1993).
[101] 2 BvR 859/15, 1651/15, 2006/15, 980/16. See discussion in Hilpold (2021).
[102] Hailbronner (2017) at 131.
[103] 2 BvR 1444/16 (2016a) at https://www.bundesverfassungsgericht.de/SharedDocs/Entscheidungen/EN/2016/12/rs20161207_2bvr144416en.html (last accessed 11 November 2022).
[104] It resembles, to an extraordinary degree, the dispute settlement bodies of the World Trade Organization (WTO). See discussion in Reinisch (2017) at 355. It also offers so modest a change in dispute resolution processes that it is unlikely to make much of a difference to arbitral outcomes, observes Lévesque (2017) at 75.

the principle of democracy, associated with German identity, would be violated, in addition to diminishing the powers of the German Parliament. The application of environmental principles, including the precautionary principle, would be inhibited as would human rights norms familiar to German and EU law. These constitutional questions were not addressed by the Court in its interim decision. Only in its decision of 2022, to which I turn later in this chapter, are the merits of these arguments addressed. It sufficed, for the meantime, for the Court to deny the interim application and to say a few things about the implications of the remedy sought by the petitioners.

Of significance to the Court was the fact that the European Commission had designated CETA a 'mixed agreement' which would have force only on a provisional basis.[105] The EU, in other words, 'did not have the necessary competence to conclude CETA on its own' and, instead, would proceed on the basis that competence was shared with member states, particularly in regard to indirect investment and enforcement via an investment court.[106] This lowered the stakes and indicated that the German delegate could vote in favour of CETA. On the other hand, the disadvantages of having the Court block the German delegate's vote were 'likely to be severe'.[107] It would 'significantly interfere with the—generally broad—legislative discretion' available to the federal government on foreign economic policy.[108] It would not only 'impair' trade relations between Canada and the EU 'but also have far-reaching effects on the negotiation and conclusion of future external trade agreements'. Heavily relying upon the implications of such an order,[109] the Court declared that the effects of a preliminary injunction 'would be irreversible', giving rise to a 'loss of reliability' in the Federal Republic of Germany, having 'lasting effects ... in the shaping of global trade relations'. It would 'seriously damage' CETA's 'potential function as a model for shaping external trade relations with other partners, or would even eliminate it completely'.[110] The foreign policy implications, of grave concern to the Court, appeared to be determinative of this constitutional outcome.

---

[105] EU Council Decision 10974/16 (5 October 2016) at https://data.consilium.europa.eu/doc/document/ST-10974-2016-INIT/en/pdf (last accessed 12 November 2022).
[106] 2 BvR 1444/16 (2016a) at paras. 13, 16.
[107] 2 BvR 1444/16 (2016a) at B.I.1. The Constitutional Court described the standard of review in an application for preliminary injunction as one of balancing: 'In case the outcome of the principal proceedings cannot be foreseen, the Federal Constitutional Court must, in the context of a weighing of the consequences, in principle only weigh the disadvantages that would arise if the preliminary injunction were not issued but the constitutional complaint or the application in *Organstreit* proceedings were successful in the principal proceedings, against the disadvantages that would arise if the preliminary injunction sought were issued but the applications in the principal proceedings were unsuccessful.'
[108] 2 BvR 1444/16 (2016a) at paras. 46–7.
[109] This argument is described as one to which the Court was 'quite sensitive ... as it explicitly refers to it no less than three times' in Miéral (2017).
[110] 2 BvR 1444/16 (2016a) at paras. 48–9.

There would be one area of concern for the Court, and it involved the considerable authority granted to the CETA committees to, for instance, 'adopt interpretations' of CETA text or add 'further elements' to the short list of CETA's fair and equitable treatment obligation.[111] This was a feature of CETA which, it will be recalled, the *Conseil constitutionnel* found unproblematic. The German Constitutional Court would not 'rule[] out' the prospect of the committee system encroaching on the principle of democracy. Committees were to be staffed by Canadian and EU representatives, giving rise to the possibility that German representatives would not have a 'seat or a vote'.[112] By excluding Bundestag representatives, it could be that the committee system violated the principle of democracy. The Court was comforted by the implausibility that Germany would be left out in the cold. Given that CETA would have only provisional application outside of dispute settlement and portfolio investment,[113] an 'inter-institutional arrangement' could ensure that EU decisions on CETA committees were unanimously approved by European member states. In addition, as a last resort, the German government could terminate application of CETA.[114]

The petitioners renewed their application in December 2016, after the CETA vote, claiming that Germany was not compliant with conditions laid down in the Court's earlier October ruling. On the contrary, the Court ruled, the Government 'did meet the requirements' laid down in their 13 October 2016 judgment. Only provisional application of CETA was approved.[115] It was even more 'unlikely' that operation of the committee would encroach on the principle of democracy as part of German constitutional identity. According to European Council Statement No. 19, 'all member state concerns' will be considered when CETA Joint Committee decisions are made.[116] Furthermore, no interpretive proposals would be forthcoming until the main proceedings had been completed before the German Federal Court.[117] I return to this final ruling in Section IV below. I turn next to the CJEU decision addressing the compliance of CETA with the laws of the EU.

---

[111] See CETA Arts. 8.44 and Art. 26.1(3).
[112] 2 BvR 1444/16 (2016a) at paras. 62–4. Member states could only be certain of possibly influencing deliberations.
[113] In addition to international maritime transport, mutual recognition of professional qualifications and labour protection (n 112) at para. 70.
[114] 2 BvR 1444/16 (2016a) at paras. 71–2. Pursuant to CETA Art. 30.7(3)
[115] 2 BvR 1444/16 (2016b) at paras. 20–1.
[116] Statement No. 19 declares 'The Council and the Member States recall that where a decision of the CETA Joint Committee falls within the competence of the Member States the position to be taken by the Union and its Member States within the CETA Joint Committee shall be adopted by common accord' in EU Council Doc. 13463/1/16 REV1 (27 October 2016) at https://data.consilium.europa.eu/doc/document/ST-13463-2016-REV-1/en/pdf (last accessed 12 November 2022).
[117] 2 BvR 1444/16 (2016b) at para. 29.

IV. Protecting 'Choices Democratically Made': EU

The CJEU had already weighed in on the authority of the EU to enter into comprehensive trade and investment agreements. Matters concerning trade and foreign direct investment fall within exclusive European competence, the Court declared in its Singapore opinion.[118] Such agreements do not require further consent from member states as these investments have a 'direct and immediate effect on trade' between the EU and third party states.[119] As regards other types of investment, such as so-called portfolio investment, competence is shared with member states.[120] This also will be the case as regards the agreement's investment court model. 'Such a regime', the CJEU concluded, 'removes disputes from the jurisdiction of the courts of the Member states', requiring their specific consent.[121]

The Court significantly disrupted the intra-EU investment treaty regime in its *Achmea* decision, the following year. On referral from the German Federal Court, its opinion concerned an arbitration award secured by the Dutch investor Achmea against the Slovak Republic under a 1992 Czech/Slovak Federative Republic–Netherlands bilateral investment treaty. The concern was that the treaty required interpretation and application of EU law, contrary to Art. 344 of the Treaty on the Functioning of the European Union (TFEU). EU states undertake, pursuant to the TFEU, not to submit disputes concerning interpretation or application of EU law to any bodies other than those authorized by EU treaties. The Court (Grand Chamber) determined that arbitral tribunals 'may be called on to interpret or indeed apply EU law, particularly the provisions concerning fundamental freedoms, including freedom of establishment and free movement of capital'.[122] Investor–state dispute settlement mechanisms, in such circumstances, 'could prevent those disputes from being resolved in a manner that ensures the full effectiveness of EU law'. This would have an 'an adverse effect on the autonomy of EU law'.[123] Member states are now proceeding to dissolve all intra-EU bilateral investment treaties (BITs), leaving only EU institutions to resolve investment disputes between EU citizens and member states.[124] What *Achmea* and related decisions of the CJEU

---

[118] Opinion 2/15 at para. 82. This authority is derived from TFEU Art. 3(1)(e) and TFEU Art. 207(1) ('based on uniform principles ... relating to trade in goods and services, and the commercial aspects of intellectual property, foreign direct investment ...').

[119] Opinion 2/15 at para. 84.

[120] Opinion 2/15 at para. 83. 'Non-direct foreign investment' is described by the CJEU as concerning, among other things, 'acquisition of company securities with the intention of making a financial investment without any intention to influence the management and control of the undertaking ("portfolio" investments), and that such investments constitute movements of capital for the purposes of Article 63 TFEU' (at para. 227).

[121] Opinion 2/15 at para. 292.

[122] Case C-284/16 at para. 42.

[123] Case C-284/16 at paras. 56, 59.

[124] See European Commission, 'Declaration of the Member States of 15 January 2019 on the Legal Consequences of the *Achmea* Judgment and on Investment Protection' at https://ec.europa.eu/info/sites/default/files/business_economy_euro/banking_and_finance/documents/190117-bilateral-investment-treaties_en.pdf (last accessed 7 December 2022).

reveal is a desire to jealously guard jurisdiction to interpret EU law.[125] The CETA ruling, however, reveals that the Court will relax its jurisdictional monopoly when the future of EU foreign economic policy is imperilled.[126]

Though CETA does not contemplate intra-EU disputes, several questions about EU law remained outstanding. Of particular interest was whether the new investment court was compliant with EU law insofar as it threatened the EU's legal autonomy. As a preliminary matter, the Court maintained that the autonomy of EU institutions was preserved as CETA did not confer on tribunals jurisdiction to 'interpret or apply EU law'.[127] They pointed to the CETA text which declares that the applicable law in CETA investment disputes was 'the Agreement ... and other rules and principles of international law applicable between the Parties' (CETA Article 8.31.1) and not EU law.[128] If a tribunal were to consider the domestic law of EU member states in determining whether there has been a breach of CETA (a question arising in innumerable investment disputes),[129] a Tribunal 'shall follow the prevailing interpretation given to the domestic law by the courts or authorities of that Party' (CETA Art. 8.31.2).

Implied in the Court's reasons is the conclusion that there should never be any doubt about '"prevailing" interpretations'.[130] This is highly unlikely.[131] There might, on occasion, be disagreement about what domestic law requires.[132] Alternatively, competing formulations may not yet have settled around a single interpretation.[133] Moreover, tribunals may be required to make judgments about the content of any prevailing interpretation. It is true, as the Court argues, that should 'serious concerns arise as regards matters of interpretation that may affect investment', the Committee on Services and Investment may recommend that the CETA Joint Committee 'adopt an interpretation binding on a Tribunal' (Art. 31.3). But absent anything more specific, the issuance of binding interpretations will occur after the fact, not during an investment dispute. The interpretive authority conferred on investment tribunals simply is not on the Court's radar. The Court

---

[125] For example, Hindelang (2015). Weiss (2020) at 27 describes the CJEU in these earlier cases as 'too critical' and, in the CETA opinion, 'too uncritical'.
[126] Gáspár-Szilágyi (2021).
[127] CJEU Opinion 1/17 (30 April 2019) at para. 119.
[128] As Titi (2019) at 527 notes, this is a departure from standard investment treaty practice, which are mostly 'agnostic' about applicable law, and the ICSID Convention Art. 42, which refers to host state law where the treaty does not otherwise stipulate applicable law.
[129] This is acknowledged by the Court at para. 131. See Douglas (2009) at 52 ('Whenever there is a dispute about the scope of the property rights comprising the investment, or to whom such rights belong, there must be a reference to a municipal law of property.').
[130] Opinion 1/17 at para. 131.
[131] Hepburn (2017) at 105–6 observes that 'treating domestic law as fact seems particularly inapt in relation to contemporary investment treaty arbitration' and that, despite attempts to guard arbitrators from interpreting domestic law, 'tribunals usually inescapably have to apply domestic law anyway'.
[132] Scheu (2022) at 734 acknowledges that 'this may occur in rare cases' but that tribunals are expected to do so 'as little as possible'.
[133] Justice Hogan in *Costello v. Ireland* [2022] IESC 44 at para. 112 referred to this possibility.

confidently brushes concerns aside, concluding that no tribunal will have 'jurisdiction' as 'powers of interpretation are confined to the provisions of CETA'.[134]

This failure to appreciate the interpretive authority of tribunals is echoed in the Court's discussion of the effect of CETA upon EU member states' policy space. The issue arises in the context of whether an investment tribunal could impede measures taken by a European member state in furtherance of the 'public interest'. The Court acknowledges that, if tribunals can question the 'level of protection' demanded by the 'public interest', the obligation to pay damages 'could create a situation where, in order to avoid being repeatedly compelled by the CETA Tribunal to pay damages to the claimant investor, the achievement of that level of protection needs to be abandoned by the Union'.[135] It might be thought that the Court is concerned with, though it does not name it as such, the chilling effects of overbroad and indeterminate rights that can be claimed against states for carrying out constitutionally authorized policy initiatives.[136] If CETA's investor protections impeded state action in other words, the ensuing regulatory chill would pose a problem for 'choices democratically made within a Party'.[137] Eckes and Ankersmit maintain, however, that the Court's anxiety is focused upon the 'ex-post effects of multiple awards'.[138] This is an interpretation that places emphasis on the EU being 'repeatedly compelled' to pay damages for violations of CETA.[139] It is these after-effects that can result in laws having to be 'amended or withdrawn'. In either case, the result would be a more cramped policy space than the EU bargained for.

Though scholars and arbitrators have identified chilling effects associated with investment treaties[140] it turned out not to be a problem for the Court. This is because the CETA text declares, in its 'General Exceptions' clause (Article 28[3]), that CETA cannot be 'construed to prevent the adoption or enforcement' of measures 'necessary to protect public security or public morals or to maintain public order,

---

[134] Opinion 1/17 at para. 134. What is denied is that which Epstein, Landes, and Posner insist upon in the US context: 'It has long been understood that American judges exercise, at least occasionally (and at the Supreme Court level much more than occasionally), a legislative or policymaking role.' See Epstein, Landes, and Posner (2013) at 28.

[135] Opinion 1/17 at para. 149. Weiss (2020) at 28–30 and Boelaert (2021) at 61 argue that the CJEU appears to be shielding 'secondary legislation' from CETA pressures rather than preserving the EU constitutional order.

[136] As did rulings in the High Court and Supreme Court of Ireland, mentioned infra in note 126.

[137] Opinion 1/17 at para. 160.

[138] Eckes and Ankersmit (2022) at 30.

[139] Justice Hogan in the Supreme Court of Ireland maintained that not just repeated damage awards but 'one single large award—or, even, perhaps, the threat of such litigation before CETA—might be enough to dissuade a Member state to review or change its own legislation' in *Costello v. Ireland* [2022] IESC 44 at para. 108.

[140] For example, Scott and Van Harten (2017) and dissenting arbitrator Donald McRae in *Clayton v. Canada*. Concerns about regulatory chill arising under CETA are addressed in Ankersmit (2020). Justice Butler of the High Court of Ireland acknowledged the threat of regulatory chill but rejected the argument, relying on CJEU Opinion 1/17, in *Costello v. Ireland* [2021] IEHC 600 at para. 138. The Supreme Court of Ireland seemed more open to the possibility in *Costello v. Ireland* [2022] IESC 44 at para. 108, per Justice Hogan.

or to protect human, animal or plant life or health' provided that such measures 'are not applied in a manner that would constitute a means of arbitrary or unjustifiable discrimination between the Parties where like conditions prevail'.[141] In addition, CETA's 'right to regulate' clause 'reaffirms' the 'right to regulate within their territories to achieve legitimate policy objectives, such as the protection of public health, safety, the environment or public morals, social or consumer protection or the promotion and protection of cultural diversity' (Art. 8.9). CETA's Annex 8-A, outlining the multi-factor analysis for determining whether an indirect expropriation has occurred, confirms the parties 'shared understanding' that measures do not require the payment of compensation expect in the 'rare circumstance when the impact of a measure or series of measures is so severe in light of its purpose that it appears manifestly excessive'. Otherwise, 'non-discriminatory measures of a Party that are designed and applied to protect legitimate public welfare objectives, such as health, safety and the environment', it is declared, 'do not constitute indirect expropriations'. From this collection of like-minded textual directives, the Court derives the conclusion that investment tribunals will have 'no jurisdiction to declare incompatible with the CETA the level of protection of a public interest established by the EU'.[142]

This conclusion simply does not follow. First, 'public interest' is nowhere mentioned in CETA. Only specific measures expressly mentioned in the text—having to do with subjects associated with traditional 'police powers' jurisdiction[143]—that are declared to be beyond the agreement's reach. This is not an open-ended list. Such measures, which in the 'general exceptions' clause mimic the content of Art. XX's chapeau of the GATT-WTO, do not encompass all measures promoting the public interest. Indeed, there is little reason to believe exceptions will be read expansively.[144] The principal mention of a 'public interest' exception appears in a clause concerning the 'right to regulate' in the Joint Interpretative Instrument. The Instrument was cobbled together in the final hours in order to secure the consent of Belgian representatives in the European Parliament.[145] The paragraph declares that 'CETA preserves the ability' of Canada and the EU to 'adopt and apply their own

---

[141] Opinion 1/17 at para. 152. The clause clearly is informed by the GATT Art. XX. See Kurtz (2016) at 175. These general exceptions are declared to be 'rare' in Bonnitcha, Poulsen, and Waibel (2017) at 119.

[142] Opinion 1/17 at para. 153.

[143] For an account of police powers in investment treaty arbitration, even if highly revisionist, see *Philip Morris v. Uruguay*, ICSID Case No. ARB/10/7 (8 July 2016).

[144] Most 'new exceptions clauses are structured on an exhaustive rather than inclusive basis' in Kurtz (2016) at 179. Nevertheless, tribunals could read these expansively. See *UPS v. Canada*, Award, UNICTRAL (24 May 2007) at para. 168.

[145] Joint Interpretative Instrument on the Comprehensive Economic and Trade Agreement (CETA) between Canada and the European Union and its Member States (7 October 2017) at https://eur-lex.europa.eu/legal-content/EN/TXT/PDF/?uri=CELEX:22017X0114(01)&rid=1#:~:text=CETA%20preserves%20the%20ability%20of,public%20health%2C%20social%20services%2C%20public (last accessed 9 February 2023).

laws that regulate economic activity in the public interest'. A list of 'legitimate public policy objectives' follows which includes the promotion of health, social services, and protection of the environment (s.2). Elsewhere in the Instrument, under the heading 'Investment Protection' (s.6[a]), it is declared that 'CETA includes modern rules on investment that preserve the right of governments to regulate in the public interest ... while ensuring a high level of protection for investments'. Both clauses appear to be declaratory statements of the party's intentions. Though the Joint Instrument is described as a 'clear and unambiguous statement' of agreement between the parties 'concerning a number of CETA provisions', falling within Article 31 of the Vienna Convention on the Law of Treaties (VCLT) (s.1[e]), it does not add new provisions but merely amplifies existing ones.[146] It simply is inartful, if not inaccurate, to conclude, as the CJEU does, that CETA protects measures taken generally in the public interest.

Second, the determination of whether a measure has to do with such things as public health, morals, or security is a matter inevitably left for tribunals. Their content is not determined conclusively by the text of CETA itself. Rather, determinations require interpretation and the only body authorized to do so, in the context of an investment dispute, will be first-instance investment tribunals constituted under CETA.[147] Arbitrators appointed to tribunals, in the course of resolving CETA investment disputes, will be called upon to characterize state action as falling within or without of these categories.[148] In so doing, tribunals will also be required to answer a variety of subsidiary questions. For instance, what test of 'necessity' is to be applied in CETA's general exceptions clause—should it be a strict test or a loose one—or what sort of proportionality analysis is called for in determining whether the impact of a measure 'is so severe in light of its purpose' as regards indirect expropriations? All of these, and other questions, are disregarded in the Court's analysis. Notions of juridical discretion, within the context of dispute resolution processes, simply evaporate in the Court's analysis.

Relatedly, even if Article 28(3)(2) exceptions are a 'threshold' consideration and so deprive arbitrators of 'jurisdiction to call into question the choices democratically made within a Party',[149] tribunals will have authority to interpret the relevant

---

[146] The instrument refers to the following CETA provisions as corresponding to the 'statement of the intention of the Parties in this Instrument' regarding the right to regulate: CETA Preamble, Article 5.4, Article 6.1.5, Article 8.9, Annex 8-A, Article 21.2.1, Article 21.2.2, Article 22.1, Article 23.3, Article 23.4, Article 24.3, Article 24.4, Article 24.5, and Article 28.3. Most of these provisions lie outside of CETA's investment chapter.

[147] In addressing questions of jurisdiction 'the tribunal must decide the relevant facts and the issues of law conclusively in its preliminary decision for the simple reason that they will not arise again if the tribunal decides to hear the merits of the dispute' in Douglas (2009) at 149. This interpretive power is not denied to tribunals simply because of the possibility of appellate review under CETA.

[148] Tribunals invariably will decide these cases based upon 'subjective perceptions' of whether the exceptions apply. See Sornorajah (2010) at 225.

[149] Opinion 1/17 at para. 160. For a discussion of exceptions, see *CMS Gas Transmission Company v. Argentina*, Decision on Application for Annulment, ICSID Case No ARB/01/8 at paras. 132–4.

treaty text. They have jurisdiction, in other words, to determine whether impugned state policies fall within the categories excepted from CETA's investment chapter.[150] Arbitrators alone will make this determination, in which case, they will have jurisdiction to 'call into question' choices democratically made. Tribunals have authority to, for instance, reject a Party's characterization of its actions as being 'designed and applied to protect legitimate public welfare measures' (Annex 8-A). In addition, there is a proviso in the exception clause that Party measures, even if falling within the mentioned categories, must not 'constitute a means of arbitrary or unjustifiable discrimination'. In order to determine whether state action rises to such a level of impropriety, tribunals, again, are expected to make judgments about such matters.[151] There is as likely to be as much controversy as consensus on what constitutes arbitrariness or unjustifiable discrimination.

Consider, again, the award on the merits in *Clayton v. Canada*, previously mentioned. Two of three arbitrators arrived at the conclusion that Canada had acted arbitrarily, and in contravention of NAFTA's investment chapter, when it adopted the recommendation of an independent environmental review panel. The Clayton tribunal was persuaded that the panel failed to apply Canadian environmental law. The dissenting arbitrator, siding with the Canadian government, found otherwise—that the environmental review panel followed Canadian law when it considered human environmental effects under the rubric of 'community core values'. This disagreement could not have been resolved by any general exceptions paragraph, expropriation annex, or right to regulate clause. Instead, it required judgement by those authorized to exercise it. By invoking the idea of jurisdiction—a term of art in investment law—and by misunderstanding the role that tribunals play in interpreting investment treaty text, the CJEU intimated that it had little familiarity with international investment law. Alternatively, if they were familiar with it, the members of the Court mistook tribunal power in the construction of investment treaty law for mere mechanical interpretation.

Was the Court more nuanced in its opinion by emphasizing that member states are entitled to choose 'levels of protection' demanded by the public interest? The Court repeatedly invokes this phrase.[152] Might they mean only that tribunals have no jurisdiction to calibrate the degree of protection provided by states—that tribunals are barred from undertaking intrusive evaluations of protective legislation? It could be that the Court is calling for curial deference when tribunals are considering such schemes. But it does not follow that CETA tribunals are deprived of the authority, already described, to apply the facts and the law as it concerns exceptions or interpretive directives. Adjudicative authority, therefore, remains within CETA

---

[150] Titi (2019) at 532 correctly characterizes this part of the CJEU opinion as 'specious'.
[151] Weiss (2020) at 25 reminds us that the same can be said of the availability of reservations in Annexes I and II of CETA ('EU law itself is the yardstick for the CETA Tribunal[']s examination as the EU reservations in CETA determine the scope of the exception').
[152] For example, at paras. 148, 153.

tribunals to question democratically authorized protective legislation when it does not pursue permitted objectives or when it can be characterized as arbitrary or unjustifiably discriminatory.

The Court similarly went out of its way to shield CETA from the implications of EU treaty law in its discussion of equal treatment. Investment treaties confer privileged rights on foreign investors to launch disputes against host states, consequently we see courts repeatedly being asked to address the constitutionality of this preferential treatment. In the case of CETA, European investors are entitled to initiate claims against Canada and, conversely, Canadian investors can initiate claims against European member states or the EU.[153] However, firms and investors making their home in EU member states and who invest within the EU cannot challenge EU laws using CETA standards of protection before an investment court. The question before the CJEU was whether CETA treated nationals of EU member states differently from Canadians with capital to invest.[154] This differential treatment, it was claimed, contravened the declaration, in Article 20 of the European Convention of Human Rights (ECHR), that 'everyone is equal before the law'.[155]

It is interesting that the Court elected not to answer the equality question in the same way as did the French *Conseil constitutionnel*: that CETA's investor protections provided no greater rights to non-nationals than those available to European citizens. The Joint Interpretative Statement was intended to provide comfort precisely on this ground.[156] As European nationals are entitled to the same protections as non-nationals, there could be no denial of equality and there would have been no differential treatment of which to complain. This might have required more work, however, than the Court was willing to undertake in its short discussion of this point.[157] There is, moreover, ample evidence to the contrary: that investor rights exceed those available to European nationals.[158]

It was easier to instead reject the comparison that was being offered up. To achieve this end, the Court redefined the proper comparator for the purposes of

---

[153] A matter to be determined by the European Union (para. 8.21).

[154] Opinion 1/17 at para. 179.

[155] The Court concluded that Article 21 of the Charter of Fundamental Rights of the European Union (that 'everyone is equal before the law') was 'irrelevant' as the complaint did not concern discrimination as between nationals of EU member states (at para. 170). For discussion, see Bekkedal (2021).

[156] Clause 6 provides that 'CETA will not result in foreign investors being treated more favourably than domestic investors.'

[157] At a minimum, it would have required undertaking a comparison of European-wide and European national rights protections with CETA and a comparison of the quality of judicial enforcement within Europe and under CETA. An assessment of accessibility and judicial independence is undertaken later in the ruling, but this discussion is far too abridged to meet even this threshold. Riffel (2020) seeks to make the argument in support of CETA by interrogating German constitutional law that nationals are not disadvantaged as compared to foreign investors. If the argument is not very convincing (as regards property rights and damage awards, see Hoffman [2022] at 69, 74), he also makes the case that it exceeds remedies available under Canadian constitutional law in addition to many other 'well-functioning' states. On the latter see de Mestral and Morgan (2017). I have addressed the claim in Schneiderman (2018).

[158] For example, Poulsen, Bonnitcha, and Yackee (2015) at 73.

discrimination analysis. European nationals should not be compared to foreign investors.[159] Instead, the proper comparator for the purposes of equality analysis were EU nationals investing in Canada. Those in a situation comparable to Canadian investors were those 'enterprises and natural persons of Member States that invest in Canada'. EU nationals simply were 'not foreign investors'.[160] As foreign investors in Canada and in the EU were treated identically, there was no differential treatment.[161]

Redefining the group with whom one will be compared is a technique familiar to high courts having to resolve constitutional equality rights claims. Equality analysis invariably requires comparison[162] and high courts may choose to replace comparators proffered by claimants with ones that are 'more like' the claimants. The worry, as articulated by the Supreme Court of Canada, is that equality analysis can be 'skewed' by claiming to be compared to a group that does not 'reflect the claimant's actual circumstances'.[163] This search for a 'mirror comparator' was later abandoned by the Supreme Court of Canada.[164] What was required, instead, 'is not formal comparison with a selected mirror comparator group, but an approach that looks at the full context, including the situation of the claimant group and whether the impact of the impugned law is to perpetuate disadvantage or negative stereotypes about that group'.[165]

By describing the comparator group to one that 'mirrored' persons identified in the request for an opinion, the CJEU chose to terminate the equality analysis at an early stage of the inquiry. Foreclosed was any fuller contextual inquiry about the claimed discrimination and preferential treatment. These are preferences granted not only to foreign investors but also to foreign investment in locally established enterprises[166] or to EU nationals who re-route their investments through Canadian companies.[167] The Court, in short, engaged in judicial interpretation—an activity, curiously, that it denies to investment tribunals when they undertake application of CETA exceptions and interpretive directives. The Court, in a single opinion, both denies and proves the point that legal text, more often than not, is not self-executing but requires judgment. It is this very power that the Court exercises in its equality analysis but disavows to investment tribunals.

---

[159] Opinion 1/17 at para. 180.
[160] Opinion 1/17 at paras. 180–1.
[161] Attorney General Bot reached the same conclusion in 'Opinion of Advocate General Bot' (29 January 2019) at para. 203. For a critique, see Schepel (2019).
[162] Equality 'is a comparative concept, the condition of which may only be attained or discerned by comparison with the condition of others in the social and political setting in which the question arises' per Justice La Forest in *Andrews v. Law Society of British Columbia* [1989] 1 SCR 143.
[163] *Hodge v. Canada (Minister of Human Resources Development)* [2004] 3 S.C.R. 357 at para. 20. See critique in Gilbert and Majury (2006).
[164] *Withler v. Canada* (Attorney General) [2011] 1 SCR 396 at para. 40.
[165] *Withler v. Canada* (Attorney General) [2011] 1 SCR 396 at para. 80.
[166] Compare De Boeck (2022) at 429–31 with Schepel (2019).
[167] Gáspár-Szilágyi (2021) at 686–7.

There were additional questions addressed by the CJEU opinion, including whether CETA tribunals were accessible to investors regardless of financial resources and whether they were composed of independent and impartial adjudicators. Neither of these principles was offended by CETA. The European Commission and Council had already committed to ensuring accessibility for small and medium-sized enterprises.[168] Nor was it a problem that the aforementioned Joint Committee could develop rules governing tribunal remuneration and issue binding interpretations on independent tribunals. It was 'neither illegitimate nor unusual, under international law', wrote the CJEU, 'for provision to be made that the Parties to an international agreement may clarify, as their joint wishes concerning the effect of that agreement develop, the interpretation of that agreement'.[169]

The CJEU elected not to stand in the way of the progress of the investment treaty regime. As Europe has committed to replace traditional ISDS with its investment court model, new treaties with old ISDS are imperilled insofar as they do not respect the autonomy of the EU legal order, do not interpret EU law, do not ensure the requisite independence of arbitrators, and do not secure access to small to medium-sized investors.[170] Even older treaties with non-EU states may be imperilled, though they have been grandfathered by EU regulation.[171] As the CJEU indicates in *Komstroy*, the EU's own arbitral mechanism established under the ECT fails to safeguard the autonomy of EU law.[172] It seems safe to assume that, after Opinion 1/17, many Bilateral Investment Treaties (BITs) based upon the traditional ISDS model are vulnerable to being declared inconsistent with EU law.

Though CETA speaks repeatedly of a 'right to regulate', an extensive range of government action is potentially caught by CETA's investment chapter. Due, in part, to the expansive definition of investment, a wide berth is granted to dispute settlement bodies to interpret and apply challenged laws and regulations. On the other hand, the CJEU appears to have reserved the right to supervise investment law's policing of European legal space. Is it likely that the Court of Justice will have the capacity or desire to perform this policing function?[173] How can Europe ensure that its values are being promoted through the aegis of an investment tribunal or court? How can a CETA tribunal or investment court, in other words, be held accountable under the EU Charter? If it is correct to say, as I have argued above, that it is the everyday business of investment tribunals to question 'levels of protection',

---

[168] Opinion 1/17 at para. 218.
[169] Opinion 1/17 at para. 233.
[170] Hindelang (2021) at 150 concludes that BITs based upon the traditional ISDS model likely 'are in violation of the principle of autonomy of EU law'. See also Ankersmit (2020) at 16.
[171] Old ISDS treaties are preserved by a legacy clause, for treaties signed into force before 1 December 2009 (the date the Treaty of Lisbon entered into force), in Regulation 1219/2012 of the European Parliament. For discussion see De Boeck (2022) at 321–3 and Brown (2021) at 75–7.
[172] CJEU Case C-741/19 at para. 62.
[173] A similar question that is raised by Van der Loo (2021) at 119.

then how is CJEU Opinion 1/17 to control future adjudication?[174] Or has the CJEU abandoned that role because investment disciplines impose seemingly tolerable limits on state action?[175]

V. Of Doubtful Democratic Legitimacy: Germany Again

The German Basic Law challenge to CETA had yet to come to an end. Only preliminary rulings had been issued. German petitioners returned to the Federal Constitutional Court to argue that, on the merits, German representatives violated the Basic Law and so exceeded their authority when they consented to the provisional application of CETA in the European Parliament.[176] As mentioned, the CJEU's advisory opinion on the Singapore agreement had clarified that the EU did not have competence in regard to certain investment matters (portfolio investments and dispute settlement). Member states would be obliged to provide consent, via their national legislatures, to accede to these investment obligations. This renewed application for constitutional review sought to pre-emptively block German consent to CETA.

The arguments on the merits were focussed upon rights to democracy (Art. 38[1]), the rule of law (Art. 20[3]), the freedom and sovereignty of citizens (Art. 2[1]), and constitutional identity (Art. 146).[177] Democratic principles were violated, it was said, by having left the Bundestag out of negotiations with Canada, producing an agreement that was solely in the English language.[178] Environmental protections would be threatened as would the precautionary principle, as part of Germany's constitutional identity (Art. 20a). The principle of equality is alleged to have been violated by conferring special privileges on foreign investors to have their disputes against host states settled before special courts using special laws (Art. 19[1] and Art. 101[1]). German investors, it was claimed, are discriminated against because they are not entitled to sue the German government on similar grounds before specialized investment courts.

The members of the parliamentary group, Die Link, offered a complaint premised upon shrinking policy space that would follow upon the ratification of CETA. It 'would lead to a substantial loss of power to the Bundestag' and would remove

---

[174] Hindelang (2021) at 140 observes that investment arbitrators 'do not have the best track record' of complying with CJEU directives. Following *Achmea*, write Jaremba and Piscitelli (2021) at 76, investment tribunals 'routinely disregarded' CJEU's claim to exclusive autonomy. In this light, it is puzzling why the CJEU appears to exhibit such confidence.

[175] Boelaert (2021) at 63 surmises that 'the limited jurisdiction the Court has over CETA has probably already been exercised'.

[176] See EU Council Decision 2017/38 (28 October 2016) at https://eur-lex.europa.eu/legal-content/EN/TXT/PDF/?uri=CELEX:32017D0038&from=EN (last accessed 12 November 2022).

[177] I am generalizing from arguments offered by individual petitioners.

[178] BVerfG, Order of the Second Senate of 9 February 2022—2 BvR 1368/16.

'decisive policy areas which are protected by constitutional identity and which are central to democratic self-determination'. Despite numerous references to a 'right to regulate' in CETA and its accompanying joint declarations, the joint committee system would leave 'essential questions of fundamental rights protection' to be decided by the executive and by dispute settlement bodies. Lastly, the dispute mechanism contemplated by CETA, namely, a new investment court, would leave national Parliaments out of the appointment processes.

The German federal government fiercely resisted these propositions. Opening markets to investments and to services did not encroach unconstitutionally upon democratic sovereignty. The mere threat of payment of compensation did not violate budgetary responsibility in the Bundestag. Also, the establishment of a committee system to supervise free trade agreements is sufficiently 'common' as to not give rise to any constitutional difficulty. 'So long as there is a democratic chain of legitimation traceable back to authorizations provided by the Bundestag', the government argued, there is no violation of democratic principle. As for the diminution of policy space, there was substantial 'democratic room to manoeuvre' that corresponds to requirements imposed by EU law and German Basic Law. The government's rejoinder was that CETA granted no greater rights to Canadian investors than those already available to German nationals.

Nor was the international protection of human rights 'impaired'. CETA is required to be interpreted in conformity with the VCLT which ensures that international human rights covenants and the Universal Declaration of Human Rights would be 'observed'. The same could be said about international environmental obligations consistent with the precautionary principle. CETA, it was claimed, would not undermine human rights, the welfare state, or ecological principles. The government insisted that there was an alignment between investment law and other international obligations despite the scant evidence to support this claim. It is, by now, fairly clear to most observers that investment treaty and arbitration law is not fit for the purpose of protecting rights, human or natural.[179]

The German federal government maintained that CETA 'has neither a legal nor a factual effect of encroaching on the domestic sphere'. By consenting to CETA, the Bundestag would not be authorizing any direct effect on German domestic law. As Canadian judges had concluded, it was argued that investment treaties operated in spheres separate from national constitutional law.

Having granted standing to some, but not all, of the petitioners, the Court ruled that all of the remaining complaints were 'manifestly unfounded'. First, the fact that the German representative had already authorized the provisional application of

---

[179] Reiner and Schreuer (2009) at 82, for instance, report that references to human rights in investment arbitration are 'sparse and infrequent' and, in the text of an investment treaty, 'highly unlikely'. The environment, too, is typically given short shrift. The 'very demanding character of investment standards ... can jeopardize the enactment of environmental policies' observe Schacherer and Hoffman (2019) at 618.

CETA did not give rise to constitutional problems. This consent was 'extended only to matters that undisputedly fall within' EU competence. Should there be any lingering concerns about CETA's committee system, EU Council directives ensured that no interpretations would be offered regarding matters beyond exclusive EU competence. There remained the possibility, however, that the consent of each member state would not be required ('it is not guaranteed' the Court observed). Instead, EU states could only influence decision-making indirectly. Because of this, the Court declared that it 'appears doubtful' that decisions taken by CETA's oversight committee 'would meet the level of democratic legitimation and oversight required' by the Basic Law (Arts. 20[1][2]).[180]

The Court, however, was content to table the question of democratic legitimacy for later. These issues, it concluded, 'need ultimately not be resolved in the present case'. So long as the EU remained bound by its commitment to seek the consent of the German representative during the provisional stage of application,[181] no encroachment on Germany's constitutional identity arose. Should the EU act in ways beyond its competence, or in violation of the Basic Law, there remained the last resort of terminating CETA's provisional application.

Shortly after the German Constitutional Court granted to CETA its provisional greenlight, a bill to approve CETA was introduced in the Bundestag.[182] According to the ruling coalition, it proposed ratification of CETA with 'minor' interpretive notes appended to the agreement.[183] The German federal government offered proposed interpretations of both fair and equitable treatment (FET) and indirect expropriation that can be submitted to the CETA Joint Committee. These proposed interpretations, while intended to lower standards of investor protection, can rightly be characterized as minor. The proposal also adds an acknowledgement that climate change obligations under the Paris Agreement may require the parties to pursue 'climate change mitigation and adaptation policies' that can upset investor expectations.[184] In the meantime, a constitutional complaint has been filed challenging the committee system in the EU–Singapore agreement analogous to the CETA one.[185] It is safe to assume that a further challenge to the whole of CETA will also be launched. The last remaining question regarding CETA's compatibility with the German Basic Law may ultimately be decided on that occasion.

---

[180] 2 BvR 1368/16 (2022) at para. 190.
[181] In EU Council Decision 19 (28 October 2016).
[182] Köller (2022a).
[183] Trade Justice Network (2022).
[184] Germany (2022). This is despite the Court's reassurance that CETA would not impede such measures.
[185] Köller (2022b).

VI. Conclusion

The European record as regards the compatibility of CETA with national and EU constitutional legal orders is one, mostly, of harmonious co-existence. Judicial opinion is united in the view that investment treaties, such as CETA, either pose no threat to these constitutional orders or, should they give rise to any concern, that discord can be managed. I have characterized this set of responses as exhibiting either hard or soft deference. Hard deference is characterized by denials that there is any encroachment on constitutional space (as in France and the CJEU). Soft deference is exemplified by reassurances that, though there might be tension with constitutional law, a court need not do much about it (as in Germany). Extrapolating from the European experience, it can be said that apex courts in capital-exporting states will behave in deferential ways so that they will not impede the spread of investment treaty law disciplines.

Should the same be expected of judges situated in the courts of capital-importing states? The next part of this book examines how apex courts in four states have responded to constitutional problems arising out of investment treaty law and arbitration. The method employed is more contextual than the preceding two chapters. In each instance, I trace the rise of the apex court, its constitutional set-up and relationship to the political branches, and the court's record in accommodating or resisting disciplines associated with economic globalization. In the final section of each chapter, a recent case is taken up for discussion that is meant to be illustrative of the court's general disposition. We learn that, while these judges have declined to serve in a vanguard role by exhibiting hard resistance, apex court judges have, in some locales, taken up this task in a sufficiently inquisitive way that they exhibit soft resistance.

PART II

4
Of Little Constitutional Interest
Peru

I. Introduction

Mining for export has been a principal source of revenue for Peru since at least the late nineteenth century and remains so today.[1] Foreign investment in mining increased 2000 per cent in Peru between 1990 and 1997.[2] It grew another 500 per cent between 2008 and 2014, accounting for almost 60 per cent of Peru's exports.[3] It has been a priority since the 1990s to enhance investment opportunities in Peru and so encouraging investor confidence is an ongoing concern. Confidence has been facilitated by easing policies that allow for mining concessions, lightening tax burdens, using force to quell opposition, all the while ramping up the number of investment protection agreements that heighten legal security for investors.[4] These policy concessions are captured by Peru's preoccupation with 'extractivism', policies that promote large-scale, capital-intensive industries premised on the extraction of commodities for export.[5] They also render Peru vulnerable to price fluctuations that are endemic to resource-intensive activities destined for foreign markets.[6]

Peru has had some success in pursuing this monolithic path to development. New Chinese investment in mining is double that of US and Canadian investors combined.[7] The United Nations Conference on Trade and Development (UNCTAD) reports that Peru was a top five developing and transition country destination for investment from BRICS countries in 2014.[8] Four years later, UNCTAD

---

[1] Himley (2019).
[2] McDonnell (2015) at 114 (as compared to 400 per cent in Latin America).
[3] Fairlie Reinoso and Herrera (2016) at 333–4. The authors appear to rely solely on company information in their account of the Bear Creek conflict.
[4] McDonnell (2015) at 114 identifies the first three but makes no mention of investment agreements.
[5] Contrasted with 'neoextractivism' where resource rents from extractive development is, in principle, redistributed. See Gudynas (2018) at 72, who describes Peru as extractivist ('nothing is produced and everything is extracted'). On neoextractivism, see Svampa (2015) at 66 and Yates and Bakker (2014) at 76. On the significance of mining to the generation of tax revenue, see Lust (2012) at 213.
[6] See the 'staples thesis' developed in Innis (1956) at 81–6.
[7] Fairlie Reinoso and Herrera (2016) at 335.
[8] UNCTAD (2016) at 12. Brazil, Russia, India, China, and South Africa are known by the acronym BRICS.

trumpeted Peru's 'improved investment environment', including six new mining projects together with 26 projects listed at the development stage.[9]

If extractivism has been a priority for the political branches, its apex court—the Peruvian Constitutional Tribunal—does not seem interested in disturbing the primacy accorded to foreign economic policy. Although the Tribunal has, in some instances, pushed back against a powerful executive branch and has enforced some social and economic constitutional commitments, it has fallen mostly into line with executive branch priorities. These include commitments made to foreign traders and investors via new free trade and investment agreements. The Tribunal's response to the threat of diminished constitutional space as a consequence of investment treaty law and arbitration is one that is best described as compliant. For the most part, the tribunal has deferred to—even embraced—the potential diminution of policy options otherwise constitutionally available to the Peruvian state. This submissive posture results in something akin to convergence between national and international commitments, a stance I associate with hard deference.

Most directly impacted by the state's embrace of investment law are the indigenous peoples of Peru. As resource extraction takes place in territories beyond the capital Lima, conflict with indigenous communities is a recurring feature of investment policy due to lack of consultation and adverse social impacts. In the year 2012 alone the Ombudsman's Office registered a total of 233 social conflicts, many of them ongoing, 123 of which concerned resource extraction.[10] Harmed by the economic impacts of resource exploitations and 'denied the opportunity to share' in its economic benefits,[11] conflict has awakened Peruvian indigenous identity that previously had lain dormant.[12] This has precipitated deepening conflict between indigenous communities, the state, and foreign investors. If the provision of confidence and security are the priority of states like Peru, it comes as little surprise that the number of declarations of states of emergency by the executive branch have increased precipitously.[13] This gives rise to disputes, such as the one discussed next, that highlight both civil society conflict and the shrinking policy scope available to the state.

II. The Bear Creek Dispute

Peru has successfully defended many of the investment claims launched against it.[14] This could help explain the disinterest its apex court has shown in the potential

[9] UNCTAD (2019) at 51.
[10] Lupaka Gold (2022) at para. 47.
[11] Lupaka Gold (2022) at para. 48 and Muñoz (2021) at 28.
[12] Merino Acuña (2015) and McDonnell (2015). On the 'revitalization' of Indigenous collective identity see Quijano (2005).
[13] Pursuant to Art. 137.
[14] Valderrama (2021) at 118. These disputes are detailed in Calvert (2022) c. 6.

erosion of policy space associated with investment treaty law and arbitration. The successful claim by Bear Creek of Vancouver, British Columbia under the Canada–Peru Free Trade Agreement serves as a warning shot, however.[15] The dispute was precipitated by a decision of the Peruvian government to revoke mining concessions granted to Bear Creek in Aymara indigenous territory. Residing on this territory, adjacent to the Bolivian border and the Lake Titicaca–Desaguadero watershed, are pre-Inca communities with deep attachments to the land.[16] Authorization to conduct mining activities was initially granted without consulting the Aymara.[17] There were further constitutional impediments. The Peruvian Constitution does not permit foreigners obtaining mining rights within 50 kilometres of the border unless there is a finding of 'public need'.[18] Public need was decreed some four years after the company's initial application.[19]

The company early on was aware of vociferous local opposition to the mining project due to its deleterious impact upon the natural, cultural, and spiritual integrity of Aymara territory.[20] Despite efforts at outreach over the course of two years, the investor obtained agreement with only four of 36 local communities. The remaining 32 claimed not to have been properly consulted and so assembled under a common indigenous front, organizing protests and blockades.[21] More than 25,000 people participated in a single day of protest in 2011.[22] Seven Peruvian nationals died in an altercation with the National Police in the following month.[23] The authorization and decree of public need was subsequently revoked by the government on the grounds that 'new circumstances' had arisen that required 'safeguarding the environmental and social conditions' of Aymara lands.[24] The reversal was occasioned by the election of a new president after a late-night meeting with local communities.[25] The investor was afforded no opportunity to be heard or to make

---

[15] Bear Creek (2017), arbitrators Pryles, Sands, and Böckstiegel (Pres). Part of the discussion that follows is drawn from Schneiderman (2022a), c. 6.
[16] Bear Creek (2017) 'Partial Dissenting Opinion' at para. 25.
[17] This is now required by a 2011 Peruvian law: see Prior Consultation Law No 29785. For a discussion of the circumstances giving rise to its enactment see Sanborn and Peredes (2014). The Peruvian Constitutional Court has also declared consultation a constitutional obligation in a series of cases, e.g. The *Cordillera Escalara* Case No 00025-2005-PI/TC at para. 31. See the helpful discussion in Flores (2015) and Flemmer (2019).
[18] Article 71provides that: 'within a distance of fifty kilometers from the borders, foreigners may not acquire or possess under any title, directly or indirectly, mines, lands, woods, water, fuel, or energy sources, whether individually or in partnership, under penalty of losing that so acquired right to the State. The sole exception involves cases of public need expressly determined by executive decree and approved by the Cabinet, in accordance with the law.' See Political Constitution of Peru, 1993 at http://www.congreso.gob.pe/Docs/files/CONSTITUTION_27_11_2012_ENG.pdf.
[19] Bear Creek (2017) at para. 149. Bear Creek's permits were obtained in suspicious fashion by its employee, a Peruvian national, who transferred rights to the foreign national company shortly afterwards.
[20] Bear Creek (2017) at para. 202.
[21] Bear Creek (2017) at para. 170. The protests are chronicled in McDonnell (2015).
[22] McDonnell (2015) at 112.
[23] Bear Creek (2017) at paras. 188, 197.
[24] Bear Creek (2017) at paras. 386, 388.
[25] Hepburn (2019c) at 152–3 and Williams (2019) at 213.

representations at the meeting.[26] After an initial victory in Peruvian courts, the Canadian investor launched its dispute, claiming damages of at least US$522.2 million from the state for its treaty violations.[27]

A key issue for the investment tribunal was whether the company had obtained a social license to undertake mining activities in traditional Indigenous territory. The tribunal determined that, for a three-year period, the Republic of Peru was satisfied that the company had done all that it needed to secure permission to operate on Aymara land. Peru was 'aware of and did not object to Claimant's outreach activities,' the tribunal concluded. Those activities were undertaken with the government's 'approval, support and endorsement.'[28] Consequently, there were no grounds for revoking the finding of public need on the alleged grounds of 'environmental and social conditions.'[29] Instead, in the tribunal's view, the government 'panicked and arbitrarily' terminated the project.[30]

Nor was Peru entitled to take advantage of the room to manoeuvre granted to states in Canada–Peru FTA's annex on expropriation.[31] These are now commonly attached to treaty prohibitions on expropriation and nationalization.[32] Typically, these annexes identify three factors that must be considered in determining whether there has been an indirect expropriation: the economic impact of the measure, interference with distinct reasonable investment backed expectations, and the character of the measure. All three factors were 'fulfilled', according to the tribunal, that is, the measures, presumably, were of sufficient magnitude to warrant an award.[33] This amounted to an indirect expropriation, not accomplished in accordance with due process, and requiring the payment of compensation.[34]

To this was added an unexpected twist. The tribunal would not entertain the possibility that Peru had acted in the exercise of its police powers jurisdiction—the inherent authority entitling states to take measures to protect the health, safety, morals, etc. of its citizens. The question presented in a typical investment claim

---

[26] Bear Creek (2017) at para. 414.
[27] Bear Creek (2017) at para. 730.
[28] Bear Creek (2017) at paras. 411, 412.
[29] Bear Creek (2017) at para. 414.
[30] Bear Creek (2017) at para. 657.
[31] Annex 812.1(b): 'The determination of whether a measure or series of measures of a Party constitutes an indirect expropriation requires a case-by-case, fact based inquiry that considers, among other factors:

  i. the economic impact of the measure or series of measures, although the sole fact that a measure or series of measures of a Party has an adverse effect on the economic value of an investment does not establish that an indirect expropriation has occurred,
  ii. the extent to which the measure or series of measures interferes with distinct, reasonable investment-backed expectations, and
  iii. the character of the measure or series of measures;'.

[32] On the origins of these annexes and their relationship to US Supreme Court jurisprudence, see Schneiderman (2018) at 265–6, 272–3.
[33] Bear Creek (2017) at para. 415.
[34] Bear Creek (2017) at paras. 446–7.

based upon expropriation or nationalization is whether the measure requires the payment of compensation or whether it was taken in the exercise of police powers authority, which calls for no-compensation. Peru argued that it was entitled to exercise its police powers authority 'in the face of months of violent protests that threatened [its citizen's] health and safety'.[35] In which case, no compensation would be due. The tribunal was resistant, however, to the idea that this argument was available in light of the treaty's exceptions clause (Art. 2202.1). This clause, modelled upon GATT Art. XX, ousted any other 'exceptions'.[36]

The list of exceptions, the tribunal surmised, was meant to be 'exclusive' and so 'no other exceptions from general international law or otherwise can be considered applicable in this case'.[37] According to the tribunal, the treaty had ousted what has long been considered an inherent element of state sovereignty—police powers jurisdiction—and a part of international law's toolkit regarding expropriations.[38] Alschner characterizes the tribunal as having erected an 'interpretive "firewall" … against state-driven change'.[39] It is a curious and potentially serious setback as states go about tweaking text to preserve policy space otherwise eroded by investment treaty commitments. Defences previously available are no longer due to alteration in treaty text.

The tribunal awarded Bear Creek damages in the amount of roughly US$18 million plus interest, representing sunk costs, substantially less than the total claimed, but no sum was awarded for future lost profits as none were foreseeable.[40] The tribunal refused to deduct any sum from the award representing Bear Creek's contribution to the political unrest. The tribunal majority concluded that, although it could have done more to secure its social license, the investor did all it legally was required to do to consult with those affected.[41] The claimant, in addition, was awarded 75 per cent of its legal costs, worth almost US$6 million.[42]

In his partial dissenting opinion, Phillipe Sands took a different view of the company's conduct. First, as to liability, the respondent state had 'no option but to

---

[35] Bear Creek (2017) at para. 469.
[36] The exceptions clause in Article 2201.1.3 reads as follows: 'For the purposes of Chapter Eight (Investment), subject to the requirement that such measures are not applied in a manner that constitute arbitrary or unjustifiable discrimination between investments or between investors, or a disguised restriction on international trade or investment, nothing in this Agreement shall be construed to prevent a Party from adopting or enforcing measures necessary: (a) to protect human, animal or plant life or health, which the Parties understand to include environmental measures necessary to protect human, animal or plant life or health; (b) to ensure compliance with laws and regulations that are not inconsistent with this Agreement; or (c) the conservation of living or non-living exhaustible natural resources.' Typically, such exceptions clauses are modelled upon Article XX of the General Agreement on Tariffs and Trade (GATT). See discussion in Henckels (2018) at 2827–8.
[37] Bear Creek (2017) at para. 473. See discussion in Hepburn (2019) at 153.
[38] *Philip Morris v. Uruguay*, ICSID Case No. ARB/10/7 (8 July 2016) reviews this arbitral jurisprudence.
[39] Alschner (2022) at 165.
[40] Bear Creek (2017) at paras. 603, 604.
[41] Bear Creek (2017) at paras. 412, 567, 668.
[42] Bear Creek (2017) at para. 736.

act in some way to protect the well-being of its citizens'. There were, however, less drastic options available other than revocation and so the state was liable for having indirectly expropriated the investment.[43] It was appropriate to reduce the award of damages, nevertheless, because of the investor's contribution to the social unrest.[44] Relying upon international obligations owed towards Indigenous Peoples in ILO Convention 169, incorporated into Peruvian law via a 1993 legislative resolution, an investor would have been encouraged to 'take into account' international obligations owed to the Aymaran people.[45] Even if the ILO Convention did not bind private foreign investors, Sands concluded, it was not 'without significance or legal effects for them'. It also was relevant to the tribunal's work and so should be taken into account as applicable law in the context of the dispute.[46] Having responded to the concerns of only some communities, and not all or most of them, the investor's outreach programme was deemed woefully 'inadequate' by Sands[47] and fell short 'largely because of its own failures'.[48] As a consequence, Sands would have cut in half the damages owed to Bear Creek. In addition, he also would have split legal costs equally between the two parties.[49] Despite this setback, the government's embrace of investment treaty law disciplines has not abated.

III. Investment Law and Policy

The Peruvian government aggressively pursued the signing of bilateral investment treaties with capital-exporting states in the 1990s. From 1993 onwards, Peru signed 33 investment treaties or free trade agreements with investment chapters, many with powerful states like the US and numerous EU member states.[50] Seven of these have since been terminated.[51] After a ten-year hiatus, Peru has turned towards signing sweeping trade and investment or regional treaties, like the Comprehensive and Progressive Agreement for Trans-Pacific Partnership (CPTPP). Such agreements are offered to Peruvian negotiators by powerful,

---

[43] Bear Creek (2017) 'Partial Dissenting Opinion' at para. 2. Sands only mentions suspension of the licence, but it is hard to see how a temporary suspension would have resolved this impasse.
[44] Bear Creek (2017) 'Partial Dissenting Opinion' at para. 6.
[45] Resolución Legislativa No. 26253 of 26 November 1993 at https://www.acnur.org/fileadmin/Documentos/BDL/2008/6747.pdf (last accessed 10 March 2023).
[46] Bear Creek (2017) 'Partial Dissenting Opinion' at para. 10, referring to Urbaser (2016) at paras. 1200, 1201.
[47] Bear Creek (2017) 'Partial Dissenting Opinion' at para. 33.
[48] Bear Creek (2017) 'Partial Dissenting Opinion' at para. 37.
[49] Bear Creek (2017) 'Partial Dissenting Opinion' at para. 39.
[50] UNCTAD (2011) at 16.
[51] And a total of nine are not yet in force. See UNCTAD Investment Policy Hub at https://investmentpolicy.unctad.org/international-investment-agreements/countries/165/peru (last accessed 15 August 2022).

capital-exporting, negotiating partners on a take-it-or-leave-it basis. Calvert, for this reason, describes Peru as a rule-taker rather than a rule-maker.[52]

The United Nations Conference on Trade and Development (UNCTAD) viewed this engagement with investment treaty law, in 2011, as having 'rendered fruits'.[53] They have served to 'improve the climate for foreign investment' even if they also have given rise to disputes.[54] The data reveals that in 2012 Peru was required to respond to 31 investment claims, 19 of which remained pending at the time.[55] Peru had a decent record of success early on, succeeding in six disputes and investors awarded damages in only two of those cases (of which Bear Creek was one).[56] This resulted in a net gain for the state by virtue of cost awards in its favour.[57] These 'wins' confirm, for Peruvian officials, the 'value of ISDS'.[58] If the record looks impressive, warns a member of Peru's legal defence team, it is still 'far from optimal'. Legal costs, reputational harm, and delay render ISDS a 'lottery', he warns, giving rise to unnecessarily long and complex proceedings.[59] There are, in addition, numerous disputes that have yet to be resolved.[60]

Prompted by the rise in claims and desirous of mitigating more disputes,[61] Peru established in 2006 an in-house agency (*Sistema de Coordinación Respuesta del Estado en Controversias Internacionales de Inversión* [SICRECI]) that would offer legal representation and coordinate defences to the myriad of disputes being launched. The agency also is mandated to prevent disputes by centralizing information, enhanced by a 'state-of-the-art online alert mechanism'.[62] This new agency has not forestalled the rise in investor claims, however. At least six known cases have been initiated since 2021 alone. UNCTAD reports that Peru was the most frequent respondent state that year.[63]

---

[52] She confirms this is an interview with a Peruvian official in Calvert (2022) at 169. Also see Gramercy (2022) at paras. 212–14 where the tribunal notes that 'public debt' was excluded from protection under the 2000 Peru model investment treaty but subsequently included in the text of the 2004 Peru–US BIT. Peru was only able to secure, in return, a concession in Annex 10-F that excludes treaty coverage if negotiated restructuring of Peruvian public debt is ongoing.
[53] UNCTAD (2011) at 15.
[54] UNCTAD (2011) at 16. Some were initiated pursuant to contract rather than investment agreement.
[55] Bullard (2012) at 513 ff. For a recent round-up of disputes, see Bohmer (2022) and Calvert and Tienhara (2022).
[56] Two were discontinued and two were settled. These are typically counted as wins for Peru. It is not obvious, however, that settled cases do not result in a payout to the investor. See Ubilava (2020) at 548 (publicly available 'settled amounts are not in any way smaller than awarded amounts'). Bregante and Ossio (2022), by comparison, declare 15 of 18 ICSID disputes were won by Peru as of March 2021. This is the same data reported in Gestión (2020) (14 of 17 disputes have been resulted in 'positive results' for Peru).
[57] Valderrama (2021) at 118.
[58] Calvert (2022) at 183.
[59] Valderrama (2021) at 119.
[60] Bohmer (2022).
[61] Cordero Hijar (2016) at 1.
[62] All described in Valderrama (2021) at 126–8 and Cordero Hijar (2016) at 1–2.
[63] UNCTAD (2022) at 74.

Such a large increase in the number of outstanding claims prompted Peru's former President, Pedro Castillo, to promise to negotiate new investment treaties and to withdraw from the International Convention on the Settlement of Investment Disputes (ICSID).[64] Castillo, however, faced a series of political crises, including ejection from the political party, Free Peru, of which he was leader and under whose banner he was elected as President.[65] He also successfully rebuffed two trials for impeachment and was predicted not to survive in office until the next general election in 2026.[66] As if to prove those predictions correct, Castillo was ousted for orchestrating a coup plot to dissolve the legislature and rule by Presidential decree in December 2022.[67]

Protests have been roiling the country, even following Castillo's ouster.[68] Social unrest due to rising prices were accompanied by protests initiated by indigenous communities opposed to mining in their traditional territories. States of emergency were declared by President Castillo in both urban and rural areas due to rising inflation, while mining activities at the Chinese-owned Las Bambas copper mine and the Mexican-operated Cuajone mine were suspended.[69] Only a new constitution could solve the problem of social unrest, the head of Free Peru declared.[70] This was a commitment that Castillo made when running for President but remained unfulfilled. In the meantime, Peru continues to be governed by a constitution imposed by President Fujimoro, following his self-coup (or *autogulpe*) in 1993.

IV. Constitutional Order

Peru's record of constitutional change is represented by numerous abridged reforms—the constitution was rewritten 12 times between 1823 and 1933[71]—punctuated by lengthy periods of military rule,[72] including military invasion by neighbouring Chile. Suspicious of the overweening authority exercised by Spain, the country's first constitution of 1823 installed a plural executive so as to fragment discretionary authority[73] and installed a unicameral legislature so as to empower the people.[74] The second constitution of 1828 has been described as a 'progressive

---

[64] Bregante and Ossio (2022).
[65] According to Free Peru, the policies adopted by the Castillo government were 'not in line with what was promised during the electoral campaign and even less with the party program, implementing a losing neoliberal program' in De Mello (2022).
[66] Economist Intelligence Unit (2022).
[67] It is said that his failed coup was 'on brand for Castillo, a fitting end to his year and a half of improvisation and incompetence' in Alarcón (2022).
[68] The Guardian (2023). Reports indicate that 48 people have been killed in the protests.
[69] Egerton-Vernon et al. (2022) and Muñoz (2021).
[70] De Mello (2022).
[71] Alba (1977) at 50.
[72] Kenney (2008) and Ríos-Figueroa (2016) at 83.
[73] Gargarella (2010) at 65.
[74] Gargarella (2010) at 63.

document' that further trimmed executive authority.[75] These more radical experiments in constitutionalism were replaced by more conservative documents in subsequent decades. The 1860 Constitution, practically in force until 1920,[76] mandated bicameralism, introduced a 'weak Congress' that met only biannually, and limited the franchise to only those with the requisite literacy.[77] Majoritarian institutions were now cabined by constitutional constraints. The 1933 Constitution, by contrast, introduced social commitments and pared back executive power.[78] By 1979, a powerful executive would be restored but coupled with constitutional conceptions of a social state. Its provisions addressed the right to equality (Art. 2), to education (Art. 24), and worker participation in the management and property of corporations (Art. 56).[79] The state was, in addition, obliged to 'provide opportunities for development to those sectors suffering from any type of inequality' (Art. 59). The Constitution recognized that property served social interests while requiring the payment of compensation in the event of its having been taken in the public interest (Art. 125). The state was obliged to guarantee economic pluralism, declared that the national economy was based on 'the democratic coexistence of various forms of property and business' (Art. 112),[80] and encouraged agrarian reform (Art. 159).

These innovations were terminated by the 1993 Constitution, the product of machinations by President Fujimori that put an end to the 'era of social security'.[81] For Fujimori, and his conservative movement, the Constitution served as an obstacle to installing neoliberal policies.[82] Constitutional Court rulings nullifying nine laws having to do with limiting benefits available to retirees, increasing the cost of public transportation, and the privatizing state-owned enterprises, contributed to this belief.[83] Mere weeks after the Court' last ruling, Fujimori declared a self-coup and dismissed all of the other political and judicial branches. Upon re-election in 1993, the Fujimori-controlled Congress, acting as constituent assembly, drafted a new constitution that would not stand in the way of his economic agenda. It was approved via popular referendum that October.

---

[75] Gargarella (2010) at 11.
[76] The Constitution of 1867, which restored progressive features of the 1856 text, was in force for merely four months. See Gargarella (2013) at 189–90. Also see Cladgett (1947) at 96–7.
[77] Gargarella (2013) at 217, fn. 16. Executive power was also consolidated in the Constitutions of 1826 and 1839 in Gargarella (2013) at 121 and 121, fn. 97. Conservative elites were also distrustful of federalism—it was associated with 'internal disorder' writes Gargarella (2013) at 109. They also disliked constitutionalism as it cabined in political power (id. at 112).
[78] Gargarella (2013) at 234, n. 14.
[79] Some of this is canvassed in Landa and Sánchez (2021).
[80] The Constitution also recognized communal property (Art. 157).
[81] Quoted in Teivainen (2002) at 157.
[82] Teivainen (2002) at 156.
[83] Finkel (2008) at 67. Also Ríos-Figueroa (2016) at 96.

Under the new constitution, Peru remains a monist jurisdiction[84] and treaties are incorporated into Peruvian national law (Art. 55). Approval of treaties is more complex, however. While the executive branch has carriage of foreign relations and may negotiate and ratify international treaties with advance notice to Congress (Arts. 118, 57), the Constitution requires that Congress approve treaties prior to their ratification by the President when they concern human rights, state sovereignty, national defense, or state financial obligations (Art. 56).[85] In addition, treaties that address taxes or that 'require modification or repeal of any law or require legislative measures for their application' require Congressional approval (Art. 56). When a treaty 'affects constitutional provisions' the Constitution's amending formula will apply (Art. 57). The same rules are triggered in the case of the denunciation of treaties (Art. 57). In the case of all other treaties, the President may negotiate and sign them with only an obligation to report to Congress. These treaty provisions are the very ones at issue in the constitutional rulings taken up for discussion below (Section VI).

There are a number of other salient provisions of the 1993 Constitution that are associated with Fujimori's programme of economic liberalization. The economic system is declared to be a 'social market economy' that promotes 'free enterprise' and 'free competition' (Arts. 58–61). The Peruvian Constitutional Tribunal subsequently characterized the social market economy as a 'third way': one that is 'opposed to the economy of planning and central management … [and] is also opposed to the economy of laissez faire, where the State cannot and should not interfere in the economic process'.[86] We can assume that this reference to the social market economy is associated with the German post-war model.[87] There are, in addition, numerous references to social and economic rights in the text of Chapter II of the Constitution, among them a right to social security (Art. 10), health benefits (Art. 11), to adequate and fair compensation for work (Art. 24), to collective bargaining (Art. 28), and to sharing in profits (Art. 29). Some of these have been the subject of pronouncements by the Constitutional Tribunal, as discussed in Section V.[88]

The rights of Indigenous Peoples are subordinated to the logic of markets as well. While the 1976 Constitution recognized their land, community control, and traditions (Art. 161), its 1993 replacement degraded those rights, recognizing

---

[84] Though the distinction between dualist and monist regimes is increasingly difficult to sustain. See, for example Vásquez (2013) and Abugattas (2009) and discussion in the Introduction, section XI.

[85] According to the Fourth Final Provision of the Constitution: 'Rules concerning the rights and freedoms recognized by this Constitution are construed in accordance with the Universal Declaration of Human Rights and the international treaties and agreements regarding those rights that have been ratified by Peru.'

[86] 0008-2003-AI/TC, f 16 (NestaBrero case) (translation by Alberto Cruces Burga).

[87] This origin is highlighted in STC 0008-2033-AI/TC at para. 16, with reference to Müller-Armack, an influential post-WWII ordoliberal who served as Under-Secretary of State in the Economics Ministry and was attracted to Mussolini's fascism in the 1930s. See Joerges (2003) at 178–9.

[88] Flores Nano (2015).

community property but permitting the state to take control over 'abandoned' lands (Art. 163). This puts untitled communities at risk, warns Kamphuis.[89] Indigenous property rights protections were weakened by removing the requirement of a two-thirds majority vote to alienate community lands (Art. 89).[90] It is unquestionably the case that the 1993 Constitution is more favourable to markets than is the 1979 Constitution, reserving to the state only a regulatory role instead of the role of protector and service provider.[91]

The Constitution endorses 'economic pluralism,' as did the 1979 Constitution, and authorizes state enterprise 'for reasons of high public interest or manifest national convenience' (Art. 60). The right to property is considered 'inviolable' and the conditions under which it can be taken, heightened: only on the grounds of national security or 'public need' accompanied by the payment of compensation of the 'appraised value,' including 'potential damages' (Art. 70). The right to contract is considered inviolable. Contractual 'terms may not be modified by laws or any other provision whatsoever' and disputes 'resolved solely through arbitration or judicial recourse, in accordance with the protective mechanisms provided for in the contract, or established by law' (Art. 62).[92] The Constitution guarantees national treatment by providing that foreign nationals 'fall under the same conditions as Peruvians'. They may not, however, 'invoke exception or diplomatic protection' (Art. 71). Nor are foreign nationals permitted to acquire or possess property within 50 kilometres of the border unless expressly authorized to do so with cabinet approval (Art. 72).[93] To similar effect, the Constitution provides that national and foreign investments are to be treated equally ('subject to the same conditions') and, in the case of state contracts, foreign investors can have no access to diplomatic protection (Art. 63, cl.2). Instead, in such cases, resident foreign nationals are subject to the jurisdiction of 'national laws and courts' (Art. 63, cl. 2). The loss of diplomatic protection resembles Calvo clause requirements that national treatment be available to non-nationals but that the privilege will be lost in cases where foreigners seek diplomatic protection.[94] This is not a robust Calvo provision, however, as the Constitution also recognizes that the state and public corporations 'may

---

[89] Kamphuis (2017) at 180.
[90] Because Fujimori left intact those statutes implementing indigenous property rights, many of the former rights are preserved by statute, rather than by constitution. See Kamphuis (2017) at 180. They have been supplemented by consultation laws (such as Law No. 29785) in addition to mining regulations (e.g. Supreme Decree No. 040-2014-EM) that impose social and economic obligations on mining operators. See Lupaka Gold (2022) at paras. 53 and 67.
[91] Kresalja (2009).
[92] Merino (2022) at 187 concludes that 'state intervention in the market is minimal and that contractual terms cannot be changed even if those laws seek to protect the public interest or human rights'.
[93] This authorization was the only necessary precondition for the Bear Creek investment to proceed, according to the tribunal (discussed above).
[94] See Shea (1955).

submit controversies arising from their contractual relations' to courts established by treaties or to 'international arbitration' (Art. 63, cl. 3).[95]

Taken together, these provisions embody a partial constitutionalization of investment law.[96] So long as investors can channel their deprivation of rights claim into a property rights, equality, or national treatment claim, they can have recourse to national courts for a remedy. The investment treaty regime, however, is designed to remove disputes from local court jurisdiction. To the extent that the Constitution accommodates jurisdiction for international investment tribunals, there will be less room for judicial defiance. There, nevertheless, remains some room for interpretive conflict insofar as treaties may modify constitutional commitments. There also remains uncertainty whether Congressional authorization is required to ratify an international investment treaty, a question that has preoccupied the Peruvian Constitutional Tribunal. Before turning to a discussion of those cases, a preliminary question arises: how has the court interacted with the other branches of government?

V. The Court

Judicial review under the Constitution was unknown to Peruvian constitutional law for most of its history. A Tribunal of Constitutional Guarantees was introduced in the 1979 Constitution but with 'severely restricted' access.[97] Ríos-Figueroa describes the court as practically 'irrelevant'.[98] The tribunal, however, by nullifying measures in furtherance of the Fujimori's neoliberal agenda, inadvertently contributed to the justification for his self-coup. The Constitutional Commission, under the control of Fujimori, initially proposed abolition of the constitutional tribunal but yielded to pressure to install a new court hoping to mollify public opinion in the upcoming referendum.[99] With the advent of the 1993 Constitution, a new apex constitutional court was established with the express power of judicial review (Art. 138).

The seven-member Tribunal would be appointed by Congress by two-thirds vote for five-year terms (Art. 201). This mode of judicial appointment produces what has been described as 'crude bargaining' among political parties. The

---

[95] In contrast to the 2008 Constitution of Ecuador, there is no question about whether the Peruvian Constitution contemplates international arbitration.
[96] The Constitution's developmentalist mindset 'coexist', in Merino's terms, with more disruptive elements. See Merino (2022) at 173. Calvert (2022) at 163–4 reveals that Fujimori 'embedded investor rights into Peru's legal system', via BITs and presidential decrees.
[97] Principally political actors, or petitions with 50,000 citizen signatures, could initiate judicial review. The Tribunal also had jurisdiction to hear appeals in habeas corpus and amparo cases. See discussion in Ríos-Figueroa (2016) at 92.
[98] Ríos-Figueroa (2016) at 92.
[99] Finkel (2008) at 68–9. The constitution was endorsed by a vote of 52 to 48 per cent (ibid.).

relatively short tenure of each judge also weakens institutional independence.[100] According to its enabling statute, a supermajority of six of seven justices is required to declare laws unconstitutional.[101] The Court has original jurisdiction to hear constitutional cases (for laws enacted after January 1996),[102] and appellate jurisdiction over habeas and amparo proceedings (Art. 202). Otherwise, authority is triggered principally by actors in the political branches or by petition of 5,000 signatures (Art. 203).

It is not farfetched to assume that judges on the Peruvian Constitutional Tribunal, as do judges on many other apex courts, act strategically. If outcomes are determined principally with reference to law, judges will be attentive to the institutional context in which they operate. They will anticipate the response of the political branches, in particular.[103] Preliminary findings suggest the Constitutional Tribunal increasingly is behaving in a strategic fashion, both in regard to review of executive and legislative powers. Turning first to executive authority, in a study of 19,289 amparo applications between 1996 and 2006—the constitutional remedy that is equivalent to a common law injunction for violation of constitutional rights[104]—the court appeared to be responsive to its institutional environment. The predominant subject matters in these amparo suits concerned pensions (63.3 per cent), employment (30 per cent), disputes over public property (6 per cent), and taxes (5 per cent).[105] In periods when public confidence in the Presidency or the share of Congressional seats held by the President's party declined, the Court was more apt to act assertively. The only exceptions concerned tax cases and public property disputes in cases where the executive controlled fewer seats in Congress.[106] It is significant, write Tiede and Ponce, that 'the Tribunal is more likely to rule against the state when the subject itself constitutes the largest share of the Tribunal's docket and when the subject areas arguably affect the largest number of citizens'. It is this willingness to exercise authority against the executive branch that has helped establish the Court's reputation 'as an independent political actor'.[107]

A subsequent study confirms that Tribunal judges behave strategically—they are more deferential in periods where political power is consolidated and less deferential when power is fragmented amongst political parties.[108] The cases under study concerned the Tribunal's jurisdiction to undertake abstract review (to issue writs of unconstitutionality) when prompted by, among others, the President, the

---

[100] Ríos-Figueroa (2016) at 117.
[101] Finkel (2008) at 72.
[102] Finkel (2008) at 78.
[103] Epstein and Knight (1998) at 10–18 and Helmke and Staton (2011).
[104] Tiede and Ponce (2011) at 109.
[105] Tiede and Ponce (2011) at 120–1.
[106] Tiede and Ponce (2011) at 125.
[107] Tiede and Ponce (2011) at 130.
[108] The 'fragmentation hypothesis' in Latin America suggests that judicial assertiveness is more likely when political power is divided. See Helmke and Ríos-Figueroa (2011) at 6.

Prosecutor General, the Ombudsmen, or 25 per cent of the members of Congress (Art. 203). In the period 2001–2011 the Tribunal undertook review in 311 cases and declared unconstitutional 33 per cent of those laws or decrees.[109] These findings confirm that it is not political attitudes but strategic behaviour that helped determine judicial outcomes. The judges were most deferential towards Congress, a little less deferential in cases of Executive action, and least deferential when reviewing sub-national (regional and municipal) laws. They were also 13 per cent less likely to find against governments 'currently in power' and 12 per cent more likely in cases where Congress was more fragmented.[110] It appears to be the case that Constitutional Tribunal authority is enhanced when political party power in Congress becomes more fragmented.[111] As Dargent states it, 'judicial independence in the region is strongly linked to political pluralism'.[112]

Ríos-Figueroa's study of judicial independence in the period 1960–2010—defined as the capacity of judges to act according to their preferences coupled with compliance by political authorities—has Peruvian courts exhibiting an uneven (or 'zigzag') pattern.[113] Regarding the prior consultation of indigenous peoples, he observes, the Constitutional Tribunal has produced 'erratic jurisprudence'.[114] That independence may be constrained, however, in cases that concern the path of economic liberalism that has been pursued by successive Peruvian administrations. Presidents have continually been elected on anti-neoliberal platforms only to reverse course once elected. President Garcia was elected on a platform critiquing the Peru–US FTA, only to sign the agreement as one of his first official acts[115] These policy reversals are a common feature of Latin American executive branch behaviour. According to Stokes, these policy switchers are likely to conceal their preferences to get elected. After the fact explanations, such as unexpectedly large fiscal deficits, look disingenuous when incumbent governments undertake sweeping economic reforms that are not confined only to fiscal reform.[116]

What the evidence of policy switches reveals is a fear, on the part of Peru's ruling elites (economic, political, legal, and bureaucratic), that departures from the path determined by powerful capital-exporting states and promoted by international financial institutions are not very well tolerated. Weak political parties and a weak civil society assure path dependence, making politicians 'wary of major policy changes'. Vergara and Watanabe observe that the Peruvian 'business community

---

[109] Tiede and Ponce (2014) at 130.
[110] Tiede and Ponce (2014) at 149.
[111] It is said that party organization has always been 'feeble' in Vergara and Watanabe (2016) at 153.
[112] Dargent (2009) at 276.
[113] Ríos-Figueroa (2016) at 168. The Court is described as having been, at times, both 'co-opted' and a 'vital actor in controlling abuses of power' in López Zamora (2021) at para. 3.
[114] Ríos-Figueroa (2016) at 204. This is confirmed by a recent ruling which, unexpectedly, retreated from the more fulsome right the Court previously has recognized. See Exp. No. 03066-2019-PA/TC (20 January 2022) and Organization of American States (2022).
[115] Vergara and Watanabe (2016) at 151.
[116] Stokes (1999) at 111, 123.

has encouraged this fear, muttering of economic disaster that would occur if the government chose to deviate from neoliberal orthodoxy'.[117] The question is whether the Peruvian Constitutional Tribunal feels similar pressure to get out of the way of reforms that move in this direction.

VI. The Record

The Constitutional Tribunal replaced the Tribunal of Constitutional Guarantees established by the 1979 Constitution. The antecedent Tribunal was composed of nine judges, three of them elected by each of the three branches (executive, legislative, and judicial). The Tribunal's decision rule required that six of nine justices vote for a declaration of constitutional invalidity to have that effect. Mostly under control of the Executive Branch which commanded a narrow majority in Congress, the Tribunal lacked legitimacy as it was unable to overcome judicial deadlock under its strict decision rule. Only between 1990 and 1993 did the Tribunal flex its muscle when it was under the control of appointees elected by parties defeated in the 1990 election.

Replaced by the Constitutional Tribunal in 1993, the new decision rule, established by a 1995 Congressional law, required that six of the seven justices, appointed for five-year terms, find a measure constitutionally invalid. Dargent concludes that the Tribunal initially had little impact, declaring five of sixteen actions partially unconstitutional between 1996 and 1997. The legislative reply was to re-enact those laws but with different wording.[118] A series of crises in the Tribunal were precipitated by Fujimori seeking a third presidential term, resulting in three justices being impeached by Congress.[119] After the fall of Fujimorismi due to corruption and internal strife, the three magistrates were reinstated and the Tribunal's decision rule reduced from six of seven to five of seven.[120] It was only after overcoming this crisis, in 2002, that the Tribunal secured a semblance of independence. In Dargent's estimation, it was in this new pluralistic and competitive political party environment that the Constitutional Tribunal emerged as an 'impartial and influential actor in Peruvian politics'.[121]

One can characterize the Constitutional Tribunal's record as unevenly progressive. The Tribunal has proven itself capable of resisting executive branch incursions into fundamental rights. For example, the Tribunal held that an executive decree fixing rates for domestic and international land travel via emergency decree, in order to combat the rise of an informal transportation sector,[122]

---
[117] Vergara and Watanabe (2016) at 154.
[118] Dargent (2009) at 269.
[119] Dargent (2009) at 270.
[120] Dargent (2009) at 271.
[121] Dargent (2009) at 271.
[122] STC 0008-2033-PI/TC at para. 48. See discussion in Landa and Sánchez (2021) at 61.

was constitutionally indefensible. This was because of the measure's lack of proportionality—there were numerous less restrictive alternatives that could have been pursued[123]—and because the measure did not respond to urgent, unforeseeable, or exceptional circumstances.[124] In its opinion, the Tribunal opined at length about what a 'social and democratic state under the rule of law' entailed. Markets could not operate unimpeded, the Tribunal declared, rejecting an 'atomistic' view of constitutional rights. Referring to the Papal Encyclical *Mater et Magistra*, the Tribunal insisted that the 'juridical order ... under the guiding influence of social justice', enable the harmonization of 'particular interests with the common good'.[125] Significantly, the Tribunal laid emphasis on the 'social functions' served by private property, which entails the qualification of market rights to create and expand the 'common good'.[126]

In another instance, the Tribunal declared unconstitutional a prohibition on public sector collective bargaining that would have resulted in wage increases.[127] The Constitution, after all, recognizes collective bargaining and the right to strike (Art. 28), a right that is extended to public servants (Art. 42). Yet the Constitution also requires that budgets 'be effectively balanced' (Art. 78). The Tribunal concluded that the prohibition emptied the essential content of a fundamental constitutional right. The state could only be justified in banning public sector collective bargaining if it were an 'exceptional measure', of limited duration, and that adequately safeguarded 'workers living standards'.[128]

Constitutional rights can also entail positive obligations. In an amparo application to secure life-saving HIV/AIDS treatment, the Tribunal acknowledged that, if social rights were programmatic rights highly dependent upon state fiscal capacity and so differentiated from traditional liberal rights, they also were 'indispensable for the enjoyment of civil and political rights'. Without 'education, health and dignified life quality in general', they announced, 'it would not be possible to talk about freedom and social equality, which makes both the legislator and the administration of justice recognize them jointly and interdependently'.[129] Because health is 'inseparably' related to the fundamental right to life (Chap. 1, Art. 1), the state was obliged to take 'concrete action' by providing 'comprehensive treatment' for HIV/AIDS, and report to the Tribunal regarding its compliance every six months.[130]

---

[123] Landa and Sánchez (2021) at 51.
[124] STC 0008-2033-PI/TC at para. 61.
[125] STC 0008-2033-PI/TC at para. 12, clause 4.
[126] STC 0008-2033-PI/TC at para. 26 (a).
[127] Exp. Nos. 025-2013-Pirre; 003-2014-PI/TC; 0008-2014-PUTC; 0017-2014-P1/1C, excerpts translated in Constitutional Tribunal of Peru (2017). Article 78 mandates that the 'Budget bill shall be effectively balanced'.
[128] Exp. Nos. 025-2013-Pirre; 003-2014-PI/TC; 0008-2014-PUTC; 0017-2014-P1/1C at 21, para. 184.
[129] 2945-2003-AA-TC (20 April 2004) at para. 11 translation available at https://www.globalhealthrights.org/wp-content/uploads/2013/08/2945-2003-AA-TC-ENGLISH.pdf (last accessed 6 September 2022). See discussion in Davies (2022) and Noriega (2012).
[130] 2945-2003-AA-TC at paras. 28, 39.

Social rights are required to be fulfilled depending on factors such as 'the severity and reasonableness of the case', their linkage or effects on 'other rights,' and the 'available State budget'.[131]

The Tribunal, nevertheless, exhibits other tendencies. For instance, Judge Landa Arroyo incorporated the doctrine of indirect expropriation into Peruvian constitutional doctrine when the Municipality of Nazca cancelled mining concessions in the vicinity of the city to expand housing construction.[132] The majority of the judges chose to characterize the municipality's action as curbing contractual freedom, not property rights, as the ordinance modified conditions in a concession contract. This gave rise to a violation of the freedom to contract and offended the constitutional rule that 'Contractual terms may not be modified by laws or any other provision whatsoever' (Art. 62). The need to expand urban housing availability was not addressed. Instead, Judge Arroyo took the occasion to read in a prohibition on regulatory expropriations as part of the doctrine of indirect expropriation (he did not carefully distinguish between the two). Confusingly, he described regulatory expropriations as instances where state regulation affects property rights through the exercise of police powers.[133] Typically, the exercise of police powers are non-compensable events that do not give rise to a regulatory expropriation. Judge Arroyo declared it was proper to incorporate this doctrine into the Constitution as it already was a part of Peru's duty to 'protect foreign investors' in its BIT programme which, after all, recognizes 'the right of such agents to be compensated'.[134] Even if unmentioned in constitutional text, the rule complemented the constitutional right to property as it 'is meaningful to the extent that it allows property to be used to the greatest advantage'.[135] A majority of the Constitutional Tribunal subsequently agreed that this international law rule should be absorbed into domestic law. The judges adopted Judge Arroyo's ruling, virtually verbatim, into the Tribunal's majority reasons.[136]

Despite indications that it is eager to accommodate investment law edicts, there is reason to suspect the Constitutional Tribunal is not inclined to always bend to the will of foreign investors but will prefer parochial political interests. This was the allegation that lay at the centre of Gramercy Funds claim against Peru.[137] Gramercy alleged that the Constitutional Tribunal was involved in machinations

---

[131] 2945-2003-AA-TC at 33. The Tribunal went so far as to recommend that the government take advantage of TRIPs flexibilities available at the WTO.
[132] 1735-2008-AA (20 May 2008) at paras. 11–13.
[133] 1735-2008-AA at para. 26 ('Basis of Vote of Judge Landa Arroyo').
[134] 1735-2008-AA at para. 27.
[135] 1735-2008-AA at para. 30, referring to Arts. 70, s. 2, para. 2, Art. 63, Art. 71, and Art. 61 (ibid at para. 31).
[136] See the Town House Case, 00239-2010-AA/TC (5 November 2012) at paras. 10–12, the *Duke Energy* Case, 834-2010-PA/TC (9 May 2011), and Resolución N° 1535-2010/SC1-INDECOPI, an interpretation of the Law of General Administrative Procedure issued by INDECOPI (the National Institute for the Defense of Competition and the Protection of Intellectual Property).
[137] See Gramercy (2018a).

to subvert the value of bonds purchased from Peruvian bond holders. These were originally provided by the state to property owners as compensation for land reform initiatives taken in 1969–1979. According to Gramercy's claim, the Tribunal issued a ruling, 'tainted by forgery', reversing an earlier determination by the Tribunal in 2001 that bonds were to be appraised at their current value using the consumer price index.[138] The Tribunal's subsequent 2013 ruling, the investor argued, rejected this method of valuation because it would cause 'severe impacts' on the Peruvian economy. Instead, the Tribunal favoured 'dollarization' which would have the effect of substantially decreasing the value of the bonds.[139] The Tribunal's 2013 ruling, secured by the Chief Justice working in tandem with the President's office, so Gramercy alleged, required the reversal of several judicial votes and conversion of a majority opinion into a dissenting one that was procured with the aid of liquid paper. By subsequently implementing the Tribunal's directive, the government committed multiple alleged treaty breaches, including a denial of justice. As criminal investigation against the clerk of the Tribunal and congressional inquiries yielded no findings of wrongdoing,[140] the 2013 ruling remained the last word on the subject, despite numerous invitations to reconsider the question of valuation.

Peru, in its defence, maintained that the Tribunal did not lay down a method of evaluation in 2001 and that there was nothing that undercut the authority of the majority ruling in 2013.[141] An investment tribunal concluded, nevertheless, that Peru acted arbitrarily, contrary to the minimum standard of treatment required under customary international law and its kindred standard of fair and equitable treatment. Peru was therefore liable to pay the amount of some US$33 million (representing Gramercy's original purchase price for the bonds) plus interest, together with a portion of the fees and legal costs of the arbitration.[142] The tribunal, 'not without some hesitation,' concluded that the Constitutional Tribunal's ruling had not been 'contaminated by undue pressure' from the executive branch.[143] The investment tribunal also acknowledged that, if the use of white-out to delete signatures was 'unconventional', it did not amount to 'forgery of court documents'.[144]

So, it turned out that the apex court's behaviour was not determinative of Gramercy's ultimate success. The Constitutional Tribunal's machinations nevertheless helped to fuel the investment tribunal panel placing the court's internal deliberations under the microscope. It also is revealing the degree to which the Constitutional Tribunal yielded to executive branch influence despite the

---

[138] Gramercy (2018a) at para. 12 and 022-96-I/TC (15 March 2011).
[139] Gramercy (2018a) at para. 13.
[140] Gramercy (2022) at paras. 1006, 1183.
[141] Gramercy (2018b) at paras. 102–3.
[142] Gramercy (2022) at para. 986. In her dissenting opinion, Professor Brigitte Stern found Gramercy's investment to be entirely speculative and abusive of international dispute processes. As the tribunal was without jurisdiction, she did not offer any views on the merits of the claim.
[143] Gramercy (2022) at paras. 1186, 1164.
[144] Gramercy (2022) at para. 1176.

probability of alienating the US-based investor. Likening the Constitutional Tribunal's task to that of a 'negative legislator', the investment tribunal conceded that the judges had a 'duty, before adopting a decision, to ascertain its effects, including on the State budget'.[145]

There is, finally, the question of the right to prior consultation of indigenous communities when their lands are affected by government action. As a consequence of doctrine developed by the Inter-American Court of Human Rights that is incorporated into Peruvian constitutional doctrine as part of the 'block of constitutionality',[146] the right to meaningful prior consultation is a part of the law of the land.[147] When it comes to large-scale projects having a major impact on those communities, the Inter-American Court of Human Rights has indicated that consent may even be required.[148] As generous as this doctrine appears to be, the Tribunal has not been vigilant in protecting those interests, particularly as they run up against investment treaty obligations. In a January 2022 decision, the Tribunal elected not to uphold the communal territorial rights of the Chila Chambilla and Chila Pucará indigenous communities, who were seeking to nullify mining concession granted to Cemento Sur.[149] Three of the six judges expressed doubts that the plaintiffs were indigenous peoples and that, in any event, there was no obligation to consult them prior to granting concession rights.[150] As the concurrence of Judge Canals explains, the company would have to secure permits to initiate exploitation of the land, at which point consultation with these communities would then be required.[151]

The right to prior consultation 'is not recognized by the Constitution, either expressly or tacitly, so it is not possible to claim protection through the amparo process, since it is not a fundamental right', the Tribunal majority declared.[152] This was

---

[145] Gramercy (2022) at para. 1182.

[146] No. 03343-2007-PA. In addition to obligations arising under ILO Convention No. 169 and rights to 'cultural identity' previously recognized by the Tribunal. See discussion in Alva-Arévalo (2020). The constitutional block refers, typically in Latin America, to the incorporation of international human rights law into constitutional interpretation. See discussion in Góngora-Mera (2017) and Colombia's constitutionality block discussed in Chapter 5. This is distinct from the constitutionality block in the Constitution of France, discussed in Chapter 3, which includes 17 articles in the 1789 Declaration, 14 principles enumerated in the 1946 Preamble, unwritten principles referred to in the 1946 Preamble (the 'general principles of law recognized by the republic'), and the 2005 Charter for the Environment.

[147] The Peruvian law on consultation, Ley No. 29785, was enacted in 2011. See Ley Del Derecho a la Consulta Previa a los Pueblos Indígenas u Originarios, Reconocido en el Convenio 169 de la Organización Internacional del Trabajo (OIT) at https://bdpi.cultura.gob.pe/sites/default/files/2019-06/Ley%20N%C2%B029785.pdf (last accessed 30 January 2023). Initially, the principle was incorporated into Peruvian law by Resolución Legislativa No. 26253 of 26 November 1993 at https://www.acnur.org/fileadmin/Documentos/BDL/2008/6747.pdf (last accessed 10 March 2023).

[148] *Mayagna (Sumo) Awas Tingni Community v. Nicaragua* (31 August 2011) at paras. 149 and 35.

[149] Cemento Sur S.A. is a subsidiary of Cemento Yura S.A. (under the control of Chilean ownership), itself a subsidiary of the Gloria Group based in Peru. See Newsbeezer.com (2016).

[150] 3066-2019-PA/TC. Three other judges acknowledged that these communities belonged to the Aymara people, in ibid. 'Singular Vote of Miranda Canals' at para. 15, 'Single Vote of Judge Ledesma Narváez,' and 'Singular Vote of Judge Espinosa-Saldaña Barrera' at para. 19.

[151] 3066-2019-PA/TC, 'Singular Vote of Miranda Canals' at para. 32.

[152] 3066-2019-PA/TC at 'Fundamentals' para. 5.

a conclusion that was fiercely resisted by the Ombudsman and numerous human rights bodies.[153] Two dissenting judges agreed, concluding that the grant of mining concessions would negatively impact these indigenous communities. According to Judge Espinosa-Saldaña, the grant of concession rights 'directly affects the collective rights of the plaintiff communities, since it modifies their legal situation with respect to the right to property'.[154] Without having undertaken prior consultation, the concession should be annulled. Judge Narváez held that it was insufficient that consultation processes occur sometime in the future, only after permits were sought, as the grant of mining rights negatively impacts these communities. To 'delay the opportunity for consultation to the next phase is, in practice, to weaken the content of the right'.[155]

There is a further reason to think that the dissenting judges were right to be concerned about delaying the right to be consulted. The majority failed to appreciate that, by conferring concession rights over indigenous lands without prior consultation, the state will have induced the company to dedicate more of its resources to the mining concession. Prolonging the investment and inducing the commitment of further funds in order to complete the permit process raises expectations that can be upset should the state seek to halt exploration and exploitation. The majority, in other words, are seemingly unaware of the demands that international investment law makes of states in these circumstances. After all, investment arbitrators have resurrected a version of vested rights doctrine under the rubric of fair and equitable treatment and its legitimate expectations doctrine, as the Gramercy dispute illustrates.[156] Investors, it will be said, have reliance rights that can only be satisfied if the state allows the investment to proceed or pays an adequate sum of damages.

VII. The Cases

The executive branch considers trade and investment treaties as being solely within the purview of the President. This has not been without controversy, however, beginning with the 2001 Peru–US FTA. Thirty-two Congressman filed a petition before the Constitutional Tribunal seeking to invalidate a legislative resolution approving the FTA, but before the US Congress had done the same.[157] The suit was brought before an increasingly emboldened Constitutional Tribunal, having

---

[153] For example, see Defensoría del Pueblo (2022) and Barnaby (2022).
[154] 3066-2019-PA/TC, 'Singular Vote of Judge Espinosa-Saldaña Barrera' at para. 48.
[155] 3066-2019-PA/TC, 'Single Vote of Judge Ledesma Narváez'.
[156] Arbitrator Zachary Douglas describes this vested rights approach as one akin to strict liability. See his partial dissenting opinion in Kruck (2022) at para. 54.
[157] The Constitution grants to 25 per cent of 'congressmen' the ability to bring a writ of unconstitutionality (Art. 203.4).

achieved (for the first time in Peruvian history) a semblance legitimacy as the final arbiter of disputes concerning constitutional rights and the separation of powers. Following upon this petition were a sequence of cases, which I take up next.

(i) Peru–US FTA (#1)

The Congressmen's petition to the Court argued that there were multiple constitutional incompatibilities of both the trade and investment chapters of the Peru–US FTA.[158] The investment chapter, however, was the principal ground for their constitutional complaint as it restricted state policy space to implement measures in the public interest, including those protecting social rights and promoting economic development.[159] By entering into the Peru–US FTA, they claim, 'Peru adheres to a model of economic growth but abdicates its obligation to achieve the integral development of the country.' The petition characterized the FTA as securing 'economic, social, political and legal reform ... across the entire institutional fabric of the Nation, which affects constitutional aspects and provisions referring to the capacity of the State to define its policies and regulations, above all negatively affecting the development of its most needy population'. As a consequence, they claimed that 'the right to enjoy a healthy and balanced environment, to well-being, to equal development opportunities for the sectors that suffer inequality, among other rights recognized in the Constitution will be violated'. Moreover, the model of economic development that is adhered to via treaty is not concerned with 'development of production for the satisfaction of human needs, in an equitable manner, within a framework of social responsibility'.[160] Their legal brief, in sum, articulates presuppositions that animate this book's research question.

Specifically, it was argued that treaty provisions on indirect expropriation generate a right to compensation broader than that available to investors in their home states.[161] It also contemplated a much broader range of takings than was available under Peruvian constitutional law.[162] Performance requirements, prohibiting the

---

[158] Case file 00033-2006-PI/TC (22 January 2007).
[159] Interpreted in conjunction with Art. 26 of the Inter-American Convention on Human Rights.
[160] Action of Unconstitutionality Against Legislative Resolution No. 28766 Approving the 'Peru–United States Trade Promotion Agreement,' Peru Constitutional Tribunal 33-2006-A1 at 7.1(c) and (d).
[161] Action of Unconstitutionality at 7.1.2(i). In fact, it was only after approval of the Peru–U.S. FTA that the Constitutional Court established that this was a violation of the property clause. See discussion of Judge Landa Arroyo's ruling in *Shougang Hierro Perú* S.A., Case File 01735-2008-AA. In the subsequent rulings of Duke Energy, Case File 00834-2010-PA/TC (concerning the taking of hydroelectric plant) and Town House, Case File 00239-2010-AA/TC (concerning change in a zoning permission), the Court gave content to the requirement to compensate in cases of indirect takings, but without reference to the earlier Shougang case. There have been few developments in the Peruvian case law since then. But this clearly is an instance of what Santos calls a globalized localism—the internalization of allegedly 'global' law.
[162] The treaty's public purpose requirement, for instance, does not comport well with the requirement that property be exercised in 'harmony with the common good' and that expropriation be permitted on the grounds of 'national security or public need' that is 'determined by law' (Art. 70).

mandatory use of local products, labour, or services, barred the state from more broadly promoting social and economic development. It amounted to a 'serious restriction' on the capacity of the state to 'manage and guide' the uses to which foreign capital will be put. The claimants took note of the double standard that economic development in the Global North was achieved using precisely the sorts of measures that were now prohibited via treaty.[163] National treatment and most-favoured nation treatment rendered the constitutional mandate to promote small business enterprise[164] also more difficult to implement. All of these protections violated the 'constitutional principle of equality'.[165] The treaty's principal mode of enforcement—investor–state dispute settlement (ISDS)—granted access to foreign investors to special tribunals operating in secret with no avenue for public participation 'despite being politically affected'.[166] In addition, the treaty violated constitutional provisions concerning the right to health, indigenous consultation, and sovereignty of natural resources, amongst others. Regarding the diminution of sovereignty, the plaintiffs claimed the treaty undermined the 'fundamental duty' of the state to defend 'national sovereignty', to promote 'general welfare based on justice', and 'comprehensive and balanced development' (Art. 44, cl.1). The free trade agreement, by contrast, served as a framework which cramps the 'room for maneuver of economic policy'.[167]

Cumulatively, this amounted to constitutional reform requiring approval using the extraordinary process outlined elsewhere in the Constitution. Either approval by two-thirds majority in two successive votes in Congress was required or, following approval by popular referendum, a simple majority in Congress.[168]

What appeared critical to the opinion of the Court was the fact that, although the treaty had been approved by the Peruvian Congress, approval from the US Congress was still pending.[169] In a very short ruling, six of the seven justices declared the claim to be 'inadmissible'—colloquially speaking, the dispute was not yet ripe—because the treaty was not yet in force.[170] Judge Gonzales Ojeda would have admitted the cause of action but provided no further opinion on the merits.

---

[163] Action of Unconstitutionality, n. 160 at 7.1.2(ii). The claimants referred to Chang (2002).
[164] Constitution, Art. 59.
[165] Action of Unconstitutionality, n. 160 at 7.1.2(iii). The parties quoted from the 2005 inauguration speech of Argentinian President Nestor Kirchner: 'Equal treatment for those who are different; equal treatment between powerful and weak countries; equal treatment between highly developed and emerging countries, is not only a lie but also a deadly trap.'
[166] Action of Unconstitutionality, n. 160 at 7.1.2.(v).
[167] The plaintiffs brief quoted Alan Fairlie, ¿Cuál TLC con EE.UU? En: Tarea Revista do Educación y Cultura No 50–Lima (August 2004) at 39. This is reminiscent of the argument that NAFTA served as a conditioning framework that lock-in reforms in much the same way as do constitutional strictures in Grinspun and Krekleweich (1994) at 39.
[168] Art. 206, cl.1.
[169] The President of the Constitutional Court consulted the Ministry of Foreign Affairs regarding this question on 11 January 2007 and was informed of the absence of Congressional approval by letter dated 18 January 2007.
[170] Case file 00033-2006-PI/TC (22 January 2007).

On a request for clarification, the claimants maintained that the Tribunal had not addressed the substance of the treaty but, instead, focussed on stages of approval. This, they claimed, was 'unclear' and 'biased'.[171] The Tribunal, again, declined to take jurisdiction, declaring it inadmissible.[172] If the treaty was not yet ratified by the US, the content of the treaty could not yet be known. Judge Ojeda, once again, issued a dissenting opinion but on this occasion provided more content. The Tribunal's reasons for declining to decide were 'artificial', he complained. Having approved the FTA by legislative resolution, it became part of the Peruvian legal system 'the day after it was published' in the official record of the legislature as required by the Constitution (Art. 109). If there were subsequent modifications to the treaty, these would require new formal acts by Parliament and, possibly, fresh applications for review.[173] Clearly, the Tribunal was not yet ready to consider the content of the treaty. Would it ever be?

(ii) Peru–US FTA (#2)

This first ruling prompted a second request from the plaintiffs.[174] Though the treaty had not yet been ratified by the US Congress, the plaintiffs argued that their principal focus was on Peru's legislative resolution of 28 June 2006 approving the FTA rather than the treaty text itself. In addition, were the Court not to rule on the question of constitutionality, it would render moot any subsequent lawsuit as the treaty text would by then have been finalized, leaving no room to renegotiate its terms. Rather than putting a halt to a future agreement, the plaintiffs sought to ensure that the treaty was constitutionally compliant before it was ratified by both state parties. Despite their more specific plea, the Congressmen were impugning the treaty text along the same lines as they had previously.

Nine months after issuing their ruling in the first case, the Constitutional Tribunal demurred.[175] It could not control the content of treaties without knowing, with confidence, its content. As the treaty has not yet been ratified by the US, its character could not be known. The Tribunal again declared the claim inadmissible. It insisted that US ratification was required to allow the claim to move forward. The plaintiffs had sought to separate the legislative resolution from the treaty text yet it 'is the treaty, and only through it, that the norm challenged in the complaint acquires legal content, which can be submitted to an examination of its constitutionality'.[176] The Tribunal concluded that its power to conduct abstract constitutional

---

[171] 33-2006-PI/TC Clarification (5 February 2007) at para. 4.
[172] 33-2006-PI/TC Clarification at para. 6.
[173] 33-2006-PI/TC Clarification (5 February 2007) 'Singular Vote of Judge Gonzales Ojeda'.
[174] Case file 00036-2007-PI/TC.
[175] 00036-2007-PI/TC (20 November 2007).
[176] 00036-2007-PI/TC at para. 5.

review was conditional 'upon the approval by the US Senate ... Only then will it constitute a valid and effective internal standard, in accordance with Article 55 of the Constitution.'[177]

As Judge Ojeda was no longer on the Court, no dissenting opinion was issued. Between the first and second cases, four of seven Constitutional Court Judges, including Judge Ojeda, had been replaced by judges who were more favorably inclined to the government that was promoting the free trade agreement.[178]

(iii) Peru–US FTA (#3)

Congressional authority over implementation of the treaty continued to generate constitutional conflict. In a complaint launched by over seven million citizens, legislative decrees purporting to implement the Peru–US FTA were challenged on the grounds that they delegated to the Executive Branch powers that were too general and not sufficiently specific, in violation of constitutional requirements (Art. 104).[179] It also was claimed that the special labour regime established by the implementing legislation contributed to precarity and inequality in public sector employment.[180] The Constitutional Tribunal found both claims were without foundation. The delegation of authority to the Executive was specific enough and the special regime for contracting labour, as declared in an earlier case, was authorized as part of the 'modernization process'.[181]

Judge Eto Cruz dissented from that part of the ruling that found the new regime, reducing public sector employment rights, compatible with constitutional obligations. Not at issue in the Tribunal's earlier ruling was whether the new regime complied with the 'principle of progressivity of social rights', he observed.[182] Having not addressed this question in the prior case, the Tribunal could take jurisdiction in this instance. Judge Cruz described the Tribunal's approach to the reduction of labour protections as being formalistic and 'slightly slippery'. The government should be expected to offer a constitutional justification for departing from the principle of progressively improving labour rights. The only justification offered in support of this diminution of public sector rights, however, was financial cost. This could assist in the government's justification obligation, Judge Cruz acknowledged,

---

[177] 00036-2007-PI/TC at para. 6.
[178] Judges Alva Orlandini, Bardelli Lartirigoyen, García Toma, and Gonzales Ojeda departed and were replaced by Judges Beaumont Callirgos, Calle Hayen, Eto Cruz, and Álvarez Miranda.
[179] Art. 104 provides that 'Congress may delegate the power to legislate to the Executive Branch through legislative decrees on specific matters and in the term established by the authorizing law.'
[180] No. 00010-20 10-Pl/TC (18 April 2011) 'III. Background'.
[181] 00010-20 10-Pl/TC at paras. 10–11, 20. The previous ruling was issued in Case No. 002-2010-PI/TC.
[182] 00010-20 10-Pl/TC, 'Vote of Judge Eto Cruz' at para. 5. This was derived from Art. 26 of the American Convention on Human Rights, incorporated into the Peruvian legal system as part of the 'block of constitutionality'.

but only when considered alongside other factors, such as whether the government was making efforts to progressively improve employment conditions. For this reason, he would have assumed jurisdiction on the question of whether the special employment regime was constitutionally compliant.[183] His was the lone dissenting voice, however. The government was given the green light to proceed as it wished.

(iv) Peru–Chile FTA

Though historic rivals, Peru and Chile signed a 1998 Economic Complementation Agreement 38 (ACE 38)[184] that was subsequently replaced by a 2006 Free Trade Agreement. It was this new agreement, superseding the older one, that 40 Congressman challenged before the Constitutional Tribunal.[185] At issue in this instance was the ability of the President of the Republic to unilaterally sign onto the new accord without Congressional approval under Article 57. It will be recalled that Congress' approval is required when a treaty concerns human rights, state sovereignty, national defense, or state financial obligations (Art. 56). The plaintiffs insisted that the consent of Congress was mandatory as the new treaty affected sovereignty, national defence, and financial obligations requiring reform of the Constitution. The government responded that it was understood by the parties to the FTA that no constitutional reform was required by either side—their intention merely was to supplement an already existing international treaty.

Among their complaints, the plaintiffs alleged that the sovereignty and territorial integrity of the state was implicated by reason of an adjustment to Peru's maritime boundaries, a long-standing irritant between Peru and Chile.[186] Realigning the border could only be achieved with the participation of Congress. In addition, the expropriation provision of the FTA differed from Peruvian constitutional law. The new text authorized expropriation only for 'public utility' or 'public purpose' and not for the additional reason of 'national security' as provided for in the Constitution (Art. 70). Compensation in the event of an expropriation was also stricter in the FTA, requiring payment of fair market value rather than an amount legally specified by a Peruvian judge (Art. 70).[187] Finally, making available ISDS without requiring the exhaustion of local remedies or having national courts play any supervisory role also ran afoul of the Constitution.[188]

---

[183] 00010-20 10-PI/TC, 'Vote of Judge Eto Cruz' at paras. 14–15, 19.
[184] Acuerdo de Complementación Económica Chile—Perú (AAP.CE No. 38) available at http://www.sice.oas.org/Trade/chilper/Chpeind.asp.
[185] Case file 00002-2009-PI/TC (5 February 2010).
[186] 00002-2009-PI/TC at para. 11. The maritime boundary dispute was partly resolved by a 2014 ruling of the International Court of Justice.
[187] 00002-2009-PI/TC at para. 26.
[188] 00002-2009-PI/TC at para. 34.

Numerous other, less salient, arguments were submitted to the Constitutional Tribunal, all of which were subject to the same government reply: none of them concerned subjects that triggered the requirement of Congressional consent. The Constitutional Tribunal agreed with government, in a brief ruling, by adopting the interpretive technique of presumptive constitutionality. Even if the Treaty did not make reference to the disputed territorial sea, extending 200 nautical miles from the coast as declared in the Constitution(Art. 54), the Court presumed that the treaty would be interpreted consistent with the Constitution.[189] Similarly, regarding expropriation, though the two texts might be inconsistent, it was assumed that the Treaty was intended to incorporate the justification of national security.[190] If the Court was wrong about this, then national security would fall, in any case, within the 'public purpose' justification. Lastly, the availability of ISDS did not deny to Peruvian citizens an ability to purse their claims in national courts. Rather, the availability of ISDS was simply a 'voluntary alternative' envisaged by the Constitution.[191]

Having dispensed with the case in favour of the executive branch, the court continued by clarifying the constitutional landscape concerning treaty approval. The plaintiffs argued that Congressional participation in treaty-making was premised on the idea that the Constitution was a deliberative one requiring dialogue between the two branches. This interpretation was rejected by the Court, preferring to distinguish sharply between those spheres permitting executive treaty authorization and those requiring legislative approval. In cases where there is doubt as to which body principally had control of the treaty process, constitutional presumptions favoured the executive branch. This is the branch 'that governs and manages the public services closest to the citizen'.[192] The Tribunal warned that there might arise, after the fact (e.g. in the course of treaty interpretation), questions indicating that Congressional approval should have been sought in advance. The Tribunal offered no solution to this problem but, instead, exhorted the President to consult with Congress using a mechanism available under Congressional regulations.[193] To this end, the Tribunal encouraged more dialogue between the two branches. The judges would not otherwise indulge the plaintiff's argument that constitutional obligations to consult were triggered in this instance.

---

[189] 00002-2009-PI/TC at 'VI. Ruling', para. 2.
[190] 00002-2009-PI/TC at 'VI. Ruling', para. 3.
[191] 00002-2009-PI/TC at 'V. Ruling', para. 41. Calvert reveals that state officials do not treats ISDS as controversial and that arbitration is preferred over domestic courts for the resolution of disputes with foreign investors. Arbitration is 'fairer' and more 'efficient', they report, than domestic courts. They also believe that investment treaties leave sufficient regulatory space for the state. See Calvert (2022) at 174, 182, 195.
[192] 00002-2009-PI/TC at 11(a) at para. 71.
[193] In a separate opinion, undertaking an impressive survey of comparative constitutional law on treaty ratification, Judge Eto Cruz raised the possibility of prior constitutional control by Congress in every instance.

(v) Peru–China FTA

The final instalment in this quintet concerns the constitutional challenge, post-ratification, of the Peru–China FTA.[194] The issue arising in this case concerns not so much diminution of constitutional space by the investment and trade chapters of the Peru–China FTA as it does the role of Congress in ratifying international treaties. A collection of Congressmen—amounting to 25 per cent membership in that body—sought a declaration of constitutional invalidity on the ground that the treaty was approved even while negotiation of the text was ongoing. The decree published on 6 December 2009 referred to the non-definitive text of 29 April 2009. By the date of the application for judicial review, the definitive text of the FTA and its annexes had yet to be published in the Official Gazette. Nor had technical or legal opinions regarding the FTA been made public. Internal communications between the Peruvian Ministry of Foreign Affairs and the Peruvian Embassy in China revealed a desire on the part of the Executive branch to sideline Congress to ensure speedy tariff reductions. The whole process, the plaintiffs complained, was conducted in an unprofessional and untransparent manner.

The Government replied less with legal than economic arguments, directed at justifying the tariff reductions that were the target of the plaintiff's ire. But there was little argument offered in support of the FTA's compatibility with the Peruvian Constitution. Instead, the Government emphasized the negative consequences of a judicial declaration of invalidity. The government's principal argument was that the treaty was not one falling within the enumerations listed in Article 56, enabling the President to unilaterally ratify the treaty.

The Tribunal, once again, unanimously deferred to the executive in an opinion focussing on the process by which the treaty was negotiated rather than addressing many of the substantive complaints, including those having to do with tariff reduction.[195] The Court accepted that the process was constitutionally unassailable:

> Any technical deficiency or insufficiency that may occur in the negotiation process, such as the alleged lack of consensus among the members of the national team that was in charge of negotiating the treaty ... is outside the scope of formal constitutional control of treaties. None of these hypotheses represents a constitutionally relevant reason that authorizes this Court to declare the Peru-China FTA unconstitutional.[196]

---

[194] Ratified by Supreme Decree 092-2009-RE and implemented via Supreme Decree 0005-2010-MINCETUR.
[195] Case file 00021-2010-PI/TC (20 March 2012).
[196] 00021-2010-PI/TC at para. 9.

Official publication of a treaty that was still under negotiation had the appearance of failing to satisfy a constitutionally 'essential' requirement (Art. 51).[197] The Tribunal chose to avoid the conflict by concluding that publication on a website was sufficient.[198] Official publication in September 2011 (almost two years after the decree) remedied the remaining defect.[199] Whatever constitutional questions remained (concerning sovereignty, discrimination, or promotion of the 'general welfare'), these were not matters deserving any further consideration:[200]

> the determination of which are those actions or public policies that may lead to the promotion of ... [the general welfare], is not a question that falls within the competence of any court of justice and, among them, within the competence of this Court. The identification of what these may be and the decision to implement them depends on the reasons for and against them that are put forward in the process of democratic deliberation and, therefore, it is up to any of the political bodies with competence in these matters to assume them.

Throughout its ruling on Peru–China FTA, the Court exhibited an inclination to quiet down contentious constitutional questions. We can infer that the intention was to smooth the path for the constitutional compatibility of all trade and investment treaties moving forward.

VIII. Conclusion

Taken together, the record of Peru's apex court reveals a stance suggestive of hard deference towards investment law's constraints. Two influences seem to be at work: First is the Tribunal's submission to the desires of Peru's powerful executive branch. Second is the influence of investment law disciplines themselves as, on at least one occasion, judges eagerly incorporated the investment law doctrine of indirect expropriation into Peruvian constitutional law. Jackson cautions against conflating the 'presumption that the Constitution does not prevent compliance with treaty obligations' with the 'presumption that the Constitution itself should be interpreted to require what the treaty requires'.[201] When given the opportunity, the Constitutional Tribunal, appears to be doing both. Yet, as the Gramercy dispute reveals, the Tribunal, when confronted with having to choose between the

---

[197] It also conflicted with Peruvian Law 26647.
[198] 00021-2010-PI/TC at para. 13.
[199] 00021-2010-PI/TC at para. 19.
[200] 00021-2010-PI/TC at para. 69.
[201] Jackson (2010) at 158 cautions against conflating the 'presumption that the Constitution does not prevent compliance with treaty obligations' with the 'presumption that the Constitution itself should be interpreted to require what the treaty requires'.

two, yields to executive prerogatives. On the whole, however, the Constitutional Tribunal mostly has agreed to elide the diminution of constitutional space.

Does this submissive stance suggest that there is convergence between national constitutional law and international economic rules? The Peruvian Constitution is sufficiently distinctive to offer distance between the two legal orders, were the Constitutional Tribunal to choose to exploit that space.[202] It may also be that movement to replace Fujimori's constitutional handiwork—devised in 1993 at the height of neoliberal supremacy—with a new constitutional model will widen that distance. More likely, however, is continued extractivist economic planning, rendering the pursuit of foreign investment a top priority and other development options inapposite. In such circumstances, it is hard to imagine Peru's current or future constitutional order standing in the way.

---

[202] Jackson (2010) at 101 makes the case, in the US context, against convergence.

5
Conditionally Constitutional
Colombia

I. Introduction

Among apex courts, the Constitutional Court of Colombia stands out as having repeatedly tested investment treaty disciplines against the demands of its constitutional order.[1] The Court is described as one of the most 'hyperactive' courts in the world and a leader among courts in Latin America.[2] Recent rulings have even upset investor expectations, giving rise to a number of pending investment disputes over impacts of resource exploitation on the environment and indigenous constitutional rights of prior consultation. It was in the course of establishing its reputation that the Court halted Colombia's investment treaty programme by declaring unconstitutional a Colombia–UK BIT in 1996. It was smooth sailing afterwards, once Congress amended the Constitution's property clause, excising its offending language that permitted, in some circumstances, expropriation without compensation.[3] The Court has since repeatedly deferred to decisions of the political branches who have negotiated common investment treaty commitments.

The Court's decision in C-252 of 2019, concerning a BIT with France (and a companion case concerning a BIT with Israel), is considered by many to be a watershed moment.[4] Multiple declarations of 'conditional constitutionality' were issued by the Court, forcing the two states back to the negotiating table. Departing from earlier precedent and adopting a more aggressive stance in the conduct of its constitutional mandate to scrutinize international treaties, the executive branch was directed to negotiate joint interpretive declarations regarding selected treaty terms so as to conform to the Constitution's commands.

The Court ended up taking sides in a number of investment arbitration controversies, endorsing textual changes that resemble new treaty language negotiated by capital-exporting states. The outcome, in most every instance, was to narrow the

---

[1] Due, in no small part, to the constitutional obligation to submit treaties for review to the Constitutional Court (Art. 241 [10]). It rivals the 17 constitutional rulings issued by the Constitutional Court of Ecuador. See Espinosa (2021) at 2659–62.
[2] Gloppen et al. (2010) at 43 and Prieto Muñoz (2019).
[3] Schneiderman (2000).
[4] The 'decision has dramatically changed the Court's longstanding position regarding IIAs' in Zuleta and Camila Rincón (2019). The two rulings are identical in many respects report Correa, Prieto-Ríos, and Álvarez (2020) at 16-17.

scope of treaty disciplines and, in theory, widen state policy space. It could be said that the Court, in comparative constitutional law terms, adopted a version of 'dialogical' reasoning, engaging with international law for the purposes of justifying its constitutional outcomes.[5] Yet the Court's dialogical reasoning resulted in quite a modest outcome, arriving at the conclusion that investment treaty law, after a few required tweaks, was entirely in conformity with Colombia's purportedly transformative constitutional order. Many controversial elements of the treaty were passed over. In most every instance, when the Court chose to intervene, it did so only where capital-exporting states had already negotiated stricter treaty terms (such as had Canada and the European Union in the Comprehensive Economic Trade Agreement [CETA]).[6] The Court, in other words, merely followed dominant trendlines in investment treaty law. It did not take issue with any of its significant details. The Court's decision, one can conclude, poses little threat to the future of international investment law.

By mainstreaming investment law disciplines into Colombia's constitutional order,[7] the ruling in C-252 of 2019 exhibits aspects of both soft deference and soft defiance. The Court, admittedly, defied expectations by adopting a more activist stance vis-à-vis the political branches in addition to scrutinizing some of the overbreadth on display in investment treaty law and arbitration. But the Court's ruling exhibits less of a push toward a 'new frontier' than a failure of the nerve. Rather than daring to resist investment law's contraction of constitutional space, the Court chose to adapt the Constitution to its demands.[8]

Disputes lodged against Colombia have been on the uptick. As revealed in Section V below the state has been required to respond to a variety of investor claims initiated by reason of Colombian Constitutional Court rulings in defence of the environment or local communities. There is good reason to worry about state success in these cases, especially after the Eco Oro award, discussed next. While it is perilous to presume widespread knowledge among various branches of government about pending and resolved investment disputes, Sands advises that 'officials and judges' involved in the dispute 'had a very high level of awareness of investment law and its implications'.[9] The tribunal's award, for this reason, should give pause to the political branches as they continue to adapt the extant investment treaty regime.

---

[5] Choudhry (1999) at 835–8.
[6] On CETA as a new model agreement, see Allee, Elsig, and Lugg (2017).
[7] As I argue in the Conclusion, describing the decision as promoting 'pluralistic dialogue', for example in Prieto Muñoz (2019), seems an overreach.
[8] For Clarkson (2003) at 147 elements of both define the semi-peripheral state (they remain 'suspended somewhere between the powerful center as rule maker and the weak periphery as rule taker' at 167).
[9] Sands (2020) at 15.

II. The Eco Oro Dispute

In 2016, the Colombian Constitutional Court declared parts of Congressional Law 1753/2015, which permitted mining activities in the ecologically sensitive and unique Santurbán paramo, unconstitutional. The páramo is situated at the upper limits of the Andean forest and serves as a primary source of fresh drinking water for 70 per cent of the country.[10] In the ruling, the Court found that any deterioration of this ecosystem would be 'irreversible'.[11] Furthermore, entitling mining companies to continue exploiting the páramo[12] offended provisions in the Constitution concerning protection of the environment.[13] These will prevail over concession contracts, the Court declared, 'when the activity is proven to cause harm, or where there is merit in applying the precautionary principle to avoid harm to non-renewable natural resources and human health'.[14] 'In this regard' the Court added, 'the Political Constitution establishes economic freedom as a right susceptible to being limited in situations in which it can be compromised for constitutionally valuable purposes, among which the right to a healthy environment and ecological balance stands out.'[15] '[E]conomic and business freedom', the Court declared, can be limited by the 'common good'.[16]

It was the duty not only of the political branches to preserve areas of special ecological importance, the ruling continued, it also was an obligation of the Court to subject the ecosystem to 'direct constitutional protection' via declarations of constitutionality.[17] Even if the judges were aware that their decision would precipitate an investment dispute—which gave rise to 'heated discussions' at the Court[18]—the risk of arbitration did not deter them from the constitutional task before them. Thus, the Colombian Mining Agency proceeded to implement the Court's ruling. This course of action prompted two separate investment claims, one by Galway Gold and the other by Eco Oro, claiming expropriation pursuant to the investment chapter of a 2011 Colombia–Canada FTA. In addition, the Canadian mining company Red Eagle Exploration Limited initiated a claim triggered by a second Court ruling revoking mining rights in an area adjacent to Santurbán páramo. The investor claimed that there was expropriation and a denial of the minimum standard of treatment, including fair and equitable treatment (FET).[19]

---

[10] For an excellent account, together with video interviews, of the dispute and of the community mobilization opposed to the mining, see Cotula (2020).
[11] C-035/16 at paras. 142, 155.
[12] Eco Oro's existing mining rights had been exempted from the ban on mining operations. It was this decision that the Court scrutinized for constitutional compliance.
[13] In Articles 1, 58, 80, and 95.
[14] C-035/16 at para. 128.
[15] C-035/16 at 130.
[16] C-035/16 at para. 170.
[17] C-035/16 at 155.
[18] Sands (2020) at 16.
[19] *Eco Oro Minerals Corp. v. Republic of Colombia*, Request for Arbitration, ICSID Case No. ARB/16/41 (8 December 2016) https://www.italaw.com/sites/default/files/case-documents/italaw9443.pdf (last

In its award addressing the merits of the Eco Oro claim (Galway Gold's proceedings continue separately), the tribunal distinguished sharply between the expropriation claim and FET claim even though both arose out of the same set of facts.[20] The first claim was rejected and the second accepted. These two parts of the tribunal ruling, however, seem hardly compatible.

The tribunal's analysis of the expropriation claim required interpretation of the Colombia–Canada FTA Annex on Expropriation.[21] Depriving the investor of its licence to exploit the Santurbán paramo fell within the terms of the Annex. It was, the tribunal acknowledged, a 'legitimate public welfare objective' in the pursuit of environmental protection and so could not be characterized as indirect expropriation.[22] The measure was 'clearly implemented to protect the paramo ecosystem'.[23] Nor was it discriminatory 'in any way'—it equally affected the foreign investor as it did artisanal miners.[24] Moreover, the investor 'should have been aware' of the importance of protecting the paramo and its fragility'.[25] The precautionary principle should have been understood by the investor as requiring the state to take measures to protect environmentally sensitive areas.[26] Though the tribunal was of the view that the responsible ministry had not proceeded in accordance with procedural protections available under domestic law,[27] the tribunal could not find that this was 'sufficiently egregious to comprise a lack of bona fides on the part of Colombia'.[28] Significantly, the tribunal refused to liken 'distinct reasonable investment-backed

---

accessed 31 July 2020); *Galway Gold Inc. v. Republic of Colombia*, Solicitud de Arbitraje, ICSID Case No. ARB/18/13 (21 March 2018) at http://icsidfiles.worldbank.org/icsid/ICSIDBLOBS/OnlineAwards/C7149/DS13353_Sp.pdf (last accessed 31 July 2020); *Red Eagle v. Colombia*, Request for Arbitration, ICSID Case No. ARB/18/12 (21 March 2018) https://www.italaw.com/sites/default/files/case-documents/italaw10949.pdf (last accessed 31 July 2020).

[20] The tribunal also accepted the investor's claim that the Court's interpretation of the Constitution had prompted the government to act in violation of the treaty.
[21] Annex 811: Indirect Expropriation of the Colombia–Canada BIT provides: '(b) Except in rare circumstances, such as when a measure or series of measures is so severe in the light of its purpose that it cannot be reasonably viewed as having been adopted in good faith, non-discriminatory measures by a Party that are designed and applied to protect legitimate public welfare objectives, for example health, safety and the protection of the environment, do not constitute indirect expropriation.'
[22] Eco Oro (2021a) at para. 641.
[23] Eco Oro (2021a) at para. 644.
[24] Eco Oro (2021a) at para. 640.
[25] Eco Oro (2021a) at paras. 645, 685.
[26] Eco Oro (2021a) at para. 683. The precautionary principle refers to states taking measures to protect the environment even without indisputable scientific proof. See Davies (2016) for its marginal role in investment law disputes. Tienhaara's observation in (2009) at 210—that the principle has not been well incorporated into investment treaty arbitration—still holds true, according to Tremblay (2022) at 938. See discussion in Foster (2012) who hypothesizes about the role the precautionary principle *could*—but has yet to—play in investment arbitration.
[27] Eco Oro (2021a) at para. 676. The tribunal summarized the Constitutional Court's findings that the Ministry had not 'respected the principle of good faith by having denied protection of the rights to environmental participation, failed to provide access to information and not ensured the community's active and deliberative participation'.
[28] Eco Oro (2021a) at para. 678.

expectations' in the Annex on Expropriation with 'legitimate expectations'. They 'cannot be the same'. they decreed, but without further explanation.[29]

Yet, the investor convinced the tribunal that it had been denied fair and equitable treatment because its expectations had been upended by government. It is bewildering that no mention is made, in the tribunal's FET discussion, that this was the consequence of a legitimate public welfare measure, as it did in its expropriation discussion. Moreover, the tribunal found that Eco Oro's expectations had been upset even though no such finding was made in its evaluation of whether there had been an indirect expropriation.[30] Though no specific representations had been made, there were general inducements, giving rise to a violation of FET's legitimate expectations doctrine. These included granting mining concessions when the government knew it had an obligation to protect the paramo[31] in addition to failing to 'ensure a predictable business environment'.[32] In so doing, the government failed to act 'coherently, consistently or definitively' and has 'shown a flagrant disregard for the basic principle of fairness'.[33] This required the payment of compensation to the investor. Such an award was warranted, a majority of the tribunal ruled, despite an exceptions clause that was intended to preclude payment to investors in cases where a state party took measures to protect the environment.[34]

This bifurcation—the relevance of legitimate environmental regulation to expropriation but not to FET, and the salience of legitimate expectations to FET but not to expropriation—is hard to reconcile. Arbitrator Philippe Sands, in his partial dissent, described the majority's reasoning on expectations 'particularly odd'[35] and its reasons on environmental protection 'difficult to comprehend'.[36] Even the Colombian government could not well explain the outcome. In its press release responding to the award, the government crowed that it had gained victory on the ground of expropriation. It could not say the same about the investor's FET claim.[37] In performing in this fashion, the tribunal hardly exhibited the high degree of deference owed to non-discriminatory regulatory measures intended to protect the environment. Nor did it offer confidence that Colombia will succeed in future defence of state action in pursuance of constitutional requirements.

---

[29] Eco Oro (2021a) at para. 681. Restated at para. 804 but without any further attempt at explanation. Annex 811: Indirect Expropriation of the Colombia–Canada BIT provides that one of the factors to be considered is 'the extent to which the measure or series of measures interfere with distinct, reasonable investment-backed expectations.'
[30] Eco Oro (2021a) at para. 645.
[31] Eco Oro (2021a) at para. 766.
[32] Eco Oro (2021a) at paras. 770, 772.
[33] Eco Oro (2021a) at para. 821.
[34] Eco Oro (2021a) at paras. 822–37 discussing Art. 2201(3). See discussion in Garden (2022) at 5–7.
[35] Eco Oro (2021b) at para. 17.
[36] Eco Oro (2021b) at para. 34.
[37] Colombia (2021). See Sierra (2021) for a discussion.

III. Investment Law and Policy

Even as it tweaks treaty text, Colombian political branches continue to maintain confidence in the regime. The state has long promoted itself as a safe and profitable environment for foreign direct investment. The country is rich with natural resources which governments have made a policy of exploiting to the fullest. Colombia also has a lengthy record of political and legal stability, even if riven by political violence, personal insecurity, and extreme poverty. This tragic history of violence remains the shared experience of both perpetrators and victims.[38] It is remarkable that the 1991 Constitution emerged as the means by which reconciliation between warring factions could be secured. Reconciliation, however, remains out of reach for Colombia as extreme precarity continues to be the lived experience for the bulk of its citizens.[39]

As a part of the plan to restore peace and prosperity via constitutional means, Colombia eagerly embarked upon an investment treaty program in the early 1990s. This was prompted by the belief, reiterated by the National Council on Economic and Social Policy, that an investment treaty programme had the capacity to improve 'foreign investment flows'.[40] Four bilateral investment treaties (BITs) were promptly signed in three years.[41] The investment treaty agenda was suspended in 1996 because of concerns that investment treaties were incompatible with the new constitutional order.[42] After a declaration of constitutional validity was issued by the Constitutional Court in regard to a Colombia–UK BIT, the Constitution was promptly amended in 1999 but plans for future treaties were postponed. Only in the past decade was the BIT programme ramped up again. '[I]nternationalization of the Colombian economy' emerged as a priority in which BITs would serve as an 'important tool for stimulating the flow of investment'.[43] This renewed effort led to an unprecedented number of pending investment disputes. The Ministry of Trade, Industry, and Tourism estimates that damages cumulatively claimed amount to US$9 billion, more than 10 per cent of the 2019 national budget.[44]

Nineteen BITs have been signed with a variety states, of which seven are presently in force, including BITs with the capital-exporting states of Japan, the United Kingdom, Spain, and China. Some 20 free trade agreements with investment chapters have been signed, of which 13 are presently in force,[45] many of them regional

---

[38] Lemaitre (2015).
[39] Lemaitre (2021) at 147.
[40] Colombia (2001) and Zuleta-Londoño et al. (2014) at 17.
[41] Zuleta-Londoño et al. (2014) at 17.
[42] C-358/96 and Schneiderman (2000).
[43] C-252/19 at para. 78.
[44] Quoted in C-252/19 at para. 60.
[45] Data from United States (2019).

trade agreements with Colombia's allies in the southern hemisphere.[46] Colombia has not been actively engaged in investment arbitration though, until recently. Investment lawyers Londoño et al. reported in 2014 that 'Colombia has never been involved in an investment treaty dispute.'[47] By 2020, 14 investment disputes were pending, and one dispute resolved in favour of the claimant.[48] Approximately five of these disputes were prompted by rulings of the Colombian Constitutional Court in defence of environmental and Indigenous rights, discussed in more detail below. In one such dispute, foreign investors Cosigo Resources and Tobie Mining are claiming more than US$18 billion in damages.[49]

It was the onslaught of new investment disputes that prompted the establishment of Colombia's National Agency for the Legal Defense of the State (ANDJE) in addition to proposing new model investment treaties, its most recent iteration in 2017.[50] Treaty text aims to identify, with more precision than in the past, obligations owed to investors, together with an accompanying list of exceptions and a 'right to regulate' clause.[51] As Vélez, former Director General of ANDJE remarked, 'it seems awfully unjust to have a dispute arise because the government is fulfilling its mandate'. 'An investment regime that allows this to happen needs to be revised', he concluded.[52]

That Colombia is committed to reforming substantive treaty obligations owed to investors is attested to in the state's 2019 submission to UNCITRAL Working Group III. ISDS reform at UCITRAL is focussed upon three concerns: consistency, arbitral independence, and costs and duration of arbitration. The mandate of the Working Group has been confined mostly to 'procedural aspects of dispute settlement rather than on the substantive provisions'.[53] There is no unanimity, however, among states that UNCITRAL's agenda should be so severely hindered.[54] Colombia, for one, has expressed its 'willingness to achieve substantive reform that responds to the interests of Governments'.[55] 'Substance and procedure are of course linked and should be approached simultaneously', adds Vélez of ANDJE.[56] To this end, Colombia proposed a new multilateral instrument, drawing upon the OECD 2018 Multilateral Convention to Implement Tax Treaty Related Measures

---

[46] Figures are derived from UNCTAD International Investments Agreement Navigator at https://investmentpolicy.unctad.org/international-investment-agreements/countries/45/colombia?type=bits (last accessed 22 July 2020).
[47] Zuleta-Londoño et al. (2014) at 20.
[48] Figures are derived from UNCTAD Investment Dispute Settlement Navigator at https://investmentpolicy.unctad.org/investment-dispute-settlement/country/45/colombia (last accessed 23 July 2020).
[49] Moore and Perez Rocha (2019) at 21.
[50] Zuleta-Londoño et al. (2014) at 19. Four such model treaties have been developed.
[51] Colombia Model BIT (2017) at https://www.mincit.gov.co/temas-interes/documentos/model-bit-2017.aspx (last accessed 23 July 2020). See discussion in Coleman et al (2017).
[52] Vélez quoted in IISD (2018).
[53] UNCITRAL (2017) at para. 20.
[54] Van Harten, Kelsey, and Schneiderman (2019) at 4.
[55] Colombia (2019) at para. 5.
[56] Vélez quoted in IISD (2018).

as precedent, granting to states flexibility to opt in or out of a menu of ISDS reforms. A model ISDS convention could address not only the three areas of concern that preoccupy the UNCITRAL working group, but also an 'illustrative list of substantive provisions' could be proposed, some of which 'would constitute minimum standards from which no state can opt out'.[57] There seems little likelihood that Colombia, and other states that view process and substance as interlinked, will have their concerns addressed by UNCITRAL in the current round of talks. Yet there seem good reasons for Colombia to have second thoughts about investment treaty commitments.

IV. Constitutional Order

Colombia's model BIT 'reaffirms' its commitment to fulfilling constitutional obligations.[58] Yet simple reaffirmations may not suffice, particularly in light of the significant number of constitutional responsibilities enshrined in the 1991 Constitution. Colombia experienced lengthy periods of constitutional stability even as violence and personal insecurity affected all sectors of political life. Supplanting the 1886 Constitution (as amended), the new constitution was the product of a special convention whose membership turned out to better reflect the diversity of Colombian political communities than have its political branches. A number of distinctive features emerged out of this atypically representative body.[59] First, the convention sought to decentre the executive, a branch of government that has long dominated Colombia.[60] The convention endowed Congress with new authority, incorporated participatory mechanisms (e.g. referenda and initiatives), and established a number of other independent checks (e.g. Office of the Ombudsman and Office of the General Prosecutor) with the aim of impeding presidential excesses.[61] The executive branch, nevertheless, continues to dominate electoral politics in Colombia. This is because the 'engine room' of the Constitution—namely, the organization of public power—remains mostly intact.[62] Colombia is not, Uprimny maintains, a 'consolidated democracy', rather, it is a state that has long faced 'high levels of violence' and 'exclusionary policies, resulting in a society with deep inequalities and oligarchic rule.'[63]

---

[57] Colombia (2019) at para. 28.
[58] Colombia Model BIT (2017), supra n. 51 at 10.
[59] The Constitution of Colombia 1991 with amendments available at https://www.constituteproject.org/constitution/Colombia_2015.pdf?lang=en (last accessed 24 July 2020). The composition of the assembly was 'radically different' from the composition of Congress quoted in Merhof (2015) at 717.
[60] Fox and Stetson (1992) at 146–7. In addition to much of Latin America.
[61] Fox and Stetson (1992) at 146–7.
[62] Gargarella (2015) at 89 and Gargarella (2017) at 225–8.
[63] Uprimny (2004) at 50.

The Presidency remains central to Colombian political life, no more so than in the case of international economic policy, where the President is conferred responsibility to 'direct international relations', conclude treaties and international agreements, and 'promote the internationalization of political, economic, social, and ecological relations on the basis of fairness, reciprocity, and the national interest' (Arts. 189, 226). As influential economists gained increasing access to each successive administration since the 1960s (overtaking in influence the legal profession and public finance specialists), the 'economic technocracy' has mostly been free to 'operate without any major interference from those in political power'.[64] Along with the absence of populist party politics,[65] and with Congress usually falling into line with the President,[66] there are few checks on executive-branch preferences. It is significant, then, that the 1991 Constitution requires that Congress either approve or reject treaties by ordinary legislation. It also confers the power of constitutional review upon the Constitutional Court to determine conformity of an international treaty with the Constitution within six days of Congressional approval (Art. 241[10]). In addition, any 'citizen may intervene to defend or challenge their constitutionality'. The Court expanded this authority by allowing written interventions and public hearings to which public entities, private organizations, and experts are invited to present their views in writing or orally.[67]

The second distinctive feature of the 1991 Constitution is that a catalogue of human rights is constitutionally entrenched, among them a number of second generation socio-economic rights.[68] The Constitution (Articles 1 and 334 declare) 'is a social state under the rule of law'.[69] Gender equality, indigenous rights, the rights of children, disabled and working persons, the right to social security, and the protection of health and the environment are acknowledged as 'rights' which the state is bound to protect. The state is authorized to intervene in the economy to promote full employment especially for the economically vulnerable ('those with low income') so that they may have 'access to all basic goods and services' (Art. 334).

There is, third, an enumeration of classical liberal rights (many of them 'fundamental rights'), among them the right to property. The Constitution also endorses the internationalization of economic relations (Art. 227) and permits Congress to sell public assets (Art. 150.9) and to privatize public services (Art. 60). While 'public health and environmental protection' are declared to be 'public services for which the state is responsible', the Constitution permits 'private entities ... to

---

[64] Uribe Mallarino (2014) at 51.
[65] Rodríguez, García-Villegas, and Uprimny (2003) at 138–9.
[66] He 'usually manages to build a comfortable majority in Congress' according to Cepeda-Espinosa (2004) at 681.
[67] C-199/2012 at 25.
[68] The significance of these enumerated rights is underscored by the fact that only after 1936 amendments to the 1886 Constitution were first-generation rights constitutionally recognized.
[69] It is an 'estado social de derecho'. On the distinction between estado social de derecho and estado de bienstar (the welfare state), see Itturalde (2013) at 362–3, fn. 3.

exercise oversight and control over them' (Art. 49). Social security is guaranteed as an 'irrevocable right which 'may be provided by public or private entities' (Art. 48). A 'rationalized' economy within a 'framework of fiscal sustainability' (Art. 334) is mandated as are balanced budgets which require the 'creation of new revenues or the modification of existing ones to finance the amount of contemplated expenditure' (Art. 347). For instance, Article 336 requires the state to 'sell or liquidate' state monopolies 'when the requirements of efficiency are not met'. No new monopolies may be established 'except through the free play of the marketplace and to promote the public or social interest' (Art. 335). The Constitution clearly contemplates privatization of both public property and public services.[70] The 1991 Constitution, in short, enables the enactment of a neoliberal programme, an ingrained feature of global public policy since the early 1990s.[71]

Though Colombia is declared to be a 'unitary republic' it is also described as 'pluralistic' (Art. 1) with rights protecting 'ethnic and cultural diversity' and linguistic and educational diversity within its territories and communities (Art. 10). The state is even required to consult with indigenous people's regarding resource exploitation in their territories.[72] Finally, a variety of procedures are now available to citizens by which individuals can enforce the Constitution, including both abstract and concrete constitutional review.[73] The latter device—the *acción de tutela*—has been 'crucial' to elevating the Constitution as relevant to the lives of its citizens.[74] The *tutela* enables any citizen to petition a judge to protect fundamental rights. All *tutelas* ultimately fall within the jurisdiction of the Constitutional Court.[75] It is hard to overstate the significance of this mechanism to enhancing the authority of Colombia's Constitution and its apex court.

Foreign investors may avail themselves of numerous constitutional rights, including a general equality right and the right to be free from discrimination on the ground of national origin (Art. 13), property rights together with prior compensation in the event of expropriation (Art. 58), intellectual property rights, and economic freedom including freedom of enterprise and competition (Art. 333).[76]

---

[70] Schneiderman (2000).
[71] It was the 1990 program of economic liberalization (*Apertura*) that signalled Colombia's openness to foreign investment and commitment to a modest program of privatization. See Pacuzzi (1994) at 443.
[72] On the rise and fall of popular consultations, see Sierra (2022).
[73] Cepeda-Espinosa (2004) at 552–7.
[74] Eslava (2009) at 294.
[75] Constitution of Colombia 1991, Art. 86 (leave to review *tutelas* is discretionary).
[76] Constitution of Colombia 1991, Art. 333: 'Economic activity and private initiative must not be impeded within the limits of the public good. For their exercise, no one may demand prior permission or licenses without authorization of an Act; Free economic competition is a right of everyone, entailing responsibilities; The enterprise, as a basis of development, has a social function that implies obligations; The state shall strengthen the joint organizations and stimulate enterprise development; The State, mandated by an Act, shall check the impediments to or restrictions of economic freedom and shall avoid or control any abuse that individuals or enterprises may create thanks to their dominant position in the national marketplace; An Act shall delimit the scope of economic freedom when the social interest, the environment, and the cultural patrimony of the nation demand it.'

'Aliens', the Constitution declares, 'shall have the same civil rights as Colombian citizens' though these rights may be abridged for reasons of 'public order'. But for political rights, aliens also 'enjoy civil rights granted to citizens' (Art. 100). Legislation, such as Decree 2080 of 2000, seeks to reassure foreign investors that 'discriminatory conditions or treatment may not be established for foreign investors vis-à-vis national resident investors'.[77] Law 963 of 2005 enables the establishment of arbitral tribunals via contract that will be governed either by Colombian national law or via applicable law under treaty. Contractual rights are considered 'acquired rights' and belong to the 'assets of a person'. The Constitution, the Constitutional Court has declared, 'prohibits ignorance or modification of consolidated legal situations under the force of law', reminiscent of investment law's legitimate expectations doctrine.[78]

There are thus two logics embedded within the 1991 Constitution: a social state that encourages state intervention in the public interest and an economic liberal charter that prioritizes competition and private enterprise.[79] These two conflicting messages give rise to a tension 'between the social content' of the Constitution and the 'development strategies' the Colombian government has implemented since the 1990s.[80] The tension is reminiscent of Schmitt's complaint about the 'jumbling of diverse principles' contained in the 1919 Weimar Constitution.[81] The core of the Weimar Constitution, for Schmitt, was its liberal *Rechstaat* principles of personal liberty, private property, and freedom of contract that gave expression to its bourgeois political order. This 'value neutral' part of the Weimar Constitution was weighed down by its 'excessive value commitments' contained in its 'socialistic' parts addressing such things as the rights of labour.[82] The bourgeois Rechstaat represented rights that were 'inalterably prior to or superior to' the state.[83] The social part of the Weimar Constitution, by contrast, represented a 'hodgepodge of programs and positive provisions ... jumbled together in a confused synthesis'.[84] Schmitt maintained that the liberal part of the Weimar Constitution deserved to be 'liberated' from its contradictory social part.[85] Schmitt could not contemplate,

---

[77] Decree 2080 of 2000 available at https://investmentpolicy.unctad.org/investment-laws/laws/52/colombia-foreign-investment-decree (last accessed 25 July 2020).

[78] C-155/07. The Court distinguishes between enforceable 'acquired rights' and 'simple expectations' arising, for example, under 'ordinary law'. In these latter circumstances, 'the legislator may modify the law; in the former, the legislator guarantees' that the state will 'abstain from exercising its constitutional powers' (at 5.2).

[79] Murillo-Castaño and Gómez-Segura (2005); Uprimny (2015) at 97. Neoliberalism 'has been accommodated, not without conflict, into the legal framework of *estado social de derecho*' observes Itturalde (2013) at 362–3, fn. 3.

[80] Uprimny and García-Villegas (2005) at 72; Velásquez Ruiz (2016) at 50, 56.
[81] Schmitt at (2008) at 201.
[82] Schmitt (2004) at 50.
[83] Schmitt at (2008) at 203, 211.
[84] Schmitt at (2008) at 83.
[85] Schmitt (2004) at 94. Scheuerman (1996) at 8–9 remarks that Schmitt is vague about the contours of the Weimar Constitution and fails to reconcile the substantive values contained in liberty rights, such as religious freedom, with a value-free constitution.

however, that the promotion of material equality, via constitutional guarantees, might contribute to the success of liberal democracy.[86] In the Colombian case, Murillo-Castaño and Gómez-Segura argue that these conflicting tendencies need to 'unite' if a 'successful constitutional regime [is] to be born'.[87] This turns out to have been a principal task of one of the most powerful institutions to emerge out of the 1991 process, namely, the Colombian Constitutional Court.

V. The Court

Judicial review under a constitution was not entirely alien to Colombian legal culture in 1991. The 1886 Constitution limited the Supreme Court's role to reviewing disputes between the President and Congress over the constitutionality of Congressional enactments. Jurisdiction to conduct abstract constitutional review initiated by citizens was granted to the Supreme Court in 1910. In 1968, a further constitutional amendment empowered the Supreme Court to undertake review of emergency decrees issued by the President.[88] Judicial independence was only achieved in 1957 by plebiscite, paradoxically initiated by the military junta then in power, granting life tenure to Supreme Court judges and relocating the power of appointment from the executive branch to the Court's sitting judges.[89] Proposals to establish a constitutional court were floated as of the late 1960s, culminating in a 1968 amendment passed by Congress though failing to achieve passage a second time in the following year as required by the Constitution.[90] The upshot is that judicial review was not unknown to Colombian constitutional culture prior to 2001. It is not obvious, however, that the consensus achieved in the Constitutional Convention was to establish a powerful Constitutional Court.

As had occurred in the past, the 1991 proposal for a new apex court emerged out of the President's office.[91] This is curious as executives typically are not eager

---

[86] As Kircheimer (1996) at 80 recognized in his reply to Schmitt. Nevertheless, Kircheimer (1923) at 58–9 maintained that the Weimar Constitution tilted in favour of the status quo—in favour of 'the most dangerous enemy of any democratic constitution, the large landlord, undisturbed in his economic power position ... it has decided which of the economic forms possible ... shall be the *real* economic form of the contemporary era'. On the ongoing difficulty of reconciling these two parts of modern constitutionalism, see Caldwell (2000).
[87] Murillo-Castaño and Gómez-Segura (2005) at 15.
[88] Cepeda-Espinosa (2004) at 538–9. Nagle (1995) at 68 maintains that the 1910 amendment was inspired by Tocqueville's *Democracy in America* (1836), citing Eder (1960) at 571. Eder reports that the drafters of the 1841 Yucatán State Constitution were inspired by Tocqueville 'to whom the Latin Americans were indebted for their first knowledge of the working of our [sic] system' by virtue of its translation into Spanish in 1837. This influence had knock-on effects throughout Latin America.
[89] Rodríguez, García-Villegas, and Uprimny (2003) at 142–3.
[90] Passage in successive Congressional sessions is required by the constitutional amending formulae. See Landau (2015) at 101.
[91] Cepeda-Espinosa (2004) at 549. Landau (2015) at 102 reports that four previous Presidents had made this effort, beginning in the late 1970s.

to institutionalize controls on the exercise of their prerogatives. Landau explains the President's motivation as stemming from a critique of the Colombian Supreme Court's record. Recent jurisprudence had impeded presidential initiatives for constitutional reform and had watered-down presidential emergency decrees.[92] President Gaviria complained that the Supreme Court's record had created 'uncertainty in an area where clarity is fundamental'.[93] Furthermore, a new process could return influence over the power of appointment to the executive. Each of three bodies—the Supreme Court, Council of State (the final court of administrative review), and President of the Republic—would be entitled to propose three candidates to the elected Senate. Candidates would be chosen by the Senate exclusively from this list who then would serve non-renewable eight-year terms.[94] The proposal to establish a new Court can be explained, Landau writes, 'as an attempt to bring the judiciary close[r] to the political regime'.[95]

Delegates to the Constitutional Convention, however, had a different motivation: to secure a future for the new Constitution that was beyond the control of the Supreme Court. The latter had proven itself unwilling to envisage judicial power as anything other than formalistic.[96] The Court exemplified the traditional view of the Colombian judiciary as being preoccupied with scrutinizing form rather than substance, even when provided with the opportunity to do otherwise.[97] The worry that the Supreme Court would undo the Convention's work inspired delegates to deprive the Supreme Court of the ability to hear any constitutional challenges after 1 June 1991, even before the Convention delegates had finished their work.[98] Cepeda-Espinosa reports that the proposal for a new court even attracted public opposition from the Supreme Court itself. The Convention moved to approve the proposal, after an 'unusually contentious' debate[99]—by a 44:26 secret vote—adopting the Presidential proposal for tripartite appointment.[100] The Convention delegates probably did not anticipate that they were establishing an activist court that would go so far as to answer 'political questions'.[101]

Despite executive branch expectations, the Court has turned out to be bold and innovative as regards the interpretation of basic rights. It has demonstrated, write

---

[92] Landau (2015) at 86.
[93] Landau (2015) at 109.
[94] Cepeda-Espinosa (2004) at 551.
[95] Landau (2015) at 105.
[96] Cepeda-Espinosa (2004) at 550–1 ascribes this motivation to the President who, in an address to delegates, announced that a new body was required to prevent 'any other powerful authority from hampering the transformations you are encouraging'. On the tradition of formalist jurisprudence in Colombia see Eslava (2009) and Landau (2005).
[97] Eslava (2009) at 195.
[98] Landau (2015) at 111. It is opined that the establishment of a constitutional convention was unconstitutional, reports Merhof (2015) at 717.
[99] Cepeda Espinosa and Landau (2017) at 9.
[100] Cepeda Espinosa (2004) at 551.
[101] Merhof (2015) at 718.

Rodríguez, García-Villegas, and Uprimny, a 'noteworthy independence and desire to interpret and apply the constitution in a progressive manner'.[102] It has proven to be one of the most activist courts in the world and the most influential court in the region. The Constitutional Court has decriminalized possession and consumption of drugs for personal use (C-221/94) and euthanasia (C-239/97), has protected gay men and those with HIV/Aids from discrimination (ST-082/94), and has ensured access to medicines (T-484/92). It has taken seriously the protection of vulnerable internally displaced people (T-025/04) by declaring an 'unconstitutional state of affairs' and retaining jurisdiction to oversee compliance with its ruling.[103] The Court has also deepened recognition of indigenous rights and the state's duty to consult in matters affecting their territories and livelihoods (ST-380/93).[104]

Though not representative of the judicial record, the Court has even, on occasion, impeded the progress of neoliberal reforms. This is because the Constitution, the Court declared, is not neutral vis-a-vis the economy but is subject to the guidance provided by the Constitution's Preamble and fundamental rights. It does not impose any particular economic model, the Court has said, but is open to whichever direction the political branches choose to pursue.[105] Nevertheless, *tutela* decisions have ordered government expenditure concerning expensive medical procedures (T-590/99), vaccination plans in the City of Bogota (SU-225/98), and financing of social housing (C-747/99). Constitutional rights can even be claimed against private actors delivering public services or utilities, for instance, in circumstances where a citizen is in a position of 'subordination' or is 'defenceless' in the face of private authority (T-524/2000).[106] The Court has connected social and economic rights with 'fundamental rights' so as to give full force and effect to the more weakly framed positive rights.[107] The Court has made use of the idea of a 'constitutionality block' (Art. 93) in order to amplify the catalogue of fundamental rights by having recourse to not only the Constitution but to international humanitarian law and international human rights treaties (Art. 94) (C-802/02).[108]

Nagle complains that Colombian judges, trained in the civil law, are expected 'to apply the law, not to create it'.[109] This is the sort of functional role inhabited by the Supreme Court, a tradition of formalism derided by Eslava as being preoccupied only with ensuring the law is 'rightly produced and interpreted'.[110] This formalistic legalism has been abandoned in favour of what Landau describes as a

---

[102] Rodríguez, García-Villegas, and Uprimny (2033) at 157.
[103] Parts of T-025/04 are translated in Cepeda Espinosa and Landau (2017) at 179–86. On its implications see Rodríguez-Garavito (2015) also Rodríguez-Garavito and Rodríguez-Franco (2015).
[104] See discussion in Bonilla Maldonado (2013) and Cepeda Espinosa and Landau (2017) at 42–4.
[105] Cepeda Espinosa (2004) at 641.
[106] Cepeda Espinosa (2004) at 645–9.
[107] Gloppen (2010) at 54.
[108] On the constitutional block see Góngora-Mera (2017).
[109] Nagle (1995) at 89.
[110] Eslava (2009) at 195.

'new constitutionalism',[111] where rights are applied, per Eslava, with 'one eye on the constitutional text and another on the social situation'.[112] For Nagle, too heavy a reliance on 'foreign legal philosophers' (for instance, there are plentiful references to Dworkin) has resulted in 'uninformed libertarian activism'.[113]

The *tutela* action is seen as the key by which the court has made constitutional rights 'meaningful'[114] even 'emancipatory', though compliance remains a problem.[115] It is an increasingly popular mechanism[116] that has enabled the Court to 'deeply impact[] most aspects of Colombian life'.[117] According to their random study of *tutela* cases decided between 1991 and 2001, Rodríguez, García-Villegas, and Uprimny identify the largest percentage of cases arising in claims against health service providers and in the provision of retirement income (11.57 per cent) with a smaller percentage having to do with labour disputes (6.18 per cent) and education (the third most important at 3.01 per cent).[118] The tutela actions most likely to succeed concern civil and political rights (31 per cent); only 19 per cent of social, economic, or cultural rights claims are successful.[119] Their data comports with Merhof's finding that health services comprise the greatest number of *tutela* actions: between 1999 and 2012 they amounted to almost 31 per cent of all actions.[120] For the most part, however, the Court's impact on the deep and persistent inequality in Colombia has not really been felt: 'it has not been 'really transformative', complains Correa Henao.[121]

The Court nevertheless feels free to impose its interpretation of the Constitution on all relevant political actors.[122] As the Court explained in T-406/92, 'unchecked growth of the executive power in the interventionist state and the loss of political leadership of the legislative organ, must be compensated, in constitutional democracy, by the strengthening of the judicial power'. Otherwise, the Court declared,

---

[111] Landau (2005) at 709 and Itturalde (2013) at 371 and, for critique, see Gargarella (2017). This does not seem to refer to the 'new constitutionalism' described by Gill and Cutler (2014) within international political economy nor the aspirational model described by Elkin and Sołtan (1993) within political theory that promotes republican constitutional forms. Rather, the new constitutionalism appears to refer to what Stone Sweet (2000) at 1 describes as innovative judicial functions offered up by new constitutional dispositions ('that legislation must conform to the dictates of the constitution—as interpreted by constitutional courts—or be invalid').
[112] Eslava (2009) at 201.
[113] Nagle (1995) at 90.
[114] Eslava (2009). See also Saffon (2007).
[115] Uprimny and García-Villegas (2005).
[116] Merhof (2015) at 729 reports 90,000 *tutelas* filed in 1999 as compared to 400,000 every year since 2010. The Constitutional Court reviews a subset of these petitions, from a high of 1,340 in 2000 to a low of 789 in 2014 in Cepeda Espinosa and Landau (2017) at 15.
[117] Cepeda Espinosa (2004) at 649.
[118] Rodríguez, García-Villegas, and Uprimny (2003) at 158–9. Their study randomly sampled 631 *tutela* cases, yielding a five per cent margin of error (ibid. at 158).
[119] Rodríguez, García-Villegas, and Uprimny (2003) at 162.
[120] Merhof (2015) at 731.
[121] Correa Henao (2019) at 332.
[122] The court operates 'in a fashion relatively independent of the political system' in Uprimny and García-Villegas (2005) at 85.

'the executive power will predominate'.[123] Yet there is also evidence of the Court behaving strategically, recognizing that its institutional relationships are key to its success and legitimacy, as is the case with other Latin American courts.[124] Uprimny's study of the Court's review of Presidential emergency decrees offers plausible evidence of this phenomenon. Colombia has been governed by a 'state of siege' regime for large chunks of its history—30 of 42 years from 1949 to 1991 under the 1886 Constitution, for instance.[125] Emergency powers remain available to the President under the 1991 Constitution as 'states of exception' (c. 6). The Court has carefully scrutinized emergency declarations, issuing more declarations of invalidity than had its predecessor, the Supreme Court.[126] The Constitutional Court indicated, in its very first ruling on the subject, that it would exercise not only 'formal' but also 'material' or substantial' control over Presidential authority (C-004/92). Among the factors to be considered by the Court was evidence that the President acted upon provable facts, with little time to evaluate them, and that no ordinary instruments of government were available to address the alleged crisis (C-802/92).[127] Much would turn on the degree to which the President could satisfy the Court that he had justification for invoking an emergency. Over time, the executive branch learned to offer better justifications for emergency decrees.[128]

Two decisions striking down emergency decrees in 1994 (C-300/94) and 1995 (C-466/95) provoked 'fierce' attacks by government officials together with legal and business elites. Charges of judicial dictatorship were accompanied by threats of retribution, including proposals to limit the ability of the Court to review states of exception.[129] After the assassination of former Presidential candidate Alvaro Gómez, a subsequent decree in 1996 was partly upheld, even though the facts invoked to justify the decree were identical to one declared void only a year earlier (C-027/96).[130] Then President Samper responded by retreating from his threat to trigger a state of exception.[131] In its subsequent review of emergency decrees, the Court has upheld them even as it purports to apply the same stringent test of material control.[132] It is hard to believe that the Court has not yielded to executive authority, and the pressure being applied by powerful actors within Colombian society, for fear that the Court's powers will be trimmed in retaliation.[133]

---

[123] Justice Barón translated and quoted in Cepeda Espinosa and Landau (2017) at 18.
[124] González-Bertomeu (2019) at 174–5.
[125] Uprimny (2004) at 51.
[126] García-Villegas (2001).
[127] Uprimny (2004) at 56.
[128] For example, concerning immediate release of dangerous prisoners in C-300/94.
[129] Uprimny (2004) at 59–60 and Rodríguez-Raga (2011) at 85–6.
[130] Uprimny (2004) at 59.
[131] Gloppen et al. (2010) at 54.
[132] Uprimny (2004) at 60.
[133] Threats to limit the Court's jurisdiction to entertain *tutelas* against judicial decisions or regarding social and economic rights or to impose 'fiscal sustainability' on such rulings have been proposed but never followed through. See discussion in Itturalde (2013) at 390–2.

Strategic decision-making also appears have played a role in separation of powers cases, outside of emergency declarations, when the Court partakes in review of ordinary legislation and executive decrees. Rodríguez-Raga empirically tests the hypothesis of strategic deference from 1992 to 2006 in cases of 'abstract review,' namely, judicial review of exercises of legislative and executive power that are not prompted by individual *tutelas* (Art. 241). These cases amounted to 82 per cent of the Court's workload in this period.[134] Deference was measured by the Court declaring no part of the law unconstitutional. This occurred 62 per cent of the time. Annulment of executive decrees was less likely to occur early in a presidential term and more likely near the end of that term. Moreover, when the executive indicated a preference for an impugned measure, the Court was more likely to defer to those political signals.[135] Significantly, declarations of constitutional invalidity were less likely to occur in challenges to executive decrees than to Congressional laws.[136] Rodríguez-Raga concludes that the Court acts strategically and defers to the executive when there are 'indications that the latter may adversely react to a decision that checks the government's power.'[137]

The Court is constitutionally mandated to provide a 'final decision on the execution of international treaties and the statutes approving them' (Art. 241[10]). International treaties will have been initiated and negotiated by the executive branch and so provide another window on how the Court may behave strategically. It is to a discussion of this evidence that I turn next.

VI. The Record

The Colombian Constitutional Court has judicially considered the implications of investment treaty law and arbitration on the Constitution perhaps more frequently than any other apex court.[138] The question of constitutional conformity arises because of the requirement that the Court certify compliance of international treaties and ratifying legislation with the Constitution.[139] Like other constitutional courts, it has been confronted with the 'permanent tension between the need to protect fundamental rights and the need to maintain the existing economic and institutional' order,[140] in short, to ensure economic success.[141] The Court has repeatedly

---

[134] The study contained 1,116 executive decrees (33 per cent) and 2,301 laws (67 per cent) in Rodríguez-Raga (2011) at 89.
[135] Rodríguez-Raga (2011) at 93. Yet the political strength of the President appears to have no statistically significant relationship to judicial outcomes. In addition, the Court defers more often in cases involving individual rights (in contrast to more successful tutela actions) in ibid. at 93–4.
[136] Rodríguez-Raga (2011) at 94.
[137] Rodríguez-Raga (2011) at 82.
[138] See the list of constitutional decisions in Table 5.1, below.
[139] According to Art. 241(10).
[140] Uprimny and García-Villegas (2005) at 87.
[141] Block (1987).

been asked either to fully respect Colombia's constitutional commitments or get out of the way of Colombia's professed path to economic success.

The Court's record has been an uneven one. The story told in this part is bookended by moments of soft defiance —not fully a rejection of international or foreign legal influences but a strategic engagement with them. More often than not, however, the Court has declared investment treaties constitutionally compliant. The Justices have chosen, in other words, not to get in the way despite investment protections confining constitutional capacity. This is despite treaty commitments that, as Professor Correa describes them, 'intensely preserve the assets of the investor, with clear unequal treatment towards national competition and privileges over the regulating power of the state'.[142]

The story begins in 1996, when the Constitutional Court was first confronted with the question of constitutional compatibility in the case of a UK–Colombia BIT (C-358/96).[143] The principal issue before the Court was whether investment treaty commitments were consistent with both the property and equality provisions of the 1991 Constitution. Private property was described in Article 58 as an 'acquired' right that also serves 'social functions'.[144] Expropriation was expressly permitted due to 'public necessity or social interest' so long as accompanied by 'means of a judicial determination and prior indemnification'. However, the Constitution also permitted expropriation without the payment of compensation 'for reasons of equity', 'public necessity or social interest', by a majority vote in both the lower and upper Chambers of Congress, which could then be subject to judicial review. This contradicted the UK-Colombia BIT. In addition, it was claimed that the investment treaty conferred greater rights on foreign investors than Colombian nationals, offending Article 13 of the Constitution. By exclusively conferring rights on foreign investors to challenge expropriations and entitling them to the payment of compensation despite 'public necessity' or 'social interest' they were granted preferential treatment.

The Court agreed with both propositions. It was 'beyond any doubt' that the BIT was inconsistent with Article 58's property clause. The treaty required the state to 'refuse in advance' to exercise power conferred upon it by the Constitution. To 'obligate, *a priori*, the legislature to close its eyes and abstain from judging whether

---

[142] Correa Henao (2019) at 329. Or, as she puts it in her intervention in C-252/19, BITs 'generate a privilege for foreign investors ... to obtain a prompt solution to their disputes with the State. In practice this alternative gives them a greater chance of obtaining a favorable resolution to the controversies of which they are a part. The violation of equality with respect to other investors is, in this sense, evident.' In Correa Henao (2018) at 19.

[143] I have told parts of this story previously in Schneiderman (2000).

[144] Art. 58 provided, in part, that: 'Property is a social function which implies obligations. As such an ecological function is inherent to it.' The UK–Colombia BIT was non-compliant because it deactivated the last paragraph of Art. 58: 'Still, the legislative, for reasons of equity, may determine those cases in which there is no ground for indemnification through an affirmative vote of the absolute majority vote of the members of both chambers. Reasons of equity, as well as motives of public necessity or social interest invoked by the legislative, will not be judicially reviewable.'

expropriation is or is not equitable in certain cases, in order to make foreign investment more attractive, to the detriment of national investors and foreigners other than those expressly favored, is something that can hardly be reconciled with the philosophy of the Constitution which from Article 2 assigns, as an essential objective of the authorities of the Republic, that of "... ensuring peaceful coexistence and the *operation of a just order*".[145] The treaty also abridged equality rights by preferring UK investors while treating Colombian nationals worse. Reciprocity, the majority of the Court maintained, is not 'equivalent to the principle of equality'. First, Colombian nationals would have to re-route their investment through the UK in order to receive equivalent treatment. Second, this gives rise to a 'new' inequality: between those who can afford to invest abroad and those who cannot. Nor was it tenable to argue that discrimination was justified because foreigners cannot participate in the political process. The Constitution, after all, prohibits the state from discriminating, even in the cases of expropriation without compensation for reasons of equity and when authorized to do so by Congress.[146] The Constitution promptly was amended to remove these offending impediments to the progress of the investment treaty regime, denying the ability of the state to expropriate without compensation.[147] Though drafted by a widely representative constituent assembly and subsequently approved by Congress, the obnoxious property rights clause was later described by the Court as having been 'widely criticized' (C-059/01) and subject to 'harsh criticism' (C-309/07).

The Court returned to the question of constitutional conformity in subsequent rulings, each of which declared Presidentially directed and Congressionally approved investment treaty obligations as constitutionally compliant. As Table 5.1 indicates, in rulings concerning BITs with Chile, Spain, Switzerland, Peru, Canada, and India, the Court ruled these were intended to integrate Colombia into the 'contemporary market economy'[148] in furtherance of the state promoting the 'internationalization' of the economy (Art. 226). Such agreements, the Court declared in the case of the Spanish BIT, are 'designed to create favorable conditions that attract Spanish capital ... in order to boost the economy'.[149] In addition, the Court approved ratification of the ICSID Convention as it was an 'ideal instrument to provide higher levels of security to foreign investors'.[150]

Consider, for example, the Court's 2011 ruling concerning a second UK BIT. National treatment obligations were now in 'harmony' with the Constitution's

---

[145] C-358/96 at 29–30 (per Carlos Gaviria Diaz and Jose Gregorio Hernandez Galindo) (emphasis in original).
[146] C-358/96 at 33 (per Carlos Gaviria Diaz and Jose Gregorio Hernandez Galindo).
[147] See Legislative Act 01 of 1999, by majority vote in both Houses in two consecutive sessions (simple majority vote in the first session and absolute majority vote in the second), pursuant to Articles 114 and 375 of the Constitution.
[148] C-123/12.
[149] C-309/07.
[150] C-442/96 at 35.

Table 5.1 International Investment Agreements Considered by the Colombian Constitutional Court[a]

International Treaty	Law Approving Treaty	Constitutionality Control Decision	Outcome
FTA Colombia–Mexico	Law 172/1994	C-178/1995	Compliant
BIT Colombia–UK	Law 246/1995	C-358/96	Non-Compliant
BIT Colombia–Cuba	Law 245/1995	C-379/96	Non-Compliant
BIT Colombia–Chile	Law 672/2001	C294/2002	Compliant
BIT Colombia–Spain	Law 1069/2006	C-309/2007	Compliant
FTA Colombia–United States of America	Law 1143/2007	C-751/08	Compliant
FTA Colombia–Northern Triangle of Central America	Law 1241/2008	C-446/2009	Compliant
BIT Colombia/Switzerland	Law 1198/2008	C-150/2009	Compliant
FTA Colombia–Canada	Law 1363/2009	C-608/2010	Compliant
BIT Colombia/Peru	Law 1342/2009	C-377/2010	Compliant
FTA Colombia-EFTA (Switzerland, Lichtenstein, Norway, Iceland)	Law 1372/2010	C-941/2010	Compliant
BIT Colombia/India	Law 1449/2011	C-123/2012	Compliant
BIT Colombia/UK	Law 1464/2011	C-169/12	Compliant
BIT Colombia/China	Law 1462/2011	C-199/2012	Compliant
BIT Colombia/Japan	Law 1720/2014	C-286/15	Compliant
FTA Costa Rica	Law 1763/2015	C-157/2016:	Compliant
BIT Colombia/Korea	Law 1747/2014	C-184 of 2016	Compliant but with restricted application[b]
BIT Colombia–France	Law 1840/2017	C-252/19	Conditional Compliance
FTA Colombia–Israel	Law 1841/2017	C-254/19	Conditional Compliance

[a]Table 5.1 by Maria Carmago.

[b]2 (a) of Annex 8C to the Colombia-Korea FTA was declared constitutionally compliant subject to its terms being interpreted as preserving Colombian Central Bank authority to direct monetary policy, in accordance with Article 371 of the Constitution.

principle of equality, honouring postulates found in Article 13 that prohibit arbitrary discrimination, the Court ruled. The BIT expropriation clause was in accord with Article 58 (as amended) as it required compensation in the event of an indirect expropriation. Such clauses, the Court ruled, 'are reasonable, as they respond to the principle of "legitimate expectations" and do not disproportionately limit state regulatory powers in matters as sensitive as public health, the environment and security, of course, as long as they are applied strictly'.[151] There was no apparent interest in drawing upon the arbitral record to support this deferential standard of review. Lastly, the Court characterized ISDS as constitutionally compatible because it promotes the 'peaceful resolution' of conflict, one of the 'fundamental purposes' of the Constitution.[152] As in previous rulings on the subject, the Court declared ISDS a 'valid and constitutionally viable mechanism' for resolving disputes.[153]

The Court, however, has not elevated investment treaties to the level of the constitutionality block. International treaties in economic and commercial matters, the Court declared in its decision approving the US FTA, 'do not display a higher normative hierarchy than ordinary laws' as they do not concern international human rights.[154] Despite claims to the contrary by scholars and arbitrators,[155] their purpose is not the recognition of human rights but the regulation of economic relations.[156] Investment laws and treaties, instead, must have regard to the Constitution, 'especially fundamental rights'.[157] Regarding the degree of 'intensity' the Court applies in scrutinizing international economic treaties, it should be 'slight, considering the wide margin of discretion enjoyed by the President of the Republic as director of international relations'. It would, however, become more 'intense in relation to those conventional clauses that affect the enjoyment of fundamental constitutional rights, such as health and work, as well as the protection of the indigenous and traditional communities'.[158] Such international treaties still have 'normative force', however, and can serve as benchmarks for the interpretation of domestic legislation.[159]

Not only has the Court been testing investment treaties for constitutionality, the Court's day-to-day work has prompted several investment disputes, many of them, at the time of writing, still pending (see Table 5.2). A selection of these disputes are discussed next.

---

[151] C-169/12 at 4.4.4.
[152] C-169/12 at 4.4.7.
[153] Also C-309/07 at 51.
[154] C-750/08 at 166.
[155] For example, Alvarez (2018).
[156] C-155/07.
[157] C-608/10 at 18–19.
[158] C-155/07.
[159] C-155/07 at 32–3.

THE RECORD   131

Table 5.2 Investment Disputes Prompted by Colombia's Constitutional Court[a]

International Treaty	C.C. Decision	Disputing Investor
Colombia–Mexico FTA	C-555/13	América Móvil
Colombia–Spain BIT	C-553/13	Telefónica
Colombia–USA TPA	SU-447/98	Carrizosa Gelzis (I)&(II)
Colombia–USA TPA	T-384A/14	Cosigo Resources and others
Colombia–Canada FTA	C-035/16	Galway Gold
Colombia–Canada FTA	C-035/16	Eco Oro
Colombia–Canada FTA	T-361/17	Red Eagle
Colombia–Canada FTA	SU-133/17	Gran Colombia

[a]Contents of Table 5.2 generated by Maria Carmago and augmented by C-252/19 at para. 62.

The Carrizosa dispute was prompted by the state taking possession of the assets of the financial institution, Corporación Grancolombiana de Ahorro y Vivienda (Banco Granahorrar), due to the bank's liquidity problems. New management was imposed upon the Bank, which was eventually nationalized. The Court's 2014 ruling that no compensation was due to the investor was challenged in parallel ICSID and UNCITRAL proceedings. It was alleged that by reversing a lower court ruling requiring compensation (by the Council of State), the Court's decision amounted to judicial expropriation and a denial of justice (as part of fair and equitable treatment) under the 2006 Colombia–US TPA.[160] The claimants described the Court's decision as an 'extreme and stark departure from national law' and an 'ethically challenged' opinion.[161]

The América Móvil dispute concerned the cancellation of a mobile phone services contract. Once the concession contract expired, Congress assured the claimant that its physical assets would not revert back to the state, only allocated radio frequencies would revert. The Constitutional Court ruled that the law could not operate retroactively.[162] This required the delivering up of telecommunications equipment that was owned by the concessionaire which was now public property

---

[160] See discussion in Peterson (2018).
[161] *Alberto Carrizosa Gelzis, Enrique Carrizosa Gelzis, Felipe Carrizosa Gelzis v. Republic of Colombia*, PCA Case No. 2018-56, Notice of and Request for Arbitration (24 January 2018) at 80–1. Both claims were rejected by ICSID and UNCITRAL tribunals on jurisdictional grounds. See *Astrida Benita Carrizosa v. Republic of Colombia*, Award, ICSID Case No. ARB/18/5 (19 April 2021) and *Alberto Carrizosa Gelzis, Enrique Carrizosa Gelzis, Felipe Carrizosa Gelzis v. Republic of Colombia*, Award, PCA Case No. 2018-56 (7 May 2021).
[162] 'Colombia Faces Second Telecoms Claim' *Global Arbitration Review* (22 February 2018).

owned by the state. The investors alleged in ICSID proceedings a violation of the FTA with Mexico, a claim that was rejected by the investment tribunal.[163]

The Gran Colombia claim (now Aris Mining Corporation) arises out of a series of strikes and disruptions initiated by traditional miners opposed to the claimant's mining project. The Constitutional Court ruled that the participation rights of traditional miners were abridged as was the right to prior consultation for affected indigenous and Afro-descendant communities. The Court ordered the state to comply with constitutional obligations by undertaking to consult with the mining communities adversely affect by the allocation of mining rights in Marmato.

Cosigo Resources and Tobie Mining are co-claimants in UNCITRAL proceedings launched under the Colombia–US TPA concerning the establishment of a national park that terminated the claimant's gold mining activities. In a ruling subsequent to filing of the claim, the Court ordered various governmental ministries to suspend mining operations until environmental and community impacts could be assessed. The Court underlined that the Yaigojé Apaporis indigenous community had a 'right to be consulted' regarding measures that 'affect them'. The requirement of prior consultation requires that they be provided with 'full knowledge' and illustrations of the impact together with the opportunity to 'freely examine the advantages and disadvantages of the project' and 'to be heard in relation to their concerns'.[164] Not only must government agencies and traditional communities co-ordinate natural resource usage but 'respond to a social process of biodiversity conservation, based on the traditions and visions of the associated indigenous peoples, which guarantee their conservation and ethnic and social and cultural survival'.[165] The claimants seek US$16.5 billion plus interest in damages for an expropriation.[166]

There is no need to revisit the claim in Eco Oro. As described above, their dispute concerns the cancellation of mining concessions in the ecologically sensitive and unique Santurbán páramo. And, as mentioned, the Eco Oro tribunal issued a bifurcated ruling, conceding that the state acted legitimately to protect the environment in respect of the investor's expropriation claim while, in respect of the FET claim, found that the state upset expectations, entitling the investor to an award of damages, yet to be determined. The related claims by Galway Gold and Red Eagle, arising out of similar prohibitions on mining in the Santurbán páramo, remain pending.

---

[163] *América Móvil S.A.B. de C.V. v. Republic of Colombia*, Laudo [Award], ICSID Case No. ARB(AF)/16/5 (7 May 2021).
[164] T-384A/14 at 60, 66, 97.
[165] T-384A/14 at 132.
[166] *Cosigo Resources, Ltd., Cosigo Resources Sucursal Colombia, Tobie Mining and Energy, Inc. v. Republic of Colombia*, UNCITRAL, Notice of Intent to Arbitrate and Statement of Claim (5 August 2015) at 15 available at https://www.italaw.com/cases/3961 (last accessed 30 July 2020). The case currently appears to be inactive.

The array of disputes launched against Colombia indicates that investment lawyers are confident that the work of the Constitutional Court generates viable grounds to launch investment claims. Though tribunals will insist that they do not sit in an appellate capacity, I have argued elsewhere that investment tribunals have, at times, misconstrued what constitutional text requires or distorted the work of apex courts in order to elide apparent constitutional conflicts.[167] They have, on these occasions, distorted national constitutional law in order to suit the imperatives of international investment law, tilting the outcome in favour of investor protection and the mitigation of political risk despite constitutional impediments. The same could well happen in any number of these claims. One indicator was the denial by the Eco Oro tribunal, in an interim ruling, to permit non-disputing party written submissions and attendance at the tribunal hearing by six environmental NGOs with expertise in both environmental law and international investment law. These petitioners, the tribunal concluded, had not satisfied 'even the most minimum requirements that would be needed to establish that issues of human rights, and particularly the right to live in a healthy environment, may be said to form a part of the scope of the dispute'. They had not established, the tribunal added, 'that issues of human rights and the right to live in a healthy environment' were at issue.[168] This is hard to square with the Constitutional Court ruling that prompted the investment dispute. The Court intervened precisely because of the state's constitutional duty to protect the 'especially vulnerable' páramo ecosystem with the aim of guaranteeing the rights to human health and well-being.[169] Absent an unreasonably narrow interpretation of the right, how could the human right to live in a healthy environment not serve as a constituent element of the dispute?[170]

Investment arbitration prompted by Colombian Constitutional Court decisions will have the effect of testing the legitimacy of the investment treaty regime not only in Colombia, but elsewhere. For this reason, we can assume that the audience for the Eco Oro award was larger than merely the parties to the dispute. Tribunals, for this reason, can be understood as behaving strategically.[171] They are producing more than law—they are participating, in some measure, in a public relations exercise. By issuing an internally inconsistent ruling, the Colombian government could

---

[167] Schneiderman (2020).
[168] *Eco Oro Minerals Corp. v. Republic of Colombia*, Procedural Order No. 6 (Decision on Non-Disputing Parties' Application) ICSID Case No. ARB/16/41 (18 February 2019) https://www.italaw.com/sites/default/files/case-documents/italaw10360.pdf (last accessed 31 July 2020) at paras. 30, 35.
[169] C-035/16 at paras. 129, 160.
[170] The non-disputing submission of Canada in Eco Oro, however, implicitly aimed to curb tribunal second guessing of the Court. Canada requested that the tribunal have a 'high degree of deference' regarding the Colombia's 'regulatory choices', particularly where 'bona fide non-discriminatory regulatory measures to protect the environment' are enacted based on the precautionary principle. See *Eco Oro Minerals Corp. v. Republic of Colombia*, Non-Disputing Party Submission of Canada, ICSID Case No. ARB/16/41 (18 February 2019) available at https://www.italaw.com/sites/default/files/case-documents/italaw11532.pdf (last accessed 31 July 2020).
[171] See discussion in Schneiderman (2010).

applaud the decision for having declared the mining ban to be a legitimate public welfare measure. The finding against the state for violating FET would be accorded less emphasis.

VII. The Case

The outcomes of the plethora of cases where investment treaties have been tested against the Colombian Constitution reveal a Constitutional Court persistently exhibiting deference to the political branches. The Court has repeatedly declared its disinterest in second-guessing not only the utility of these agreements but also their standards of protection and processes for dispute resolution. The treaties generally were found in conformity with the Constitution because they 'satisfy a need for integration of the national economy that is imposed as a consequence of the globalization of the world economy'.[172] The Court has been deferential not only due to the exigencies of economic globalization but also due to the technical nature of investment rules. They can only be verified 'in practice' which would require an 'abstract and objective judgment', the Court previously warned.[173] The Court's jurisprudence turns out to have been highly detached and formalistic, reminiscent of the pre-1991 style of judicial review. The law need not be effective, as Eslava has written about this period, 'it is sufficient that it is rightly produced and interpreted to formally exist'.[174] The problem moving forward is that this case law serves as precedent and, in cases of abstract review, has *erga omnes* effects against all.[175] The Court treats the matters decided as *res judicata*—the Court cannot 'rule again in this matter', it is said.[176] This practice has, until recently, stood in the way of any deeper interrogation of investment treaty law by the judges.

The earlier case law was deficient in two further respects. First, the Court's review of the process by which the treaty proceeds from Presidential negotiations to its final adoption by Congress, has proven to be superficial. The Court has expressed little interest in the quality of the debate leading to the treaty's adoption. Second, as mentioned, by examining only the terms of investment instruments without also delving into how those terms have been interpreted and applied by investment tribunals, constitutional review has been conducted at a safe remove from experience. The intervention by the University of Externado, led by the head of the law department Professor Magdalena Correa, argued for greater scrutiny

---

[172] C-309/07.
[173] C-031/09 quoted in C-252/19 at para. 48.
[174] Eslava (2009) at 195.
[175] T-292/06 per Justice Manuel José Cepeda Espinosa, quoted in Cepeda Espinosa and Landau (2017) at 37, 38. Cepeda Espinosa and Landau describe Colombia's system of precedent as 'much closer to the common-law system' than in other Latin American civil law systems at 41.
[176] C-228/15 quoted in C-252/19 at para. 66.

of both elements in C-252/19, the ruling under discussion in this section. In respect of treaty terms, the Court had started from 'excessively general premises that ignore the[ir] practical implications' and, as a consequence, the 'negative experience' of other countries 'in these international forums is ignored'.[177] Greater judicial scrutiny to preserve legislative ratification of international treaties also is called for particularly as Congress has no ability to amend or modify treaty terms. As the 'powers of Congress are more limited in this process, the control exercised by the Constitutional Court must be stricter and more complete to guarantee compliance with constitutional purposes', Professor Correa maintained.[178]

Practically speaking, the Court accepted both premises in C-252/19 concerning a Colombia–France BIT in majority reasons authored by Judge Carlos Bernal.[179] The Court purports to have adopted a greater standard of scrutiny than in earlier cases of *ex ante* review[180] and accepted that constitutional review was 'an opportunity to enrich' the deliberative process by which international treaties are concluded. In this way, the Court could 'complement from the point of view of constitutional supremacy and deliberation' the decisions of the political branches.[181] The Court also agreed that it was constitutionally 'relevant' to take into account arbitral rulings in order to determine constitutional compliance.[182] Whilst previously the Court could not foresee 'vicissitudes related to interpretation and application of BITs', in this case their 'practical effects ... are currently partially perceptible'.[183] Earlier Court rulings are considered 'absolute *res judicata*'—the Court is barred from ruling on the 'same instruments'. But the Court was authorized to constitutionally scrutinize the clauses in the relevant BIT, in its particulars, without reversing these earlier decisions.[184] The present case, the Court added, could even serve 'as binding force as a precedent in relation to the constitutionality control of future BITs'.[185] For these and related reasons, decision C-252 of 2019, concerning the constitutionality of the Colombia–France BIT, has been described as 'unprecedented', and 'truly transformative'.[186] However significant in the annals of Colombian constitutional law, the ruling offers only mild push back— something between soft deference and soft defiance —to the effects of international investment law on state policy space. The ruling has the effect

---

[177] Correa Henao (2019) at 2.
[178] Correa Henao (2019) at 3.
[179] An English language translation of the ruling can be found in Correa, Prieto-Ríos, and Álvarez (2020). A companion case concerning the Colombia–Israel FTA (C-254/19) will not be discussed here as C-252/19 is the more comprehensive and consequential ruling.
[180] Ochoa-Sánchez (2022) at 853.
[181] C-252/19 at para. 55.
[182] C-252/19 at para. 57.
[183] C-252/19 at para. 58.
[184] In her dissenting opinion, Judge Fajardo Rivera complained that none of the conditions authorizing departure from precedent were present in this case in 'Partial Dissenting Opinion of Judge Diana Fajardo Rivera' at para. 1.3 referring to SU-075/18.
[185] C-252/19 at para. 72.
[186] Prieto Muñoz (2019) and Tamayo-Álvarez (2020) at 478.

of trimming some of its excesses by adopting treaty language embraced by capital-exporting states. In the following paragraphs, I examine aspects of the Constitutional Court's reasoning in support of this less enthusiastic reading.

(i) Generally

The Court, first, applied a 'reasonableness' test to determine whether the treaty's 'overall purposes' were in conformity with the Constitution: that its 'overall purposes' were 'legitimate' and that the treaty was a suitable means for achieving its ends.[187] Adopting a form of proportionality analysis, the Court was interested in inquiring into the 'reasons and evidence' offered to 'justify' adoption of this treaty.[188] It is significant that the Court accepted the intervenors' argument that there was 'no empirical evidence' to support the claim that signing the treaty contributes to increasing the stock of new inward FDI 'unfailingly'.[189] But this finding was undercut by the Court's grumbling that there was no empirical evidence to the contrary: that 'this BIT does not have the potential to generate FDI'. '[N]one' of the intervenors, the Court complained, 'provided evidence to justify such questioning'.[190] This seems an indefensible way of determining reasonableness. The intervenors were asked to prove a negative: that the treaty, on balance, would not generate new investment. The proportionality analysis also looks defective. Typically, the onus is on the government to prove the efficacy of the means adopted to pursue a chosen end. Meeting this burden is key to any successful defence of a measure. It should have been sufficient to argue, in other words, that there was no reliable evidence showing a correlation between signing treaties and attracting new investment. The Court chose to abandon a more rigorous inquiry and, instead, to defer to dominant understandings. The Justices accepted that the treaty was reasonably justified given the support of the political branches, whose 'political legitimacy ... reasonably supplement the lack of concrete empirical evidence' that the treaty increases FDI.[191]

(ii) Equality

The Court appeared to be more interested in the argument that the treaty offended the Constitution on the ground of equality. Professor Correa argued that

---

[187] C-252/19 at para. 92. Judge Fajardo Rivera described the Court's reasonableness analysis as resembling the intense scrutiny applied in fundamental rights cases, rather than the mild intensity expected of free trade agreements in 'Partial Dissenting Opinion of Judge Diana Fajardo Rivera' at para. 1.5, quoting Judgement C-031/99 (RJ Humberto Antonio Sierra Porto).
[188] C-252/19 at para. 65.
[189] C-252/19 at para. 108.
[190] C-252/19 at para. 108.
[191] C-252/19 at para. 108.

the treaty was incompatible with 'formal equality', privileging French foreign investors over Colombian nationals, and 'material equality' by providing special protections to 'powerful economic actors' without benefiting society's most 'vulnerable groups'.[192] Justice Bernal observed that the treaty actually fulfilled the constitutional mandate of equality by advancing the idea of non-discrimination. The Court remained concerned, however, that there was no text guaranteeing that foreign nationals would not be preferred over Colombian nationals, thereby granting 'more favorable unfair treatment' to foreigners and their investments.[193] Tapping into debates in capital-exporting states about ensuring that investors are granted 'no greater rights' than locals, a commitment incorporated into CETA's Joint Interpretive Declaration, the Court conditioned constitutionality on the adoption of a similar joint interpretive declaration with France.[194] It was this interpretive fix that also convinced the French Constitutional Court to accept that CETA's text was in conformity with Article 6 of the 1789 Declaration of the Rights of Man and Citizen.[195] Nothing more was said about how the treaty protected only the most powerful actors and failed to contribute to the material equality of the poor and other marginalized groups who attract special attention under the Constitution's equality clause (Art. 13).[196]

(iii) FET

The Court also exhibited interest in the treaty's indeterminate language. The tables, in some ways were turned. Rather than vindicating only an investor's interest in transparency and predictability, the Court identified features of investment treaty text that provide little clarity about the conduct expected of states in order to avoid liability under international law. Article 4 (1) of the BIT expected state parties to 'accord fair and equitable treatment in accordance with applicable international law'. Did this refer to 'customary or conventional law,' the Court asked? Applicable international law did not sufficiently delineate the parameters of the obligation. It is 'impossible for the State to determine or foresee what is ordered, prohibited or permitted, as well as the specific obligations whose breach may give rise to its international responsibility'. Such uncertainty violated Article 9 of the Constitution respecting the attributes of state sovereignty.[197] This precipitated an order of

---

[192] C-252/19 at para. 109.
[193] C-252/19 at para. 113.
[194] C-252/19 at para. 122 referring to s. 6(a) of the CETA's Joint Interpretative Instrument. The Court also referred to the example of the US Trade Act (2002) at C-252/19 at para. 115.
[195] C-252/19 at para. 117.
[196] The argument is powerfully laid out in Correa Henao (2018) at 22–3. De Boeck (2022) at 422 describes this differential treatment as concerning effects-based discrimination. This preferential treatment, however, is intentional and not the result of unintentional discrimination.
[197] C-252/19 at paras. 205–6.

'conditional constitutionality'. The government was expected to clarify the scope of this treaty obligation or, otherwise, invite a declaration of unconstitutionality.[198]

Similarly, the expression 'inter alia' in Article 4, though intended to provide greater specificity to the FET obligation (by including the examples of denial of justice, non-discrimination, and non-arbitrariness), did not indicate FET's 'basic parameters' thereby generating 'uncertainty for national authorities'.[199] The few examples enumerated in Article 4 indicate that FET was meant to be an open rather than a closed obligation, in contrast to the 2017 Colombian model BIT which 'refers solely' to a closed list of FET obligations. Given this open-endedness, the Court demanded that the phrase inter alia be 'interpreted restrictively' enabling only grounds analogous to those enumerated.[200] The text of the FET obligation in Article 4, however, was 'consistent' with the constitutional obligation to consider the 'legitimate expectations of investors'. Taking note of the vagaries of the arbitral jurisprudence on legitimate expectations—'one of the most controversial developments' in this sub-field of international law—the Court insisted on a narrow interpretation.[201] A declaration of constitutionality was conditional on the Parties defining what was understood by legitimate expectations 'taking into account' that they arise only if they are the product of 'specific and repeated acts ... that induce the investor in good faith to make or maintain the investment, and that there are sudden and unexpected changes made by public authorities, that affect its investment'.[202] Delimiting the scope of legitimate expectations is entirely 'consistent with recent developments', Justice Bernal added, pointing to CETA and TPP which both confine the variety of government action capable of offending FET.[203]

(iv) National Treatment

The Court turned next to the wide discretion available to tribunals in identifying comparators for the purposes of national treatment analysis.[204] The phrase 'in like circumstances' was too ambiguous, the Court concluded, and so its declaration of constitutional validity was conditional on the parties defining 'its content in a manner consistent with the principle of legal certainty'.[205] What about departures from equal treatment—are they justifiable under the BIT? Tribunals have occasionally admitted that a public interest exception typically qualifies the national

---

[198] C-252/19 at para. 207.
[199] C-252/19 at para. 208.
[200] C-252/19 at para. 209.
[201] C-252/19 at para. 211, quoting Lim, Ho, and Paparinskis (2018) at 269. As in *Continental Casualty v. Argentina* ICSID Case No. ARB/03/9 Award (5 September 2008) at para. 252.
[202] C-252/19 at para. 212.
[203] C-252/19 at para. 211.
[204] See the discussion of this practice in Schneiderman (2023).
[205] C-252/19 at para. 246.

treatment obligation, and this analysis is typically done in the context of determining 'like circumstances'.[206] The Colombia–France BIT appears to close the door on such departures unless they are measures 'designed to ensure public order in the event of threats to the fundamental interests of the State'. Such measures are defensible so long as they are not 'arbitrary' and are 'justified, necessary, and proportionate to the objective pursued'.[207] While shrinking the space available to depart from the principle of national treatment, did this exception incorporate a strict test of 'necessity', requiring that measures be 'indispensable' and that no other alternative means are available? Or was a more deferential test appropriate, one that asks whether the measures are 'reasonable and appropriate'? Or perhaps something in between these two alternatives? Apex courts continually address this key question of the standard of proof, being more attuned to the issue than are investment arbitrators. The first interpretation, the Court concluded, is incompatible with the Constitution's margin of appreciation in 'economic matters'. The Court contrasts the lower threshold with the stricter standard applied in the case of fundamental rights.[208] A looser standard of scrutiny was more constitutionally compatible in a BIT as it conferred 'broad freedom in terms of regulatory autonomy' to secure public order by intervening in economic matters. The President, therefore, was directed to take the necessary steps to ensure the adoption of a joint interpretive declaration serving that end.[209]

(v) MFN

Even though the MFN clause – which ensures equal treatment for all foreign investors protected by Colombia under treaty – excluded dispute settlement processes from its scope,[210] consistent with recent developments, the standard was adjudged to be overbroad.[211] The problem was the ability to import standards from other treaties, irrespective of whether Colombia had adopted measures that, in actuality, preferred investors from third party states.[212] That is, French investors could incorporate better standards of protection based merely upon facial differences between treaties. Replacing the treaty's terms without anything further compromised the President's competence to conduct international relations (Art. 189.2). Instructive for the Court were 'recent developments' in new treaty practice

---

[206] S.D. Myers at para. 250.
[207] Article 5(3) of the BIT quoted in C-252/19 at para. 216.
[208] C-252/19 at para. 248.
[209] The Court was encouraged to do so by reason of Colombia's 2017 model BIT which does not incorporate the standard of necessity and proportionality.
[210] Prompted by the decision in *Maffezini v. Spain*.
[211] The Court's reasoning in this section, however, is not so clear. I am extrapolating from the reasons offered.
[212] A problem more fully explained in Yilmaz Vastardis (2023).

limiting an investor's ability to incorporate substantive protections via MFN in CETA, USMCA, and Colombia's 2017 model BIT.[213] Constitutionality, for the Court, was conditioned on the parties jointly limiting MFN's 'cascade effect' to circumstances in which the state actually has preferred an investor under a third-party treaty. MFN would only be available where, as in Colombia's 2017 model BIT, the state has taken measures having a 'concrete effect' so that investors from third States 'enjoy differential treatment.' This would result, it was claimed, in the preservation of the President's bargaining power going forward.[214]

(vi) Expropriation

Among the factors to consider in determining whether an indirect expropriation has occurred were an investor's 'legitimate expectations.' Legitimate public policy objectives that were, among other things, 'necessary and proportionate' were deemed not to give rise to indirect expropriation (Art. 6.2.c.). Both expressions, as the Court previously explained, were problematic, giving rise to an order of conditional constitutionality.[215] All else in the BIT's expropriation clause was acceptable from a constitutional point of view, including incorporation of the high standard of 'prompt, adequate and effective compensation.'[216] This result was no great surprise. As earlier Constitutional Court decisions had declared, this was the expected outcome after amendment to Article 58's property clause in 1999.

(vii) ISDS

Was the investor–state dispute settlement clause (ISDS) also compatible with the Constitution? Earlier rulings had so affirmed (e.g. C-358/96). Professor Correa argued that, by conferring the 'significant privilege' of dispute resolution on foreign investors and allowing for a 'generous interpretation' of their 'substantial rights,' there was breach of the Constitution's equality rights.[217] This equality argument was rejected by the Court as it was premised upon a faulty comparison. The proper comparator for the purposes of equality analysis in the context of ISDS, the Court ruled, were 'Colombians in France' and not Colombians in Colombia.[218] This

---

[213] C-252/19 at para. 241. For instance, CETA Art. 8.7(4): 'Substantive obligations in other international investment treaties and other trade agreements do not in themselves constitute "treatment", and thus cannot give rise to a breach of this Article, absent measures adopted or maintained by a Party pursuant to those obligations.'
[214] C-252/19 at para. 254.
[215] C-252/19 at para. 280.
[216] C-252/19 at para. 274.
[217] Correa Henao (2019) at 17.
[218] C-252/19 at para. 377.

formalistic equality analysis, illustrative of how equality problems can be defined away by manipulating the comparator analysis, was identical to the move deployed by the Court of Justice of the European Union in their CETA ruling. Nor was lack of transparency a problem as the parties had committed to applying UNCITRAL rules on transparency, if neither party objected, within a year after entry into force. This would also have the effect of 'ensur[ing]' participation by third party interveners. Any further interpretive declarations were deemed 'innocuous and unnecessary'.[219]

The Court's analysis of ISDS elides many of the weaknesses that have given rise to controversy. The fact that investor–state dispute is central to the continued 'success' of investment treaty arbitration would not have escaped the Court. It seems hard to square the many interventionist aspects of the ruling, where the Court weighed into various controversies over the wording of BIT clauses, with its quietude regarding ISDS. It likely was viewed as imperative to the various members of the Court that the regime's centrepiece remain intact. This is underscored by the 'clarification' issued by Justice Bernal, the principal author of the Court's decision, who took issue with his colleagues for failing to address transparency in ISDS and the enormous compensation awards that 'menace the financial sustainability of the State'.[220] Not much else was of concern to Judge Bernal.[221]

VIII. Conclusion

Tamayo-Álvarez has grounds to say that aspects of ruling C-252/19 are 'truly transformative', while other elements remain 'embedded within the parameters laid down by dominant narratives on investment protection'.[222] Insofar as the Court intervened by issuing conditional constitutional orders premised on new joint interpretive declarations clarifying some treaty commitments, the Court appeared to bravely stare down terms that had been dictated by the executive branch. Yet, the Court chose to issue such orders only when other agreements, like the Canada–EU CETA or the CPTPP, had offered a template for the Court's intervention. It was as if the Court insisted that Colombia catch-up to 'recent developments' in the Global North. As had Latin American jurists in the nineteenth and early twentieth centuries, the Constitutional Court exhorted the executive branch to 'modernize' its approach to international law. The aim was to ensure equality of arms vis-à-vis

---

[219] C-252/19 at para. 386.
[220] 'Clarification of the Vote of Judge Carlos Bernal Pulido in Judgement C-252/19' at para. 3.
[221] Concern also was expressed about the effect of the European Court of Justice opinion in *Achmea* which may have an impact on European member state capacity to enter into treaties in 'Clarification of the Vote of Judge Carlos Bernal Pulido in Judgement C-252/19' at paras. 4–6 ('The judgement has generated a *huge global discussion*') (emphasis in original).
[222] Tamayo-Álvarez (2020) at 478.

more powerful states (like France). The consequence is to steer international investment law in directions desired by powerful capital-exporting states.[223]

Tamayo-Álvarez also expressed the worry that France would be 'unwilling to negotiate' new interpretive declarations.[224] Because the Court has sought out to mainstream, and make more palatable, Colombia's investment treaty commitments, French negotiators had every incentive to go along. So long as the Court did not depart too radically from the status quo, France would not be asked to do so either. This verdict is borne out by the newly negotiated texts of both the Colombia–France BIT and the Colombia–Israel FTA.[225] Approximately one year later, the parties agreed to revised terms regarding key provisions, such as legitimate expectations doctrine and the MFN clause.[226]

While the Court was motivated to preserve Colombian regulatory space, by reading some treaty commitments narrowly, many other investment disciplines were left intact. In this respect, the Court did not stray far from the centre of gravity of investment treaty law and arbitration. For these reasons, the Court's ruling does not stand in the way of the pursuit of new international investment agreements. It only calls upon Colombian negotiators to make commitments that mirror capital-exporting state 'best practices'. There is, otherwise, little daylight between investment law and Colombian constitutional law.

---

[223] See Obregón (2008). On the allied 'myth' of development, see Furtado (2021), and on Europe as the source for universally valid norms, see Quijano (2000).

[224] A hypothesis floated by Tamayo-Álvarez (2020) at 477.

[225] See 'Joint Interpretative Declaration Between the Republic of Colombia and the French Republic on The Agreement on The Reciprocal Promotion and Protection of Investments Between Colombia and France, Signed on 10 July 2014' (5 August 2020) at https://edit.wti.org/document/show/b1f4e650-ab74-4bf5-91fd-4d876cf86b0f?textBlockId=ee58d4d2-8c31-4fcc-9758-bece8ee70ba5&page=2 (last accessed 24 February 2023) and 'Exchange of Letter Between the Republic of Colombia and the Israeli Ministry of Foreign Affairs (27 April 2020) at https://edit.wti.org/document/show/f6561c5f-f384-4fe7-875b-4f71bcd98174?textBlockId=7cbfe76b-8a20-4c05-b072-968639cb1d0a&page=11 (last accessed 24 February 2023). Titi (2020) worried that the changes requested by the Court would 'significantly alter' the treaties. This turned out not to be the case.

[226] For discussion, see Correa, Prieto-Ríos, and Álvarez (2020) at 17–18. They express concern that the revised legitimate expectations clause in the FTA with Israel may not comply with C-254/19.

6
The People's Voice
Indonesia

I. Introduction

The case of Indonesia exhibits both similarity and difference with the other country studies discussed in this book. The Constitution emerges out of a history of colonialism, promotes economic nationalism, and endorses religious belief in its preamble. Its Constitution establishes a new constitutional court that has not shied away from exercising its review functions and, in this way, resembles the Colombian case. The state has also exhibited a great deal of ambivalence about the investment treaty regime, aggressively withdrawing from treaties due to near losses in significant investment disputes but then making regional commitments to protect investors. When confronted with a constitutional challenge to an exclusively executive role in signing and ratifying investment and trade treaties, the Constitutional Court insisted that the legislative branch have a role to play in treaty ratification, relying upon democratic principle and political process. In this way, the Court's performance allows it to remain, as does Indonesian public opinion, ambivalent about the impact of economic globalization.[1] By addressing concerns raised by investment law's constraints on constitutional capacity in this indirect manner, the Court exhibits less deference and more soft defiance.

The significance of investment treaty law to Indonesian political debates reached its crescendo with the Churchill Mining claim.[2] This dispute was precipitated by the withdrawal of mining rights that had been conferred on the UK-based mining conglomerate. The investment tribunal adjudicating the claim concluded that it had jurisdiction to proceed to the merits of the claim, despite Indonesia intimating that the mining licences were not genuine but were secured by 'large scale' fraud.[3] Four years after initiation of the claims[4] the tribunal held that the claims were

---

[1] On the ambivalence of public opinion, see Damuri and Pangestu (2018) at 110 and of elite opinion, see Hill and Pane (2018) at 272.
[2] Lumbantobing (2022) at 74. Though its first investment treaty including ISDS was with the Netherlands in 1968, Indonesia began to aggressively negotiate new treaties in the early 1990s.
[3] Churchill Mining (2016) at para. 510.
[4] Proceedings were initiated in May 2012 and ran until the issuance of an award in December 2016. Proceedings to annul the award were then commenced in April 2017 and concluded in March 2019.

barred—they were 'inadmissible'—by reason of the investor's reliance upon forged documents.[5] Only then was it determined that the investor could proceed no further with its claim for damages. It is said that the dispute shook the 'confidence of Indonesian policy-makers in the IIA [international investment agreement] regime'.[6] The government 'genuinely thought that it could have lost' the case.[7] 'Imagine if such cases happened in hundreds of regencies in the country ... especially when we're on the wrong side and lose, it's a remarkable implication', a vexed President Yudhoyono declared in 2012.[8]

Indonesia successfully rebuffed the investor's claim yet, as the dispute was still pending, gave notice to terminate many of Indonesia's BITs. Indonesian officials clearly were exasperated with the investment treaty regime. Why worry so much about investor–state dispute settlement (ISDS)? Could this have been a consequence of the ways in which the regime comforts investors, no matter how tenuous their allegations? A more detailed discussion of those proceedings helps to illuminate the answer to this question. It also illustrates the ways in which investment arbitration is structured to limit state policy capacity.

II. The Churchill Mining Dispute

Churchill Mining, together with its wholly owned subsidiary, Planet Mining, sought to extract coal in the East Kutai Regency on the island of Kalimantan (Southern Borneo). With the aid of a local business partner, Ridlatama, the investor applied for a succession of licences to explore and then exploit coal seams in what, it was predicted, would be the seventh largest coal deposit in the world. Survey and exploration licences were ostensibly granted but then revoked in May 2010 by the Regency. The reasons for that revocation lay in Ridlatama operating without permission of the Ministry of Forestry (in violation of forestry law), using allegedly forged licences on territory which overlapped with permits previously granted to another operator.[9]

Indonesian dismay with ISDS would have been compounded when the tribunal, constituted to resolve two joined disputes, concluded in February 2014 that it had

---

[5] Churchill Mining (2016) at para. 528.
[6] Losari and Ewing Chow (2016) at 140.
[7] Butt and Lindsey (2018) at 376.
[8] Quoted in Saragih (2012) and Price (2017) at 138.
[9] Churchill Mining PLC (2014a) at para. 35 and Planet Mining (2014) at para. 35. The competing permits were granted to Nusantara, an enterprise under the control of a former candidate for Indonesian President. There were indications, early on, that the investor was relying on forged documents to pursue its claim against the state. In materials filed at the State Administration Court of Samarinda in 2012, the companies mentioned that a police investigation had been conducted into the forgery of five documents. These suspicions of criminal activity, they reported, had been 'eliminated'. This turns out not to have been the whole story. See Churchill Mining PLC (2012).

jurisdiction to continue with the proceedings.[10] Expanding upon 'indications' made in previous submissions, Indonesia made mention during the hearing that the investors' claims were aided by forged documents.[11] The tribunal appears to have been persuaded, though it did not say so, by the claimants' arguments that, though there may have been 'clerical errors', the state had not acted on these suspicions. This was sufficient, they argued, to rebut doubts about the legality of their licenses.[12] The tribunal concluded that, in any event, the legality requirements in the treaty had been satisfied by the investor.[13]

One month after Indonesian legal counsel had the opportunity to inspect the original documents that were in the possession of the investor, the state moved to dismiss both claims. They argued that these were founded on forgeries and requested a hearing before the tribunal to determine this conclusively as soon as possible. The tribunal rejected this request in its procedural order of 27 October 2014. The tribunal was not convinced that a finding of forgery would be dispositive of the investor's entire case. There were lingering concerns, for instance, that there had been a denial of justice by Indonesian courts.[14] Twenty-one days later, on a motion to reconsider this procedural order, the tribunal changed its mind. Aided by a table cataloguing how a finding of forgery would dispense with all of the investor's allegations, the tribunal granted the request and agreed to treat the authenticity of documents as a 'matter of priority'. Argument regarding the legal consequences of a finding of forgery would also be made at that time.[15] The investors, though given the opportunity, failed to rebut Indonesia's arguments. Upon a further motion by the investors to reconsider the order to bifurcate the proceedings (separating the question of the tribunal's jurisdiction from the merits of the investor's claim), the Tribunal indicated that Indonesia had satisfied the requisite 'burden of persuasion' to proceed with its expedited hearing regarding the alleged forgeries.[16]

In the award, where the authenticity of the documents and the legal consequences of finding forgery were assessed, the tribunal concluded that a 'large scale fraudulent scheme [was] implemented' to obtain the coal mining licences.[17] Even if the investor was not responsible for the fraud, it failed to conduct itself in a manner that obviated its reliance on fraudulent behaviour. The investor knew of the 'risks' associated with mining concessions due to the 'disorganization' of governmental

---

[10] Churchill Mining PLC (2014a) at para. 57.
[11] Churchill Mining PLC (2014a) at para. 247 and Planet Mining (2014) at para. 227.
[12] Churchill Mining PLC (2014a) at para. 282 and Planet Mining (2014) at para. 261.
[13] As the proceedings continued, Indonesia refused to produce police files concerning the alleged forgery as the criminal investigation had not been terminated but was 'ongoing'. Suspicions that the investment had been facilitated by forgery and deceit, however, were not convincingly refuted. See Churchill Mining PLC (2019) at para. 79.
[14] Churchill Mining PLC (2014b) at para. 47.
[15] Churchill Mining PLC (2014c) at para. 28.
[16] Churchill Mining (2015) at para. 25.
[17] Churchill Mining PLC (2016) at para. 510.

agencies, overlapping claims, and the decentralization of power to local authorities since 2001.[18] Indeed, the investors chose their business partner, Ridlatama, precisely because of this operator's 'connections' with government officials. In such a dubious regulatory environment, the investors failed to conduct 'proper due diligence' in its local partner's reliability.[19] In other words, the investors conducted their affairs with a proverbial head buried in the sand. All of the claims before the tribunal were deemed to be inadmissible.[20]

The saga of Churchill Mining undoubtedly helped to sour Indonesian officials on ISDS. Suspicions concerning the authenticity of the documents authorizing mining activities arose early on, and were raised repeatedly, though not in a sufficiently comprehensive fashion.[21] The forgery issue ordinarily would have been relevant to the jurisdictional phase, but the tribunal chose to adopt a narrow view of the legality requirement in the treaty. Once the forged documents were made available for inspection, the respondent state moved immediately to dismiss the claim yet, again, the tribunal dragged its heels. It was not convinced that other allegations would be resolved by a conclusive finding of forgery. The tribunal's default position, in other words, was that the investor's claim should proceed unless persuaded otherwise. Yet, within a matter of weeks, the tribunal changed course. The panel of arbitrators seemed to place a great deal of emphasis on a chart, presented by Indonesia, illustrating the impact of a finding of forgery on the investors' allegations.[22] If the legal impact of the forgeries could be resolved by argument at an expedited hearing, why was that not a good reason to grant the request for that hearing in the first place? Indonesia warned, after all, that proceeding in the usual manner to the merits phase of the dispute, with a claim premised upon forgeries, would impose 'enormous expense[s]' upon the state.[23] It would, they predicted, bring 'the interests of justice and integrity of the ICSID system' into doubt.[24]

This was not mere hyperbole. The dispute, which was launched in 2012 and continued until 2016, cost US$1.6 million in arbitral and facility fees. The respondent's legal costs alone amounted to US$11 million. The claimants bore the whole cost of the former and 75 per cent of the latter (US$8,646,528).[25] The investor subsequently sought annulment of the award under the ICSID Convention, ending with dismissal of these proceedings in 2019. Fees and costs have been utterly enormous.

---

[18] Churchill Mining PLC (2016) at para. 517. The CEO characterized the state of government in the Regencies as the 'wild west'.
[19] Churchill Mining PLC (2016) at para. 518–19. The investors would have been expected to exercise a 'heightened degree of diligence'.
[20] Churchill Mining PLC (2016) at para. 528.
[21] Ahmad (2018) at 202 suggests that the issue was 'undeveloped.' See also Le Moullec (2016) at 147.
[22] Churchill Mining (2015) at para. 7 (claimants alleging that the tribunal 'simply ignored' their arguments, 'relying instead on the table appended' to a single piece of Indonesian correspondence).
[23] Churchill Mining (2014b) at para. 19.
[24] Churchill Mining (2014b) at para. 18.
[25] Febriani and Hertanti (2019). These costs have not been recovered according to Hertanti (2019) at 46.

III. Investment Law and Policy

Indonesia had an active bilateral investment treaty programme until, as mentioned, it soured on the experience two years into the Churchill Mining proceedings in 2014. Indonesia, that year, began terminating a number of its 67 investment agreements with ISDS.[26] The process began with the Netherlands BIT, the first investment treaty containing ISDS with the very state that colonized Indonesia and from whom it secured its independence in 1945.[27] Indonesia had been the subject of seven ISDS-based claims[28] and lost one under contract-based arbitration. In the Amco dispute, for instance, Indonesia paid out US$3.2 million as part of a US$12.5 million damages claim.[29] Indonesia also succumbed to foreign mining company pressures when it reversed a decision to prohibit open-pit mining in protected forests. Companies that had threatened ISDS were subsequently exempted from the ban.[30] More sensational, however, were the disputes in which Indonesia prevailed, including Churchill Mining, which received a lot of media attention. The case of *Newmont v. Indonesia* 'added to' this sense of crisis around ISDS.[31]

On the eve of a presidential election in January 2009, the Yudhoyono government introduced a new mining law that required natural resources to be domestically processed.[32] Mining companies operating in Indonesia would have to process minerals into semi-finished or finished products within the country before exporting them abroad. According to a 2010 regulation, this would have to be achieved within five-year's time. Mining companies engaged in the export of raw gold or copper, such as Newmont, would have to begin construction of smelters and other processing facilities so as to meet the five-year deadline or otherwise pay a punitive export tax. Rather than face a ban on the export of copper, Newmont's subsidiary, PT Newmont Nusa Tenggara (PTNNT), under the control of its Dutch

---

[26] Thirty have been terminated, as of the time of writing, according to the UNCTAD Investment Policy Hub at https://investmentpolicy.unctad.org/international-investment-agreements/countries/97/indonesia (last accessed 12 May 2020). Some have been replaced (e.g. Singapore) while 16 of these agreements have never entered into force.

[27] Price (2017) at 11 and Venzke and Günther (2022) at 1206–7. Crockett (2017) at 847 argues that Indonesia was a sophisticated and careful negotiator, able to secure numerous concessions from the Netherlands, in their 1968 BIT.

[28] According to the UNCTAD Investment Policy Hub at https://investmentpolicy.unctad.org/investment-dispute-settlement/country/97/indonesia (last accessed 12 May 2020). See also Crockett (2017).

[29] *Amco Asia Corp. v. Indonesia* (1990) Award, Merits, ICSID Case No ARB/81/1 at para. 280 (31 March). Indonesia has lost other contract-based disputes, including a US$500 million claim in favour of CalEnergy Himpurna, another for US$261 million in favour of Karaha Bodas. See discussion in Wells and Ahmed (2007) c. 13 and 14.

[30] Van Harten (2020) at 108 reports that 13 companies were provided with exemptions in 2004. Gross (2003) at 896–8 details the bases upon which the foreign mining companies (23 in total) sought to reverse protected forest designations. Indonesian government officials attributed their reversal to the threat of ISDS (at 895).

[31] Losari and Ewing Chow (2016) at 140.

[32] Mining Law No. 4 of 2009 discussed in Batubara (2014) at 3.

subsidiary Nusa Tenggara Partnership BV (NTPBV), threatened to shut down its Batu Hijau gold and copper mine. It also filed an investment dispute under the 1994 Indonesia–Netherlands bilateral investment treaty.[33] The company's mining concession, they claimed, was authorized under a Contract of Work with the Indonesian government, specifically 'designed to provide assurance and stability to encourage significant, long-term investments'.[34] The investor alleged that their Contract of Work was protected by the treaty's umbrella clause and that the mining regulations amounted to an indirect expropriation and a denial of fair and equitable treatment.[35]

At the same time, the Indonesian government had come to agreement with another large mining company, Freeport, allowing their operations to continue uninterrupted so long as the company would make some progress in the direction of refining metals in country. A settlement of the investment dispute initiated by Newmont followed not too long after. Lumbantobing reports that the government had not been aware that the introduction of the statute in 2009 would render the state vulnerable to investment disputes. However, that certainly would not have been the case by 2017, when Newmont and Freeport began their pressure campaign. Though there are no references to the pending investment dispute in subsequent public statements, 'behind the scenes,' Lumbantobing observes, the state was wary of new disputes, particularly as the Churchill mining claim remained pending before an investment tribunal.[36]

That Indonesia settled the matter with both Freeport, which threatened but did not initiate an investment dispute,[37] and Newmont, which did do so, weakens, but does not vitiate, complaints that ISDS chills state regulatory capacity.[38] It is difficult, however, not to acknowledge that the threat of ISDS was lurking in the background and likely influenced the outcome of negotiations with both foreign investors. Newmont's lawyers, after all, were quoted as pointing to the 'effectiveness of treaty protections' and that 'ICSID arbitration provides a good background' for the conduct of settlement negotiations.[39] If so, it cannot be said that 'Indonesian BITs have not had a "chilling effect"'.[40]

---

[33] *Nusa Tenggara Partnership B.V. and PT Newmont Nusa Tenggara v. Republic of Indonesia*, ICSID Case No. ARB/14/15, discontinued 29 August 2014.
[34] PTNNT (2014).
[35] The Newmont claim has not been made public, however, Lumbantobing (2022) at 90 has identified the substance of the investor's claims in interviews.
[36] Lumbantobing (2022) at 91.
[37] Lumbantobing (2022) at 90 referring to Jensen and Asmarini (2017).
[38] Regrettably, van der Pas and Damanik (2014) fail to acknowledge this weakness in their argument that the 'mere threat of a billion-dollar claim' can scuttle government policy intended to promote economic development.
[39] Quoted in Van Harten (2020) at 110. Also see Gross (2003) at 895 who attributes reversal of protected forestry designations that would have shut down foreign-owned mining concessions to the government's fears of international arbitration.
[40] Crockett (2021) at 123.

If Indonesia had been able to successfully attract foreign investment in the past, it was feared that termination of BITs would threaten those investment flows.[41] This has been described as an 'unjustified concern' which, nevertheless, continues to preoccupy the regime.[42] The fear of capital flight would be dampened by reassurances provided by the Indonesian Investment Law, discussed further below.[43]

Accompanying the strategy of BIT terminations was the formulation of a new model investment treaty for Indonesia. According to the Director for Treaties in the Ministry of Foreign Affairs, Abdulkadir Jailani, there were numerous reasons that prompted the state to begin reviewing its investment policy. First, there was a need to strike a better balance between 'investor protection and national sovereignty'; second, to restore policy space; and third, to reconsider the state's commitment to ISDS. Jailani singled out Churchill Mining as having 'encouraged' undertaking this review of BIT policy. This was a 'frivolous claim' which prompted then President Yudhoyono to say that multinationals will not be entitled to 'do as they please with their international back-up and put pressure on developing countries such as Indonesia'.[44] Fourth, there was the added worry that investment agreements 'may potentially override national legislation' and even 'supersede the decisions of domestic courts'.[45]

The Indonesian model treaty text, drafts of which have been under discussion since 2014, has not been made public.[46] But we get a sense of what Indonesia may have settled upon in the United Nations Conference on Trade and Development (UNCTAD) 2015 World Investment Report.[47] According to UNCTAD, the model BIT would contemplate excluding portfolio (non-direct) investment from the definition of investment and require a contribution to economic development within the country to have the benefit of the treaty's protections. It was also indicated that the anti-discrimination norm of national treatment would carve out special privileges for small- to medium-sized enterprises, in addition to measures 'affecting' natural resources. In addition, the model treaty would seek to 'clarify' fair and equitable treatment (FET) and prohibit denial of justice claims prompted

---

[41] So concludes a World Bank study (2017) at 8–9. Contrariwise, Public Citizen (2018) at 7 found an increase in new inward investment even after the termination of BITs in 2014.
[42] Jailani (2016) at 118.
[43] Investment Law of 2007 (at https://investmentpolicy.unctad.org/investment-laws/laws/93/indonesia-investment-law) discussed, infra, in Section IV in text associated with nn. 111–18.
[44] Jailani (2016) at 114–15.
[45] Jailani (2016) at 116. He seemed reluctant to acknowledge that this remains the regime's principal objective, as discussed further in the Conclusion (c.8).
[46] According to Lumbantobing (2022) at 70, the model 'only serves as internal guidance for future treaty negotiations'.
[47] Crockett (2021) at 124, also Jailani (2015) at 4–5. This 2015 Report was a watershed moment for UNCTAD, as it announced that ISDS had 'generated unanticipated (and at times inconsistent) interpretations . . . and has resulted in a lack of predictability as to what IIAs actually require from States'. This has precipitated what UNCTAD labelled a 'legitimacy crisis'. See UNCTAD (2015a) at 126, 128.

by judicial and administrative proceedings and, finally, require specific consent of the host state.[48]

One has to closely examine subsequent free trade agreements signed with Australia, New Zealand, China, Japan, South Korea, and India, or the ASEAN Comprehensive Investment Agreement to find traces of these proposals. Each agreement entitles investors to sue for violation of laconic investment treaty obligations.[49] Some innovations associated with a newer generation of investment treaties, such as highlighting the right to regulate or refining FET obligations can be discerned, but much remains undisturbed. The 2018 treaty with Singapore, for instance, adopts minimal criteria for what constitutes an investment[50] and does not carve out exceptions for small- or medium-sized Indonesian businesses.[51] Nor does it omit denial of justice claims or require the specific consent of the host state. Expectations, in other words, have yet to align with negotiating realities. Yet Indonesia is also encouraging ISDS reform in its submissions to UNCITRAL's Working Group III, tasked with improving the regime. Proposing some procedural hurdles, like mandatory mediation (included in the Singapore–Indonesia BIT) and exhaustion of local remedies, Indonesia insists that 'maintaining the conventional approach of ISDS is hardly an option, given today's criticism of the existing ISDS mechanism'.[52]

IV. Constitutional Order

At its origins in 1945, Indonesia's constitutional regime concentrated its authority in the executive. Its first two strongmen Presidents, Sukarno and Suharto, were supplanted in 1998 following waves of discontent and demands for democratization.[53] Two interim Constitutions—the first, in 1949, a federal design adopted under Dutch supervision and the second, in 1950, rejecting federalism in favour of a unitary state[54]—incorporated liberal democratic elements, including limits on 'arbitrary' expropriations. These elements were abandoned when the 1945 Constitution was revived in 1959.[55] It was only after the 1997 Asian financial crisis,

[48] UNCTAD (2015a) at 109 10.
[49] Butt and Lindsey (2018) at 376.
[50] Agreement Between the Government of the Republic of Indonesia and the Government of the Republic of Singapore on the Promotion and Protection of Investments (11 October 2018), p. 2, fn. 1 ('commitment of capital, expectation of gain or profit, the assumption of risk or certain duration' [sic]). These same observations hold true for the 2022 Indonesia–Swiss BIT. See Accord entre le Conseil fédéral suisse et le Gouvernement de la République d'Indonésie concernant la promotion et la protection réciproque des investissements (24 May 2022).
[51] Exceptions to national treatment appear in 'Agreement Between the Government of the Republic of Indonesia and the Government of the Republic of Singapore,' ibid., Annex 1 (at 34).
[52] Indonesia (2018) at 3.
[53] Butt (2018a) at 54–9.
[54] Butt and Lindsey (2012) at 3.
[55] Taufik (2020) at 7–8.

triggering the fall of Suharto, that the People's Consultative Assembly (*Majelis Permusyawaratan Rakyat Republik Indonesia* or MPR)[56] proposed four sweeping amendments. These aimed at installing a semblance of a separation of powers by limiting Presidents to two five-year terms, shrinking presidential and MPR authority and, conversely, enhancing the legislative authority of the lower house (*Dewan Perwakilan Rakyat* or DPR).[57] In addition, a panoply of human rights was incorporated in addition to installing a new Constitutional Court (*Mahkamah Konstitusi*).[58] Amendments, however, did not touch upon the sensitive role of religious belief, which remained confined to one of five principles in the Preamble to the Constitution (the *Pancasila*).[59]

Nor was the complex relationship between the executive and legislative branches in the realm of treaty ratification well addressed. The executive is granted authority, with the approval of the legislature, to make war and peace and to make international agreements without approval of the DPR but for those agreements having 'an extensive and fundamental impact on the lives of the people which is linked to the state's financial burden, and/or that requires an amendment to or the enactment of a law'.[60] The circumstances in which approval of treaties must be secured from the legislative assembly were only filled out in the International Treaty Law 24 of 2000.[61] Legislative ratification is required if the subject matter of the treaty concerns:

a. political, peace, defense and state security issues;
b. regional or regional changes in the Republic of the country of Indonesia;
c. sovereignty or sovereign rights of the state;
d. human rights and environmental life;
e. the establishment of new legal rules;
f. foreign loans and/or grants.

In so far as a proposed treaty addresses matters falling outside of this list, ratification can be achieved by Presidential decree alone.[62] If Butt concludes that the

---

[56] This is the legislative body composed of a lower house of representatives and an upper house representing the regions.
[57] As a bill cannot be voted upon in the legislature without presidential approval, the President exercises an 'effective veto' over parliament's activities. See Kawamura (2013) at 165.
[58] See the description of the amendment process in Indrayana (2010), also Butt (2018a) at 59–61. Authorized by constitutional amendment in 2002, the Court was established by the Constitutional Court Law of 2003.
[59] A reference to 'belief in the One and Only God' will be found in the Preamble. Today, Pancasila has been reengineered, assert Butt and Lindsey (2012) at 247, as an emblem of religious and social pluralism. In addition to a further declaration that the 'State shall be based upon the belief in the One and Only God' (Art. 29[1]), religious freedom is guaranteed (Art. 29[2]).
[60] Article 10 of the Constitution.
[61] Article 10 of the Treaty Law.
[62] Article 11 of the Treaty Law.

system is 'primarily dualist in practice',[63] this has not been so in the case of trade and investment agreements. Investment protection agreements have been ratified by Presidential Decree ever since the first Indonesian BIT was signed in 1968, including 12 agreements signed since the Treaty Law of 2000.[64] That the division of labour between the political branches remains contested is made evident in the constitutional case discussed below in Section VI.

Determining the degree to which Indonesian constitutional law will be fitted to the exigencies of economic globalization is also made complicated by numerous provisions in the 1945 Constitution. At its origins, the constitution exemplified features of an anti-colonialist document founded upon social justice, the primacy of the family, and community.[65] In practice, however, it has meant collusion between public and private actors based upon 'corruption and nepotism' under previous authoritarian rule.[66] An expression of this constitutional ambition is found in Article 33, which declares the economy to be organized 'as a common endeavour based upon the family principle' (Art. 33[1]). Sectors of 'production' that are 'important for the country and affect the life of the people shall be under the powers of the state' (Art. 33[2])[67] and, in the case of land, water, and natural resources, shall also be 'used to the greatest benefit of the people' (Art. 33[2]). Two additional paragraphs were added to Article 33 in 2002, including the declaration that organization of the 'national economy is to be run on the basis of economic democracy upholding the principles of togetherness, efficiency with justice, continuity, environmental perspective, self-sufficiency, and keeping a balance in the progress and unity of the national economy' (Art. 33[4]). The concept of 'efficiency with justice,' Taufik argues, was intended to promote privatization and replace the 'command economy' with a 'regulated free market'.[68] The ambiguities associated with Article 33, nevertheless, remain. The amendment exhibits Indonesian reluctance to submit unqualifiedly to global trade and investment rules and institutions.[69] The Constitutional Court has frequently had recourse to Article 33 to forestall some features associated with the 'Washington consensus', as discussed in Section VI. Yet it also has under-enforced socioeconomic rights, such as the right to education, included in the Second Amendment to the Constitution.[70]

Foreign investors are given no special solicitude in the Constitution, in fact, it could be said that they are deprived of rights available to Indonesian nationals. For

---

[63] Butt (2014) at 27. See also Savitri (2019) at 64.
[64] Evidence of Abdulkadir Jailani before the Constitutional Court in Decision No. 13/PUU-XVI/2018 at p. 183
[65] Butt and Lindsey (2012) at 251.
[66] Taufik (2020) at 9.
[67] Butt and Lindsey (2012) at 251 translate the clause as referring to branches of production 'important to the state' and not, as do other translations, production that is 'important for the country'.
[68] Taufik (2020) at 5.
[69] Hill and Pane (2018) at 272.
[70] See Article 28H (1) and discussion in Hendrianto (2016).

instance, only 'citizens' are declared to be 'equal before the law' (Art. 27 [1]), though this provision was amended in 2002 so that every 'person' has the right to 'equal treatment before the law' (Art. 28D [1]). Property rights are conferred on every person (Art. 28G [1]) though, under a 1960 statute, foreigners are not permitted to hold title to land (there are some well-practised methods for circumventing this restriction).[71] Significantly, there are no constitutional guarantees around compensation in the event of an expropriation. Instead, these are provided under statute, as is the declaration that land rights serve a 'social function'.[72] Despite very relaxed standing rules for Indonesian nationals to bring petitions before the Constitutional Court, foreign nationals are denied standing to raise constitutional claims directly to the Court.[73] Indonesian anxieties about foreign influence and its 'place in the world' continue to shape constitutional developments.[74]

V. The Court

Prior to the formation of the Constitutional Court in 2003,[75] judicial review under the Indonesian Constitution was unavailable.[76] The Supreme Court had authority to undertake only statutory judicial review and it did so timidly. Nor did the Supreme Court have the ability or legitimacy to serve as a constitutional check on the other branches.[77] Precipitated in part by the need for a forum to hear pending impeachment proceedings against President Wahid, it was deemed imperative that there be established, via constitutional reform, an independent and credible check on the political branches.[78] Not that the Constitutional Court, itself, has been bereft of scandal. Chief Justice Mochtar was arrested in 2013 and imprisoned for life for taking bribes in an election law case. Judge Akbar was arrested in 2017 and convicted of corruption for accepting bribes in constitutional cases.[79] After the arrest of Mochtar, President Yudhoyono issued an interim emergency measure (a

---

[71] Basic Agrarian Law 5/1960. On methods of circumvention though contract, see Tan (2004) at 104–5.
[72] See Law 5/1960 (on social function) Land Acquisition Law 2/2012, Arts. 31–4 (on compensation), supplemented by Government Regulation No. 19 of 2021. See Bedner (2016) at 73 and Butt and Lindsey (2018) at 146. Robinson (2016) reports that the state has used its power of eminent domain in heavy-handed ways to, for instance, displace local communities to enable mining development. See Robinson (2016) and Butt and Lindsey (2018) at 150.
[73] Butt and Lindsey (2018) at 104 per the majority in Constitutional Court Decision 2-3/PUU-V/2007.
[74] Aspinall (2018) at 36.
[75] The Court was established by statute in 2003, while constitutional authority was granted via the third (9 November 2001) and fourth (10 August 2002) amendments.
[76] Butt (2018a) at 54; Butt and Lindsay (2009) fn. 115.
[77] Siregar (2015) at 213 heavy handed 14; Butt and Parsons (2014). Under Suharto, the Court was 'little more than ... servants of the executive' in Pompe (2005) at 471.
[78] On impeachment as a catalyst, see Hendrianto (2010) at 162. Butt (2015) at 15–16 argues that the need to have such a forum for impeachment proceedings has been greatly exaggerated.
[79] Butt and Lindsey (2018) at 101 and Hendrianto (2018) at 59.

PERPU, eventually re-enacted by the DPR) requiring, among other things, that justices have no links to a political party seven years prior to their appointment and are screened by an independent selection panel.[80] The Court likely overreached in declaring these regulations constitutionally invalid for encroaching on judicial independence.[81]

Despite these setbacks, the Constitutional Court has sustained levels of diffuse support likely sufficient to ensure its longevity.[82] This can be attributed, in part, to the fragmentation of Indonesian political parties. Horowitz places emphasis on political party competition as generating 'a more secure environment for judicial independence'— independence 'is an offshoot of moderate pluralism'.[83] In the immediate aftermath of Sohorto's departure, and as constitutional amendments were being formulated in 2002, the House of Representatives was divided along five major party lines.[84] Moreover, no President has since had control of the DPR via majority party rule.[85] A splintered political party system has generated a semblance of equipoise in the country's constitutional politics.

As in the case of Peru, three judges are appointed by each of the branches for five-year terms that are renewable only once (Art. 24 [3]).[86] The Chief Justice and Vice-Chair are elected by, and from among, their fellow justices for renewable 30-month terms.[87] In the period between 2004 and 2018, a third of those appointed were career justices, while those with executive branch experience were the second largest group. There has always been at least one justice on the court with an academic background.[88]

This is a court of first instance regarding applications for constitutional review—it does not serve as a court of appeal—and has the final word in testing laws against the Constitution (Art. 24 [1]). Jurisdiction is limited to reviewing the constitutionality of statutes and so regulations, executive decrees, and sub-national laws are beyond its purview.[89] The Court also is granted jurisdiction to resolve a variety of different political conflicts including those arising between state institutions,

---

[80] Dressel and Inoue (2018) at 163; and Lindsey (2015) at 39–40.
[81] The emergency measure amended the Constitutional Court Law of 2003. Constitutional Court Decision 1-2/PUU-XII/2014. See discussion in Roux and Siregar (2016) who complain about the Court rejecting these reasonable accountability measures (at 15).
[82] Horowitz (2013) at 243 (the Court has 'built up a stock of political capital because of its apparent integrity and good faith, despite much criticism of individual decisions'). On diffuse support, see Easton (1965) at 273–4.
[83] Horowitz (2013) at 237, 239.
[84] Hendrianto (2010) at 163.
[85] Horowitz (2013) at 283.
[86] Hendrianto (2018) at 57, interprets the five-year term limit as intended to 'restrict' the power of Constitutional Court judges. The mandatory retirement is at age 70. As regards appointment, budget, and autonomy of the Constitutional Court, see Mahfud (2011).
[87] Nardi (2018) at 251. The term was formerly three years.
[88] Dressel and Inoue (2018) at 170.
[89] Butt (2015) at 78 and Xi (2019) at 178, though it has on occasion circumvented these limitations as in Constitutional Court Decision No. 85/PUU-XI/2013 (Water Resources Law II case) at 144.

dissolution of political parties, disputes in general elections (Art. 24 [1]), and alleged violations of the Constitution by the President and Vice-President (Art. 24 [2]). It is said that the Court is modelled upon the South Korean Constitutional Court, yet its jurisdiction is more severely circumscribed and hears far fewer cases than its Korean counterpart.[90]

The Court's docket has been a busy one, even if small in number comparatively speaking,[91] particularly during election periods. Election disputes comprise the largest agenda item on the Court's docket.[92] Applications for judicial review under the Constitution have been steadily rising, comprising the second largest group of cases. The Court has granted about 25 per cent of these petitions for unconstitutionality.[93] The statistics are reversed in high profile 'megapolitical' cases.[94] Dressel and Inoue conclude, in their study of 80 high profile cases between 2004 and 2018, that there is little evidence to support claims that the Court is politicized and lacks independence.[95] Instead, they find that the Court has responded to its institutional environment in a strategic fashion. The closer the decision is to the end of a Presidential term, the more likely the Justices will vote against the administration. In addition, the closer Justices get to retirement, the more likely they are to rule against the government.

Prior professional experience appears to play no role in decision-making except for those Justices with an 'executive background'—they are more likely to vote with the administration.[96] In cases addressing separation of powers questions and executive prerogatives, the Court is more likely to decide against the government (80 per cent in each instance). In most 'economic' cases, they are likely to rule in favour of government action (57 per cent).[97]

The empirical evidence suggests that the Court's decision-making is heavily influenced by non-governmental organizations (NGOs) who are repeat players before the Court in socioeconomic and individual rights claims. Because the Court has no authority to issue damage awards but only declarations, NGOs are the more likely candidates to launch such claims. They will not be seeking compensation for 'past harms' but endeavouring to prevent 'future constitutional violations'.[98] In a study of 524 cases between 2003 and 2013, Nardi attributes to NGOs 'more of the content' of the Court's agenda in regard to socioeconomic rights (for example, 'labour, education, agriculture, human rights, welfare and economics' claims) and

---

[90] Hendrianto (2010) at 169. The fear may be opening the litigation floodgates.
[91] Hendrianto (2010) at 164.
[92] Nardi (2018) at 252.
[93] Dressel and Inoue (2018) at 164.
[94] Dressel and Inoue (2018) at 168, 171.
[95] Dressel and Inoue (2018) at 161.
[96] Dressel and Inoue (2018) at 177.
[97] Dressel and Inoue (2018) at 172.
[98] Nardi (2018) at 257. The most an applicant can hope for, write Butt and Lindsey (2018) at 107, is 'to prevent future constitutional damage to themselves or others by having the Court remove the offending statute from the books'.

so credits them for playing an important agenda setting role.[99] Second, the Court is 'more likely to quote from the text of petitions submitted by NGOs' as compared to other petitioners. Nardi infers from this disproportionate influence that the justices treat petitions submitted by NGOs 'as more credible and informative' than other petitions.[100] What the record suggests is that the Court has generated a constituency among NGOs who help sustain its diffuse support. Notably by issuing positive rulings in cases 'having broad popular support'[101] the Court generates specific support among NGOs that helps to sustain its overall legitimacy and independence.[102]

We can conclude that the Court acts strategically in its constitutional review cases—that it is 'influenced by Indonesia's political conditions'.[103] However, the Court's decision-making is not as efficacious as might be assumed. The record indicates that the legislative branch does not prioritize implementing Constitutional Court decisions. The political branches, on occasion, simply ignore Court rulings.[104] According to the data compiled by Laksono, Sudarsono, Hidayat, and Safaat, only 11 of 29 decisions were implemented via legislation between 2003 and 2016.[105] The executive has gone so far as to negate Court rulings on electricity regulation and water resources. Responding to the Electricity Law case of 2003, in which the Court halted privatization of state-owned electricity as a component of IMF loan conditionality,[106] the government responded via regulation, rather than statute (placing it beyond the Court's jurisdiction), allowing for private sector participation in electricity provision, practically nullifying the Court's decision.[107] Such occasions, Butt maintains, are exceptional. Government 'usually' respects Court decisions and rarely defies them.[108] The Court has responded reflexively by crafting decisions that are 'self-enforcing', tolerating few 'legal vacuums', and leaving the legislature with little left to do.[109]

---

[99] Nardi (2018) at 264.
[100] Nardi (2018) at 269.
[101] Nardi (2018) at 271.
[102] On specific support, as compared to diffuse support, see Easton (1965) at 268.
[103] Hastuti (2019) at 334.
[104] Horowitz (2013) at 246 ('the DPR has rarely produced new legislation in response to decisions of the Constitutional Court rendering legislative provisions unconstitutional').
[105] Laksono et al. (2017) at 156. According to Chief Justice Usman in 2020, only approximately 50 per cent of the court's rulings between 2013 and 2019 had been 'adhered to', while a third appear to have been ignored. Quoted in Butt and Murharjanti (2022) at 429.
[106] Lindsey (n.d.) at three surmises that, because the IMF were 'heavily involved' in steering Soharto's corrupt regime, its reputation likely was severely damaged by this cozy relationship.
[107] Butt and Lindsey (2009) at 286 in Constitutional Court Decision 001-021-022/PUU-I/2003.
[108] Butt (2015) at 72; Siregar (2015) at 209.
[109] Butt (2015) at 73 and Horowitz (2013) at 246. Apex courts typically do not issue self-enforcing rulings but require cooperation and enforcement of their rulings from the executive branch.

VI. The Record

The Constitutional Court has not shied away from thwarting plans intended to liberalize the economy. Much of this work has been done under the auspices of Article 33 which gives expression to 'Indonesian Socialism'.[110] Propping up international economic directives has not been a priority. For this reason, the Indonesian Constitutional Court offers a case study of an apex court on the 'soft defiance' end of the continuum.

The Electricity Law case,[111] just mentioned, offers an early example of this defiance when confronted with an IMF induced scheme to denationalize Indonesia's electricity sector. For the Court, the plan to privatize and unbundle the state monopoly offended Article 33(2)'s requirement that the important sectors of production be 'under the powers of the state'.[112] The Court conceded that private enterprise could participate in the electricity sector but that the power to regulate, supervise, and monitor the sector, in the pursuit of the people's welfare, could not be abandoned by the state.[113] There was the nagging worry, the Court explained, that expansion of electricity service would be frustrated and affordability sacrificed in the interests of retaining profits.[114] In a subsequent ruling on the subject concerning the 2009 Electricity Law—which sought to allow for private participation in electricity production and delivery without giving up state control—the Court declared the law 'conditionally unconstitutional'.[115] Hendrianto describes this remedy as a 'phenomenon unique' to the Court, which he associates with quasi weak-form judicial review.[116] But the remedy is pretty common among apex courts as Butt acknowledges.[117] It is one adopted by the Colombian Constitutional Court, for instance, as discussed in Chapter 5.[118] It is a remedy that leaves the state, in this case, ultimately in control of the electricity sector.[119]

---

[110] Butt and Lindsey (2012) at 252. Article 33 is discussed in nn. 64–7, supra.
[111] Constitutional Court Decision 001-021-022/PUU-I/2003.
[112] Butt and Lindsey (2012) translate this phrase as 'controlled by the state' at 251.
[113] The Court identified five forms of state control: the power to regulate, govern, manage, supervise, and create policy (at 334). Al'Afghani observes that the Court was likely incorporating Friedmann's four functions served by mixed economies: regulator, umpire, entrepreneur, and provider in Friedmann (1971). Friedmann there rejects laissez faire as unworkable: 'the philosophy of the free play of economic forces is thus no longer accepted by any contemporary democracy' (at 23). Al'Afghani (2014) at 10 maintains that Friedmann's ideas about state functions is 'pervasive among Indonesian jurists and among one of the mandatory basic courses studied by first year law students' (at 11).
[114] Butt and Lindsey (2012) at 261. In a subsequent ruling, the Court affirmed the role of the state electricity company (PLN). See Constitutional Court Decision No. 149/PUU-VIII/2009.
[115] Constitutional Court Decision No. 111/PUU-XIII/2015.
[116] Hendrianto (2019) at 105. On weak-form judicial review, see Tushnet (2009).
[117] Butt (2015) at 123.
[118] It is a technique familiar to other courts (see Roux and Siregar [2016] at 12) and what Dixon and Issacharoff (2016) at 687 label 'judicial deferral' (permitting laws to operate so long as they are implemented in accordance with constitutional rulings).
[119] Constitutional Court Decision No. 111/PUU-XIII/2015. See discussion in Hendrianto and Siregar (2016).

The Investment Law Case of 2007 offers another example of the Court's lack of inhibition in thwarting conformity with the commands of international economic law. The stated object of Indonesia's new investment law was to improve the country's 'investment climate' by providing, in its statement of principles, legal certainty, impartiality, and equal treatment for foreign investors.[120] Several provisions replicated investment treaty obligations, by requiring national treatment, compensation based on market value in the case of nationalization, and the free transfer and patriation of profits.[121] But the law went further by obliging investors to be attentive to the welfare of workers and to environmental concerns. Moreover, in those instances where the government supports an investment (by the provision of concessions such as tax holidays or property tax reductions), investors are expected to employ local workers, transfer technology, preserve the environment, and enter into partnerships with local enterprise.[122] If the law offers the opportunity for interface—an 'interlocking' law—between national legal commitments and international ones, it is discordant with a number of investment treaty commitments.[123]

At issue in the constitutional challenge was the path that was smoothed for investors to acquire state-owned land rights. Previously, foreign nationals could apply for renewals of up to 20 to 30 years, entirely at the discretion of government. Under the Investment Law of 2007, newly acquired land rights were automatically renewed in advance.[124] The law was challenged under Article 33(3) for removing a 'natural resource' (or land) from state control. The Court ruled that the extension of land rights per se did not violate 33(3) as the state reserved the right to 'regulate' and 'manage' the land. But the automatic extension of land rights in advance, potentially 'reduce[d] or remove[d]' state control. This loss of control was underscored by the Court observing that, should rights automatically granted be subsequently revoked,[125] this could prompt international arbitration at the behest of a disgruntled investor.[126] Easy recourse to arbitration, the Court worried, exhibits a level of 'distrust' in the Indonesian judiciary and 'reduc[es] the meaning of the legal

---

[120] Indonesia (2007) and summary in Butt (2011).
[121] Indonesia (2007) at Arts, 4, 7, 8. For this reason, it is clear that investment treaties provide more protections to foreign investors than is available under Investment Law of 2007, though Butt (2011) at 118 believes they do not 'add much' while Knörich and Berger (2014) at 66 describe the law as 'not too different' from investment agreements.
[122] Indonesia (2007) at Art. 18.
[123] On the investment law as 'interlocking law', see Knörich and Berger (2014) at 66. Consider their discussion of fair and equitable treatment at 86. National and international commitments do not line up well (they do 'not appear to be fully consistent').
[124] Indonesia (2007) at Art. 22 and discussion in Butt and Lindsey (2012) at 258–9.
[125] Under conditions outlined in Indonesia (2007), Art. 22(4) (for example, abandonment, inflicting damage to the public interest or using land in ways that violates the land grant's purpose and object).
[126] Constitutional Court Decision No. 21/22/PUU-V/2007 at 261 (referring to Art. 32(4): 'In the event of dispute in investment sector between Government and any foreign investors, the two parties may settle it through international arbitration based on agreement between them.') This concern is summarized in Butt and Lindsey (2012) at 259.

sovereignty of the Unitary State of the Republic of Indonesia based on the 1945 Constitution'.[127]

Butt and Lindsey complain that the Court's rulings in these, and other, cases exhibit 'ideological left-over[s] from another era' that conflict with attempts to 'liberalize' the economy.[128] By impeding law reform in economic domains aimed at improving efficiency and attracting high-level investment, they write, the Court strayed far from its knowledge base, upsetting major planks of economic policy that it 'does not seem to fully understand'. The Court failed to appreciate 'the complex economic issues involved or ... articulate a consistent and economically sophisticated rationale for its understanding'.[129] This seems a particularly harsh verdict, particularly when international financial institutions such as the IMF admit that the social context of their reform efforts are more important than previously acknowledged.[130] Moreover, it turns out that there are many other determinants for attracting new inward investment other than privatizing state-owned enterprise.[131] It may be that the Court simply had a sense of what the discourse on 'sustainable development' might mean, namely, 'growth that benefits all, including the poorest'.[132]

These Constitutional Court rulings, however, have resulted in the unintended consequence of shrinking the state. If neoliberal reform yielding state control to private firms is rejected, the state nevertheless is in retreat by virtue of what Al'Afghani calls 'disguised privatization'. The Court, he maintains, is more interested in ensuring that the state maintains its entrepreneurial/share ownership function rather than its role as regulator or umpire.[133] In which case, the government response to these constitutional rulings has been to discreetly give up regulatory control to business firms operating within relevant sectors. While this outcome avoids further declarations of constitutional invalidity it also deprives citizens of regulation in the public interest or remedial outlets by which to seek redress for public wrongs.

VII. The Case

The Court's ruling on the Treaty Law of 2007 exhibits some of the muscularity seen in these earlier cases. The constitutional challenge, launched by nine NGOs and five individuals (including social justice and farm organizations in addition to

---

[127] Butt and Lindsey (2012) at 262.
[128] Butt and Lindsey (2012) at 266.
[129] Butt and Lindsey (2009) at 288.
[130] IMF (2019) at 13 ('Since the 1990s, IMF policy advice has increasingly recognized that there need not always be a trade-off between growth and distributional objectives, and the key role of social spending in achieving inclusive growth').
[131] On determinants of FDI see Chanegriha, Stewart, and Tsoukis (2017).
[132] As formulated by UNCTAD (2015b) at 32.
[133] Al'Afghani (2014) at 13 and Friedman (1971). See discussion in n. 113, supra.

individual farmers), disputed the constitutional authority of the President to ratify FTAs and BITs[134] without the participation of the legislature as the people's representative. Every trade and investment agreement, both before and subsequent to the 2007 law, was signed and ratified exclusively by the President and was not subject to legislative scrutiny or consent. The ASEAN–China agreement, and BITs with Singapore BIT and India, for instance, were all ratified by Presidential decree[135] and this has been the continuous practice since the first investor protection agreements were signed in 1968.[136]

The executive branch defence to this practice was that both the Constitution (Art. 11[2]), in general terms, and the six enumerations in the Treaty Law (Art. 10), did not require DPR (House of Representatives) consent. That is, these treaties did not 'produce an extensive and fundamental impact' on people's lives. They did not require amendment or enactment of any law, did not have an impact on the state's financial burden (Constitutional requirements), nor did they concern, among other subject matters, state sovereignty, human rights, or the environment (Treaty Law requirements). Moreover, the consultation mechanism in the Treaty Law enables the executive to determine the DPR's opinion, in advance, regarding any particular treaty.

But is consultation sufficient when legislative approval is required? The Petitioners principal argument was that trade and investment treaties triggered constitutional thresholds, having a broad and fundamental impact, necessitating legal changes and consequences for state finances, requiring the approval of the DPR.[137] In so far as the Treaty Law specifically enumerated the range of treaties necessitating legislative consent, these were not compliant with the Constitution (e.g. those having broad and fundamental impacts).[138] Loss of control by the DPR deprived representatives from participating in the decision of determining what was in the best interests of the people's welfare.

Among the Petitioner's experts, Lutfiyah Hanim argued that investment treaties have an impact on state finances given the broad obligations owed to investors under, for instance, fair and equitable treatment. Successful investment claims can give rise to an award of damages that enhance indebtedness and hobble state capacity.[139] It followed that FET commitments could precipitate a number of 'bad

---

[134] Called Agreements to Increase Investment Protection or P4M.
[135] Constitutional Court Decision No. 21/22/PUU-V/2007 [The International Treaties Case] at 13.
[136] Constitutional Court Decision No. 21/22/PUU-V/2007 at 183. Further examples are provided ibid., at 58–60 (Claimant's Expert Evidence of Irfan R. Hutagalang). Knörich and Berger (2014) at 56 suggest that Parliamentary views were 'often sought during negotiations'. This likely is a reference to the consultation mechanism in Article 2 of the Law of International Treaties.
[137] Constitutional Court Decision No. 21/22/PUU-V/2007 at 6. The Petitioners also claimed that Article 2 (requiring consultation with the DPR), Article 9(2) (permitting ratification by way of a law or a presidential decree), and Article 11 (enabling ratification by Presidential decree not outlined in Article 10) were incompatible with the Constitution. See infra, n. 106.
[138] Constitutional Court Decision No. 21/22/PUU-V/2007 at 38.
[139] See Paparinskis (2020) and Schneiderman (2022).

impacts' that negatively affect state finances.[140] If the harms caused by investment (and trade) treaties were at the centre of the petitioner's complaints, the fact that there was 'no involvement of the people in any process of making and ratifying' those treaties, via their representatives in the DPR, triggered constitutional incompatibility.[141]

The evidence of Ifran R. Hutagalung advanced the argument that depriving the legislative branch from scrutinizing and ratifying treaties precipitated a 'loss of constitutionality'. That is, if the Constitution's Article 10 conferred on citizens the right, via their representatives, to be provided with the 'opportunity to stop the government's move to bind itself to international treaties that have the potential to harm the constitutional rights of citizens', then ignoring this requirement gave rise to 'a direct loss' in citizens' constitutional rights. Though this loss would be felt only indirectly, 'the resulting loss is real'.[142] The petitioners' experts emphasized the harms suffered as a consequence of entering into these binding treaties and the consequential narrowing of Indonesian policy space otherwise secured by the Constitution, particularly under Article 33(4). However, this was not the constitutional point on which the judges of the Court would hang their hats. Instead, these claims provided the foundation for the finding that the President had departed from the constitutional obligation to secure legislative participation in regard to treaties having so fundamental an impact on Indonesian citizens.

Of particular significance, to both sides to the dispute, was the expert evidence of Abdulkadir Jailani in support of the government. Jailani, Director Treaties in the Ministry of Foreign Affairs, had authored a paper for the South Centre complaining about the shrinking policy space produced by BITs and called for a new balance to be struck between investor protection and 'national sovereignty' (I have referred to this publication above).[143] While the petitioners relied upon Jailani's argument, he resisted the implication that it gave aid to their cause. Instead, Jailani described his analysis as modestly consistent with the opinions of some investment law experts who view BITs as having surrendered broad rights to foreign investors.[144] This did not mean, however, that the Treaty Law criteria in Article 10 were constitutionally invalid. No new laws are required to be enacted or amended nor is the content of international investment agreements directly related to 'sovereignty or sovereign rights'. This refers only to 'territoriality' and rights over the territorial seas, he maintained. It would be unreasonable to infer from this language an 'unqualified' concept of sovereignty, as rules of international law, by definition, constrain state sovereignty.[145]

---

[140] Constitutional Court Decision No. 21/22/PUU-V/2007 at 85.
[141] Constitutional Court Decision No. 21/22/PUU-V/2007 at 195.
[142] Constitutional Court Decision No. 21/22/PUU-V/2007 at 63–4.
[143] Jaliani (2015) at 1.
[144] Jaliani (2016) at 182 refers to Aikaterini Titi in support .
[145] Jailani relied upon Bonnitcha's argument. See Jailani, (2016) at 184 and Bonnitcha (2014) at 32.

His defence of the status quo hardly comports with the proposals for wholesale reform accompanying Jailani's hard-hitting, previously published critique. While insisting that Indonesia has not lost faith in the value of investment treaty commitments and will continue to offer certainty and security to investments (as promised in the National Law on Investment),[146] Jailani there outlined a series of radical proposals for reform. These include limiting the definition of protected investment, public interest defences to the national treatment rule, shrinking the scope of the FET to only denials of justice, and excluding indirect (or regulatory) expropriations to 'preserve a greater degree of regulatory space'.[147] As discussed above, very few of these of ambitious proposals would get taken up in new investment treaties with, for instance, Singapore and Australia.[148]

The Court agreed with the petitioners that the President's conduct, together with the statute governing ratification, were not constitutionally compliant.[149] The Justices began by noting that the fourth paragraph of the preamble to the 1945 Indonesian Constitution declares that the state of Indonesia is tasked with 'carrying out a world order based on independence, eternal peace and social justice'.[150] Signing international treaties could only be in the pursuit of these objectives and the executive would be obliged to oppose any treaty not advancing the just world order contemplated in the preamble. Looking to comparative constitutional practice, the Court declared that, as regards treaties that it characterized as 'technical or administrative', the approval of the legislative branch was not necessary.[151] By contrast, those having a 'political dimension' (as outlined in Article 11 of the Indonesian Constitution) require some legislative consultation or approval. Generally, the executive branch will make these determinations—they must have 'sufficient freedom of movement' to determine if the legislature should get involved.[152]

The conditions stipulated in Article 10 of the Treaty Law, triggering DPR approval, were too narrow in scope to conform to the constitution. The law was inconsistent with the requirements of the Constitution's Article 11 (2), the Justices concluded.[153] International relations, the Court declared, were 'becoming more intense,' rendering members of the international community 'more interdependent,' 'greatly' and 'significantly affect[ing]' Indonesia's 'national interests.' The 'formulation of norms contained in Article 10', consequently, 'will not be able to answer

---

[146] Jailani (2015) at 2.
[147] Jailani (2015) at 4–5.
[148] Limiting FET to denial of justice, it turns out, is a desirable reform and gets taken up in recent Indonesian bilateral investment treaties such as the Singapore-Indonesia BIT of 2018.
[149] Constitutional Court Decision No. 21/22/PUU-V/2007 at 244.
[150] Constitutional Court Decision No. 21/22/PUU-V/2007.
[151] Constitutional Court Decision No. 21/22/PUU-V/2007 at 254.
[152] Constitutional Court Decision No. 21/22/PUU-V/2007 at 255.
[153] The Court rejected arguments that Articles 2, 9, 11 of the Treaty Law were constitutionally invalid (ibid. at 262–3).

the needs' of the Indonesian people. This was no mere technical problem but was 'directly related to the fulfillment of the mandate of the Constitution'.[154]

The Court, regrettably, did not specify what in Article 10 is meant by an 'extensive and fundamental impact on the people which is linked to the state's financial burden'. The Court's ruling, nevertheless, can be understood as requiring, at a minimum, that trade and investment agreements be ratified by the legislature. For this reason, Indonesia for Global Justice, the lead petitioner in the case, could call for a review of all international agreements, particularly trade and investment agreements, to ensure their compliance with the Constitution's pledge of social justice, together with impact assessments on the economic, social, environmental, and human rights implications of new agreements moving forward.[155] Having required ratification by the people's representatives, the Court indirectly exhibited something that looks like soft defiance.

VIII. Conclusion

By rendering executive branch treaty-making accountable to the legislature, the Court enhanced democratic practice in Indonesia.[156] Whatever one's views about the merits of shrinking constitutional space due to international economic law's edicts, the ruling enables scrutiny by the people's representatives of investment treaty obligations. Adopting Ely's terminology, the Court undertook representation reinforcement review, ensuring that there was an ability on the part of the DPR to participate in political processes having to do with ratification of significant commitments made pursuant to international treaty.[157]

Though it has successfully policed elections to ensure that they are 'free and fair'[158]—serving as the 'main driver of democratic reforms'[159]—the Court has not always been keen to vindicate other democratic interests. It has rejected 'reasonable accountability measures' in the past, observe Roux and Siregar.[160] What helps to explain the Court's interest in doing so on this occasion? Could it be that it was the only constitutional remedy available to the Court considering the stinging critique of Indonesian trade and investment policy that was proffered by NGOs? The Court hinted that larger questions could arise in subsequent litigation. Unanswered, for

---

[154] Constitutional Court Decision No. 21/22/PUU-V/2007 at 264.
[155] Indonesia for Global Justice (2019).
[156] For a discussion of how courts in transitional democracies need to 'step back and allow the democratic system to function', see Roux and Siregar (2016).
[157] Ely (1980) at 77.
[158] Butt (2012) at 111.
[159] Mietzner (2010) at 418.
[160] Roux and Siregar (2016) at 3 ('There is some doubt … about the Court's democracy supporting capacity' at 18). The authors point to Court rulings in 2011 and 2014 overturning amendments to the regulation of judicial conduct on the Constitutional Court. They write that in 2014 the Court 'adopted an essentially dogmatic position on the requirement of judicial independence' (at 15).

instance, is the degree to which the regimes of international economic law are consistent with the Constitution's Article 33. How compliant are treaties that make up the investment law regime with the principles of economic democracy, sustainability, or development? What about the Constitution's preamble, mentioned in passing by the Constitutional Court in its reasons? Does the regime contribute to the 'establishment of a world order based on independence, eternal peace and social justice'?

It would be difficult for investment law norm entrepreneurs to argue that the regime has these precise aims in mind. Does it not exhibit, instead, a single-minded focus on shielding investors and their investments from states reducing their profitability in violation of something associated with the 'rule of law'?[161] By improving 'governance' along the lines exemplified by investment treaty standards of protection, it is said that treaties can improve the country's 'investment climate.'[162] Even if treaties had these good governance outcomes,[163] they are only second-order effects. Norm entrepreneurs will, of course, acknowledge that there is always 'room for improvement'.[164] For this reason, the regime will continue to self-correct, as it has continually been doing so since its take-off in the 1990s. The question is whether this will be good enough for apex courts who choose to closely scrutinize treaties for constitutional compatibility.

---

[161] Vandevelde (2010) at 113 and Calamita and Berman (2022) at 3 (described as the 'rule of law' thesis').

[162] Echandi (2013) at 298.

[163] A highly doubtful proposition as illustrated by eight country case studies in Calamita and Berman (2022). According to their summary, at 303, 'the impact of investment treaties on governmental decision making has been minimal'.

[164] Reinisch (2020) at 128.

7
Shackling the Future
Israel

I. Introduction

Can states constitutionally pre-commit not to upset investor expectations? Forcing the hands of newly decolonized states, who insisted upon 'permanent sovereignty' over natural resources, investors sought to include stabilization clauses in state contracts in order to shield their investments from regulatory change.[1] Freezing the regulatory environment would 'neutralise' the sovereignty of the host state. Together with a choice of law clause that made international law applicable law in any future dispute, optimum legal protection from legal change could be secured. From a constitutional point of view, however, 'a stabilisation clause may not be able to achieve what it sets out to do'.[2] Municipal law might have a different orientation than the single-minded protection of foreign investors. Once apex courts are seized with jurisdiction, they might conclude that it is beyond the capacity of present governments to bind the hands of future ones, at least not without the requisite legal foundation.[3] The judiciary in both common law and civil law jurisdictions, Walede and Ndi observe, may apply doctrines that render *ultra vires* commitments to freeze the regulatory environment.[4]

Consider a 2007 Nigerian Federal High Court ruling. A stabilization commitment was made via statute that was intended to benefit a Niger Delta gas processing company. The government's promise to make 'no new laws' not otherwise generally applicable was ruled by the High Court to be unconstitutional.[5] Because the stabilization clause fettered the National Assembly's legislative powers, it offended the 'tenets of the Rule of Law' and the ability of the legislature to 'make laws for the good of all people of this country'.[6] 'This cannot stand', Justice Nwodo insisted. The Nigeria Court of Appeal vacated this part of the ruling, characterizing Justice Nwodo's ruling on constitutionality of the commitment as *obiter dicta*.[7] There is no

---

[1] Sornarajah (2010) at 281.
[2] Sornarajah (2010) at 282.
[3] de Vries (2017) at 339.
[4] Waelde and Ndi (1996) at 235.
[5] Niger Delta Development Commission (2009); Sotonye (2014) at 245; and Gjuzi (2018) at 195.
[6] Niger Delta Development Commission (2009) at 59; and Adaralegbe (2008) at 240.
[7] Niger Delta Development Commission had not specifically sought a declaration of constitutionality in Niger Delta Development Commission (2011) at 2 and discussion in Elebiju (2011) at 2.

evidence that the Nigerian Courts were aware of the threat of an investment dispute, although some shareholders in the company would have had such remedies available to them in the circumstances.[8]

What investors desire is a means by which contracts can be 'internationalized' so as to 'bypass ... the heavy impact of state sovereignty'.[9] This could simply be achieved via interpretation of investment treaty umbrella clauses – treaty provisions that incorporate contractual commitments. Nevertheless, elevating contractual breaches into international treaty breaches remains not only 'highly controversial',[10] but 'lacking in clarity'.[11] The circumstances in which a contractual breach will give rise to a treaty breach turn on fuzzy distinctions between states acting as 'traders' or market actors and states acting in their sovereign capacity.[12] The distinction has proven to be not only dissatisfying but mostly unworkable. It is pretty clear, however, that investment tribunals, channelling investor's wishes, will find commitments to regulatory stability either under a treaty's umbrella clause or as a part of an investor's legitimate expectations. Both can have the effect of trimming regulatory flexibility.

How might apex courts, confronted with this choice—preserving policy space granted under the constitutional order or honouring contractual commitments to investors—respond to this threat? In the ruling taken up for discussion later in this chapter, the Israeli High Court of Justice answered this question but elided the impact their decision could have on investment treaty commitments. Indeed, they preferred not to worry about that threat, though it was made clear to the Justices that good grounds for launching a dispute would be available to the investor were the Court to decide in favour of the state. This is why some have characterized the ruling in *The Movement for Quality Government v. Prime Minister of Israel* (2016) as 'striking'[13] and 'earth shaking'.[14] It is true that the High Court of Justices relied not on Israel's Basic Laws (Israel's 'incomplete constitution')[15] but upon a reading of administrative law principles that places limits on executive authority binding the legislative branch.[16] The decision nevertheless offers up an opportunity to

---

[8] Adaralegbe (2008) at 243.
[9] Waelde and Ndi (1996) at 237.
[10] Ho (2018) at 180. Ho (2018) at 217 identifies three reading of umbrella clauses: the first refuses to raise mere contractual breach to a treaty breach; the second elevates a contractual breach only if the state acts in its sovereign capacity (*jure imperii*); while the third elevates any contractual breach to an international breach. Ho (2018) at 221 endorses the qualified use of the umbrella clause that 'enhances' contract protections.
[11] Ortino (2013) at 448 (it is the 'institutional character of the actor and [not] the nature of the function being performed' that should be determinative).
[12] For example, see *Hamester v. Ghana* (2010) Award, ICSID Case No. ARB/07/24 (18 June) at para. 328 and discussion in Schneiderman (2022c).
[13] de Vries (2017) at 338.
[14] Reich (2018) at 64.
[15] Vogelman et al. (2016).
[16] It is described as a basic principle of administrative law, by Justice Rubinstein, that an administrative authority cannot, in advance, release itself from responsibility when the public interest requires it. See Movement for Quality Government (2016b) at paras. 106–8. On administrative review in Israel

consider how apex court judges respond to the diminishing policy space offered up by aspects of international economic law, exemplifying what I regard as soft resistance.

Claims about the contraction of constitutional capacity are not mere hyperbole. So as to illustrate the diminution of policy space, I turn to a dispute, one of a number of investment claims launched against Argentina (following upon measures taken in response to a grave economic crisis). The tribunal's award exemplifies how contractual commitments receive special solicitude under international investment law's edicts.[17]

II. Stabilizing Investment Commitments

The Suez dispute arose from cessation of a contract to provide water and sewage services to metropolitan Buenos Aires. Aguas Argentina, part of a consortium led by the French-based multinational water companies Suez and Vivendi, was awarded a 30-year concession contract, the largest privatization initiative of its kind.[18] According to *The Economist*, this was not only the world's largest water concession, it also was one of the most profitable.[19] Water rates rose significantly afterwards which were well beyond the ability of an impoverished populace to pay. Unhappy with the rate of progress in connecting users to city utilities, the municipal government asked the concessionaire to accelerate expansion ahead of schedule and to expand connections beyond its original target. Rather than cross-subsidizing new connections, the company chose to impose further rate hikes. It also preferred more borrowing so that the company incurred greater indebtedness, in excess of that contemplated in the concession contract.[20]

By 2001, the Argentinian economy became unglued, experiencing an economic crisis that was likened to the great depression of the 1930s.[21] The country was plunged into political crisis once the government, by decree, froze bank deposits and prohibited cash withdrawals of more than $250 per week (Argentinian currency was pegged to the US dollar).[22] Thirty civilians died after one day of riots in

---

that is 'outside the reach of traditional administrative law in the UK', see Barak-Erez (2021) at 166. On the rise of common law constitutionalism in Israel that animates the Court's work, and which goes well beyond procedural questions and reaches into substantive ones, see Weill (2020).

[17] I have drawn upon a previous discussion of the Suez dispute in Schneiderman (2013a) at 48-49. There is no record of Israel being a respondent in an investment dispute.
[18] Suez (2010) at para. 26.
[19] Approaching a 40 per cent rate of return. See Artana, Navajas, and Urbiztondo (2001).
[20] Cassaron et al. (2007) at 245.
[21] Emmott (2003).
[22] The tribunal described the crisis as 'one of the most severe of its [Argentina's] history ... characterized by extreme social disturbance, riots, violence and almost total breakdown of the political system' in Suez (2010) at para. 257.

December 2001. Argentina defaulted on its sovereign debt by announcing deferral of over US$100 billion of external bond debt that was owed to both domestic and foreign creditors. In January 2002, Argentina enacted Emergency Law No. 25.561 which unpegged the peso to the dollar ('pesification'), precipitating an economic meltdown. With the collapse of the peso, thousands were thrown out of work, and foreign investors lost hope of reaping high returns on their investments that had been promised in privatization's heydays. Those at the bottom suffered the most: the population living in 'extreme poverty' more than tripled between 2000 and 2003.[23]

An investment tribunal was tasked with adjudicating the investor's claim, under three different bilateral investment treaties signed with France, Spain, and the UK. The investor claimed that Argentina had expropriated its investment, failed to provide full protection and security, and denied the investor fair and equitable treatment. For our purposes, it is this latter claim that is most instructive. It is worth mentioning, however, the lip service the tribunal paid to the 'right to regulate' in the context of the investor's allegation that there had been an expropriation. This phrase, common to a later generation of investment treaties, was considered an implied source of sovereign authority under earlier generations of treaty text.[24] The Suez tribunal declared that it was 'important to recognize a State's legitimate right to regulate and exercise its police power'[25] (the authority to take measures to protect public morals, health, and safety). The measures taken by Argentina, having the effect of significantly diminishing the value of the investment, were within the state's police powers jurisdiction and therefore did not rise to a compensable expropriation.[26]

Also, Argentina had not failed to provide full protection and security of the investment. This standard, common to all three investment treaties, was meant to shield investors from 'physical injury'. Claims to legal stability were not encompassed under this standard of treatment.[27] It was, instead, under the fair and equitable standard of treatment that the investor could lay claim to damages for violation of its legitimate expectations. The legal terms (regulatory, statutory, and contractual) under which an investor is induced to make an investment create expectations about future state behaviour.[28] It is these legal conditions that determine whether protected expectations have been upset. The tribunal warned that it was important

---

[23] UNDP (2005) at 36.
[24] Titi (2014). It is not at all clear that the proliferation of these clauses has changed the evaluation of what constitute violations of investment treaty standards. See the discussion in Sierra and Suarez (2023).
[25] Suez (2010) at para. 139.
[26] Suez (2010) at para. 140. It did not amount to a 'substantial deprivation' of the investment, for instance, the investor remained in control of the investment (ibid.). Nor was the state's behaviour outside the realm of normal contractual behaviour and so did not rise to the level of an expropriation (ibid. at para. 154).
[27] Suez (2010) at para. 179.
[28] Suez (2010) at para. 222.

to not look 'single-mindedly at the Claimant's subjective expectations'. Rather, the tribunal should adopt an 'objective' viewpoint, that of the 'reasonable investor'.[29] Nor was the state expected to satisfy every element of an investor's expectations but, instead, only those that are 'legitimate and reasonable in the circumstances' that are not associated with mere business risk or normal regulatory patterns of behaviour.[30] The investor's expectations were captured by the concession contract and legal framework—it played a 'central role' in establishing the investment. The problem was that Argentina had 'abruptly' terminated the concession contract.[31] The investor's expectations that 'Argentina would respect the Concession Contract throughout the thirty-year life of the Concession was legitimate, reasonable and justified'.[32] The tribunal continued, that 'without such belief in the reliability and stability of the legal framework the Claimants—indeed no investor—would ever have agreed to invest in the water and sewage system of Buenos Aires'.[33] Frustration of these expectations entitled the investor to damages in the sum of US$383.5 million plus interest.[34]

It is curious that the tribunal seemed oblivious to the investment's early profitability.[35] The tribunal concluded, moreover, that the investor had acted reasonably even as it sought tariff increases as the Argentinian economy went into nosedive. Argentina, by contrast, had not acted reasonably despite its right to regulate.[36] The state could have adopted 'more flexible means' in responding to the requests for tariff increases, such as relieving the concessionaire of further investment commitments, passing on tariff increases to consumers who could pay, and having governmental bodies pay overdue tariffs to the concessionaire.[37] The tribunal, however, nowhere addressed what proportion of the paying population of Buenos Aires could have offset those losses. The tribunal also took for granted that it was more appropriate, in the face of a US$100 billion sovereign default, for the state to give priority to investors, by requiring them to pay overdue tariffs, than addressing other economic priorities such as assisting economically desperate Argentinians.[38]

---

[29] Suez (2010) at para. 228.
[30] Suez (2010) at para. 229.
[31] Suez (2010) at para. 146.
[32] Suez (2010) at para. 231.
[33] Suez (2010) at para. 231.
[34] From and after I November 2014. See Suez (2015) at 60–2.
[35] Suez (2010) at paras. 35, 124.
[36] This is not unlike the reasoning in the *Eco Oro v. Colombia* tribunal award, discussed in Chapter 6.
[37] Suez (2010) at paras. 235–8. This also was relevant to the question of whether Argentina could take advantage of the customary international law defence of necessity (no treaty defence of necessity was available). It could have taken less drastic measures, the tribunal concluded, while Argentina itself had contributed 'substantially' to the circumstances giving rise to the crisis. Two of requisite four conditions for invoking the customary international law defence would not have been met. See Suez (2010) at paras. 260, 64.
[38] It was admitted by IMF staff that it was difficult even for non-poor households to have managed the economic shocks in Argentina, therefore, 'social intervention'—including public works programs and direct transfers—is 'useful ... to assist households during macroeconomic crises at' in Corbacho et al (2003) 27, 33.

The state's 'reasonable right to regulate' did not extend to operating outside the detailed rules laid down in the legal framework for the Concession Contract.[39] Contracts, under this reasoning, amount to an 'exception to the exercise of the regulatory power of the state'.[40]

III. Investment Law and Policy

Unlike the other country studies in this part of the book, Israel is a relatively wealthy country and exhibits both capital-importing and capital-exporting state characteristics. In 2021, however, its inward foreign direct investment (FDI) was almost triple that of its outbound investment, making it more dependent on (and vulnerable to) foreign capital.[41] Israel is a minor player in the investment treaty world, having about 45 international investment agreements currently in force. All of them, but one, include ISDS.[42] Only a handful are signed with capital-exporting states. The motivation seems to have been to protect Israeli investors abroad rather than to protect foreigners in Israel.[43] It was also considered unnecessary for Israel, a developed state, to pre-commit not to engage in expropriation or arbitrary conduct. It could send a 'bad signal' that the rule of law is weakly respected in Israel.[44] This perception, together with 'bad experience' in past negotiations, an insistence on maintaining flexibility in currency control, and a desire to avoid paying damages to investors, advises Reich, steered Israeli officials away from expanding its network of IIAs.[45] At the same time, Israel has chosen to impede economic development in the region. Restrictions imposed by Israel on the occupied territories has taken a toll. The cost of these restrictions between 2000 and 2020, in the West Bank alone, was estimated at US$50 billion.[46]

The state has yet to respond to an investment claim, though Israeli nationals have been claimants in seven disputes.[47] An indicator of the Israeli view on ISDS was placed before UNCITRAL Working Group III in a submission authored jointly with Chile and Japan. The 'Proposal for a Workplan' lays out a series of steps, together with a suite of issues, by which the Working Group could proceed with

---

[39] Suez (2010) at 237.
[40] Sornarajah (2015) at 287.
[41] See http://unctadstat.unctad.org/countryprofile/generalprofile/en-gb/376/index.html (last accessed 15 February 2023).
[42] Reich (2018) at 50.
[43] Reich (2018) at 45.
[44] Reich (2018) at 47.
[45] Reich (2018) at 47.
[46] UNCTAD (2022). The study focuses on Area C, comprising the bulk of Palestinian territory. At the time of publication, the raising of Gaza by Israeli Defence Forces has contributed untold costs to economic development.
[47] UNCTAD Investment Policy Hub at https://investmentpolicy.unctad.org/investment-dispute-settlement/country/102/israel (last accessed 18 May 2020).

its agenda of suggested reforms to ISDS. The joint submission expresses passing complaint about older generation treaties and how a newer generation may resolve these problems.[48] A disposition to replace old with new treaties lines up with Chriki, Broude, and Haftel's observation that Israeli investment treaties impede regulatory space and that Israel would be well advised to renegotiate new treaties that enable a wider range of public intervention.[49]

There are no constitutional or statutory rules regarding treaty-making and ratification in Israel. Following British constitutional practice, the executive branch has freedom to conduct foreign affairs including the making of trade and investment treaties.[50] Implementation of international obligations, however, follow a dualist model, requiring legislation by the Knesset.[51] The Israeli judiciary exhibits an ambivalence towards international law, largely because of the supervisory role it purports to provide to the occupation of the West Bank and Gaza. The Court prefers to undertake its own assessments of national security rather than being directed by international legal principle. Benvenisti argues that this 'apprehensive' and 'restrictive' approach to international law extends well beyond national security to 'matters of international trade and economic cooperation'.[52]

The legal regime for investment in Israel is governed by the Capital Investment Encouragement Law which is intended to attract foreign investment into Israel. This is accomplished mainly by grants and tax incentives.[53] There are few other specific protections available to foreign investors other than the general commitments to property, liberty, and freedom of occupation found in the Basic Laws, to which we turn next.

IV. Constitutional Order

It is said that Israel first became a constitutional democracy with the passage of two Basic Laws on 'Freedom of Occupation' and 'Human Dignity and Liberty'.[54] The 'gestation and delivery' of the constitution, however, may have arrived only with a second event, the Israeli High Court of Justice opinion in *United Mizrahi Bank* (1995).[55] Both constitutional moments[56] are the product of determined

---

[48] UNCITRAL (2019b).
[49] Chriki, Broude, and Haftel (2019).
[50] Cohen (2019) at 520.
[51] Cohen (2019) at 521; Kretzmer (2002) at 31 (an approach adopted 'long before the occupation of West Bank and Gaza').
[52] Benvenisti (1993) at 182.
[53] Shetreet and Homolka (2017) at 519–22.
[54] Barak (1997). These were preceded by nine Basic Laws including ones on the Knesset (1950) and on Government (1968). See full texts of the Basic Laws at https://www.knesset.gov.il/description/eng/eng_mimshal_yesod1.htm (last accessed 19 March 2020).
[55] Porat (2018) at 269.
[56] Though not the type that mobilizes the people as described in Ackerman (1991).

strategizing by a small number of key players. These constitutional accomplishments are compromised, moreover, by the degree to which Israeli constitutional law is implicated in the politically and legally fraught occupation and dispossession of Palestinians. The logic of 'settler-colonialism' writes Masri, is 'one of the central features that animate Israeli constitutional law'.[57]

The Knesset, sitting as a constituent assembly, passed the two Basic Laws in 1992 on the back of simple legislative majorities and without public consultation.[58] On this occasion, the Knesset was wearing one of its 'two hats'.[59] Having failed to reach consensus sitting as a Constituent Assembly after independence, a Knesset committee was authorized to draft a series of laws (the 'Harari Resolution') which would then be submitted to the whole of the Knesset for approval.[60] The first Basic Law: The Knesset, entrenched provisions concerning elections, requiring that they be general, national, proportional, and equal, and subject to an absolute majority (61 of 120) vote. It could be amended only by another Basic Law.[61] In 1992, with the passage of a Basic Law: Freedom of Occupation (together with a revised Basic Law: The Government) another law was entrenched, guaranteeing 'the right to engage in any occupation, profession or trade'.[62] The Basic Law on Human Dignity and Liberty, however—guaranteeing a limited set of personal rights comprising 'life,' 'body,' 'dignity,' 'privacy,' and 'property of a person'—was not entrenched.[63] It instead incorporated a limitations clause modelled upon the Canadian one, in addition to a legislative override.[64] This rendered the Basic Law: Human Dignity and Freedom 'quasi-entrenched', declared Justice Barak.[65]

The constitutional 'revolution' was only partly achieved, however. In order to enshrine constitutional supremacy, it required an act of judicial audacity exhibited by Israeli High Court decision in *United Mizrahi Bank*, the second constitutional moment. Though the Court denied the petition, the case, Weill claims, 'changed everything'.[66] All Basic Laws were now treated as if they were

[57] Masri (2017) at 389. Palestinians occupy the place of 'negative exemplar', per Fitzpatrick (1992) at 63. To similar effect Shinar (2018) prefers to invoke the friend/enemy distinction as does Jamal (2019).
[58] Lerner (2011) at 80. Basic Law: Freedom of Occupation was approved 23:0 and Basic Law: Human Dignity and Liberty by a vote of 32:21.
[59] Barak (1992).
[60] See the 'Harari Resolution' in Gavison (2006) at 367, fn. 49. On the 1950 debates leading to the Harari Resolution, see Lerner (2011) at 60–5.
[61] Entrenchment here refers to an inability to amend the Basic Law without an extraordinary majority. See Gavison (2003) at 60 (section 4 of the Basic Law: The Knesset). See discussion in *Bergman v. Minister of Finance and State Comptroller* (1969) 23 (1) PD 693 (per Landau J.) reprinted in Zamir and Zysblat (1996) at 310–71.
[62] Gavison (2006) at 367. Though the language in the Basic Law: Freedom of Occupation is 'stronger' than section of the Basic Law: The Knesset as it requires an absolute majority rather than a majority of the Knesset to effect change, observes Kretzmer (1992) at 241.
[63] Sapir (2018) at 38.
[64] Sections 1 and 33 of the Constitution Act, 1982. See Kahana (2013) and Segal (1997). This 'notwithstanding' mechanism was added to Basic Law: Freedom of Occupation two years later.
[65] A limitations clause is 'entrenched [only] against legislation' that does not observe these limits, wrote Barak (1992) 11–13. This move was predicted in Kretzmer (1992) at 242.
[66] Weill (2012) at 498; Weill (2020) at 21.

entrenched.[67] At issue was debt relief ('Gal Law') for agricultural farms that was challenged by creditors under the property right guaranteed by the Basic Law: Human Dignity and Liberty. The panel of nine Justices agreed that the law violated the right to property but was salvaged by the limitations clause. All also agreed that an entrenched basic law has supremacy over the political branches and can only be amended by another Basic Law.[68] President Shamgar read property as encompassing 'the right to make one's own decisions' and which 'ought to be interpreted in a general and broad manner'.[69] Shamgar resisted, however, transforming the Court into a 'designer of economic policy' and so chose to preserve a law that is not a 'severe burden'—it did not have 'substantive personal implications'.[70] Justice Barak's opinion has been likened to a *Marbury* v. *Madison* moment.[71] Barak invokes the 'people' as the source of authority for undertaking judicial review, in which case, the judges stand in the shoes of the people when they enforce the Basic Law's commitments.[72] 'In this manner' he writes, 'the Court actualizes democracy and the separation of powers.' 'Indeed' he adds, 'if the constitution itself is democratic, then judicial review is democratic.'[73]

As for the right of property, Barak J. described the right to property as encompassing 'every interest that has a financial value'.[74] This was no mere right to property, ordinarily understood (in the 'classic sense'), but constitutional protection of any economic interest including freedom of contract.[75] Justice Barak elsewhere wrote that 'free competition' is constitutionalized via 'freedom of occupation' in the Basic Law. 'If the state intervenes in free competition', he wrote, then 'it infringes on freedom of occupation' and must be justified under the limitations clause.[76] Although property was a robust right, it was subject to a proportionality analysis demanded by the limitations clause, including an inquiry into whether the law was in pursuit of a 'worthy purpose' and did not impair the right more than was necessary. Legislation in pursuit of human rights or serving 'social economic goals' such as the 'welfare state or protection of the public interest' were sufficiently worthy purposes.[77] The Gal Law satisfied all elements of the proportionality analysis.

---

[67] Sapir (2018) at 39 (labelled 'substantive entrenchment').
[68] Only Justices Barak and Shamgar insisted that non-entrenched Basic Laws also are supreme.
[69] United Mizrahi Bank (1995) at 774 (per Shamgar CJ).
[70] United Mizrahi Bank (1995) at 774 (per Shamgar CJ).
[71] Porat (2013) at 168. Justice Barak referred to *Marbury v. Madison* 5 US (1 Cranch) 137 (1803) at Mizrahi Bank (1995) at para. 75. See discussion in Rabin and Gutfel (2007). A different reading of Marbury that is contrary to the mythological one that inaugurates judicial review can be found in Ackerman (2005).
[72] United Mizrahi Bank (1995) at 781 (per Barak J).
[73] United Mizrahi Bank (1995) at 785 (per Barak J).
[74] United Mizrahi Bank (1995) at 785 (per Barak J).
[75] Gross (1997) at 90.
[76] Quoted in Gross (1997) at 96.
[77] United Mizrahi Bank (1995) at 788 (per Barak J).

With evidence of judicial exuberance around protecting traditional economic rights, and the absence of socio-economic rights from the texts of the Basic Laws, a concern was expressed that a 'neo-liberal worldview which emphasizes the autonomy of the economic sphere from state intervention and the withdrawal of the state from formerly regulated economic arenas' would triumph.[78] Constitutionalism would serve 'as a vehicle for Israel's brand of neoliberalism', Gross worried.[79] The High Court came around to the view that the right to dignity in the Basic Law incorporated welfare rights, but this was an unusually weak form of socio-economic rights. Not even a 'significant reduction' in income supplement benefits would 'itself indicate a violation of dignity'.[80] What was lacking in that case, complained President Barak, was an evidentiary record to support the petitioners' claims, taking into account all income and expenses.[81] Not only was there no loss of dignity, he concluded, it was inadvisable for the Court to intervene in 'a major piece of social and economic policy'.[82]

V. The Court and the Record

The Israeli High Court of Justice (also serving as the Supreme Court) is one of the most accessible courts in the world. Petitions to the Court are welcome concerning all grievances against the Government.[83] The Court serves as the judicial forum of first and final instance regarding these complaints. The observable trend has been to jettison jurisdictional 'boundaries'.[84] Without strict rules about standing, most everything is justiciable.[85] '[A]nyone can approach the court', wrote Justice Zamir, in any matter of public concern.[86] Responding to the charge of judicial interference in political matters, Zamir admitted to 'the facts but plead[ed] not guilty'.[87] Though divided on the question, the Court has tended not to 'interfere in matters which are predominantly political' even as it has taken a stand in many 'legal matters of a political nature'.[88] These interventions have been beneficial, Zamir claims, as Israel's political culture is still an immature one—democracy is 'not well-rooted.'[89]

---

[78] q (1997) at 146; also Mandel (1999).
[79] Gross (1997) at 107.
[80] Commitment to Peace and Social Justice (2005) at 128.
[81] Commitment to Peace and Social Justice (2005) at 131.
[82] Commitment to Peace and Social Justice (2005) quoted in Gavison (2006) at 374–5; also Segal (2011) at 327 ('the Supreme Court stands on the sidelines' in the social sphere). For an updated discussion see Ziv (2013).
[83] In order to reduce the High Court's workload, its jurisdiction was confined to human rights matters while other administrative questions were offloaded to new administrative courts. See Navot (2014) at 196–7.
[84] Navot (2014) at 197.
[85] Barak (2006b) at 33 ('major violation[s]' of the rule of law' grant to 'every person' standing to sue); Friedmann (2016) at 306; Weiss (2020) at 13.
[86] Zamir (1996) at 1.
[87] Zamir (1996) at 1.
[88] Zamir (1996) at 1–2.
[89] Zamir (1996) at 3.

This open-door policy provoked a backlash of sorts, particularly among religious communities and nationalist conservatives, causing the Supreme Court to absorb 'the most sustained political attack in its history'.[90] Legislative proposals to restrict standing before the High Court, in addition to a new override clause, and reform of appointment processes were tabled.[91] Due to personnel changes on the court, new remedial tactics such as a ripeness doctrine and suspended declarations of invalidity were adopted by the Court as a way of forestalling this counter-reaction.[92] Nonetheless, an amendment to the Basic Law: The Judiciary to curb the Court's jurisdiction to adjudge the reasonableness of the decisions of government (this was severed from a plan to hand control of judicial appointments to the ruling political coalition[93]) was passed by the Knesset without opposition party support.[94] The High Court of Justice ruled, subsequently, by a bare majority of 8:15 to be in violation of the separation of powers and the rule of law.[95] It is hard to explain enactment of the new 'Basic Law: Israel as the Nation-State of the Jewish People' in 2018 other than as a response to the constitutional revolution of the 1990s.[96]

For Hirschl, the Israeli case is the archetypical instance of 'hegemonic preservation'. A cross-party coalition of secular Israeli intelligentsia, Hirschl writes, agreed to enact Basic Laws in order to shield their policy preferences 'from the vicissitudes of democratic politics'.[97] Once seized upon by the judiciary, the High Court has 'advanced an explicitly anti-collectivist and deregulatory' agenda.[98] It is significant that a consensus could only be achieved in the Knesset around a selected set of rights, drawing even the support of the National Religious Party.[99] Two other Basic Laws, addressing such matters as equality, religious freedom, free speech, and social rights, did not generate similar support.[100] Other interests, particularly those of marginalized Israeli Arabs, simply are not cognizable. Some describe the constitutional revolution of 1992 as an effort to institutionalize liberal rights, overtaking the collectivist ideology that was predominant at Israel's origins, and thereby thwarting a neo-conservative counter-revolution.[101] Others hypothesize

---

[90] Jacobsohn and Roznai (2020) at 217.
[91] Jacobsohn and Roznai (2020) at 217.
[92] Mautner (2018) at 156–7, Roznai (2018a) at 361, 363, and Segev (2022).
[93] Judges are nominated by a nine-member judicial selection commission on which judges and legal professionals have a majority vote. See Shetreet (1994) at 259 and, on the proposals for reform, see Cohen and Shany (2023b).
[94] Cohen and Shany (2023a).
[95] See Movement for Quality Government v. Knesset, HCJ 5658/23 (1 January 2024). For a translation of the official abstract into English, see Sharon (2024).
[96] Mautner (2020).
[97] Hirschl (2004) at 17, 43. Gavison's explanation of the Israeli constitutional process is not that different in (2006) at 368–70. See also Mautner (2011) at 1–2.
[98] Hirschl (2004) at 67.
[99] They were pleased, Gavison reports in (2003) at 64, to have secured a declaration that Israel was a 'Jewish and democratic state' in the preamble to the Basic Law: Freedom of Occupation.
[100] Weill (2020) at 20. A variety of unenumerated rights came to be judicially incorporated via *The Basic Law: Human Dignity and Liberty in Movement for Quality Government v. The Knesset* (2006) HCJ 6427/02, PD 6(1) 619 [in Hebrew]. See Porat (2018) at 282–3.
[101] Navot and Peled (2009) at 430.

that it is decline in electoral support for the Ashkenazi elite (the ruling Labour Party), the corresponding rise of Sephardi political power (in the Likud Party), and the splintering of political support in favour of multiple sectarian interests that has precipitated a 'governability' problem.[102] Fragmented and shifting coalitions that rule Israeli politics result in 'instability and gridlock'. It is this crisis of governability that helps to explain the shift of power from the political branches to the judicial branch.[103]

Relaxation of standing rules prompted a vast rise in applications to the Court for relief. Among the 2,869 petitions filed between 2000 and 2006, the majority were directed at the Ministry of the Interior who has responsibility for family, immigration, and citizenship matters, amongst others.[104] The High Court intervened, however, in only 18 per cent of all the petitions filed in this period.[105] So despite the appearance of being highly activist, the High Court exercises more caution than its reputation suggests. Another study of 9,072 judicial decisions from 1995 (the year of *United Mizrahi Bank*) to 2015, yielded an acceptance rate of only 10 per cent.[106] The authors of this study find the data revealing that governmental stability plays a role in these results. There is significantly greater likelihood that the Court will uphold appeals against governments that endure for lengthy periods[107] (in Dahl's terms, coalitions that represent the 'dominant national alliance').[108] Comparing rulings in human rights cases from national security cases in the years between 2000 and 2008, Hofnung and Margel find the Court is marginally more likely to intervene in 'terror-related' human rights cases than in other human rights ones.[109] Moreover, the Court is less likely to second-guess terror-related human rights violations if the decision is handed down in the aftermath of a terrorist attack or during a military operation.[110] When it comes to the claims of the Arab minority, the Court 'refuses to rule' on cases 'with significant political implications' or that will result in 'important legal and material remedies'.[111] Lurie and Shany reveal that the success rate of petitions has been steadily declining since the late 2000s,

---

[102] Barzilai and Shain (1991) at 365.
[103] Meydani (2011a) at 79; (2011b) at 177.
[104] Meydani (2011a) at 14; (2011b) at 182.
[105] Fifty per cent were rejected, 21 per cent were postponed, and 11 per cent were retracted in Meydani (2011a) at 15; (2011b) at 185.
[106] These decisions are drawn from '2,800 court rulings' (the methodology is opaque). See Rosenthal, Barzilai, and Meydani (2016) at 14–15.
[107] This is described as the 'Constitutional Inter Election Period (CIEP)' in Rosenthal, Barzilai, and Meydani (2016) at 33–4.
[108] Dahl (1957) at 293.
[109] Often using the 'latent' strategy of granting interim relief without forcing a showdown with government. See Hofnung and Margel (2010) at 679, 688. Weill (2020) at 32 describes this strategy as intervening in 'public life mainly through the potent threat of invalidating statutes' which is enough to 'influence the drafting of statutes'.
[110] These variables have a 'strong effect' on decisions in Hofnung and Margel (2010) at 685.
[111] Sallon (2005) at 298; Al-Salem (2019) at 232–3; Lahav (1993) at 145.

consistent with the embrace of a more chastened judicial role since the heady days of the Barak-led court.[112]

The extant empirical studies suggest that the Court is more restrained than appears, nullifying few laws.[113] Weill attributes this to former Justice Barak's strategic behaviour that was intended to 'gain and maintain legitimacy'.[114] The Knesset, Navot surmises, has also been content deferring to the Court's exercise of judicial review regarding politically divisive issues, thereby 'having someone else to blame'.[115] With such a modest record of intervention, the Knesset has 'largely accepted' judicial rulings that invalidate legislation under the Basic Laws.[116] The appearance of activism, however, has attracted 'fierce criticism'. President Barak's methods were described as 'tantamount to legislation'.[117] Former Chief Justice Moshe Landau described matters as 'having gone too far'—the Court's conduct as 'tantamount to judicial dictatorship'. The Supreme Court, Landau complained, behaved as if they were 'governing sages'.[118]

Early and controversial interventions in political and religious affairs drove public opinion in a downward direction. Polling reveals a continual decline in confidence in the Court.[119] This 'dramatic' drop in confidence held by Jewish majority opinion has seen no corresponding increase in confidence among the non-Jewish minority.[120] Orthodox Jewish anxieties were prompted by one of the Court's early post-1992 decisions concerning a prohibition on licenses to import non-kosher meat. This measure, the Court ruled, deprived the importer of the freedom to pursue a vocation and so was *ultra vires* under the Basic Law: Freedom of Occupation.[121] It is said that the ruling woke the religious parties from their 'slumber', prompting Barak's proposal to add a notwithstanding clause, renewable for four years, similar to the one found in the Canadian Charter of Rights and Freedoms (s. 33).[122] This compromise helped to forestall immediate attacks on the 'constitutional revolution' but it also triggered waves of opposition to a number of High Court rulings that would follow. Disillusionment with the constitutional project continues to prompt various measures to trim the High Court's power including court packing proposals, removal of subject-matter jurisdiction,

---

[112] Lurie and Shany (2022) at 19–20.
[113] Legislative provisions in only 20 cases have been invalidated from 1995 to 2017, according to Lurie and Shany (2022) at 19–20. An earlier count by Navot (2014) at 199 reveals that 10 laws were nullified over an 18-year period.
[114] Weill (2020) at 32.
[115] Navot (2014) at 199; also Barak (2006) at 20.
[116] Weill (2012) at 499–500.
[117] Friedmann (2016) at 303.
[118] Friedmann (2016) at 304.
[119] Friedmann 2016 at 304, Meydani (2011a) at 113, Lerner (2011) at 220.
[120] Givati and Garber (2023) at 3.
[121] HCJ 3872/93 (*Mitral v. Prime Minister and Minister of Religious Affairs*). See Reichman (2013) at 245. In obiter, Justice Or suggested that legislation would have to satisfy the supermajority requirement in the Basic Law: Freedom of Occupation, which seems incorrect.
[122] Sapir (2018) at 79; Segal (1995).

and establishment of a constitutional court.[123] A bare majority was finally able to push one such proposal over the finish line in the Knesset. In July 2023, The Basic Law: The Judiciary was amended to preclude Israeli courts from reviewing the 'reasonableness' of executive action.[124] The amendment was described by the Attorney General, in a submission to the High Court of Justice, as part of a 'broad campaign aimed at effecting ... the elimination of checks and balances on the Government's power'.[125] As mentioned, the Israeli Supreme Court ruled the amendment a violation of Israeli constitutional principles.[126] It is considered the first instalment in a larger package of reforms, tabled for the moment, that are intended to truncate the power of courts.

VI. The Case

Sornarajah presciently raised the question whether, as a matter of constitutional theory, a state could fetter its legislative authority by entering into concession contracts with private parties.[127] A new theory of precommitment had to be devised by international lawyers to solve the problem that could operate outside of, but parallel to, national constitutional legal mechanisms. The internationalization of contracts via the umbrella clause provided one such mechanism while legitimate expectations doctrine under BITs served similar ends but without the need for a contract.

This question—of whether a parliamentary democracy could commit its legislature not to legally upset investor expectations—was put to the Israel High Court of Justice in *The Movement for Quality Government v. Prime Minister of Israel* (2016). The petitioners challenged a commitment made by the government of then Prime Minister Netanyahu not to make regulatory changes to the gas industry for a period of 10 years in exchange for the development of four natural gas fields in the Mediterranean Sea by Houston-based Noble Energy in partnership with the Delek Group of Israel. Noble was to initially invest US$7 billion and insisted upon what the Minister of Energy described as a 'stable environment ... for the next decade

---

[123] See discussion of the 'counterrevolution' in Lerner (2011) at 82–6.
[124] Section 15 (D1) was added to the Basic Law: 'Notwithstanding what is stated in this Basic Law, those who hold judiciary powers by law, including the Supreme Court when sitting as the High Court of Justice, will not discuss the reasonableness of decisions made by the government, the prime minister, or any other minister, and will not issue orders in this regard. In this section, "decisions" refers to any decision made, including those relating to appointments, or decisions to refrain from utilizing any given powers.' Barak (2006a) at 71 describes this judicial function as 'locat[ing] the relevant values' that are at stake and 'balancing' them on the 'basis of the weight' that is assigned to them given 'their relative importance in society'.
[125] Quoted in Navot (2023).
[126] Movement for Quality Government v. Knesset, HCJ 5658/23 (1 January 2024) and Sharon (2024).
[127] Sornarajah (2010) at 282. For a discussion, see Goldsworthy (2010) c. 5.

at least'.[128] This required specific commitments by the Government to Noble, declaring 'its intention to refrain from making substantial changes in the arrangements that have been set in the coming decade, and to carefully examine required regulatory changes while considering their effect on the profitability of the investment'.[129] The Government promised not only to not 'initiate any changes' in the revenue available to Noble but also to 'oppose any private bills aimed at promoting' such changes.[130]

Israel had taken a reputational hit in the oil and gas industry by reason of its evolving tax policy and small market.[131] This had the effect, according to an industry report, of reducing it, among oil exporters, to a rank below 'Indonesia, Angola, Mozambique and other third world countries'. Only 'Nigeria is worse' than Israel, according to the report's authors.[132] Reich surmises that it was the two Sheshinski Committees—examining tax policy and proposing a rise in royalties—that caused 'so many changes in a short time' and the ensuing uncertainty in gas exploration.[133]

The commitment was controversial from the start. Concessions made to Noble and Delek had already attracted the attention of the Israeli Public Utilities Authority. Chairperson Frakash-Hacohen had smoothed the path for private participation in the electricity sector but was alarmed by the monopoly position granted to the gas operators for a 10-year period without a public tender.[134] The pricing of gas in US dollars, in addition to annual increases tied to the US consumer price index, would have a significant effect on Israeli consumers, resulting in the steady increase of prices as it was not tied to international markets.[135] Frakash-Hacohen describe the contracts as the 'most inefficient and expensive possible' with a 'very high and uncommon return on investment'.[136] An independent report confirmed these concerns, particularly with respect to the price index formula,

---

[128] Minister of Energy Yuval Steinitz (30 May 2015) at https://www.youtube.com/watch?v=LpJrOUsy2F0 (starting 1:30:40).

[129] Israel, Ministry of Energy, at http://my.ynet.co.il/pic/news/gas.pdf, at slide 14 (last accessed 10 March 2019) [in Hebrew].

[130] Israel (2015) at 12. Depriving the opposition of this authority is no small matter. It is one of few outlets available to opposition parties in the Knesset to express disagreement with the government, even though few of these bills receive legislative approval. See Galnoor and Blander (2018) at 113–14 and Lis (2019) and discussion of Justice Landau in Bergman, supra n. 62, reprinted in Zamir and Zysblat (1996) at 312, on the ability of every Knesset member to introduce a private bill.

[131] Horesh (2016).

[132] The report was prepared by the consulting firm HIS CERA and commissioned by the Association of Oil and Gas Workers of Norway. See Cohen (2014). One wonders whether the Niger River Delta Commission case, discussed in text associated with nn. 5–9, supra, contributes to this impression.

[133] Reich (2018) at 71. A constitutional challenge to the Oil Profits Taxation Law of 2011 was dismissed in HCJ 3734/11 (*Davidian v. Knesset*).

[134] Farkash-Hacohen (2018) at 10, 17.

[135] Farkash-Hacohen (2018) at 14.

[136] Farkash-Hacohen (2018) at 23, 50.

which was out of sync with common practice, would deter future investors, and allocate the risk of cost increases upon consumers and not gas suppliers.[137]

The grant of this concession without the prior approval of the Israeli anti-trust authority (as required by law) also prompted an investigation by the Commissioner for Restrictive Trade Practices, Professor David Gilo.[138] Gilo declared in 2012 that the Noble–Dalek deal amounted to the grant of a monopoly.[139] Ongoing negotiations between the government and Noble prompted Gilo's resignation in 2015. If approved, the deal 'would not lead to competition in the natural gas market', Gilo warned.[140] The executive took control of matters and declared Noble–Dalek exempt from anti-trust laws and promised regulatory stability for 10 years. The Minster of the Economy (Aryeh Deri), who was empowered to invoke the anti-trust exemption, also resigned in protest and assumed the reins of a different ministry.[141] All powers over the economy were then assigned to Prime Minister Netanyahu. The Chair of the Public Utilities Authority, Frakash-Hacohen, also was asked to resign. The Minister responsible described her as 'too professionally independent ... for the prime minister's taste'.[142] Rather than listening to professional and independent authorities, the government kept ignoring them.

Even the Knesset was being uncooperative. Two separate votes on legislation to approve the scheme were postponed, the Knesset eventually approving the framework agreement only by way of legislative resolution (by a vote of 59:51).[143] Thousands protested in 2015 and civil society groups mobilized to fight the deal led by the principal petitioners in the case, the Movement for Quality Government.[144] Multiple arguments were submitted to the Israel Supreme Court sitting as the High Court of Justice, including contravention of anti-trust laws (already mentioned), defective legal processes, and harms to democracy. In regard to this last point, the petitioner complained that roles had been reversed. The state is expected to supervise gas exploitation in the public interest yet, in this case, the gas monopoly 'determines policy' and the conduct of government ministries.[145] The outcome of the

---

[137] Farkash-Hacohen (2018) at 25–7 and Shameh (2014). This remains the case, observes Ascari (2021) at 212, as prices in Israel 'are consistently higher than reasonable cost estimates, and allow twice as normal rates of return'.
[138] Farkash-Hacohen (2018) at 16.
[139] The official announcement is at http://www.antitrust.gov.il/files/11525/%D7%94%D7%9B%D7%A8%D7%96%D7%94%20%D7%AA%D7%9E%D7%A8.pdf (last accessed 10 March 2019).
[140] Bar-Eli and Koren (2015) and Farkash-Hacohen (2018) at 34. Reich (2018) at 73 complains that no new investment entered the natural gas market after the Sheshinski Committee recommended the raising of royalties. This was as likely the product of the anti-competitive nature of the Noble–Dalek arrangement, as Farkash-Hacohen (2018) predicted.
[141] Reich (2018) at 64 and Singer (2015).
[142] Farkash-Hacohen (2018) at 40.
[143] Reich (2018) at 63.
[144] Klein (2015); Greenberg (2016). The petitioners also included 'Headquarters of the Gas Struggle'.
[145] Movement for Quality Government Petition (2016c) (AA); the argument is also made in Farkash-Hacohen (2018) at 70. The argument is reminiscent of Foucault (2008) at 116.

case would 'determine the balance of power between the State of Israel and private companies', the petitioner warned.

Two related legal grounds were the principal ones upon which the High Court decision turned. First was argument that the Government had not anchored the Gas Outline in properly authorized law and, second, that the stabilization commitment improperly shackled future governments and so was beyond the government's capacity. Turning to the first 'anchoring' point, the High Court decided (3:2) that the Government need not have done anything further to implement the Gas Outline plan.[146] That is, the Government was entitled to rely upon a 'secondary arrangement' (namely, regulations issued by the executive branch) to implement a plan having important and substantial implications for the Israeli economy. It was not obliged to implement such changes via 'primary arrangements' involving the legislative branch.[147] The distinction between primary and secondary arrangements, admitted Justice Sohlberg, is not 'free from difficulties'.[148] Nevertheless the Government decision was properly anchored in already existing legislation.[149] The Court would not insist upon participation by the people's representatives in the Knesset.[150]

By contrast, Deputy President Rubinstein in dissent, maintained that this could not be done without an independent primary arrangement involving the Knesset.[151] Given the 'huge economic implications' and the fact that the subject was of 'deep public dispute', the 'Government deviated from the limits of its powers and authorities.' Even when it had 'good intentions,' as it was regulating an 'important' and 'sensitive' matter, the Government had to do so by way of legislation.[152] The

---

[146] The division on the High Court regarding the necessity for a new primary arrangement reproduced an earlier split, between the same justices, regarding a challenge to gas export quotas in HCJ 449/13 (*College of Law & Business v. Government of Israel*). See discussion in Reich (2018) at 56–9.

[147] This is how Justice Barak describes primary arrangements (in *Rubinstein v. Minister of Defense* (1998) HCJ 3267/97 at para. 19 [English translation at https://versa.cardozo.yu.edu/opinions/rubinstein-v-minister-defense (last accessed 11 December 2022)]: 'A basic rule of public law in Israel provides that where governmental action is enshrined in a regulation or an administrative guideline, then the general policies and basic criteria constituting the basis of the action must be established in legislation, pursuant to which the regulation was enacted or the administrative decision adopted. In more "technical language," —under this basic rule, "primary arrangements" that determine general policy and the guiding principles, must be enshrined in statute (Knesset Legislation), whereas regulations or administrative guidelines must only determine "secondary arrangements."' On the distinction between primary and secondary arrangements see Roznai (2018b) at 417–18. It is 'one mechanism', he writes, 'for the court to protect the role of the Knesset' at 418.

[148] Movement for Quality Government (2016b) at para. 132 (NK). Also see discussion on the distinction in Barak (2006a) at 228. I am grateful for supplemental translations of the ruling provided by Amos Atzmon, Nir Kremerman, and Meir Kuba.

[149] For example, section 52 of the Antitrust Law and section 33(a) of the Oil and Gas Law. Movement for Quality Government (2016a) at 5.

[150] Unlike the Indonesian Constitutional Court decision discussed in Chapter 6.

[151] As mentioned, Justices Rubinstein and Jubran also dissented, on similar grounds, in the earlier gas export case, in HCJ 449/13 (*College of Law & Business v. Government of Israel*).

[152] Movement for Quality Government (2016a) at 3.

Gas Outline Plan, for this reason, was beyond the capacity of the executive and *ultra vires*, according to Rubinstein.[153]

The High Court (4:1) instead relied upon the 'shackling' of future legislatures argument, concluding that the stabilization clause was *ultra vires*. Their conclusion was founded upon a basic principle of administrative law that restricts limiting of discretion granted to public authorities.[154] The executive cannot 'undertake in advance to not change its position'.[155] Government cannot impose this 'sweeping restraint' without leaving room to consider 'future relevant and specific consideration ... in accordance with the changing needs of the hour'.[156] In other words, 'should the public interest require it', the Government should be entitled to resile from this promise.[157] One is reminded of Bickel's observation that the 'power to accomplish a reversal' in a democracy 'is of the essence, and no less so because it is often merely held in reserve'.[158]

This does not mean that Government has unlimited power to renege on promises, only that it should have a 'wider scope of discretion' than the one undertaken here.[159] When the law establishes a duty to exercise discretion, the 'government has no authority not to decide'. This 'could lead to the shackling' of not only future governments but also of the legislature concerning matters 'that are at the center of political discourse'.[160]

Justice Rubinstein identified two principal models for securing regulatory stability for investors: freezing clauses (full or partial) and economic balancing (or 'equilibrium') clauses. The latter did not prevent the introduction of regulatory change but promised compensation in the event of such a change. This was the type that was ubiquitous in OECD states. Freezing clauses, by contrast, were typically found in developing states where 'the rule of law is shaky', he opined. In other words, the 'partial freezing' clause at issue in this case was unusual for an economically developed state.[161] Such a strict stabilization commitment was not appropriate for 'developed countries with a stable democratic regime'.[162] A 'proper democratic

---

[153] Reich (2018) at 68, complains that the logic of Justice Rubinstein's position would result in a framework legislation that was 'entrenched by legislation'. It would have been a preferable outcome, from Rubinstein's perspective, to have preserved flexibility by refraining from passing legislation. But this ignores the democracy-promoting nature of the ruling—sending it back to the Knesset would have required a legislative vote, which had failed twice previously.
[154] Movement for Quality Government (2016a) at 2. On administrative law principles in Israel based upon common law constitutionalism, see Weill (2020).
[155] Movement for Quality Government (2016b) at para. 106.
[156] Movement for Quality Government (2016b) at para. 107.
[157] Movement for Quality Government (2016b) at para. 109.
[158] Bickel (1986) at 17.
[159] Movement for Quality Government (2016b) at para. 113. Deputy President refers to the doctrines of 'lawful justification' or 'reasonable reason' (ibid.).
[160] Movement for Quality Government (2016b) at para. 119–20.
[161] This is the view that, Reich (2018) at 65 reports, has shaped Israel's BIT policy—that Israel is a stable democracy with the rule of law and so does not require investment protections to attract investment.
[162] Movement for Quality Government (2016b) at para. 25, per Sohlberg J.

regime' would never 'agree to a complete constraint' of an authority's future discretion, he maintained.[163] The stabilization commitments 'restrict the arms and legs of government', Justice Hayut agreed, crossing 'all permissible boundaries in a parliamentary democracy'.[164] This, she declared, was a 'negation of the Knesset's power to enact laws that contradict the government's guidelines'.[165]

Justice Sohlberg, in dissent, disagreed that the Knesset's power was now limited. It formally had the power to reconsider its commitment (even if the Government was committed to opposing changes for 10 years).[166] This was not a 'total restriction of discretion'.[167] Nor did it impose a 'chilling effect' on future governments.[168] The commitment was like any other made by international treaty.[169] Justice Sohlberg preferred not to undermine the 'package deal', the product of 'long and complex professional negotiations' among experts (even though the record reveals the executive being continually hostile to professional advice).[170] The state only would have to pay damages if it changed its mind, collapsing the distinction between freezing and balancing clauses. 'It will certainly be very expensive' to do so admitted Sohlberg J. It was 'only reasonable that the State shall be forced to bear a significant monetary cost to rescind' its promise, after all, the 'greater the reward the greater the risk'.[171]

Of particular salience to this discussion is that, looming in the background, was a potential investment claim under an Israel–Cyprus BIT.[172] In his appearance before the Knesset Economics Committee, Avi Licht, Deputy Attorney General, admitted having seen a secret legal opinion addressing Noble Energy's ability to sue Israel under the treaty for reneging on the Gas Outline. Licht identified two types of risks that would arise: the first, if the Plan was not approved and, the second, if it was approved but then the state reneged on its commitment. Under the first scenario, he explained, 'if this outline doesn't pass, we are exposed to international arbitration'. A similar outcome held for the second scenario. He did 'not want to present them [these risks] in public' but admitted that the Government had 'examined [the prospect], including the use of an American law firm specializing in international arbitration'. 'I'll say it gently', he added, '[t]hey claim they have cause . . . based [not] on the laws of the State of Israel [but on] on international trade

---

[163] Movement for Quality Government (2016b) at para. 24, per Sohlberg J.
[164] Movement for Quality Government (2016a).
[165] Movement for Quality Government (2016a) at para. 8.
[166] Movement for Quality Government (2016a).
[167] Movement for Quality Government (2016b) at para. 26, per Sohlberg J.
[168] Movement for Quality Government (2016b) at paras. 33–4, per Sohlberg J.
[169] Did he have in mind investment treaties, such as the Israel-Cyprus BIT, discussed in the next paragraph?
[170] Farkash-Hacohen (2018) at 68.
[171] Movement for Quality Government (2016a) at 5.
[172] Cohen (2014) and Chriki, Broude, and Haftel (2019) at 23–5 [in Hebrew]. But see de Vries (2017) at 341, fn. 20.

agreements'.[173] The petitioner acknowledged this threat, one the Prime Minister had been publicly relying upon for many months but whose significance he chose to minimize.[174]

Deputy Attorney General Licht is reported to have introduced this threat in oral argument before the Court.[175] Justice Rubinstein also mentioned, in passing, the existence of the danger, but declined to address it. 'We have not forgotten the American legal opinion submitted by the State regarding the consequences that may or may not be the subject of a change in future policy in the context of international law,' Rubinstein J. acknowledged. 'However', he concluded, 'since we have reached the result we reached, we do not find [the need] to address the question of the implications of international law' in this case.[176] The threat apparently did not 'chill' the High Court Justices into submission. There is no telling, however, what influence this risk may have had on internal government decision-making.[177]

The Court suspended its declaration of invalidity for one year in order to provide the Netanyahu government time to renegotiate the terms of the Gas Outline with Noble Energy. Talks between the government and investors ensued and agreement was reached several months later. The Government resolved, in the case of legislation or regulations that 'materially impact' on the investment, to 'positively consider solutions to maintain the economic feasibility' of the project. The Government also would 'strive' to behave in accordance with generally accepted standards in 'OECD countries where there is an oil and gas industry'.[178] The ruling, nevertheless, was declared as 'bizarre' by the Prime Minister—an 'exaggerated legal interference ... [that] makes doing business hard,' he broadcast via Twitter. Noble Energy CEO David Stover announced that the ruling undermined Israel's 'stable investment climate'.[179] After the newly renegotiated deal, gas prices elsewhere continued to decline while those in Israel continued to increase. Profits on the Tamar gas field remain unusually elevated—its rate of return 'extremely high'.[180] In 2017 alone, it yielded record profits of US$1.1 billion and US$3 billion between 2015 and 2017.

The secrecy surrounding the gas deal was unsettling. Without the requisite support from well-informed professionals and cabinet ministers, the Prime Minister

---

[173] Knesset Economics Committee, Protocol No. 98 60–1 (29 November 2015). They are referring to an investment agreement not a trade agreement.
[174] Movement for Quality Government Petition (2016c). The second risk, presumably, would also give rise to international liability.
[175] Cohen (2014).
[176] Movement for Quality Government (2016b) at para. 113. The attorney for the State of Israel referred the Court to Weiler and Laird (2008).
[177] Sharvit (2016).
[178] Government Resolution No. 1465 (22 May 2016), paras. 5 (a) and (f) at http://www.energysea.gov.il/English-Site/Pages/Regulation/Decision%201465%20English%20translation%20with%20disclaimer.pdf (last accessed 24 May 2020).
[179] Henderson (2017).
[180] Farkash-Hacohen (2018) at 48, 64.

personally took control, pushing the deal forward despite an inability to find legislative support from the Knesset. The Prime Minister even personally appeared before the Court, for the first time in Israeli history, to plead for the agreement's legal validity. It also is clear that the executive used the threat of ISDS as a cudgel to have the High Court fall into line behind the government's policy.[181] The Court could not stop the deal from moving forward. It did, however, throw some sand in the wheels.

VII. Conclusion

By preventing the political branches from committing to stabilization clauses that mirror investment treaty commitments, the Israeli High Court of Justice exhibited soft defiance in response to exigencies associated with international investment law. The Court, however, did not weigh in on the constitutionality of any particular investment treaty text. The Justices might behave differently in circumstances where the executive and legislative branches express a consensus about the need to commit to promises of this nature.[182] Moreover, as we have seen in apex courts in capital-exporting states (the European Court of Justice stands out in this regard), there is reason to anticipate that new treaty language—for instance, declaring that the 'right to regulate' is preserved while cabining other standards of treatment, like FET—will help to forestall declarations of judicial invalidity. This may even be more likely in capital-importing states eager to be seen as open to trade and investment. For instance, in a constitutional dispute concerning the constitutionality of the Philippines signing on to strictures imposed by having joined the World Trade Organization, the Supreme Court declared that the Philippines Constitution 'did not intend [for the country] to pursue an isolationist policy'.[183] To the contrary, as one commentator put it, the Philippines Constitution, was intended to facilitate the 'enlightened use of profit' and to enable the economy 'to expand and to grow'.[184]

On the other hand, the reasoning of the High Court of Justice may empower future Israeli governments to resist some investment treaty law disciplines that are viewed as incongruous, even if accepted by other capital-importing states. Some of these may not be appropriate for 'developed countries with a stable democratic

---

[181] Sharvit (2016).
[182] Would the amendment to The Basic Law: The Judiciary (discussed in n. 125, supra) that was intended to preclude courts from evaluating the reasonableness of executive branch actions have precluded judicial review in the gas case? Only dissenting Justice Sohlberg spoke in the language of reasonableness (for example, 'We are not convinced that the government's decision is extremely unreasonable' in Movement for Quality Government [2016b] at para. 50). The majority justices declined to invoke reasonableness doctrine relying, instead, on administrative law principles to declare the gas outline plan *ultra vires*.
[183] Tañada (1997) at 39. For further discussion, see Schneiderman (2022b).
[184] Villegas (1987) at 175. Villegas was Chairman of the Committee on the National Economy and Patrimony. The Commission did not, however, constitutionalize 'neo-liberal capitalism' (ibid.).

regime', as Justice Sohlberg put it.[185] With these words, one gets the impression that the Court's soft defiance was motivated, in part, by a desire not to be treated like other capital-importing states in the Global South. This could be pertinent in resisting other of investment law's constraints which are intended, in part, to recreate conditions associated with rule under informal empire.[186]

Any ability to resist these encroachments on Israeli jurisdiction will ultimately reflect Israel's bargaining power as a capital-exporting state.[187] One can foresee Israel exercising some leverage, in other words, so as to be able to impose its will at the negotiating table.[188] This ability to resist encroachments based upon both policy and public law grounds is a paradoxical outcome for a constitutional system whose foundation is obscure, where market rights are expressly recognized in its Basic Laws, and which continues to experience stress generated by political forces from within and without.

---

[185] Movement for Quality Government (2016b) at para. 25, per Sohlberg J.
[186] See Bedjaoui (1979) at 92. I discuss such connections in Schneiderman (2022), c. 2.
[187] For a study that addresses the bargaining of power available to capital-importing states in negotiations with more powerful capital-exporting ones, see Schneiderman (2009) (tracing failed negotiations between South Africa and the United States for a new trade and investment treaty).
[188] This does not appear to have been Israel's objective in the final Israel–Japan investment treaty. See the laconic wording on 'fair and equitable treatment' in Article 4 on 'General Treatment'. See 'Agreement Between the State of Israel and Japan for the Liberalization, Promotion and Protection of Investment' (1 February 2017) at https://investmentpolicy.unctad.org/international-investment-agreements/treaty-files/5849/download (last accessed 29 September 2022).

8
Conclusion

I. First, A Brief Summary

With the country studies that comprise the bulk of this book now complete, it remains first to sum things up and then to address normative concerns prompted by some of the scholarship in this field. The accumulated observations derived from variable constitutional experiences are, of course, partial ones.[1] Each of the country and regional case studies in this book demand further investigation and refinement. The more general inquiry, which concerns the interaction between the local constitutional complexities and international legal norms, also calls for more study. My hope is that this book prompts further thinking along some of the lines of inquiry laid down here. This is not to say that interesting work is not, at present, being produced. I propose engaging with some of this literature in the balance of this conclusion. First, I turn to a summary of the book's main findings.

Readers will have learned that apex courts in capital-exporting states are more likely to tolerate the disciplines by which investment law constrains state capacity. This may be the case for any number of reasons. Courts may be of the view that, by having their home states author the international ties that bind, investment law is in alignment with constitutional commitments made to their own citizens, as in France. Or it may be that judges prefer to prioritize movement in the direction of more intense international economic cooperation, breaking down boundaries that inhibit the movement of goods and capital, as in Canada. In some cases, doing otherwise can impede regional global leadership that lays down the rules of the game, as the Court of Justice of the European Union worried. The desire to improve the investment climate for economic development helps to explain why some courts in capital-importing states respond in similar ways—for example, in Peru. Judges may not wish to be seen to be standing in the way of capital flows that improve the economic conditions of citizens in their own states.[2]

We have also seen judicial push back in the interests of vindicating democratic values.[3] This has the consequence of ensuring that investment law commitments

---

[1] Weber (2010) at 119 insists that knowledge of 'cultural reality is always knowledge from specific and *particular points of view*' (italics in original).
[2] As the Colombian Constitutional Court in C-358/96 (5 August 1997) explained, the 'internalisation of economic relations becomes a necessity for the survival and development of States that transcends ideologies and political programs', quoted in Fandiño-Bravo (2015) at 700 (economic protectionism 'can only lead to . . . ostracism and to becom[ing] a sort of pariah of the international society').
[3] What Guinier (2008) labels 'demosprudence'.

have their origins in democratic chains of legitimation. To this end, apex courts serve as a backstop to ensure that processes associated with self-government, including legislative checks on executive action, offer opportunities for fulsome deliberation upon, and vetting of, international investment law's limits on state policy capacity, as in Indonesia. While this can be interpreted as obstructionist it also can lend legitimacy to the regime if approved after being duly vetted by elected bodies. Finally, apex courts in capital-importing states are motivated, in some instances, to ensure that there is tolerable conformity between commitments made to foreign investors and national constitutional law. Constitutional obligations can modulate treaty terms so that they mirror best practices in the field of investment treaty law, as in Colombia, or even bar promises that constrain state capacity into the future, as in Israel. In these instances, we see apex courts serving as a modest check on, and softly defying, international legal processes. These courts also exhibit some humility, attentive to the institutional limits of the judiciary meddling in foreign affairs.

With this range of responses in hand, it is possible to begin to theorize the relationship between the local and the international—between national constitutional law and a regime that some consider an emergent supranational constitutional law.[4] Theory will always be '*for* some purpose', Cox reminds us.[5] He draws contrasts between problem-solving theory—having the object of making existing 'relationships and institutions work smoothly'—and critical theory—which 'does not take institutions and social and power relations for granted but calls them into question by concerning itself with their origins and how and whether they might be in the process of changing'.[6] We might understand problem-solvers as adopting seemingly value-free methods aiming to smooth friction between the local and the global. Critics, on the other hand, maintain that normative choices are required to be made and thereby envisage feasible changes to the prevailing order in the pursuit of a more just state of affairs. If the qualitative method adopted in this book resembles the style associated with problem-solving theory, it has been in the service of critique, which I pursue in the remaining parts of this conclusion.

II. Democracy (Not) Vindicated

Among the principal concerns of problem solvers is that, in contemporary times, there is a disjuncture between the authors and addressees of law.[7] Law-making

---

[4] Thornhill (2016).
[5] Cox (1986) at 207.
[6] Cox (1986) at 208-10.
[7] Habermas (1996) at 104 and Von Bogandy and Venzke (2014) at 19. Dahl (1970) at 64 called this the 'principle of affected interests' in thinking about authority within a democratic polity. It is 'the best general principle of inclusion that you are likely to find' (Dahl (1970) at 64).

institutions are not necessarily congruent with those who are governed by law, unsettling the democratic foundation upon which the idea of self-government has been built. This gives rise to a 'gap' between those who authorize rules and those who are subjected to them.[8] It is a problem recognized within international relations theory: that growing interdependence gives rise to increased capacity for states to 'exercise power over'—even to 'injure'—others.[9] Much of the literature on law, globalization, and economic integration is preoccupied with having politics catch up with new governance structures established to oversee state behaviour. At the same time, states are expected to internalize the impact their decisions will have on foreigners. The judicial branch, as we have seen, is wrapped up in this network of institutions that advance norms associated with free trade and the free movement of capital.[10] Constitutional interpretation that disrupts this dominant trendline, it is often presumed, will be resisted in favour of interpretation that smooths integration in accordance with value system associated with economic globalization.

Somek describes the process as one where international law serves as a form of 'peer' review that speaks on behalf of those without a voice within national legal and political orders. Labelled 'Constitutionalism 3.0', national legal orders are described as constrained by international legal obligations that serve to check local decision-making. Somek characterizes this as the 'darling dogma' of Europeanists—treating impacts on unrepresented foreigners as a problem for democracies that can only be cured by external legal devices.[11] Investment dispute settlement mechanisms, such as ISDS, serve precisely this purpose, even in operative democracies. Democratic processes within host states are flawed, it is alleged, as the interests of unrepresented foreign investors do not get taken into account in decision-making by the political branches. Foreigners also are unlikely to get a fair hearing before the judicial branches. Even where 'sophisticated' legal systems are in place, ISDS serves as a 'last option', write Bungenberg and Reinisch, so as to ensure that foreign investors are dealt with in a non-discriminatory and non-arbitrary manner.[12]

This is not entirely an accurate portrayal of ISDS. Dispute settlement typically is available in the very first instance, even before local courts are given an opportunity to scrutinize an investor's claim under local law.[13] This is justified, the experts claim,[14] because national judicial systems are biased and lacking independence. By

[8] Neyer (2012) at 68.
[9] Young (1969) at 747 and Young (1983) at 103.
[10] Slaughter (2004) at 101.
[11] Somek (2014) at 28.
[12] Bungenberg and Reinsich (2021) at 456.
[13] This is exemplified by the *Clayton v. Canada* award, where dissenting arbitrator McRae speculated whether the investor possibly could even succeed in gaining an award of damages under Canadian law. It should be mentioned as well that there is also likely a requisite cooling-off period in the treaty before a dispute can be launched.
[14] I am referring to investment lawyers, scholars, and arbitrators—investment law's norm entrepreneurs.

contrast, investment tribunals, they argue, are undistracted by complex and countervailing constitutional considerations and so are the preferred locales for the adjudication of foreign investment disputes. So, unless an investor chooses otherwise, national courts are deprived of jurisdiction to settle their claims, in addition to resolving the legal questions that touch upon violation of their alleged rights (in investment treaty terms, standards of treatment). If such investor–state dispute mechanisms are meant to serve as a 'substitute' for allegedly defective national legal systems, this amounts to another limit on constitutional space, this time that of jurisdiction to address investor claims within local legislative and constitutional contexts.[15] The law that is applied in investment disputes typically is not national law but international law, a law whose content is derived from treaty and custom and interpreted and applied by investment arbitrators. Rather than keeping disputes within the legal regimes that enforce compromises reflected in constitutional text or national legislation, they are placed in locales that are decidedly unfriendly to those who are not investors, host states, or their legal advisors.

Having relocated investment disputes to spheres of privatized dispute resolution, apex court judges are now confronted with the task of managing the interface between local law and international regimes. This turns out to be more contentious than many initially presumed. Where political forces are attentive to complaints about such things as large damages awards or cramped policy space, and this is brought to the attention of local courts, then regime conflict gains salience. Non-governmental organizations, campesino movements, or indigenous peoples—otherwise neglected in investment dispute settlement processes[16]—also can be expected mobilize to challenge investor–state dispute settlement. Yet, these sub-national communities are often simply ignored or, if heard, are not believed by investment tribunals. Being on the front lines of, and thereby most vulnerable to, poorly planned foreign investment activity, the voices of the disempowered simply are left out of the regime's institutional logic. To the extent that they enter into it, they are often portrayed by investment arbitrators as the dupes of rent-seeking competitors or paid hooligans.[17]

Heightened legitimacy concerns have rendered investment arbitration vulnerable to complaints from both capital-exporting and capital-importing states. Scholars have therefore been prompted to think about how local courts should respond. Benvenisti and Downs offer an account of national court strategic behaviour that corresponds, in some ways, to what has been described herein as soft

---

[15] The point is more fully elaborated upon in Ginsburg (2005). This concern is well represented by the judicial responses mentioned in the Introduction to this book, in text associated with nn. 12-18.
[16] See Cotula and Perrone (2021).
[17] For example see final awards in *Metalclad Corp v. Mexico*, (2000) Award, Ad hoc—ICSID Additional Facility Rules, ICSID Case No ARB(AF)/97/1 (30 August) and *Técnicas Medioambientales Tecmed SA v Mexico* (2003) Award, ICSID ARB(AF)/00/2 (29 May), also discussed further below. For a fuller discussion, see Schneiderman (2013a) at 119–25.

resistance. They identify a 'newly found judicial courage' among apex courts having the effect of protecting democratic processes and judicial autonomy from domination by the 'economic forces of globalization'.[18] They document the strategic use of foreign and international law by national courts in three distinct areas: judicial review of global counterterrorism measures, protection of the environment in developing states, and the status of asylum seekers in destination countries.[19] What Benvenisti and Downs highlight is judicial resistance to actions of the political branches which yield too easily to the influence of global law authored by powerful states.[20]

The lesson that emerges out of their case studies is that national courts are reluctant to outright limit legislative action on constitutional grounds but, instead, 'engage the political branches in an ongoing dialogue'. Declarations of unconstitutionality, they write, are 'used only sparingly'.[21] Courts, they insist, are not sitting 'idly by while their authority to review the actions of the political branches is eroded'.[22] They provide not a lot of evidence, however, that this judicial reaction is intended to 'resist the depletion of domestic democratic space'.[23] Dialogue is also encouraged among judiciary operating at different levels. They favour a model of judicial cooperation which ensures that, at 'both domestic and international levels[,] ... the interests of a greater proportion of relevant stakeholders (both within rich democratic countries and within poorer countries) are taken into account by decision makers and that the resulting outcomes are more informed and balanced'.[24] Such a project of 'shared interpretation' lends legitimacy to both levels of judicial oversight—both will be 'better off',[25] they claim—giving rise to 'greater mutual respect' and 'fewer jurisdictional confrontations'.[26]

Together, they say, international and national courts can overcome the counter-majoritarian difficulty, described by Bickel in the US constitutional context.[27] By conferring power upon judges to 'construe the Constitution, in matters of the greatest moment, against the wishes of a legislative majority', Bickel famously described judicial review as a 'deviant institution'.[28] Rather than subverting

---

[18] Benvenisti and Downs (2017) at 105, 110, 116.
[19] Benvenisti and Downs (2017) at 122. It is only in the realm of protecting the environment, however, could it be said that there is evidence of courts fighting back against the 'economic forces of globalization'.
[20] Benvenisti and Downs (2017) at 127 (courts are 'refusing to simply rubber stamp the actions of the political branches of government').
[21] Benvenisti and Downs (2017) at 128.
[22] Benvenisti and Downs (2017) at 148.
[23] Benvenisti and Downs (2017) at 147.
[24] Benvenisti and Downs (2017) at 149. Also see Benvenisti (2014) at 121. It is said that national courts can contribute to the production of international norms in numerous ways, for instance, to the content of customary international law. See Benvenisti and Downs (2017) at 151 and Roberts (2011).
[25] Benvenisti and Downs (2017) at 154.
[26] Benvenisti and Downs (2017) at 164.
[27] Bickel (1986) and Benvenisti and Downs (2017) at 168.
[28] Bickel (1986) at 20, 18.

democratic choice, Benvenisti and Down recommend that courts at both levels work symbiotically to reinforce democratic processes. This can be accomplished in two ways: first, by generating information that promotes accountability and deliberation[29] and, second, by taking into account interests that otherwise are neglected within domestic political processes. It is this second effect that is of particular interest here.[30] Advancing the principle that, in an age of economic globalization, all affected interests should be considered by decision-makers,[31] investment law has the virtue of insisting that the welfare of foreign economic actors get taken into account in national policy-making. The concern is to reinforce the representation of those otherwise without a voice or influence in domestic political outcomes.[32] Benvenisti and Downs point to the tribunal decision in *Tecnicas Medioambientales* (Tecmed) as illustrative of this positive effect.[33] There were no grounds, they argue, for the international tribunal to be deferential to defective democratic processes within Mexico. The tribunal was correct, they say, to order the state to pay damages for depriving the investor an ability to operate a hazardous waste facility site near the border city of Hermosillo.

Caution is called for here as the Tecmed tribunal ruling exhibits numerous flaws.[34] The circumstances suggest that the investor had colluded with government in order to secure its original and ongoing privileges. Permits were issued and renewed, and environmental transgressions neglected, at the investor's behest. Even if Tecmed was ultimately denied renewal of its permit to operate the hazardous waste site, empirical studies confirm that foreign investors have a wide variety of mechanisms available to mitigate political risk. They are not, as are national firms, without a vote and therefore voiceless. They can lobby, exercise influence, and take steps to mitigate the effects of policy changes.[35] There turn out to be many methods available to foreign economic actors to have their voices heard. Measures that mitigate political risk serve as a preferred substitute for ISDS—they are more reliable and probably less expensive. They also have the benefit of not conferring a veto on state policy on behalf of foreign investors nor warranting occasionally enormous damage awards.[36]

It is particularly troubling to claim that investment law and arbitration vindicate democratic values. There simply is little empirical evidence to sustain it. This international legal regime is premised, instead, upon distrust of democratic processes.

---

[29] Benvenisti and Downs (2017) at 169–70.
[30] I have considered such an alternative—that all those affected (including investors) be listened to—in Schneiderman (2017a).
[31] Somek (2014).
[32] See also Benvenisti (2016) at 63.
[33] Benvenisti and Downs (2017) at 182; Técnicas Medioambientales (2003), supra (n. 17) at para. 122, referring to *James and Others v. The United Kingdom* (1986) 98 Eur.CtH.R. (Ser. A) 8 EHRR 123 at para. 63.
[34] Schneiderman (2013) c. 5; Schneiderman (2010b) at 915–21.
[35] Schneiderman (2013) at 134.
[36] On likening investment tribunals to exercising veto points, see Schneiderman (2020).

Whatever passing interest tribunals have expressed in democratic values, they mostly provide cover for the solicitude that is conferred upon foreign investors by the regime. Van Harten's content analysis of 162 arbitral awards confirms this suspicion. He finds that where 'elections or democracy were mentioned by arbitrators ... it was often to suggest that politics had contributed to unsound decisions and that the arbitrator's role was to ensure that investors were compensated'.[37] Arbitrators, for the most part, appear more comfortable disparaging democratic politics. National court judges, without much evidence, are treated with equal suspicion. All are guilty of preferring their own nationals over foreigners. This renders the 'organized uncertainty' associated with democracy a permanent threat. So long as democracies 'offer all of the relevant political forces real opportunities to improve their material welfare', it will pose an ongoing peril to the international economic legal order.[38] It is not without significance, then, that soft resistance exhibited by some apex courts in this study are motivated, in part, by democratic principles. It cuts against the grain of the regime's underlying premises.[39] But it will not have the effect of upsetting international economic law's preoccupation with constraining state authority. In the next two sections I take a closer look at proposals intended to promote dialogue between courts and the actors and institutions of international investment law.

III. (Un)Easy Coexistence

On what grounds should judges yield to preferences granted to some of the most powerful economic actors in the world today despite the complex and sometimes delicate compromises that are entrenched in constitutional text? Is it not, after all, the 'province and duty' of apex court judges to enforce constitutional obligations in the face of obvious constitutional transgressions? Or do judges, as some suggest, have an obligation to yield to international investment law, irrespective of national constitutional settlements, in the interests of promoting 'dialogue'?

Prieto Muñoz, for instance, advances an argument for 'conditional coexistence' between constitutional courts and investment arbitration. Courts are expected to 'manage normative conflicts ... by defining a set of minimum conditions' investment law must satisfy before entering into force within host states.[40] These courts enter into conversation with international law by 'voic[ing] discontent ... without undermining the system as a whole'.[41] By harmonizing the interaction between courts and investment law, apex courts can exert 'greater influence' over the content

---

[37] Van Harten (2013) at 73.
[38] Przeworski (1991) at 13, 32.
[39] For more on investment law's tension with democracy see Schneiderman (2018b).
[40] Prieto Muñoz (2022) at 151.
[41] Prieto Muñoz (2022) at 156.

of international investment law.[42] Paradoxically, he claims that by tolerating inroads into constitutional space, courts can better protect constitutional values.

Prieto Muñoz offers up the Colombian Constitutional Court ruling in C-252 of 2019 (discussed in Chapter 5) as illustrative of this model of conditional coexistence. It will be recalled that the Court there issued findings of conditional constitutionality regarding several provisions of the Colombia–France bilateral investment treaty (BIT). If conditions laid down by the Court were satisfied—modifying the treaty's terms so that it was compliant with the Constitution—the treaty could then enter into force. Some of the standards of treatment, advantageous to investors, required trimming in order to be constitutionally compliant. The practical outcome was that the newly negotiated Colombia–France BIT would resemble newer treaties being signed between Global North states—like that between Canada and the EU (CETA) which is described as the 'gold standard' of trade and investment protection agreements.[43] All that the Colombian Constitution mandates, it turns out, was the incorporation of global best practices into Colombian BITs. These were the 'minimum conditions' that were needed to pass constitutional muster. It is noteworthy that other constitutional complaints concerning, for instance, violations of the principle of equality as between national and foreign economic actors were dismissed out of hand. Prieto Muñoz maintains (even if not precisely in these terms) that, by acceding to the demands of the investment treaty system, the 'Court gained more influence' over the future of BITs signed by Colombia.[44]

This is contrasted with the 1996 Colombian Constitutional Court decision concerning a Colombia–UK BIT, where the Court concluded that the BIT violated both constitutional property rights and equality rights.[45] Prieto Muñoz complains that the Court 'forfeited its own influence' by 'rigidly' interpreting the Constitution.[46] The Constitution was thereafter swiftly amended so that the constitution conformed to investment treaty edicts. Similarly, Prieto Muñoz alleges that when the Ecuadorian Constitutional Court issued 17 rulings declaring that BITs in force were non-compliant with Article 422 of the 2010 constitution— holding that 'sovereign jurisdiction' could not be yielded to 'international arbitration'—the Court lost an opportunity to 'influence' the 'shape' of international investment law.[47] This opened up an opportunity for investment tribunals to offer interpretations of the Ecuadorian Constitution, fulfilling a function the Court declined to perform.[48] In both instances, these Courts 'lost influence over the content and interpretation of their respective Constitutions and the future development

---

[42] Prieto Muñoz (2022) at 151–2.
[43] Douma (2021).
[44] Prieto Muñoz (2022) at 168.
[45] Decision No. 358/96, discussed in Chapter 6.
[46] Prieto Muñoz (2022) at 161.
[47] Prieto Muñoz (2022) at 172.
[48] Prieto Muñoz (2022) at 176.

of international investment law'.[49] They gave up the 'advantages that accrue' when apex courts pursue conditional coexistence.

Numerous problems associated with this set of claims arise. For one thing, Prieto Muñoz fails to elucidate the structure of constitutional argument that would entitle apex courts to achieve these harmonious outcomes, particularly when constitutional text pushes them in an opposing direction.[50] This requires detailed examination of constitutional text, history, and precedent—the contexts of meaning that produce constitutional understanding—for particular jurisdictions (something I have endeavoured to do in the case studies that appear in Part II of this book).[51] Prieto Muñoz also fails to explain why this obligation to influence investment law generally falls within the mandate of national courts. Nor does he explain how Courts will 'influence' the 'development' of investment law beyond redrafting clauses in discrete treaties that operate at high levels of generality. There is an absence of evidence that courts—particularly those in capital-importing states—can 'influence' the future direction of investment treaty text and interpretation. This is illustrated by the Colombian Constitutional Court ruling which Prieto Muñoz applauds as a model of conditional coexistence. The Court will have no influence over the development of investment law other than to insist that Colombian negotiators better preserve regulatory capacity as have capital-exporting states in their own agreements. What is missing from this account, in short, is an appreciation of how power and influence operate within the investment treaty system. It is a regime shaped by political and economic elites that make their home mostly in the Global North.

Not only does his prescription exonerate political branches of responsibility for giving up constitutional capacity, Prieto Muñoz also reveals an impoverished understanding of what national legal norms get channelled by international investment law and arbitration.[52] It is not Colombian or Ecuadorian constitutional standards that get incorporated into the content of international investment law. Rather, it is the constitutional law of capital-exporting states that receives the imprimatur of international law. As indicated in the Introduction of this book, the content of investment treaties is driven by developed country models often offered to developing states on a take-it or leave-it basis. Data compiled by Alschner and Skougaerskiy reveals that 'developing countries seem to have little say over the content of the treaties they sign and are therefore exposed to a more diverse array of legal commitments'.[53] As treaty text evolves and more legal precision is attained,

---

[49] Prieto Muñoz (2022) at 178.
[50] This is notwithstanding the ambit of discretion available to apex court judges. See Posner (2005) at 39 who describes the US Supreme Court as 'political in the sense of having and exercising discretionary power as capacious as a legislature's'.
[51] On contexts of meaning, see Weber (1978) at 8–9.
[52] Principally those of influential capital-exporting states as I have argued elsewhere. See, for example, Schneiderman (2018c).
[53] Alschner and Skougaerskiy (2016) at 574.

report Manger and Peinhardt, reforms are 'driven primarily by capital-exporting states' who 'change the content of treaties to reduce ambiguity in order to avoid outcomes that contradict their interests'.[54] It is evident that capital-exporting countries have had a firm grasp of the pen during investment treaty negotiations.

IV. (Mono)Cultural Dialogue

International law is constructed by appealing to the universality of the particular case.[55] Typically, such claims to universality are unaccompanied by any acknowledgement of the access available only to the privileged few to contribute to its content. For example, American political leadership unambiguously acknowledged that US constitutional law was a proper candidate for take-up in negotiations for a new trade and investment agreement with Europe (TTIP). By determining the content of investment treaty law, Americans triumphantly could legitimately claim to have their own law represent 'universal' standards.

Seeking to smooth the path by which investment tribunals and local courts can interact, some promote 'dialogue' between institutional actors. These interventions operate under the shadow of European Union practice, where discourse about judicial dialogue and constitutional pluralism dominate the scholarly literature.[56] Fandiño-Bravo, for instance, encourages a priori control of investment treaties by constitutional courts as the 'perfect stage' at which to scrutinize conformity with national constitutional law. These rulings, in turn, will 'enlighten arbitrators' by alerting them to specific constitutional contexts and reducing concerns about arbitrations' 'lack of embeddedness in the national context affected by their decisions'.[57] The object is to 'bring them [tribunals] closer' so as to produce not only better decision-making but to satisfactorily balance the 'public and private interests at stake'.[58] As between tribunals and courts, Schill and Tams encourage 'complementarity and cross-fertilization' and 'constructive engagement' by apex courts by stressing an 'openness toward' ISDS.[59]

Witte similarly invokes the dialogue metaphor so as to bring constitutional courts and investment arbitration into closer cooperation. She advances an argument for heterarchy rather than hierarchy as between these adjudicative settings. The two fora end up standing 'on more or less equal footing, each with valid claims from the logic of their system'.[60] Aiming to enhance reasoned decision-making on

---

[54] Manger and Peinhardt (2017) at 921.
[55] This paragraph draws upon Schneiderman (2018c).
[56] Dyevre (2017) at 457.
[57] Fandiño-Bravo (2015) at 737. Constitutional law rulings also inform tribunal proportionality analyses or may even be worthy of 'a certain degree of deference' on the part of tribunals (ibid.)
[58] Fandiño-Bravo (2015) at 673.
[59] Schill and Tams (2022) at 36.
[60] Witte (2018) at 519.

the international plane,[61] Witte asks that courts and tribunals 'adopt a spirit of co-operation and deference, in line with the heterarchical conceptualization of their relationship'.[62] She applauds the French *Conseil constitutionnel* for constitutionally endorsing CETA, on this basis.[63]

Witte's plea for heterarchy lines up well with a systems–theoretical approach to the management of conflict. Consider Teubner's portrait of societal constitutionalism, upon which diagnoses of the fragmentation of international law have been constructed.[64] This account envisages self-constituting systems functioning at all levels and no longer exclusively the product of state action.[65] Each operates as a closed system free to pursue its own logic, yet open to irritations from other systems.[66] The rationality pursued by any one system produces collisions, even permanent conflict.[67] There is no central authority, however, to resolve these conflicts. Instead, each system attends to responses best befitting its own stripped-down sensibility. For Teubner, what emerges is the 'equal authority of colliding discourses'.[68] The expansionist fervour of these closed systems—the urge to control cognate systems—is creating 'real problems of global society,' however.[69] What is required is self-restraint and better listening devices in order to ascertain harms caused by the single-minded pursuit of a system's partial rationality. The question is whether 'sufficient external pressure [can] be brought to bear on the subsystems so that self-limitation of their possible courses of action becomes effective'.[70]

I have argued elsewhere that the self-understanding of relevant actors operating in investment law's domains correspond relatively well to a systems–theoretic account.[71] How well has investment law responded to perturbations emanating from other systems—has it developed its own 'collision law'?[72] I have suggested that there is some learning and adapting to these system collisions. The movement to embrace proportionality in investment law, for instance, can be viewed as a response to critique that the regime fails to incorporate public interest concerns. Overall, however, the regime's sensors have proven to be faulty. Investment

---

[61] The impetus for promoting dialogue, it seems, is to 'enhance the legitimacy of investment arbitration as an exercise of public authority' (Witte [2017] at 475). Witte unqualifiedly accepts many of the premises and promises of investment law, for instance, that it offers a 'depoliticized' enforcement mechanism and is 'conducive to economic development' (2017 at 515).
[62] Witte (2018) at 521.
[63] Witte (2018) at 491–2.
[64] International Law Commission (2006).
[65] Teubner (1997a).
[66] Fischer-Lescano and Teubner (2004) at 1006. In Luhmann's famous formulation, sub-systems, though 'normatively closed' respond to their environment by being 'cognitively open.' See Luhmann (2004) at 106.
[67] Teubner (1997b) at 158.
[68] Teubner (1997) at 159.
[69] Fischer-Lescano and Teubner (2004) at 1007.
[70] Teubner (2010) at 20.
[71] Schneiderman (2011).
[72] Teubner (2015) at 235.

arbitrators instead single-mindedly are concerned with the protection of foreign investors that are advanced by investment law's standards of treatment.

It is noteworthy that, for these problem-solving theories, there is an expectation that constitutional courts will yield to the power of international investment law instruments and bodies. The 'controversial plurality' associated with permanent conflict between colliding discourses, which Teubner portrays, is not that welcome.[73] There is also an expectation of some reciprocity: investment tribunals, for instance, should be expected to issue reasons attentive to local constitutional conditions. The centre of gravity of these proposals, however, is upon apex courts—the guardians of national constitutional law—to succumb to the regime of investment law. The rationale for this is not well explained. In the few remaining pages, I offer a few reflections on a key supposition operating in this mode of problem-solving theory.[74]

Some apex courts, particularly but not exclusively those in capital-exporting states, treat constitutional law as mostly in harmony with investment law. In such instances, the rationalities pursued by each regime are considered compatible. Other courts express concern that the logic of these regimes are in discord, possibly incompatible. Systems theory counsels that, in either case, the rationality of each be respected as if they were operating on a roughly equal footing. Systems theory, however, elides important qualitative differences between these regimes. It is in light of these differences that investment law proves to be significantly inferior to constitutional law enforced by apex courts. The differences principally have to do with the presence—and in the case of investment law, absence—of the people.

Modern constitutions are the product of compromises fashioned in the course of the high politics associated with constitution-making. Liberal constitutions exhibit common features to be sure: democratic elections,[75] a semblance of a separation of powers, and judicial independence, among other things.[76] They also will be nested within complex constitutional compromises, serving differing and, oftentimes, conflicting objectives. It is more accurate to comprehend modern constitutions as serving multiple purposes—carriers of assorted ideal types.[77] They are tapestries comprised of variable combinations of ideal–typical constitutions. Indeed, it is rare for a constitution to pursue exclusively one type to the exclusion of others.[78] Instead, they might as often incorporate 'contradictory institutional initiatives' and 'tensions' in the articulation of structure and rights.[79] Baxi, for instance, describes 'constitutional texts' as 'multidimensional spaces of inscription',

---

[73] Teubner (1997a) at 157–8.
[74] This resembles what Bourdieu (2000) at 15 describes as a 'repressed presupposition'.
[75] However episodic the depth of their 'intensity'. See Marks (2000) at 53 ff and Thornhill (2021) at 3.
[76] Law (2004) associates these with 'generic' constitutional law.
[77] On constitutions as 'archetypes' see Frankenberg (2018) at 30 and Schneiderman (2022b).
[78] Tushnet (1999) at 1229.
[79] Gargarella (2018) at 182–3.

that constitute sites of 'contradiction,' conjoining 'many narratives' that concern the past and engage the present.[80] Even sophisticated accounts of 'constitutional identity'—identity claims tend to serve as focal points for uniformity[81]—can be understood as exhibiting 'constitutional disharmony', giving expression to varying 'communities of meaning'.[82] From this angle, constitutions serve not as mechanisms to impose uniformity but spaces for dialogue and negotiation over constitutional meaning.[83]

International investment law is not like that. It is built to run as a prophylactic for foreign firms to guard against political risk, namely, state action that renders their investments less profitable.[84] Privatized arbitral processes have the advantage of shrinking the law applicable to the dispute so that claims are adjudicated 'outside' the laws of the host state.[85] They are the equivalent, writes Yilmaz Vastardis, of 'justice bubbles' for privileged foreign investors.[86] The law applicable to such disputes is not intended to be local law—this is deemed suspect as are local judges—but a species of international law, whose content is pronounced by investment arbitrators and lawyers in privatized dispute settings. It is a body of law so favourable to investors that it offers the kind of 'certainty [that is not] available in any other realm of economic activity', observes Waldron.[87]

Because the regime is structured to protect investors, state action is treated as suspect. So long as legal change runs afoul of laconic treaty protections (the regime's standards of treatment), the likelihood of a claim for compensatory damages, including lost profits, becomes more likely.[88] Its legal imaginary is best described as a 'curious amalgam of welfare economics', 'sporadic empiricism', the identification of 'best practices', and 'informal deference to the attitudes of the foreign investor community'.[89] The public benefits to be gained by state measures running afoul of commitments made to investors do not weigh heavily in the equation, despite efforts at 'recalibration'.[90] Not only are public interest defences hardly effective, they

---

[80] Baxi (2003) at 574.
[81] Fabbrini and Sajo (2019), and Sholtes (2023).
[82] Jacobsohn (2010) at 4. Wolin (1989) at 10 on describes American political identity being 'essentially ... contested'.
[83] Tully (1995) at 183–4.
[84] On the use of ISDS to manage political risk, see Jandhyala (2021).
[85] Boue (2022) at 9.
[86] Yilmaz Vastardis (2020) at 630.
[87] Waldron (2012) at 73. '[H]onest jurists', he cautions, 'should have nothing to do with cynical uses of the [rule of law] ideal that are designed to do nothing more than underwrite the investor-profits of predatory and extractive enterprises'.
[88] I am mindful that empirical evidence suggests that investors lose their disputes as often as do states. When settlements are included—often than not they entail the payment of compensation by states to investors—the odds of success turn out to be more favourable to investors. Settlement sums roughly are equivalent (32 per cent of the amount claimed) to the pay-out for successful claims (31 per cent of the amount claimed). See Ubliava (2020) at 548.
[89] David Kennedy (2006) at 142.
[90] Alvarez (2010) at 143. This is despite the proliferation of 'right to regulate' clauses. On the limited functions they serve in CETA, see Douma (2021) and Sierra and Suarez (2023).

also barely register on those occasions where states change their minds. States are expected to live by their commitments to foreign investors regardless of the merits of a change of direction. The 'power to accomplish a reversal', subject to governing national rules, is something that democratic states usually take for granted. This power, declared Bickel, forms the 'essence' of democratic government.[91] It is a privilege denied to states and their citizens by the regime to protect foreign investors.

That the regime promotes other values—such as hackneyed claims about promoting 'good governance'[92] or 'sustainable development'[93]—is belied by its everyday results. The regime is laser-focussed on the sole objective of protecting investments abroad. In furtherance of this goal, investment law imposes a single and homogenous view of the functions government should be expected to perform, namely, promoting inward capital and securing profits for risk-takers. Few other values are treated as legitimate—all else becomes subservient to that overriding goal. Little attention needs to be paid to the compromises a polity will have enshrined in its constitutional text. Why should investor rights be crowded in by conflicting interests, whether they be a minimum wage, environmental protection, or indigenous land rights? Instead, only certain state functions are preferred, namely, those associated with nineteenth-century conceptions of acquired rights under property and contract.[94] The object is to 'unplug foreign investment relations from domestic public imperatives and plug[them]into global business imperatives' with accompanying strict liability rules.[95] Consider how the harvesting of tropical forests for timber requires the rejection of agricultural practices and people that do not fit that goal. Vandana Shiva describes this practice as a 'false universalization' which prefers 'narrow commercial interests' over local knowledge. It amounts to the erasure of diversity in favour of the 'monoculture of the mind'.[96]

It is the monoculture of vested economic rights which renders investment treaty law and arbitration anaemic as compared to those arrangements and interests enshrined in constitutional text. Judges in apex courts surely are aware of this order of priority. Even in those instances where constitutions direct that international law take precedence, it will be the duty of apex court judges, as guardians of constitutional norms, to vindicate the communal interests memorialized in constitutional text. This book's analysis suggests that this change of course is less likely to occur in courts in capital-exporting states. As for capital-importing states—the principal addressees for investment law's strictures—so long as apex court judges fear

---

[91] Bickel (1986) at 18.
[92] For example, Sattorova (2018) and the case studies collected in Calamita and Berman (2022), in particular, see chapters by Atanasova and Bonnitcha.
[93] An ambivalent evaluation is provided by Schacherer and Hoffmann (2019).
[94] Rights associated with what Duncan Kennedy (2006) calls the 'first globalization' of classical legal thought.
[95] Perrone (2021) at 10.
[96] Shiva (1993) at 18–19.

executive reprisal or believe that their interests align with those of foreign entrepreneurs or even wish to join the ranks of investment arbitrators upon retirement, citizens may have to wait longer for a more robust change of course. It will take some time yet for apex court justices in the Global South to admit, in their public transcripts, that the interests of footloose foreign economic actors deserve less solicitude than the most vulnerable constituencies served by a country's constitution.

Bibliography

Abugattas, Gattas (2006) Sistemas de incorporación monista y dualista: ¿tema resuelto o asignatura pendiente? *Agenda Internacional Año XII* 23: 439–61

Ackerman, Bruce (1991) *We the People: Foundations* (Harvard UP)

—— (2005) *The Failure of the Founding Fathers: Jefferson, Marshall, and the Rise of Presidential Democracy* (Harvard UP)

Ackerman, Bruce and David Golove (1995) 'Is NAFTA Constitutional?' *Harvard Law Review* 108: 799–929

Adaralegbe, Bayo (2008) 'Stabilising Fiscal Regimes in Long-Term Contracts: Recent Developments from Nigeria' *Journal of World Energy Law & Business* 1: 239–46

Ahmad, Jawad (2018) 'Complicity in Forgery and Investor Due Diligence over Local Partners' *Journal of World Trade & Investment* 19: 293–304

Al'Afghani, Mohamad Mova (2013) 'The Elements of "State Control"' *The Jakarta Post* (14 January) 6

—— (2014) 'The State Retreats and Never Returns: Consequences of Neoliberal Reforms on Administrative Law Protection in Indonesia' (19 April) at https://ssrn.com/abstract=2426804 (last accessed 9 May 2020)

—— (2015) 'Court Decision Brings Water Governance Reforms to a Halt (Part 1)' *The Jakarta Post* (9 March) 6

Alarcón, Daniel (2022) 'What Pedro Castillo's Failed Coup Attempt Means for Peru' *The New Yorker* (9 December)

Alba, Victor (1977) *Peru* (Westview Press)

Alexy, Robert (2002) *A Theory of Constitutional Rights*, translated by Julian Rivers (Oxford UP)

Allee, Todd and Clint Peinhardt (2014) 'Evaluating Three Explanations for the Design of Bilateral Investment Treaties' *World Politics* 66: 47–87

Allee, Todd, Manfred Elsig, and Andrew Lugg (2017) 'Is the European Union Trade Deal with Canada New or Recycled? A Text-as-data Approach' *Global Policy* 8: 246–52

Al-Salem, Rouba (2019) *Security, Rights and Law: The Israeli High Court of Justice and the Israeli Settlements in the Occupied West Bank* (Routledge)

Alschner, Wolfgang (2022) *Investment Arbitration and State-Driven Reform* (Oxford UP)

Alschner, Wolfgang and Dmitriy Skougaerskiy (2016) 'Mapping the Universe of International Investment Agreements' *Journal of International Economic Law* 19: 561–88

Alter, Karen J. (2018) 'National Perspectives on International Constitutional Review: Diverging Optics' in Erin Delaney and Rosalind Dixon (eds) *Comparative Judicial Review* (Edward Elgar) 244–71

Alva-Arévalo, Amelia (2020) 'The Relevance of the Inter-American Court of Human Rights' Standards on the Right to Prior Consultation in the Domestic Sphere: A Review of the Jurisprudence' *International Journal on Minority and Group Rights* 27: 603–24

Alvarez, José E. (2010) 'Why Are We "Re-Calibrating" Our Investment Treaties?' *World Arbitration & Mediation Review* 4: 143

—— (2018) 'The Human Right to Property' *U. Miami L. Rev* 72: 580

American Law Institute (2018) *Restatement of the Law Fourth, The Foreign Relations of the United States: Selected Topics in Treaties, Jurisdiction, and Sovereign Immunity* (The American Law Institute)

Anghie, Anthony (2004) *Imperialism, Sovereignty and the Making of International Law* 249 (Cambridge UP)

Ankersmit, Laurens (2020) 'Regulatory Autonomy and Regulatory Chill in Opinion 1/17' *Europe and the World: A Law Review* 4(1) DOI: 10.14324/111.444.ewlj.2020.25

Argentina, Republic of v. BG Group PLC (2012) 665 F. 3d 1363 (USDCA)

Artana, Daniel, Fernando Navajas, and Santiago Urbiztondo (2001) 'Regulation and Contractual Adaptation in Public Utilities: The Case of Argentina' *The Quarterly Review of Economics and Finance* 41: 585–607

Arthurs, Harry (2003), 'Constitutional Courage' *McGill Law Journal* 49: 3–19

Ascari, Sergio (2021) 'The Middle East and Africa' in Sergio Ascari (ed) *Natural Gas Price Control: Theoretical Issues and World Case Studies* (European University Institute) 177–214 at https://cadmus.eui.eu/bitstream/handle/1814/71599/QM-04-21-053-EN-N.pdf?sequence=1 (last accessed 11 December 2022)

Aspinall, Edward (2018) 'The New Nationalism in Indonesia' in Arianto A. Patunru, Mari Pangestu, and M. Chtaib Basri (eds), *Indonesia in the New World* (ISEAS–Yusof Ishak Institute) 35–51 at https://library.fes.de/pdf-files/bueros/bruessel/12662.pdf (last accessed 12 November 2022)

Bakan, Joel, Bruce Ryder, David Schneiderman, and Margot Young (1995) 'Developments in Constitutional Law: The 1993–94 Term' *The Supreme Court Law Review* 6: 76–126

Baker, Peter and Susan Glasser (2022) *The Divider: Trump in the White House, 2017–2021* (Doubleday)

Barak, Aharon (1992) 'The Israeli Constitutional Revolution: Protected Basic Rights' [on file with the author] translation of 'The Israeli Constitutional Revolution: Protected Human Rights' *Mishpat Umimshal: Law and Government in Israel* (1992) 1:1 (translated by Hillel Neuer)

—— (1993) 'A Constitutional Revolution: Israel's Basic Laws' *Constitutional Forum* 4: 83–4

—— (1997) 'The Constitutionalization of the Israeli Legal System as a Result of the Basic Laws and its Effect on Procedural and Substantive Criminal Law' *Israel Law Review* 31: 3–23

—— (2006a) *The Judge in a Democracy* (Princeton UP)

—— (2006b) 'Human Rights in Israel' *Israel Law Review* 39: 12–34

Barak-Erez, Daphne (2021) 'English Administrative Law in the Holy Land: Tradition and Independence' in Swati Jhaveri and Michael Ramsden (eds) *Judicial Review of Administrative Action Across the Common Law World: Origins and Adaptation* (Cambridge UP) 159–70

Baranger, Denis (2019) 'French Constitutional Law' in Roger Masterman and Robert Schütze (eds) *The Cambridge Companion to Comparative Constitutional Law* (CUP)

Bar-Eli, Avi and Ora Koren, '"I Can Not Do It Anymore": A Dramatic Resignation of David Gilo, The Antitrust Commissioner—The Full Letter' *The Marker* (25 May) at https://www.themarker.com/news/1.2643938 (last accessed 23 May 2020)

Barnaby, Bruce (2022) 'Derecho a la Consulta Previa: ¿Es suficiente reconocerlo como parte de nuestro bloque de constitucionalidad?' (15 March 2022) at https://idehpucp.pucp.edu.pe/notas-informativas/derecho-a-la-consulta-previa-es-suficiente-reconocerlo-como-parte-de-nuestro-bloque-de-constitucionalidad/ (last accessed 30 January 2023)

Barzilai, Gad and Yossi Shain (1991) 'Israeli Democracy at the Crossroads: A Crisis of Non-governability' *Government and Opposition* 26: 345–67

Batubara, Bosman (2014) 'Indonesian Government Continues to Serve Extractive Companies' Siftung Asienhaus (March 13) at https://www.asienhaus.de/archiv/asienhaus/kattermann-stiftung/user_upload/asienhaus-hintergrundinformation4-2014.pdf (last accessed 30 September 2022)

Baxi, Upendra (1980) *The Indian Supreme Court and Politics* (Eastern Book Company)

—— (1985) 'On How Not to Judge the Judges: Notes Towards Evaluation of the Judicial Role' *Journal of Indian Law Institute* 26: 211–37

—— (2000) 'The Avatars of Indian Judicial *Activism*: Explorations in the Geographies of (In)Justice' in Shashi Kant Verma and Kusum Kumar (eds) *Fifty Years of the Supreme Court of India: Its Grasp and Reach* (Oxford UP) 156–209

—— (2003) '"A Known but an Indifferent Judge": Situating Ronald Dworkin in Contemporary Jurisprudence' *International Journal of Constitutional Law* 1: 557–89

—— (2005) 'Postcolonial Legality' in Henry Schwartz and Sangeeta Ray (eds) *A Companion to Postcolonial Studies* (Blackwell) 540–55

—— (2006) *The Future of Human Rights*, 2nd edn (Oxford UP)

—— (2007) 'The Promise and Peril of Transcendental Jurisprudence: Justice Krishna Iyer's Combat with the Production of Rightlessness in India' in C.R. Kumar and K. Chockalingam (eds) *Human Rights, Justice, and Constitutional Empowerment* (Oxford UP) 3–25

Bear Creek Mining Corporation v. Republic of Peru (2017) Award, ICSID Case No. ARB/14/21 (30 November)

Bedjaoui, Mohammed (1979) *Towards a New International Economic Order* (Holmes & Meier)

Bedner, Adriaan (2016) 'Indonesian Land Law: Integration at Last? And for Whom?' in John F. McCarthy, J. and Kathryn Robinson (eds) *Land and Development in Indonesia* (ISEAS–Yusof Ishak Institute) 63–88

Bekkedal, Tarjei (2021) 'Autonomy or Unity? Investment Protection (ISDS) and the Principle of Equality Before the Law' *European Papers: A Journal on Law and Integration* 6: 713–39

Bell, John, Sophie Boyron, and Simon Whittaker (2008) *Principles of French Law*, 2nd edn (Oxford UP)

Bellak, Christian (2015) *Economic Impact of Investment Agreements*' Department of Economics, Vienna University of Economics and Business, Working Paper No. 200 (August) https://epub.wu.ac.at/4625/1/wp200.pdf (last accessed 1 July 2020)

Benvenisti, Eyal (1993) 'Judicial Misgivings Regarding the Application of International Norms: An Analysis of Attitudes of National Courts' *European Journal of International Law* 14: 159–83

—— (2008) 'Reclaiming Democracy: The Strategic Uses of Foreign and International Law by National Courts' *American Journal of International Law* 102: 241–74

—— (2014) *The Law of Global Governance* (Hague Academy of International Law)

—— (2016) 'Democracy Captured: The Mega-Regional Agreements and the Future of Global Public Law' *Constellations* 23: 58–70

Benvenisti, Eyal and George W. Downs (2009) 'National Courts, Domestic Democracy, and the Evolution of International Law' *European Journal of International Law* 20: 59–72

—— (2017) *Between Fragmentation and Democracy: The Role of National and International Courts* (Cambridge UP)

BG Group PLC v. Argentine Republic (2007) Final Award, Ad hoc, UNCITRAL, (24 December)

—— (2014) 572 US 25

Bickel, Alexander M. (1986) *The Least Dangerous Branch: The Supreme Court at the Bar of Politics*, 2nd edn (Yale UP)

Block, Fred (1987) 'Beyond Relative Autonomy: State Managers as Historical Subjects' in Fred Block, *Revising State Theory: Essays in Politics and Postindustrialism* (Temple UP)

Boelaert, Sonja (2021) 'Opinion 1/17 of the Court of Justice on the Legality, Under EU Law, of the Investor-to-State Dispute Settlement Mechanism Included in the CETA Agreement: A Case of Legal Pragmatism or the Dawn of a New Era?' in Andrea Bondi and Giorgia Sangiuolo (eds) *The EU and the Rule of Law in International Economic Relations: An Agenda for Enhanced Dialogue* (Elgar) 37–68

Bohmer, Lisa (2022) 'Peru Round-Up: New Cases, Threats, Awards, and Tribunals' *IA Reporter* (18 August)

Bonilla Maldonado, Daniel (2013) 'Self-Government and Cultural Identity: The Colombian Constitutional Court and the Right to Cultural Minorities to Prior Consultation' in Daniel Bonilla Maldonado (ed) *Constitutionalism in the Global South: The Activist Tribunals of India, Africa, and Colombia* (Cambridge UP) 243–90

Bonnitcha, Jonathan (2014) *Substantive Protection Under Investment Treaties: A Legal and Economic Analysis* (Cambridge UP)

Bonnitcha, Jonathan, Lauge N. Skovergaard Poulsen, and Michael Waibel (2017) *The Political Economy of the Investment Treaty Regime* (Oxford UP)

Boue, Juan Carlos (2022) 'Much More than a Footnote (or Three): Frank C. Hendryx and an Untold Story of Petroleum Concessions and the Genesis of ICSID' *Journal of International Dispute Settlement* 13: 1–40

Bourdieu, Pierre (2000) *Pascalian Meditations*, translated by Richard Nice (Stanford UP)

Boyron, Sophie (2013) *The Constitution of France: A Contextual Analysis* (Hart)

Brauch, Martin Dietrich (2021) 'Should the European Union Fix, Leave or Kill the Energy Charter Treaty?'(February) at https://scholarship.law.columbia.edu/sustainable_investment_staffpubs/190

—— (2022) 'The Agreement in Principle on ECT "Modernization": A Botched Reform Attempt that Undermines Climate Action' *Kluwer Arbitration Blog* (17 October) at http://arbitrationblog.kluwerarbitration.com/2022/10/17/the-agreement-in-principle-on-ect-modernization-a-botched-reform-attempt-that-undermines-climate-action/ (last accessed 10 November 2022)

Bregante, Pablo Mori and Micaela Ossio (2022) 'What if Peru (or Another Country) Leaves the ICSID Convention? Possible Recourses for Investors Facing a Potential Change in the Game' *Kluwer Arbitration Blog* (5 February) at http://arbitrationblog.kluwerarbitration.com/2022/02/05/what-if-peru-or-another-country-leaves-the-icsid-convention-possible-recourses-for-investors-facing-a-potential-change-in-the-game/ (last accessed 15 August 2022)

Breyer, Stephen (2015) *The Court and the World: American Law and the New Global Realities* (Alfred A. Knopf)

Brower, Charles N. (2021) 'Foreword' in José Rafael Mata Dona and Nikos Lavranos (eds) *International Arbitration and EU Law* (Elgar) xix–xx

Brown, Colin (2018) 'The European Union's Approach to Investment Dispute Settlement' The 3d Vienna Investment Arbitration Debate (22 June) at https://trade.ec.europa.eu/doclib/docs/2018/july/tradoc_157112.pdf (last accessed 30 June 2020)

—— (2021) 'The First Years of the European Union's Policy on Investment Dispute Settlement: From Initial Reforms to the Multilateral Investment Court' in Michael Hahn and Guillaume Van der Loo (eds) *Law and Practice of the Common Commercial Policy* (Brill) 73–97

Bullard, Alfredo (2012) 'Peru' in Jonathan C. Hamilton, Omar E. Garc'ia-Boli'var, and Hernando Otero (eds) *Latin American Investment Protections* (Martinus Nijhoff) 485–534

Bungenberg, Marc (2017) 'A History of Investment Arbitration and Investor–State Dispute Settlement in Germany' in Armand de Mestral (ed) *Second Thoughts: Investor–State Arbitration Between Developed Countries* (Centre for International Governance and Innovation) 259–84

Bungenberg, Marc and August Reinisch (2021) 'A Paradigm Change: The CETA Investment Chapter' *Zeitschrift für europarechtliche Studien* 24: 437–84

Butt, Simon (2011) 'Foreign Investment in Indonesia: The Problem of Legal Uncertainty' in Vivienne Bath and Luke Nottage (eds) *Foreign Investment and Dispute Resolution Law and Practice in Asia* (Routledge)

—— (2012) 'Indonesia's Constitutional Court: Conservative Activist or Strategic Operator?' in Björn Dressel (ed) *The Judicialization of Politics in Asia* (Routledge) at 112–30

—— (2014) 'The Position of International Law within the Indonesian Legal System' *Emory International Law Review* 28: 1–28

—— (2015) *The Constitutional Court and Democracy in Indonesia* (Brill Nijhoff)

—— (2018a) 'Constitutions and Constitutionalism' in Robert W. Hefner (ed) *Routledge Handbook of Contemporary Indonesia* (Routledge) 54–67

—— (2018b) 'Judicial Reasoning and Review in the Indonesian Supreme Court' *Asian Journal of Law and Society* 6: 67–97

Butt, Simon and Nicholas Parsons (2014) 'Judicial Review and the Supreme Court in Indonesia: A New Space for Law?' *Indonesia* 97: 55–85

Butt, Simon and Prayekti Murharjanti (2022) 'What Constitutes Compliance? Legislative Responses to Constitutional Court Decisions in Indonesia' *International Journal of Constitutional Law* 20: 428–53

Butt, Simon and Tim Lindsey (2009) 'The People's Prosperity? Indonesian Constitutional Interpretation, Economic Reform, and Globalization' in John Gillespie and Randall Peerenboom (eds) *Regulation in Asia: Pushing Back on Globalization* (Routledge) 270–95

—— (2012) *The Constitution of Indonesia: A Contextual Analysis* (Hart)

—— (2018) *Indonesian Law* (Oxford UP) 355–78

Cadilhac, Marie-Cécile and Cécile Rapoport (2018) '"In Between Seats …" The *Conseil Constitutionnel* and the CETA' *European Papers* 3: 811–32

Calamita, N. Jansen and Ayelet Berman (eds) (2022) *Investment Treaties and the Rule of Law Promise: The Asian Experience* (Cambridge UP)

—— (2022) *Investment Treaties and the Rule of Law Promise: An Examination of the Internalisation of International Commitments in Asia* (Cambridge UP)

Caldwell, Peter C. (2000) 'Is a "Social Rechsstaat" Possible? The Weimar Roots of a Bonn Controversy' in Peter C. Caldwell and William E. Scheuerman (eds) *From Liberal Democracy to Fascism: Legal and Political Thought in the Weimar Republic* (Humanities Press) 136–53

Calvert, Julia (2022) *The Politics of Investment Treaties in Latin America* (Oxford UP)

Calvert, Julia and Kyla Tienhaara (2022) 'Beyond "Once BITten, Twice Shy": Defending the Legitimacy of Investor–State Dispute Settlement in Peru and Australia' *Review of International Political Economy* at https://doi.org/10.1080/09692290.2022.2134172

Cameron Peter D. (2010) *International Energy Investment Law: The Pursuit of Stability* (Oxford UP)

Canada (2015) *Joint Review Panel Report on the Proposed White Points Quarry and Marine Terminal Project* (October 2007) (Queens Printer) at www.novascotia.ca/nse/ea/whites pointquarry/WhitesPointQuarryFinalReport.pdf (last accessed 13 August 2015)

—— (n.d.) 'How CETA Will Benefit Canada's Key Economic Sectors' at https://www.international.gc.ca/trade-agreements-accords-commerciaux/assets/pdfs/ceta-aecg/final_sectors_content-eng_v11.pdf (last accessed 16 December 2022)

Canada, Minister of Foreign Affairs (2013) 'Memorandum of Fact and Law of the Respondent, Minister Of Foreign Affairs Canada' Federal Court File No. T-153-13 (15 May) at http://www.international.gc.ca/trade-agreements-accords-commerciaux/assets/pdfs/disp-diff/ccfipa-03.pdf (last accessed 16 October 2022)

Carcassonne, Guy (1998) 'The Principle of Equality in France' *St. Louis–Warsaw Transatlantic Law Journal* 1998: 159–72

Cassarin, Ariel A., José Delfino, and María Eugenia Delfino (2007) 'Failures in Water Reform: Lessons from the Buenos Aires's Concession' *Utilities Policy* 15: 234–47

Cepeda Espinosa, Manuel José and David Landau (2017) *Colombian Constitutional Law: Leading Cases* (Oxford UP)

Cepeda-Espinosa, Manuel José (2004) 'Judicial Activism in a Violent Context: The Origin, Role, and Impact of the Colombian Constitutional Court' *Washington University Global Studies Review* 3: 529–700

Chan, Alexsia T. and Beverly K. Crawford (2017) 'The Puzzle of Public Opposition to TTIP in Germany' *Business and Politics* 19: 683–708

Chanegriha, Melisa, Chris Stewart, and Christopher Tsoukis (2017) 'Identifying the Robust Economic, Geographical and Political Determinants of FDI: An Extreme Bounds Analysis' *Empirical Economics* 52: 759–76

Chang, Ha-Joon (2002) *Kicking Away the Ladder: Development Strategy in Historical Perspective* (Anthem Press)

Choudhry, Sujit (1999) 'Globalization in Search of Justification: Toward a Theory of Comparative Constitutional Interpretation' *Indiana Law Journal* 74: 819–92

—— (2009) 'Migration as a New Metaphor in Comparative Constitutional Law' in Sujit Choudhry (ed) *The Migration of Constitutional Ideas* (Cambridge UP) 1–35

—— (2013) 'How to Do Comparative Law in India: Naz Foundation, Same Sex Rights, and Dialogical Interpretation' in Sunil Khilnani, Vikram Raghavan, and Arun K. Thiruvengadam (eds) *Comparative Constitutionalism in South Asia* (Oxford UP)

Choudhry, Sujit (1999) 'Globalization in Search of Justification: Toward a Theory of Comparative Constitutional Interpretation' *Indiana Law Journal* 74: 819–92

—— (2022) 'Domestic Public Law vs. Investor State Dispute Settlement: Comparing Remedies' IISD Working Paper [draft on file with the author]

Chriki, David, Tomer Broude, and Yoram Z. Haftel (2019) 'International Investment Agreements and their Impact on State Regulatory Space: The Case of Israel' forthcoming in Haifa Law Review [in Hebrew] at https://ssrn.com/abstract=3349255

Churchill Mining PLC (2012) 'Translated Decisions from the Appeal to the Supreme Court of Indonesia' *Transnational Dispute Management* (31 May)

Churchill Mining PLC and Planet Mining Pty Ltd v. Republic of Indonesia (2014a), Decision on Jurisdiction, ICSID Case No. ARB/12/14 and 12/40 (24 February)

—— (2014b) Procedural Order No. 12, ICSID Case No. ARB/12/14 and 12/40 (27 October)

—— (2014c) Procedural Order No. 13, ICSID Case No. ARB/12/14 and 12/40 (18 November)

—— (2015) Procedural Order No. 14, ICSID Case No. ARB/12/14 and 12/40 (12 January)

—— (2016) Award, ICSID Case No. ARB/12/14 and 12/40 (6 December)

—— (2019) Decision on Annulment, ICSID Case No. ARB/12/14 and 12/40 (18 March)

Cladgett, Helen Lord (1947) *Guide to the Law and Legal Literature of Peru* (Library of Congress)

Clarkson, Stephen (2003) 'Locked In? Canada's External Constitution under Global Trade Governance' *American Review of Canadian Studies* 33: 145–72

Clarkson, Stephen and Matto Mildenberger (2011) *Dependent America? How Canada and Mexico Construct U.S. Power* (University of Toronto Press)

Cohen, Amichai (2019) 'International Law in Israeli Courts' in Curtis Bradley (ed) *The Oxford Handbook of Comparative Foreign Relations Law* (Oxford UP) 519–36

Cohen, Amichai and Yuval Shany (2023a) 'The New Israeli Government's "Constitutional Law Reforms": Why Now? What Do they Mean? And What Will Happen Next?' *Lawfareblog.com* (14 February) at https://www.lawfareblog.com/new-israeli-governments-constitutional-law-reforms-why-now-what-do-they-mean-and-what-will-happen (last accessed 17 February 2023)

—— (2023b) 'The Fight Over Judicial Appointments in Israel' at https://www.lawfareblog.com/fight-over-judicial-appointments-israel (last accessed 21 February 2023)

Cohen, Benjamin J. (2008) *International Political Economy: An Intellectual History* (Princeton UP)

Cohen, Hedi (2014) 'The Israeli Gas and Oil Sector is Not Attractive for Investment' (2 November) at https://www.globes.co.il/news/article.aspx?did=1000983192 (last accessed 23 May 2020)

Coleman, Jesse, Lise J. Johnson, Lisa E. Sachs, and Nathan Lobel (2018) 'International Investment Agreements, 2017: A Review of Trends and New Approaches' in Lisa Sachs, Lise J. Johnson, and Jesse Coleman, *International Investment Law & Policy Yearbook 2017* (Oxford UP) 99–129

Colombia, República de, Departamento Nacional de Planeación (2001) 'Lineamientos de Política Para las Negociaciones Internacionales de Acuerdos de Inversión Extranjera' Documento 3135 (9 October) at https://www.mincit.gov.co/ministerio/normograma-sig/procesos-misionales/administracion-profundizacion-y-aprovechamiento-de/documentos-conpes/documento-conpes-3135-de-2001.aspx (last accessed 25 July 2001)

—— (2019) 'Possible Reform of investor-State Dispute Settlement (ISDS)' A/CN.9/WG.III/WP.173 (14 June) at https://documents-dds-ny.un.org/doc/UNDOC/LTD/V19/049/53/PDF/V1904953.pdf?OpenElement (last accessed 27 January 2024)

—— (2021) communicado de prensa (10 September)

Comella, Victor Ferreres (2021) *The Constitution of Arbitration* (Cambridge UP)

Commitment to Peace and Social Justice v. Minister of Finance (2005) HCJ 366/03 (all references are to the full English translation at https://versa.cardozo.yu.edu/opinions/commitment-peace-and-social-justice-society-v-minister-finance) (last accessed 21 May 2020)

Conant, Lisa (2018) 'Missing in Action? The Rare Voice of International Courts in Domestic Politics' in Marlene Wind (ed) *International Courts in Domestic Politics* (Cambridge UP) 11–42

Constitutional Tribunal of Peru (2017) 'Collective Bargaining in the Public Sector in Relation to the Civil Service Act: Exp. Nos. 025-2013-Pirre; 003-2014-PI/TC; 0008-2014-PUTC; 0017-2014-P1/1C, 26 April 2016' *International Labor Rights Case Law* 3: 14–22

Cope, Kevin L. and Hooman Movassagh (2018) 'National Legislatures: The Foundations of Comparative International Law' in Anthea Roberts, Paul B. Stephan, Pierre-Hugues Verdier, and Mila Versteeg (eds) *Comparative International Law* (Oxford UP) 271–91

Corbacho, Ana, Mercedes Garcia-Escribano, and Gabriela Inchauste (2003) 'Argentina: Macroeconomic Crisis and Household Vulnerability' *IMF Working Paper* WP/03/89 (April) at http://www.imf.org/external/pubs/ft/wp/2003/wp0389.pdf (accessed 28 January 2024)

Cordero Hijar, Magrit F. (2016) 'Peruvian State's Strategy for Addressing Investor State Disputes' *South Centre Investment Policy Brief* No. 6 at https://www.southcentre.int/wp-content/uploads/2016/11/IPB6_Peruvian-State%E2%80%99s-Strategy-for-Addressing-Investor-State-Disputes_EN.pdf (last accessed 16 August 2022)

Correa Henao, Magdalena (2018) 'Citizen Intervention in C-252/19' (4 December)

—— (2019) 'Tranformative Constitutionalism and Extreme Inequality: A Problematic Relationship' in Richard Albert, Carlos Bernal, and Julian Zaiden Benvindo (eds) *Constitutional Change and Transformation in Latin America* (Hart) 311–38

Correa, Magdalena, Enrique Prieto-Ríos, and José Manuel Álvarez (eds) *Foreign Investment Between International and Domestic Law: Translation of Judgement C-252/2019 of the Colombian Constitutional Court on the BIT Between France and Colombia* (Externado) at https://publicaciones.uexternado.edu.co/media/pageflip/acceso-abierto/pdf/foreign-investment-v3.pdf (last accessed 24 February 2023)

Côté, Christine (2016) 'Is it Chilly Out There? International Investment Agreements and Government Regulatory Autonomy' *AIB Insights* 16: 14–16

Cotula, Lorenzo (2020) Investment Disputes From Below: Whose Rights Matter' *IIED Blog* (23 July) at https://www.iied.org/investment-disputes-below-whose-rights-matter (last accessed 13 August 2022)

Cotula, Lorenzo and Nicolás M Perrone (2021) 'Investors' International Law and its Asymmetries: The Case of Local Communities' in Jean Ho and Mavluda Sattorova (eds) *Investor's International Law* (Hart) 71–88

Council of Canadians et al. v. Canada (Attorney General) (2005) CanLII 28426 (Ontario Superior Court of Justice)

—— (2006) CanLII 40222 (Ontario Court of Appeal)

Cox Robert W. (1986) 'Social Forces, States and World Orders: Beyond International Relations Theory' in Robert O. Keohane (ed) *Neorealism and Its Critics* (Columbia UP) 204–54

—— (1991) 'The Global Political Economy and Social Choice' in Robert W. Cox with Timothy J. Sinclair, *Approaches to World Order* (Cambridge UP, 1996) 191–208

—— (2002) 'Reflections and Transitions' in Robert W. Cox with Michael G. Schechter, *The Political Economy of a Plural World: Critical Reflections on Power, Morals and Civilization* (Routledge) 26–43

Crawford, James (2004) 'Affidavit of James Crawford' Ontario Superior Court of Justice, Court File No. 01-CV-208141 (15 July) at https://www.international.gc.ca/trade-agreements-accords-commerciaux/assets/pdfs/disp-diff/cupw-08.pdf (last accessed 16 October 2022)

Crockett, Antony (2017) 'The Termination of Indonesia's BITs: Changing the Bathwater, But Keeping the Baby' *Journal of World Investment & Trade* 18: 836–57

—— (2021) 'Investment Agreements and Regulatory Space in Indonesia' in Mahdev Mohan and Chester Brown (eds), *The Asian Turn in Foreign Investment* (Cambridge UP) 118–35

Cyr, Hugo (2009) *Canadian Federalism and Treaty Powers: Organic Constitutionalism at Work* (Peter Lang)

Dahl, Robert A. (1957) 'Decision-Making in a Democracy: The Supreme Court as a National Policy-Maker' *Journal of Public Law* 6: 279–95

—— (1970) *After the Revolution? Authority in a Good Society* (Yale UP)

Damuri, Yose Rizal and Mari Pangestu (2018) 'Who is Afraid of Economic Openness? People's Perceptions of Globalisation in Indonesia' in Arianto A. Patunru, Mari Pangestu, and M. Chtaib Basri (eds), *Indonesia in the New World* (ISEAS–Yusof Ishak Institute) 109–29

Dana, David A. and Thomas W. Merrill (2002) *Property: Takings* (Foundation Press)

Danzman, Sarah Bauerle (2019) 'The Political Economy of Bilateral Investment Treaties' in Markus Krajewski and Rhea Tamara Hoffman (eds), *Research Handbook on Foreign Direct Investment* (Edward Elgar) 11–38

Dargent, Eduardo (2009) 'Determinants of Judicial Independence: Lessons from Three "Cases" of Constitutional Courts in Peru (1982–2007)' *Journal of Latin American Studies* 41: 251–78

Davies, Hadyn (2016) 'Investor–State Dispute Settlement and the Future of the Precautionary Principle' *British Journal of American Legal Studies* 5: 449–86

Davies, Lowri (2022) 'Advancing a Human Rights-Based Approach to Access to medicines: Lessons Learned from the Constitutional Court of Peru' *Health and Human Rights Journal* 24: 49–58

De Boeck, Michael (2022) *EU Law and International Investment Arbitration: The Compatibility of ISDS in Bilateral Investment Treaties (BITs) and the Energy Charter Treaty (ECT) with the Autonomy of EU Law* (Brill)

De Mello, Michele (2022) 'Peruvian President Pedro Castillo Leaves Free Peru Party' *People's Dispatch* (translated from Portuguese) (1 July) at https://peoplesdispatch.org/2022/07/01/peruvian-president-pedro-castillo-leaves-free-peru-party/ (last accessed 15 August 2022)

de Mestral, Armand and Robin Morgan (2017) 'Does Canadian Law Provide Remedies Equivalent to NAFTA Chapter 11 Arbitration?' in Armand de Mestral (ed) *Second Thoughts: Investor–State Arbitration Between Developed Countries* (Centre for International Governance and Innovation) 155–86

de Vries, Rachel Frid (2017) 'Stability Shaken? Israeli High Court of Justice Strikes Down the Stabilization Clause in the Israeli Government's Gas Plan' *Journal of World Trade and Investment* 18: 332–41

Defensoría del Pueblo (2022) 'Defensoría del Pueblo rechaza sentencia del Tribunal Constitucional que desconoce consulta previa a los pueblos indígenas como derecho fundamental' (3 May 2022) at https://idehpucp.pucp.edu.pe/notas-informativas/derecho-a-la-consulta-previa-es-suficiente-reconocerlo-como-parte-de-nuestro-bloque-de-constitucionalidad/ (last accessed 30 January 2023)

Deutsches Institut für Entwicklungspolitik/German Development Institute (Deutsches Institut für Entwicklungspolitik)

Dimopoulos, Angelos (2019) 'European Union' in Markus Krajewski and Rhea Tamara Hoffman (eds), *Research Handbook on Foreign Direct Investment* (Edward Elgar) 434–56

Dixon, Rosalind and Samuel Issacharoff (2016) 'Living to Fight Another Day: Judicial Deferral in Defense of Democracy' *Wisconsin Law Review* 683–732

Dolzer, Rudolf and Christoph Schreuer (2012) *Principles of International Investment Law*, 2nd edn (Oxford UP)

Douglas, Zachary (2009) *The International Law of Investment Claims* (Cambridge UP)

Douma, W. Th. (2021) 'CETA: Gold Standard or Greenwashing?' in W. Th. Douma, C. Eckes, P. Van Elsuwege, E. Kassoti, A. Ott, and R. A. Wessel (eds) *The Evolving Nature of EU External Relations Law* (T.M.C. Asser Press) 61–99

Dressel, Björn and Tomoo Inoue (2018) 'Megapolitical Cases Before the Constitutional Court of Indonesia Since 2004: An Empirical Study' *Constitutional Review* 4: 157–87

Dunn, John (1969) *The Political Thought of John Locke: An Historical Account of the Argument of the 'Two Treatises of Government'* (Cambridge UP)

Dyevre, Arthur (2017a) 'Domestic Judicial Defiance and the Authority of International Legal Regimes' *European Journal of Law and Economy* 44: 453–81

—— (2017b) 'The French Constitutional Council' in András Jakab, Arthur Dyevre, and Giulio Itzcovitch (eds) *Comparative Constitutional Reasoning* (Cambridge UP) 323–55

Easton, David (1965) *A Systems Analysis of Political Life* (John Wiley & Sons, Inc.)

Echandi, Roberto (2013) 'Complementing Investor–State Dispute Resolution: A Conceptual Framework for Investor–State Conflict Management' in Roberto Echandi and Pierre Sauvé (eds), *Prospects in International Investment Law and Policy: World Trade Forum* (Cambridge UP) 270–305

Eckes, Christina and Laurens Ankersmit (2022) 'The Compatibility of the Energy Charter Treaty with EU Law' Amsterdam Centre for European Law University of Amsterdam (21 April) at https://www.clientearth.org/media/2n2po04j/report-on-ect-compatibility-with-eu-law.pdf (last accessed 9 February 2023)

Eco Oro Minerals Corp. v. Republic of Colombia (2021a), Decision on Jurisdiction, Liability and Directions on Quantum, ICSID Case No. ARB/16/41(9 September)

—— (2021b) Partial Dissent of Professor Philippe Sands (9 September)

Economist Intelligence Unit (2022) 'Peru: Country Report' (15 August)

Eder, Phanor J. (1960) 'Judicial Review in Latin America Comparative Constitutional Law' *Ohio State Law Journal* 21: 570–615

Egerton-Vernon, James et al. (2022) 'Peru's Struggle to Balance Foreign Investor's Rights and Local Communities Demands' *JD Supra* (25 May) at https://www.jdsupra.com/legalnews/peru-s-struggle-to-balance-foreign-3648838/ (last accessed 15 August 2022)

Elebiju, Afolabi (2011) 'NDDC v Nigerian LNG: Echoes and Lessons' *Lexology* (22 March 2019) at **https://www.lexology.com/library/detail.aspx?g=3a9fc159-f37d-4a50-81f0-b9ca9022cd36** (last accessed 10 June 2020)

Elkin, Stephen L. and Karol Edward Sołtan (eds) (1993) *A New Constitutionalism: Designing Political Institutions for a Good Society* (University of Chicago Press)

Elkins, Zachary, Andrew Guzman, and Beth Simmons (2006) 'Competing for Capital: The Diffusion of Bilateral Investment Treaties, 1960–2000' *International Organisation* 60: 811–46

Elster, Jon (1992) 'Intemporal Choice and Political Thought' in George Lowenstein and Jon Elster (eds) *Choice Over Time* (Russell Sage Foundation)

—— (2000) *Ulysses Unbound* (Cambridge UP)

Ely, John Hart (1980) *Democracy and Distrust: A Theory of Judicial Review* (Harvard UP)

Emmott, Bill (2003) 'A Survey of Capitalism and Democracy: Liberty's Great Advance' *The Economist* (28 June) 4: 4

Epstein, Lee and Jack Knight (1998) *The Choices Justices Make* (Congressional Quarterly Press)

—— (2000) 'Toward a Strategic Revolution in Judicial Politics: A Look Back, a Look Ahead' *Political Research Quarterly* 53: 625–61

Epstein, Lee, William M. Landes, and Richard A. Posner, *The Behavior of Federal Judges: A Theoretical and Empirical Study of Rational Choice* (Harvard UP 2013)

Erkan, Mustafa (2011) *International Energy Investment Law: Stability Through Contractual Clauses* (Kluwer)

Eslava, Luis (2009) 'Constitutionalization of Rights in Colombia: Establishing a Ground for Meaningful Comparisons' *Revista Derecho del Estado* 22: 185–229

Espinosa Velasco, Sebastián Xavier (2019) 'Ecuador and International Investment Law and Policy: Between Constitutional Sovereignty and State Responsibility', Doctoral dissertation, Masstricht University. https://cris.maastrichtuniversity.nl/en/publications/63379914-0d14-40fc-a3da-95579b27f96a (last accessed 7 February 2024)

—— (2020) 'The Evolution of the System of Foreign Investment Protection in Ecuador' in Julien Chaisse, Leïla Choukroune, and Sufian Jusoh (2021) *Handbook of International Investment Law and Policy* (Springer) 2645–76

European Commission (2010) 'Communication from the Commission to the Council, The European Parliament, the European Economic and Social Committee and the Committee of Regions: Toward a Comprehensive European International Investment Policy' COM (2010) 343 (Brussels, 7 July) at http://trade.ec.europa.eu/doclib/docs/2010/july/tradoc_146307.pdf (last accessed 10 November 2010)

—— (2023) 'Non-paper from the European Commission: Next Steps as Regards the EU, Euratom and Member States' Membership in the Energy Charter Treaty' (n.d.) at https://www.euractiv.com/wp-content/uploads/sites/2/2023/02/Non-paper_ECT_nextsteps.pdf (last accessed 25 February 2023)

European Union, Council of the (2010) 'Conclusions on a Comprehensive European International Investment Policy' (3041st Foreign Affairs Council meeting) (Luxembourg, 25 October) at http://www.consilium.europa.eu/uedocs/cms_data/docs/pressdata/EN/foraff/117328.pdf (last accessed 10 November 2010)

Fabbrini, Federico and András Sajó (2019) 'The Dangers of Constitutional Identity' *European Law Journal* 4: 457–73

Fach Gómez, Katia (2012) 'Ecuador's Attainment of the Sumak Kawsay and the role Assigned to International Arbitration' *Yearbook on Investment Law & Policy* 2010/11 451–87

Fairlie, Alan (2004) ¿Cuál TLC con EE.UU? *Tarea: Revista do Educación y Cultura* 50: 39

Fairlie Reinoso, Alan and Esthefany Herrera (2016) 'Canadian Mining Companies in Peru: Barrick and Bear Creek' *Latin American Policy* 7: 333–55

Fandiño-Bravo, Juan Camilo (2015) 'The Role of Constitutional Courts in International Investment Law and Investment Treaty Arbitration: A Latin American Perspective' *Max Planck UN Yearbook* 2015: 669–745 (LL.M. Thesis)

Farkash-Hacohen, Orit (2018) 'Facing a Gas Monopoly: The Power Game' Mossavar-Rahmani Center for Business & Government Associate Working Paper Series No. 2 (December) at https://www.hks.harvard.edu/centers/mrcbg/publications/awp/awp102 (last accessed 27 May 2020)

Favoreu, Louis (1992) 'The Principle of Equality in the Jurisprudence of the Conseil Constitutionnel' *Capital University Law Review* 21: 165–98

Febriani, Rika and Rachmi Hertanti (2019) 'Mining Permit Revocation Leads to the 1 Billion Dollar Lawsuit' in *Indonesia for Global Justice, ISDS Lawsuit: When Corporation Ignores State Sovereignty—The Compilation of ISDS Case Stories in Indonesia* (Indonesia for Global Justice) 25–28

Finer, S.E. (ed) (1979) *Five Constitutions: Contrasts and Comparisons* (Penguin)

Finkel, Jodi S. (2008) *Judicial Reform as Political Insurance: Argentina, Peru, and Mexico in the 1990s* (University of Notre Dame Press)

Fischer-Lescano, Andreas and Gunther Teubner (2004) 'Regime–Collisions: The Vain Search for Legal Unity in the Fragmentation of Global Law' *Michigan Journal of International Law* 25: 999–1046

Fitzpatrick, Peter (1992) *The Mythology of Modern Law* (Routledge)

Flemmer, Riccarda (2019) 'Prior Consultation as Door Opener: Frontier Negotiations, Grassroots Contestation, and New Recognition Politics in Peru' in Claire Wright and Alexandra Tomaselli (eds) *The Prior Consultation of Indigenous Peoples in Latin America: Inside the Implementation Gap* (Routledge) 107–18

Flores Nano, Lourdes (2015) *Economía Social de Mercado: Pasado, presente y futuro* (Lima: Instituto Pacífico)

Foster, Caroline E. (2012) 'Adjudication, Arbitration and the Turn to Public Law "Standards of Review": Putting the Precautionary Principle in the Crucible' *Journal of International Dispute Settlement* 3: 525–58

Foucault, Michel (2008) *The Birth of Biopolitics: Lectures at the Collège de France, 1978–1979*, translated by Graham Burchell (Palgrave Macmillan)

Fox, Donald T. and Anne Stetson (1992) 'The 1991 Constitutional Reform: Prospects for Democracy and the Rule of Law in Colombia' *Case Western Reserve Journal of International Law* 24: 139–63

Franck, Thomas M. (1968) *The Structure of Impartiality: Toward the Organization of World Law* (Macmillan)

Frankenberg, Günther (2018) *Comparative Constitutional Studies: Between Magic and Deceit* (Edward Elgar)

French, Chief Justice R.S. (2014) 'Investor-State Dispute Settlement—A Cut Above the Courts?' Supreme and Federal Courts Judges' Conference, Darwin (9 July 2014) at https://cdn.hcourt.gov.au/assets/publications/speeches/current-justices/frenchcj/frenchcj09jul14.pdf (last accessed 24 June 2020)

—— (2015) 'ISDS—Litigating the Judiciary' Chartered Institute of Arbitrators Centenary Conference, Hong Kong (21 March 2015) at https://cdn.hcourt.gov.au/assets/publications/speeches/current-justices/frenchcj/frenchcj21mar15.pdf (last accessed 24 June 2020)

Frieden, Jeffry and Lisa Martin (2003) 'International Political Economy: Global and Domestic Interactions' in Ira Katznelson and Helen V. Milner (eds) *Political Science: The State of the Discipline* (W.W. Norton) 118–46

Friedmann, Daniel (2016) *The Purse and the Sword* (Oxford UP)

Friedmann, Wolfgang (1971) *State and the Rule of Law in a Mixed Economy* (Steven and Sons)

Fromage, Diane and Bruno de Witte (2021) 'National Constitutional Identity Ten Years on: State of Play and Future Perspectives' *European Public Law* 27: 411–24

Furtado, Celso (2021) 'The Myth of Economic Development and the Future of the Third World' *Review of Political Economy* 33: 16–27

Galnoor, Itzhak and Dana Blander (2018) 'The Knesset: First among Equals?' in *The Handbook of Israel's Political System* (Cambridge UP) 99–142

García-Villegas, Mauricio (2001) 'Constitucionalismo Preverso: Normalidad y anormalidad constitucional en Colombia: 1957–97' in Boaventura de Sousa Santos and Mauricio García-Villegas (eds) *El caleidoscopo de las justicias en Colombia: Análisis socio-juridico*, Tomo 1 (Siglo del Hombre Editores) 317–70

Garden, Robert (2022) 'Eco Oro v Colombia: The Brave New World of Environmental Exceptions' *ICSID Review–Foreign Investment Law Journal* 38: 17–24.

Gargarella, Roberto (2010) *The Legal Foundations of Inequality: Constitutionalism in the Americas, 1776–1860* (Cambridge UP)

—— (2013) *Latin American Constitutionalism, 1810–2010: The Engine Room of the Constitution* (Oxford UP)

—— (2015) 'Latin American Constitutionalism: Social Rights and the "Engine Room" of the Constitution' in César Rodriguez-Garavito (ed) *Law and Society in Latin America* (Routledge) 83–92

—— (2017) 'The "New" Latin American Constitutionalism: Old Wine inn New Skins' in Armin Von Bogdandy, Eduardo Ferrer Mac-Gregor, Mariela Morales Anatoniazzi, and Flávia Piovesan (eds) *Transformative Constitutionalism in Latin America: The Emergence of a New Ius Commune* (OUP) 212–34

—— (2018) 'Latin American Constitutions in Trouble' in Mark A. Graber, Sanford Levinson, and Mark Tushnet (eds) *Constitutional Democracy in Crisis?* (Oxford UP) 177–90
Gáspár-Szilágyi, Szilárd (2021) 'Between Fiction and Reality: The External Autonomy of EU Law as a "Shapeshifter" After Opinion 1/17' *European Papers: A Journal on Law and Integration* 6: 675–92
Gavison, Ruth (2003) 'Constitutions and Political Reconstruction? Israel's Quest for a Constitution' *International Sociology* 18: 53–70
—— (2006) 'Legislatures and the Quest for a Constitution: The Case of Israel' *Review of Constitutional Studies* 11: 345–400
German Magistrates Association (2016) 'Opinion on the establishment of an investment tribunal in TTIP—the proposal from the European Commission on 16.09.2015 and 11.12.2015' No. 04/16 (February) at https://www.foeeurope.org/sites/default/files/eu-us_trade_deal/2016/english_version_deutsche_richterbund_opinion_ics_feb2016.pdf (last accessed 3 May 2016)
Germany, Federal Ministry for Economic Affairs and Climate Protection (2022) 'German Non-Paper Proposing Draft Decision of the CETA Joint Committee' (26 October 2022) at https://www.bmwk.de/Redaktion/DE/Downloads/G/german-non-paper-proposing-draft-decision-of-the-ceta-joint-committee.pdf?__blob=publicationFile&v=4 (last accessed 12 November 2022)
Géstion (2020) 'Los casos por los que Perú recibió US$ 110 millones tras ganar arbitrajes en el CIADI' *Gestión* (5 February) at https://gestion.pe/economia/los-casos-por-los-que-peru-recibio-us-110-millones-tras-ganar-arbitrajes-en-el-ciadi-fotos-nndc-noticia/ (last accessed 15 August 2022)
Getman, Julius (1988) *Labor Arbitration and Dispute Resolution Yale Law Journal* 88: 916
Gilbert, Daphne and Diana Majury (2006) 'Critical Comparisons: The Supreme Court of Canada Dooms Section 15' *Windsor Y.B. Access Just.* 24: 111
Gill, Stephen and A. Claire Cutler (eds) (2014) *New Constitutionalism and World Order* (Cambridge UP)
Ginsburg, Tom (2003) *Judicial Review in New Democracies: Constitutional Courts in Asian Cases* (Cambridge UP)
—— (2005) 'International Substitutes for Domestic Institutions: Bilateral Investment Treaties and Governance' *International Review of Law and Economics* 25: 107–23
Ginsburg, Tom, Mark D. Rosen, Georg Vanberg (2019) 'Introduction: Liberal Constitutions During Financial Crises' in Tom Ginsburg, Mark D. Rosen, and Georg Vanberg (eds) (2019) *Constitutions in Times of Financial Crisis* (Cambridge UP) 3–17
Givati, Yehonatan and Aharon Garber (2023) 'Juristocracy and Confidence in Courts' [unpublished]
Gjuzi, Jola (2018) *Stabilization Clauses in International Investment Law: A Sustainable Development Approach* (Springer)
Gloppen, Siri, Bruce M. Wilson, Roberto Gargarella, Elin Skaar, and Morten Kinander (2010) *Courts and Power in Latin America and Africa* (Palgrave Macmillan)
Golove, David M. and Daniel Hulsebosch (2010) 'A Civilized Nation: The Early American Constitution, The Law of Nations, and the Pursuit of International Recognition' *NYU Law Rev.* 85: 932–1066
Góngora-Mera, Manuel Eduardo (2017) 'The Block of Constitutionality as the Doctrinal Pivot of a *Ius Commune*' in Armin Von Bogdandy, Eduardo Ferrer Mac-Gregor, Mariela Morales Anatoniazzi, and Flávia Piovesan (eds) *Transformative Constitutionalism in Latin America: The Emergence of a New Ius Commune* (Oxford UP) 235–53

González-Bertomeu, Juan F. (2019) 'Judicial Politics in Latin America' in Rachel Sieder, Karina Ansolabehere, and Tatiana Alfonso (eds) *The Routledge Handbook of Law and Society in Latin America* (Routledge) 169–86

Gramercy Funds Management LLC. v. The Republic of Peru (2018a) 'Claimants' Third Amended Notice of Arbitration and Statement of Claim' (18 July), ICSID Case No. UNCT/18/2

—— (2018b) 'Respondent's Statement of Defense' (14 December) ICSID Case No. UNCT/18/2

—— (2022) 'Final Award' ICSID Case No. UNCT/18/2 (6 December)

Gramsci, Antonio (1971) *Selections From the Prison Notebooks of Antonio Gramsci*, Quentin Hoare and Geoffrey Nowell Smith (eds) (International Publishers)

Greenberg, Joel (2016) 'Israel's Supreme Court Blocks Leviathan Gasfield Deal' *The Financial Times* (28 March)

Grierson-Weiler, Todd and Iain Laird (2008) 'Standards of Treatment' in Peter Muchlinski, Federico Ortino, and Christoph Schreuer (eds) *The Oxford Handbook of International Investment Law* (Oxford UP) 260–302

Grinspun, Ricardo and Robert Kreklewich (1994) 'Consolidating Neoliberal Reforms: "Free Trade" as a Conditioning Framework' *Studies in Political Economy* 43: 33–61

Gross, Aeyal M. (1997) 'The Politics of Rights in Israeli Constitutional Law' *Israel Studies* 3: 80–118

Gross, Stuart G. (2003) 'Inordinate Chill: BITs, Non-NAFTA MITs, and Host-State Regulatory Freedom: An Indonesian Case Study' *Michigan Journal of International Law* 24: 893–960

Guardian, The (2023) 'Peru's president renews call for elections this year to bring end to protests' (30 January) at https://www.theguardian.com/world/2023/jan/30/perus-president-renews-call-for-elections-this-year-to-bring-end-to-protests (last accessed 1 February 2023)

Gudynas, Eduardo (2018) 'Extractivisms: Tendencies and Consequences' in Ronaldo Munck and Raúl Delgado Wise (eds) *Reframing Latin American Development* (Routledge) 61–76

Guinier, Lani (2008) 'Foreword: Demosprudence Through Dissents' *Harvard Law Review* 122: 6

Guzman, Andrew T. (1998) 'Why LDCs Sign Treaties that Hurt Them: Explaining the Popularity of Bilateral Investment Treaties' *Virginia Journal of International Law* 38: 639–88

Haas, Ernst B. (1983) 'Words Can Hurt You; or, Who Said What to Whom About Regimes' in Stephen D. Krasner (ed) *International Regimes* (Cornell UP) 23–59

Habermas, Jürgen (1996) *Between Facts and Norms: Contributions to a Discourse Theory of Law and Democracy*, translated by William Rehg (MIT Press)

Hacking, Ian (1990) *The Taming of Chance* (Cambridge UP)

Hailbronner, Michaela (2017) *Traditions and Transformations: The Rise of German Constitutionalism* (Oxford UP)

Hamida, Walid Ben (2009) 'Investment Treaties and Domestic Courts: A Transnational Mosaic Reviving Thomas Wälde's Legacy' in Jacques Werner and Arif Hyder Ali (eds) *A Liber Amicorum: Thomas Wälde—Law Beyond Conventional Thought* (Cameron May) 69–85

Hamilton, Alexander, James Madison, and John Jay (1961) *The Federalist Papers*, Introduction by Clinton Rossiter (New American Library)

Hastuti, Proborini (2019) 'Shifting the Character of the Constitutional Court Decision Influenced by Political Constellation in Indonesia' *Constitutional Review* 5: 330–57

Hathaway, Oona (2008) 'Treaties' End: The Past, Present, and Future of International Lawmaking in the United States' *Yale Law Journal* 117: 1236–373

Hee-jin, Kim (2012) 'Second Facebook Judge Disciplined' *Korean Joongang Daily* (15 February) at http://koreajoongangdaily.joinsmsn.com/news/article/article.aspx?aid=2948487&cloc=joongangdaily%7Chome%7Cnewslist1 (accessed 16 February 2012)

Heller, Hermann (1928) 'Political Democracy and Social Homogeneity' in Arthur Jacobson and Bernhard Schlink (eds) *Weimar: A Jurisprudence of Crisis* (University of California Press, 2008) 256–65

Helmke, Gretchen and Jeffrey K. Staton (2011) 'The Puzzling Judicial Politics of Latin America: A Theory of Litigation, Judicial Decisions, and Interbranch Conflict' in Gretchen Helmke and Julio Ríos-Figueroa (eds) *Courts in Latin America* (Cambridge UP) 306–31

Helmke, Gretchen and Julio Ríos-Figueroa (2011) 'Introduction: Courts in Latin America' in Gretchen Helmke and Julio Ríos-Figueroa (eds) *Courts in Latin America* (Cambridge UP) 1–26

Henckels, Caroline (2018) 'Should Investment Treaties Contain Public Policy Exceptions?' *Boston College Law Review* 59: 2825–44

Henderson, Simon (2017) 'Natural Gas Judgement Casts Shadow Over Israel's Energy Plans' The Washington Institute, at http://www.washingtoninstitute.org/policy-analysis/view/natural-gas-judgement-casts-shadow-over-israels-energy-plans (last accessed 26 April 2017)

Hendrianto, Stefanus (2010) 'Institutional Choice and the New Indonesian Constitutional Court' in Andrew Harding and Penelope Nicholson (eds) *New Courts in Asia* (Routledge) 158–77

—— (2016) 'The Divergence of a Wandering Court: Socio-Economic Rights in the Indonesian Constitutional Court' *Australian Journal of Asian Law* 16: 173–93

—— (2018) *Law and Politics of Constitutional Courts: Indonesia and the Search for Judicial Heroes* (Routledge)

Hendrianto, Stefanus and Fritz Siregar (2016) 'Developments in Indonesian Constitutional Law: The Year 2016 in Review' *iconnectblog.com* (8 October 2017) at http://www.iconnectblog.com/2017/10/developments-in-indonesian-constitutional-law-the-year-2016-in-review/#_edn19 (last accessed 9 May 2020)

Hepburn, Jarrod (2017) *Domestic Law in International Investment Arbitration* (Oxford UP)

—— (2019) '2017 Developments in Investment Treaty Arbitration' *Yearbook on Investment Law & Policy* 2017 (Oxford UP) 150–73

Hertanti, Rachmi (2019) 'Investment Disputes Bankrupting the State' in *Indonesia for Global Justice, ISDS Lawsuit: When Corporation Ignores State Sovereignty—The Compilation of ISDS Case Stories in Indonesia* (Indonesia for Global Justice) 44–7

Hill, Hal and Deasy Pane (2018) 'Indonesia and the Global Economy: Missed Opportunities?' in Arianto A. Patunru, Mari Pangestu, and M. Chtaib Basri (eds), *Indonesia in the New World* (ISEAS–Yusof Ishak Institute) 267–93

Hill, Jess (2015) 'ISDS: The Devil in the Trade Deal', Background Briefing, ABC Radio National Australia (26 July) at: http://www.abc.net.au/radionational/programs/backgroundbriefing/isds-the-devil-in-the-trade-deal/6634538 (last accessed 9 March 2023).

Hilpold, Peter (2021) 'So Long *Solange*? The PSPP Judgement of the German Constitutional Court and the Conflict Between the German and the European "Popular Spirit"' *Cambridge Yearbook of European Legal Studies* 23: 159–212

Himley, Matthew (2019) 'Mining and Development in Late-Nineteenth and Early-Twentieth-Century Peru' *Latin American Perspectives* 46: 27–46

Hindelang, Steffen (2015) 'Repellent Forces: The CJEU and Investor–State Dispute Settlement' *Archiv Des Völkerrechts 53*: 68–89
—— (2021) 'The Price for a Seat at the ISDS Reform Table: CJEU's Clearance of the EU's Investment Protection Policy in Opinion 1/17 and its Impact on the EU Constitutional Order' in Andrea Bondi and Giorgia Sangiuolo (eds) *The EU and the Rule of Law in International Economic Relations: An Agenda for Enhanced Dialogue* (Elgar) 127–53
Hirschl, Ran (1997) 'The "Constitutional Revolution" and the Emergence of a New Economic Order in Israel' *Israel Studies* 2: 136–55
—— (2004) *Towards Juristocracy: The Origins and Consequences of the New Constitutionalism* (Harvard UP)
—— (2014) 'The Origins of the New Constitutionalism: Lessons From the "Old" Constitutionalism' in Stephen Gill and A. Claire Cutler (eds) *New Constitutionalism and World Order* (CambridgeUP) 95–107
Hoffman, Rhea Tamara (2022) 'International Investment Law, Democratic Legitimacy, and the Protection of Human Rights: Transforming Constitutional Property Protection' in Stephan W. Schill and Christian J. Tams (eds) *International Investment Protection and Constitutional Law* (Elgar) 56–93
Hofnung, Menachem and Keren Weinshall Margel (2010) 'Judicial Setbacks, Material Gains: Terror Litigation at the Israeli High Court of Justice' *Journal of Empirical Legal Studies* 7: 664–92
Horesh, Hadar (2016) 'Why Do the Giant Companies for Gas and Oil Exploration Refuse to Invest in Israel?' Forbes (9 September) [in Hebrew] at http://www.forbes.co.il/news/new.aspx?Pn6VQ=K&0r9VQ=EIDDJ (last accessed 28 May 2020)
Horowitz, Donald L. (2013) *Constitutional Change and Democracy in Indonesia* (Cambridge UP)
Hunt v. T&N PLC [1993] 4 SCR 289
Hupacasath First Nation v. Canada (2013) FC 900 CanLii
—— (2015) FCA 4
IISD (2018) 'An Interview with Luis Guillermo Vélez—Director-General of Colombia's National Agency for the Legal Defense of the State' Investment Treaty News (24 April) 11–12 at https://cf.iisd.net/itn/2018/04/24/an-interview-with-luis-guillermo-velez-director-general-of-colombias-national-agency-for-the-legal-defense-of-the-state/ (last accessed 23 July 2020)
Indonesia (2007) 'Law Concerning Investment, No. 25 of 2007' *UNCTAD Compendium of Investment Laws* at http://investmentpolicyhub.unctad.org (last accessed 7 May 2021)
—— (2018) 'ISDS Reform: A Brief Perspective from Indonesia' (9 November) A/CN.9/WG.III/WP.156 at https://undocs.org/en/A/CN.9/WG.III/WP.156 (last accessed 8 May 2020)
Indonesia for Global Justice (2019) 'Statement of the Advocacy Team for Economic Justice in the Post-Court Verdict Concerning International Treaty Law' (9 January) at https://www.bilaterals.org/spip.php?page=print-art&id_article=38174 (last accessed 10 May 2020)
Indrayana (2010) 'In Search for a Democratic Constitution: Indonesian Constitutional Reform 1999–2002' *Media Hukum* 17: 115–31
Innis, Harold A. (1956) 'Government Ownership and the Canadian Scene' in Mary Quayle Innis (ed) *Essays in Canadian Economic History* (University of Toronto Press)
—— (1995) 'Unused Capacity as a Factor in Canadian Economic History' in Harold A. Innis, *Staples, Markets and Cultural Change: Selected Essays* (ed. Daniel Drache) (McGill-Queen's UP)

International Law Commission, Report of the Study Group (2006) *Fragmentation of International Law: Difficulties Arising From the Diversification and Expansion of International Law* (UN Doc A/CN.4/ L682)

International Monetary Fund (IMF) (2019) 'A Strategy for IMF Engagement on Social Spending' *IMF Policy Papers* 2019:16 (June 14)

Israel, Ministry of Energy (2015) 'Framework for Increasing the Quantity of Natural Gas Produced from the Tamar Natural Gas Field and Rapid Development of The Leviathan, Karish and Tanin Natural Gas Fields and Others' at http://www.energy-sea.gov.il/English-Site/Pages/Regulation/Gas%20Outline%20and%20Appendices%20and%20Explanatory%20Remarks%2016%20August%202015%20-English%20ver.%20with%20dislaimer.pdf (last accessed 23 May 2020)

Itturalde, Manuel (2013) 'Access to Constitutional Justice in Colombia: Opportunities and Challenges for Social and Political Change' in Daniel Bonilla Maldonado (ed) *Constitutionalism in the Global South: The Activist Tribunals of India, Africa, and Colombia* (Cambridge UP) 361–402

Jackson, Vicki C. (2010) *Constitutional Engagement in a Transnational Era* (Oxford UP)

Jacobsohn, Gary Jeffrey (2010) *Constitutional Identity* (Harvard UP)

Jacobsohn, Gary Jeffrey and Yaniv Roznai (2020) *Constitutional Revolution* (Yale UP)

Jailani, Abdulkadir (2015) 'Indonesia's Perspective on Review of International Investment Agreements' *South Centre Investment Policy Brief* No. 1 (July 2015); and South Centre, *Investment Treaties: Views and Experiences from Developing Countries* (South Centre 2015)

—— (2016) 'Indonesia's Perspective on Review of International Investment Agreements' in Kavaljit Singh and Burghard Ilge (eds) *Rethinking Bilateral Investment Treaties: Critical Issues and Policy Choices* (Both Ends/Madhyam/Somo) 113–27

Jamal, Amal (2019) 'Israel's New Constitutional Imagination: The Nation State Law and Beyond' *Journal of Holy Land and Palestine Studies* 18: 193–220.

Jandhyala, Srividya (2021) 'The Politics of Investor–State Dispute Settlement: How Strategic Firms Evaluate Investment Arbitration' in Julien Chaisse, Leïla Choukroune, and Sufian Jusoh (eds) *Handbook of International Investment Law and Policy* (Springer) 647–64

Jaremba, Urszula and Giancarlo Piscitelli (2021) 'Investment Tribunals vis-à-vis National Courts: Lessons on Judicial Dialogue from the EU' in Andrea Bondi and Giorgia Sangiuolo (eds) *The EU and the Rule of Law in International Economic Relations: An Agenda for Enhanced Dialogue* (Elgar) 69–88

Jensen, Fergus and Wilda Asmarini (2017) 'Freeport warns of arbitration as Indonesia mining dispute escalates' *Insider* (20 February) at https://www.businessinsider.com/r-freeport-warns-of-arbitration-as-indonesia-mining-dispute-escalates-2017-2 (last accessed 13 October 2022)

Jeong-pil, Kim (2011) 'Support for Judge Lambasted for Facebook Post' *The Hankyoreh* (29 November) at http://english.hani.co.kr/arti/english_edition/e_national/507657.html (accessed 16 February 2012)

Joerges, Christian (2003) 'Europe as Grossraum? Shifting Legal Conceptualisations of the Integration Project' in Christian Joerges and Navraj Singh Ghaleigha (ed) *Darker Legacies of Law in Europe: The Shadow of National Socialism and Fascism over Europe and its Legal Traditions* (Hart Publishing) 167–91

Johnson, Daniel (1968) 'What Quebec Wants' in *The Government of Québec and the Constitution* (L'office d'information et de publicité du Québec) 60–89

Kahana, Tsvi (2013) 'Majestic Constitutionalism? The Notwithstanding Mechanism in Israel' in Gideon Sapir, Daphne Barak-Erez, and Aharon Barak (eds) *Israeli Constitutional Law in the Making* (Hart) 73–90

Kahler, Miles (2001) 'Conclusion: The Causes and Consequences of Legalization' in Judith L. Goldstein, Miles Kahler, Robert O. Keohane, and Anne-Marie Slaughter (eds) *Legalization and World Politics* (MIT Press) 277–99

Kamphuis, Charis (2017) 'Litigating Indigenous Dispossession in the Global Economy: Law's Promises and Pitfalls' *Brazilian Journal of International Law* 14: 165–225

Kaufmann-Kohler, Gabrielle and Michele Potestà (2020) *Investor State Dispute Settlement and National Courts: Current Framework and Reform Options* in European Yearbook of International Economic Law (Springer)

Kawamura, Koichi (2013) 'President Restrained: Effects of Parliamentary Rule and Coalition Government on Indonesia's Presidentialism' in Yuko Kasuya (ed) *Presidents, Assemblies and Policy-Making in Asia* (Palgrave) 156–93

Keene, Edward (2002) *Beyond the Anarchical Society: Grotius, Colonialism and Order in World Politics* (Cambridge UP)

Kelsey, Jane (1999) 'Global Economic Policy-Making: A New Constitutionalism?' *Otago Law Review* 9: 535–55

Kennedy, David (1997) 'New Approaches to Comparative Law: Comparativism and International Governance' *Utah Law Review* [1997] 545–637

—— (2006) 'The "Rule of Law", Political Choices, and Development Common Sense', in David M. Trubek and Alvaro Santos (eds), *The New Law and Economic Development: A Critical Appraisal* (Cambridge UP) 95–173

—— (2009) 'The Mystery of Global Governance' in Jeffrey L. Dunoff and Joel P. Trachtman (eds) *Ruling the World? Constitutionalism, International Law and Global Governance* (Cambridge UP) 37–68

Kennedy, Duncan (2006) 'Three Globalizations of Law and Legal Thought: 1850–2000' in David M. Trubek and Alvaro Santos (eds), *The New Law and Economic Development* (Cambridge UP) 19–94

—— (2020) 'A Political Economy of Contemporary Legality' in Poul F. Kjaer (ed) *The Law of Political Economy: Transformations in the Function of Law* (Cambridge UP) 89–124

Kenney, Charles D. (2008) 'Peru, Constitutions' in Jay Kinsbruner and Erick D. Langer (eds) *Encyclopedia of Latin American History and Culture*, vol. 5, 2nd edn (Charles Scribner & Sons)

Keohane, Robert O. (1983) 'The Demand for International Regimes' in Stephen D. Krasner (ed) *International Regimes* (Cornell UP) 141–71

—— (1984) *After Hegemony: Cooperation and Political Discord in the World Political Economy* (Princeton UP)

Keohane, Robert O. and Joseph S. Nye, Jr. (2011) *Power and Interdependence*, 4th edn (Pearson)

Kim, Younsik (2017) 'Investor-State Arbitration in South Korean International Trade Policies: An Uncertain Future, Trapped by the Past' in Armand de Mestral (ed) *Second Thoughts: Investor-State Arbitration Between Developed Democracies* (Centre for International Governance Innovation) 447–81

Kindleberger, Charles P. (2000) ''International Public Goods Without International Government' in Charles P. Kindleberger, *Comparative Political Economy: A Retrospective* (MIT Press) 441–61

Kircheimer, Otto (1969) 'Weimar—And What Then? An Analysis of the Constitution' in Frederic S. Burin and Kurt L. Shell (eds) *Politics, Law, and Social Change: Selected Essays of Otto Kircheimer* (Columbia UP) 33–74

—— (1996) [1933] 'Remarks on Carl Schmitt's Legality and Legitimacy' in William E. Scheuerman (ed) *The Rule of Law Under Siege: Selected Essays of Franz L. Neumann and Otto Kircheimer* (University of California Press) 64–98

Klein, Yael (2015) 'Watch: Thousands Demonstrated Against the Natural Gas Outline' Jerusalem Online (8 November) at https://www.jerusalemonline.com/watch-thousands-demonstrated-against-natural-gas-outline-16989/ (last accessed 24 May 2020)

Kleinheisterkamp, J (2015) 'No Greater Rights ... But Still Meaningful Protection?' YouTube LSE Law (30) at https://www.youtube.com/watch?v=Drv0NmytvRU (last visited 1 April 2017)

Knop, Karen (2000) 'Here and There: International Law in Domestic Courts' *New York University Journal of International Law and Politics* 32: 501–35

Knörich, Jan and Axel Berger (2014) 'Friends or Foes? Interactions between Indonesia's International Investment Agreements and National Investment Law' Studies

Köller, Thomas (2022a) 'Ceta: Schmutzige Werte' *Telepolis* (14 July 2022) at https://www.heise.de/tp/features/Ceta-Schmutzige-Werte-7178860.html (last accessed 12 November 2022)

—— (2022b) 'Demokratie vs. Freihandel' *Telepolis* (9 April 2022) at https://www.heise.de/tp/features/Demokratie-vs-Freihandel-6667143.html (last accessed 12 November 2022)

Koshan, Jennifer and Jonnette Watson Hamilton (2011) 'Meaningless Mantra: Substantive Equality after Withler' *Review of Constitutional Studies* 16: 31–62

Krajewski, Markus and Rhea Tamara Hoffmann (2017) 'The European Commission's Proposal for Investment Protection in TTIP' Friedrich-Ebert-Stiftung

Krasner, Stephen D. (1983) 'Structural Causes and Regime Consequences: Regimes as Intervening Variables' in Stephen D. Krasner (ed) *International Regimes* (Cornell UP) 1–21

Kratochwil, Friedrich and John Gerald Ruggie (1986) International Organization: A State of the Art on an Art of the State' *International Organization* 40: 753–75

Kresalja, Baldo y César Ochoa (2009) *Derecho Constitucional Económico* (Lima: Fondo Editorial de la Pontificia Universidad Católica del Perú)

Kretzmer, David (1992) 'The New Basic Laws on Human Rights: A Mini-Revolution in Israeli Constitutional Law?' *Israel Law Review* 26: 238–46

—— (2002) *The Occupation of Justice: The Supreme Court of Israel and the Occupied Territories* (SUNY Press)

Kruck v Kingdom of Spain (2022) Partial Dissenting Opinion of Prof. Zachary Douglas KC, ICSID Case No. ARB/15/23 (13 September 2022)

Kumm, Mattias (2015) 'An Empire of Capital? Transatlantic Investment Protection as the Institutionalization of Unjustified Privilege' *Verfassungsblog* (27 May) at https://verfassungsblog.de/an-empire-of-capital-transatlantic-investment-protection-as-the-institutionalization-of-unjustified-privilege/ (last accessed 17 December 2022)

Kuo, Ming-Sung (2021) 'Whither Judicial Dialogue After Convergence? Finding Transnational Public Law in Nomos-Building' *International Journal of Constitutional Law* 19: 1536–58

Kurtz, Jürgen (2016) *The WTO and International Investment Law: Converging Systems* (Cambridge UP)

Lahav, Pnina (1993) 'Rights and Democracy: The Court's Performance' in Ehud Sprinzak and Larry Diamond (eds) *Israeli Democracy Under Stress* (Lynne Reiner) 125–52

Lajoie, Andrée (2003) 'Affidavit of Andree Lajoie' Ontario Superior Court of Justice, Court File No. 01-CV-208141 (14 May)

Laksono, Fajar, Sudarsono, Arief Hidayat, and Muchammad Ali Safaat (2017) 'Relation Between the Constitutional Court of the Republic of Indonesia and the Legislators

According to the 1945 Constitution of the Republic of Indonesia' *Constitutional Review* 3: 141–70

Landa, César and Isabel Sánchez (2021) 'The Social Issue in Peruvian Constitutionalism of the 20th Century and in the Case of the Constitutional Court: Influence of Socialist Constitutionalism?' *Russian Law Journal* 9: 44–69

Landau, David (2005) 'The Two Discourses in Colombian Constitutional Jurisprudence: A New Approach to Modeling Judicial Behavior in Latin America' *George Washington International Law Review* 37: 687–744

—— (2015) 'Beyond Judicial Independence: The Construction of Judicial Power in Colombia', Doctoral dissertation, Harvard University, Graduate School of Arts & Sciences, at http://nrs.harvard.edu/urn-3:HUL.InstRepos:14226088 (last accessed 25 July 2020)

Landau, Toby (2018) 'Arbitration in a Changing World' *Asian Dispute Review* 20: 154–9

Larik, Joris (2017) 'Prêt-à-Ratifier: The CETA Decision of the French Conseil Constitutionnel of 31 July 2017' *European Constitutional Law Review* 13: 759–77

Lasser, Mitchel de S.-O.-L'E. (2004) *Judicial Deliberations: A Comparative Analysis of Judicial Transparency and Legitimacy* (Oxford UP)

—— (2008) *Judicial Transformations: The Rights Revolution in the Courts of Europe* (Oxford UP)

Latour, Bruno (2010) *The Making of Law: An Ethnography of the Conseil d'État*, translated by Marina Brilman and Alain Pottage (Polity)

Law, David S. (2004) 'Generic Constitutional Law' *Minnesota Law Review* 89: 652–742

—— (2022) *Constitutionalism in Context* (Cambridge UP)

Lawrence, Sonia and Patrick Macklem (2000) 'From Consultation to Reconciliation: Aboriginal Rights and the Crown's Duty to Consult' *The Canadian Bar Review* 79: 252

Le Moullec, Caroline (2017) '*Churchill Mining Plc and Planet Mining PTY LTD v Republic of Indonesia*, ICSID Case No. ARB/12/14 and 12/40, Award, 6 December 2016' *European Investment Law and Arbitration Review* 2: 137–50

Leaver, Richard (1994) 'International Political Economy and the Changing World Order: Evolution or Involution?' in Richard Stubbs and Geoffrey Underhill (eds) *Political Economy and the Changing Global Order* (McClelland and Stewart) 130–44

Legum, Barton (2001) 'Federalism, NAFTA Chapter Eleven and the Jay Treaty of 1794' *ICSID News* 18(1) (Spring)

—— (2002) 'The Innovation of Investor-State Arbitration Under NAFTA' *Harvard International Law Journal* 43: 531–9

Lemaitre, Julieta (2015) 'Constitution or Barbarism? How to Rethink Law in "Lawless" Spaces' in César Rodriguez-Garavito (ed) *Law and Society in Latin America* (Routledge) 43–62

—— (2021) 'War' in Veena Das and Didier Fassin (eds) *Words and Worlds: A Lexicon for Dark Times* (Duke UP, 2021)

Leonard, Jenny (2017) 'Lighthizer: NAFTA 2.0 Could Shift "Paradigm", Win Over Labor and Business' *Inside US Trade* 35: 42 (20 October)

Lerner, Hanna (2011) *Making Constitutions in Deeply Divided Societies* (Cambridge UP)

Létourneau Tremblay, Laura (2022) 'In Need of a Paradigm Shift: Reimagining *Eco Oro v. Colombia* in Light of New Treaty Language' *Journal of World Investment & Trade* 23: 915–46

Lévesque, Céline (2017) 'The European Commission Proposal for an Investment Court System: Out with the Old, In with the New?' in Armand de Mestral (ed) *Second*

Thoughts: Investor–State Arbitration Between Developed Democracies (Centre for International Governance and Innovation) 59–88
Lighthizer, Robert (2023) *No Trade is Free: Changing Course, Taking on China, and Helping American Workers* (Broadside Books)
Lim, C.L., Jean Ho, and Martin Paparinskis (2018) *International Law and Arbitration: Commentary, Rewards and Other Materials* (Cambridge UP)
Lindsey, Tim (n.d.) 'IMF: Its Role in the Asia Pacific Region—Response to William Holder, Deputy Chief Counsel, IMF' at https://law.unimelb.edu.au/__data/assets/pdf_file/0005/1546304/imf1.pdf (last accessed 14 May 2020)
Lipson, Charles (1983) 'The Transformation of Trade: The Sources and Effects of Regime Change' in Stephen D. Krasner (ed) *International Regimes* (Cornell UP) 233–71
Lis, Jonathan (2019) 'Israel's Last Knesset Had Record-breaking Number of Bills Passed' Haaretz (29 April)
Locke, John (1964) *Two Treatises of Government*, critical edition by Peter Laslett (Cambridge UP)
López Zamora, Luis A. (2021) 'Constitutional Court of Peru' *Max Planck Encyclopedia of Comparative Constitutional Law* (Oxford UP)
Losari, Junjianto James and Michael Ewing-Chow (2016) 'Assessment of Indonesia's Recent Investment Policies and Recommendations for Its International Investment Agreements' in Kavaljit Singh and Burghard Ilge (eds) *Rethinking Bilateral Investment Treaties: Critical Issues and Policy Choices* (Both Ends/Madhyam/Somo 2016) 129–40
Luhmann, Niklas (2004) *Law as a Social System*, translated by Klaus Ziegert (Oxford UP)
Lumbantobing, John (2022) 'The Impact of Investment Treaties on the Rule of Law in Indonesia' in N. Jansen Calamita and Ayelet Berman (eds) *Investment Treaties and the Rule of Law Promise: An Examination of the Internalisation of International Commitments in Asia* (Cambridge UP) 67–95
Lupaka Gold Corp. v. Republic of Peru (2022) 'Republic of Peru's Memorial on Jurisdiction and Counter-Memorial on the Merits,' ICSID Case No. ARB/20/46 (24 March) at https://www.italaw.com/sites/default/files/case-documents/italaw170376.pdf (last accessed 24 September 2022)
Lurie, Guy and Yuval Shany (2022) 'The Institutional Role of the Judiciary in Israel's Constitutional Democracy' in Aharon Barak, Barak Medina, and Yaniv Roznai (eds) *Oxford Handbook on the Israeli Constitution* (Oxford UP, forthcoming), at https://ssrn.com/abstract=3762937
Lust, Jan (2012) 'Peru: Mining Capital and Social Resistance' in Henry Veltmeyer and James Petras (eds) *The New Extractivism: A Post-Neoliberal Development Model or Imperialism of the Twenty-First Century?* (Zed Books) 192–221
Made in the USA Foundation v. United States (1999) 56 F. Supp. 2d 1226 (N.D. Ala.)
—— (2001) 242 F.3d 1300 (11th Cir.)
Maffett, Mark, Mario Milone, and Wejia Rao (2023) 'The Impact of Foreign Investors' Challenges to Domestic Regulations' (18 May) *University of Miami Business School Research Paper No. 4451762* at SSRN: https://ssrn.com/abstract=4451762 (last accessed 28 January 2024)
Magnon, Xavier (2018) 'L'AECG devant le Conseil constitutionnel: Much ado about quite nothing!' *Revue française de droit constitutionnel* (2018) 113: 173–94
Mahfud, Moh (2011) 'Separation of Powers and Independence of Constitutional Court in Indonesia' (16–18 January) at https://www.venice.coe.int/WCCJ/Rio/Papers/INA_Mahfud_E.pdf (last accessed 11 May 2020)

Mandel, Michael (1999) 'Democracy and the New Constitutionalism in Israel' *Israel Law Review* 33: 259–321

Manger, Mark S. and Clint Peinhardt (2017) 'Learning and the Precision of International Investment Agreements' *International Interactions* 43: 920–40

Mansfield Jr., Harvey C. (1989) *Taming the Prince: The Ambivalence of Modern Executive Power* (The Free Press)

Marks, Susan (2000) *The Riddle of All Constitutions: International Law, Democracy and the Critique of Ideology* (Oxford UP)

Martinez, Jenny S. (2019) 'The Constitutional Allocation of Executive and Legislative Power Over Foreign Relations: A Survey' in Curtis A. Bradley (ed) *The Oxford Handbook of Comparative Foreign Relations Law* (Oxford UP) 97–114

Masri, Mazen (2017) 'Colonial Imprints: Settler–Colonialism as a Fundamental Feature of Israeli Constitutional Law' *International Journal of Law in Context* 13: 388–407

Mautner, Menachem (2011) *Law and the Culture of Israel* (Oxford UP)

—— (2018) 'Protection of Liberal Rights amidst War of Cultures (Kulturkampf) between Secular and Religious Groups' *Israel Yearbook on Human Rights* 48: 125–60

—— (2020) 'The Nation-State Law, the Escalation of the War of Cultures, and the Need for Declaring a Draw (13 October) [Hebrew] at https://ssrn.com/abstract=3710810

Maveety, Nancy (2002) 'The Study of Judicial Behavior and the Discipline of Political Science' in Nancy Maveety (ed) *The Pioneers of Judicial Behavior* (UMichigan Press)

McCann, Michael (1999) 'How the Supreme Court Matters in American Politics: New Institutionalist Perspectives' in Howard Gillman and Cornell Clayton (eds), *The Supreme Court in American Politics: New Institutionalist Interpretations* (UKansas Press)

McDonnell, Emma (2015) 'The Co-Constitution of Neoliberalism, Extractive Industries, and Indigeneity: Anti-Mining Protests in Puno, Peru' *The Extractive Industries and Society* 2: 112–23

McDougal, Myres S. and Asher Lans (1945) 'Treaties and Congressional-Executive or Presidential Agreements: Interchangeable Instruments of National Policy: I.' *Yale Law Journal* 54: 181–351

McGinnis, John O. and Mark L. Movsesian (2000) 'The World Trade Constitution' *Harvard Law Review* 114: 511–605

McLachlan, Campbell (2014) *Foreign Relations Law* (Oxford UP)

—— (ed) (2022) *The Institute of International Law's Resolution on the Equality of Parties Before International Investment Tribunals: Introduction, Text and Commentaries* (Cambridge UP)

McLachlan, Campbell, Laurence Shore, and Matthew Weiniger (2017) *International Investment Arbitration: Substantive Principles*, 2nd edn (Oxford UP)

Mercredi, Ovide (1998) 'The MAI and First Nations' in Andrew Jackson and Matthew Sanger (eds) *Dismantling Democracy: The Multilateral Agreement and its Impact* (Lorimer) 63–82

Merhof, Katrin (2015) 'Building a Bridge Between Reality and the Constitution: The Establishment and Development of the Colombian Constitutional Court' *International Journal of Constitutional Law* 13: 714–32

Merino Acuña, Roger (2015) 'The Politics of Extractive Governance: Indigenous Peoples and Socio-Environmental Conflicts' *Extractive Industries and Society* 2: 85–92

Merino, Roger (2022) 'Extractive Constitutions: Constitutional Change and Developmental Paths in Latin America' *Law and Development Review* 15: 169–200

Mertins-Kirkwood, Hadrian (2022) 'On the Offensive: How Canadian Companies Use Trade and Investment Agreements to Bully Foreign Governments for Billions' Canadian

Centre for Policy Alternatives (19 May) at https://policyalternatives.ca/sites/default/files/uploads/publications/National%20Office/2022/05/On%20the%20Offensive.pdf (last accessed 16 October 2022)

Meydani, Assaf (2011a) *The Israeli Supreme Court and the Human Rights Revolution* (Cambridge UP)

—— (2011b) 'The Intervention of the Israeli High Court of Justice in Government Decisions: An Empirical, Quantitative Perspective' *Israel Studies* 16: 174–90

Miéral, Julien (2017) 'The CETA, the German Federal Constitutional Court and the Distribution of Competences Between the EU and its Member States' (7 November 2017) at https://rsiblog.blogactiv.eu/2017/11/07/the-ceta-the-german-federal-constitutional-court-and-the-distribution-of-competences-between-the-eu-and-its-member-states/

Mietzner, Marcus (2010) 'Political Conflict Resolution and Democratic Consolidation in Indonesia: The Role of the Constitutional Court' *Journal of East Asian Studies* 10: 397–424

Millet, François-Xavier (2019) 'Constitutional Identity in France: Vices and—Above All—Virtues' in Christian Calliess and Gerhard van der Schyff (eds) *Constitutional Identity in a Europe of Multilevel Constitutionalism* (Cambridge UP) 134–52

Moehlecke, Carolina (2020) 'The Chilling Effect of International Investment Disputes: Limited Challenges to State Sovereignty' *International Studies Quarterly* 64: 1–12

Moore Jr., Barrington (1966) *Social Origins of Dictatorship and Democracy: Lord and Peasant in the Making of the Modern World* (Beacon Press)

Moore, Jen and Manuel Perez Rocha (2019) 'Extraction Casino: Mining Companies Gambling with Latin American Lives and Sovereignty Through International Arbitration' (Mining Watch Canada, Institute for Policy Studies and Center for International Environmental Law) (April) at https://ips-dc.org/wp-content/uploads/2019/07/ISDS-Mining-Latin-America-Report-Formatted-ENGLISH.pdf (last accessed 23 July 2020)

Moore, John Bassett (1898) *History and Digest of the International Arbitrations to Which the United States Has Been a Party*, Vol. 1 (Government Printing Office)

Moran, Theodore H. (1998) 'The Changing Nature of Political Risk' in Theodore H. Moran (ed) *Managing International Political Risk* (Blackwell)

Movement for Quality Government v. Prime Minister of Israel (2016a) HCJ 4374/15 English-language summary, at https://versa.cardozo.yu.edu/opinions/movement-quality-government-v-prime-minister (last accessed 8 December 2022) and https://supremedecisions.court.gov.il/Home/Download?path=EnglishVerdicts/15/740/043/t63&fileName=15043740.T63&type=4 ((last accessed 8 December 2022)

—— (2016b) HCJ 4374/15 (27 March) [in Hebrew]

—— (2016c) 'Petition' in HCJ 4374/15

Muñoz, Paula (2021) 'Peru's Democracy in Search of Representation' in Thomas Carothers and Andreas Feldmann (eds) *Divisive Politics and Democratic Dangers in Latin America* (Carnegie Endowment for Peace) 27–31 at https://carnegieendowment.org/2021/02/17/peru-s-democracy-in-search-of-representation-pub-83787 (last accessed 15 August 2022)

Murillo-Castaño, Gabriel and Victoria Gómez-Segura (2005) 'Institutions and Citizens in Colombia: The Changing Nature of a Difficult Relationship' *Social Forces* 84: 1–18

Murphy, Walter F. (1964) *Elements of Judicial Strategy* (University of Chicago Press)

Nardi, Dominic J. (2018) 'Can NGOs Change the Constitution? Civil Society and the Indonesian Constitutional Court' *Contemporary Southeast Asia* 40: 247–78

Navot, Doron and Yoav Peled (2009) 'Towards a Constitutional Counter-Revolution in Israel?' *Constellations* 16: 429–44

Navot, Suzie (2014) *The Constitution of Israel: A Contextual Analysis* (Hart)

—— (2023) 'The Supreme Court Hearing on Reasonableness: Law without Enforcement' Israeli Democracy Institute (20 September) at https://en.idi.org.il/articles/50943 (last accessed 26 September 2023)

Newsbeezer.com (2016) 'Grupo Gloria: Yura sold 70% of its stake in Industrias Cachimayo to Enaex' https://newsbeezer.com/perueng/grupo-gloria-yura-sold-70-of-its-stake-in-industrias-cachimayo-to-enaex/ (last accessed 9 September 2022)

Neyer, Jürgen (2012) *The Justification of Europe: A Political Theory of Supranational Integration* (Oxford UP)

Niger Delta Development Commission v. Nigeria Liquified Natural Gas Company (2009) 1 Tax Law Reports of Nigeria 25 (Federal High Court of Nigeria)

—— (2011) 4 Tax Law Reports of Nigeria 1; (2010) LPELR-CA/PH/520/2007 (Court of Appeal of Nigeria)

Noriega, Illari Aragon (2012) 'Judicial Review of the Right to Health and its Progressive Realization: The Case of the Constitutional Court of Peru' *UCL Journal of Law and Jurisprudence* 1: 166–87

Obama, President Barack (2016) 'President Obama: The TPP Would Let America, not China, Lead the Way on Global Trade' *The Washington Post* (2 May)

Obregón, Liliana (2008) 'Latin American International Law' in David Armstrong, Jutta Brunée, Michael Byers, John H. Jackson, and David Kennedy (eds) *Routledge Handbook of International Law* (Routledge) 154–64

Ochoa-Sánchez, Juan Carlos (2022) 'Constitutional Review of Negotiated International Investment Agreements: Strengths and Shortcomings of the Colombian Constitutional Court's Approach' *International Journal of Constitutional Law* 20: 844–68

Organization of American States [OAS] (2022) 'IACHR Concerned About Peru's Constitutional Court Decision Affecting the Rights of Indigenous Peoples' IACHR Press Release (April 6) at https://www.oas.org/en/IACHR/jsForm/?File=/en/iachr/media_center/PReleases/2022/071.asp (last accessed 23 August 2022)

Ortino, Frederico (2013) 'The Investment Treaty System as Judicial Review' *The American Review of International Arbitration* 24: 437–68

Ostřanský, Josef (2018) 'An Exercise in Equivocation: A Critique of Legitimate Expectations as a General Principle of Law under the Fair and Equitable Treatment Standard' in Andrea Gattini, Attila Tanzi, and Filippo Fontanelli (eds) *General Principles of Law and International Investment Arbitration* (Brill/Nijhoff) 344–77

Pacuzzi, David J. (1994) 'International Trade and Foreign Investment in Colombia: A Sound Economic Policy Amidst Crisis' *Florida Journal of International Law* 10: 449–50

Paparinskis, Martins (2020) 'A Case Against Crippling Compensation in International Law of State Responsibility' *The Modern Law Review* 83: 1246–86

Peck, Jamie (2010) *Constructions of Neoliberal Reason* (Oxford UP)

Perrone, Nicolás (2021) *Investment Treaties and the Legal Imagination: How Foreign Investors Play by Their Own Rules* (Oxford UP)

Peters, Anne (2009) 'Supremacy Lost: International Law Meets Domestic Constitutional Law' *Vienna Online Journal on International Constitutional Law* 3: 170–98

Peterson, Luke Eric (2018) 'Colombia Faces Two New Investment Treaty Claims Dating to Late 1990s Banking Crisis' *Investment Arbitration Reporter* (12 March) (last accessed 29 July 2020)

Planet Mining Pty Ltd v. Republic of Indonesia (2014), Decision on Jurisdiction, ICSID Case No. ARB/12/14 and 12/40 (24 February)
Pompe, Sebastiaan (2005) *The Indonesian Supreme Court: A Study of Institutional Collapse* (Cornell UP)
Porat, Iddo (2013) 'The Use of Foreign Law in Israeli Constitutional Adjudication' in Gideon Sapir, Daphne Barak-Erez, and Aharon Barak (eds) *Israeli Constitutional Law in the Making* (Hart) 151–72
—— (2018) 'The Platonic Conception of the Israeli Constitution' in Rosalind Dixon and Adrienne Stone (2018) (eds) *The Invisible Constitution in Comparative Perspective* (Cambridge UP) 268–97
Porritt, Edward (1992) *The Fiscal and Diplomatic Freedom of the British Overseas Dominions* (Oxford UP)
Porter, Bruce (2007) 'Application for Leave to Appeal in *Bruce Porter on his own behalf and on behalf of all Members of the Charter Committee on Poverty Issues v. The Queen* (19 January) at http://www.povertyissues.org/documents/CCPI%20NAFTA%20SCC%20%20Leave%20Application.pdf (last accessed 16 October 2022)
Posner, Richard A. (2005) 'Foreword: A Political Court' *Harvard Law Review* 119: 32–102
—— (2008) *How Judges Think* (Harvard UP)
Poulsen, Lauge N. Skovegaard (2015) *Bounded Rationality and Economic Diplomacy: The Politics of Investment Treaties in Developing Countries* (Cambridge UP)
Poulsen, Lauge N. Skovergaard, Jonathan Bonnitcha, and Jason Yackee (2015) 'Transatlantic Investment Treaty Protection' in Daniel S. Hamilton and Jacques Pelkmans (eds) *Rule-Makers or Rule-Takers? Exploring the Transatlantic Trade and Investment Partnership* (Rowman and Littlefield)
Price, David (2017) 'Indonesia's Bold Strategy on Bilateral Investment Treaties: Seeking an Equitable Climate for Investment?' *Asian Journal of International Law* 7: 124–51
Prieto Muñoz, Jose Gustavo (2022) 'Constitutional Courts and International Investment Law in Latin America: Between Escalation and Conditional Coexistence' in Stephan Schill and Christian J. Tams (eds) *International Investment Protection and Constitutional Law* (Edward Elgar) 149–79
—— (2019) 'The Colombian Consitutional Court Judgment C-252/19: A New Frontier for Reform in International Investment Law' EJIL Talk (29 July) at https://www.ejiltalk.org/the-colombian-constitutional-court-judgment-c-252-19-a-new-frontier-for-reform-in-international-investment-law/ (last accessed 19 August 2020)
Przeworski, Adam (1991) *Democracy and the Market: Political and Economic Reforms in Eastern Europe and Latin America* (Cambridge UP)
PT Newmont Nusa Tenggara (PTNNT) (2014) 'Arbitration Filed Over Export Restrictions in Indonesia' Press Release (1 July) at https://www.sec.gov/Archives/edgar/data/1164727/000119312514256613/d749754dex991.htm (last accessed 30 September 2022)
Ptak, Ralf (2009) 'Neoliberalism in Germany: Revisiting the Ordoliberal Foundations of the Social Market Economy' in Philip Mirowski and Dieter Plehwe (eds) *The Road from Mont Pèlerin: The Making of the Neoliberal Thought Collective* (Harvard UP) 98–138
Public Citizen (2018) 'Research Brief: Termination of Bilateral Investment Treaties Has Not Negatively Affected Countries' Foreign Direct Investment Inflows' (August) at https://www.citizen.org/wp-content/uploads/pcgtw_fdi-inflows-from-bit-termination_1.pdf (last accessed 21 January 2023)
Quijano, Aníbal (2000) 'Coloniality of Power, Eurocentrism, and Latin America' *Nepantla: Views from the South* 1: 533–80

—— (2005) 'The Challenge of "Indigenous Movement" in Latin America' *Socialism and Democracy* 19: 55–78

Rabin, Yoram and Arnon Gutfel (2007) '*Marbury v. Madison* and Its Impact on Israeli Constitutional Law' University of Miami *International and Comparative Law Review* 15: 303–35

Rahn, Kim (2011) 'Judges Revolt Against FTA Gaining Momentum' *The Korea Times*, at http://english.hani.co.kr/arti/english_edition/e_national/507657.html (accessed 16 February 2012)

Rajput, Aniruddha (2021) 'National Courts as Actors in Investment Arbitration' in Catherine Titi (ed) *Public Actors in International Investment Law in European Yearbook of International Economic Law* (Cambridge UP) 37–56

Ratner, Stephen R. (2020) 'International Investment Law and Domestic Investment Rules: Tracing the Upstream and Downstream Flows' *Journal of World Investment & Trade* 21: 7–33

Reich, Arie (2018) 'Israel's Foreign Investment Protection Regime in View of Developments in its Energy Sector' *Journal of World Investment and Trade* 19: 41–94

Reichman Amnon (2013) 'Judicial Constitution Making in a Divided Society: The Israeli Case' in Diana Kapiszewski, Gordon Silverstein, Robert A. Kagan (eds) *Consequential Courts: Judicial Roles in Global Perspective* (Cambridge UP) 233–61

Reiner, Clara and Christoph Schreuer (2009) 'Human Rights and International Investment Arbitration' in Pierre-Marie Dupuy et al. (eds) *Human Rights in International Investment Law and Arbitration* (Oxford UP)

Reinisch, August (2017) 'The European Union and Investor–State Dispute Settlement: From Investor-State Arbitration to a Permanent Investment Court' in Armand de Mestral (ed) *Second Thoughts: Investor-State Arbitration Between Developed Democracies* (Centre for International Governance and Innovation) 333–76

—— (2020) *Advanced Introduction to International Investment Law* (Edward Elgar)

Riffel, Christian (2020) 'Does Investor-State Dispute Settlement Discriminate Against Nationals?' *German Law Journal* 21: 197–222

Riles, Annelise (1999) 'Wigmore's Treasure Box: Comparative Law in the Era of Information' *Harvard International Law Journal* 40: 221–83

Ríos-Figueroa, Julio (2016) *Constitutional Courts as Mediators: Armed Conflict, Civil–Military Relations, and the Rule of Law in Latin America* (Cambridge UP)

Robert-Cuendet, Sabrina (2022) 'Investor–State Dispute Settlement and French Constitutional Law: The *Conseil constitutionnel*'s Decision of 31 July 2017 on CETA' in Stephan Schill and Christian Tams (eds) *International Investment Protection and Constitutional Law* (Elgar) 119–48

Roberts, Anthea (2011) 'Comparative International Law? The Role of National Courts in Creating and Enforcing International Law' *International and Comparative Law Quarterly* 60: 57–92

Roberts, Anthea and Christina Trahanas (2014) 'Judicial Review of Investment Treaty Awards: *BG Group v. Argentina*' *The American Journal of International Law* 108: 750–63

Robinson, Kathryn (2016) 'Mining, Land and Community Rights in Indonesia' in John F. McCarthy, J. and Kathryn Robinson (eds) *Land and Development in Indonesia* (ISEAS–Yusof Ishak Institute) 141–64

Rodríguez, César, Mauricio García-Villegas, and Rodrigo Uprimny (2003) 'Justice and Society in Colombia: A Sociolegal Analysis of Colombian Courts' in Lawrence M. Friedman and Rogelio Pérez-Perdomo (eds) *Legal Culture in the Age of Globalization: Latin America and Latin Europe* (Stanford UP) 134–83

Rodriguez-Garavito, César (2015) 'Constitutions in Action: The Impact of Judicial Activism on Socioeconomic Rights in Latin America' in César Rodriguez-Garavito (ed) *Law and Society in Latin America* (Routledge) 112–40

Rodríguez-Garavito, César and Diana Rodríguez-Franco (2015) *Radical Deprivation on Trial: The Impact of Judicial Activism on Socioeconomic Rights in the Global South* (Cambridge UP)

Rodríguez-Raga, Juan Carlos (2011) 'Strategic Deference in the Colombian Constitutional Court, 1996–2006' in Gretchen Helmke and Julio Rios-Figuerora (eds) *Courts in Latin America* (Cambridge UP) 81–98

Rosenthal, Maoz, Gad Barzilai, and Assaf Meydani (2016) 'Constitutional Judicial Review, Chief Justices, and Judges' Preferences: Institutional Lessons and Israel's High Court of Justice' prepared for the 2016 Annual Meeting of the Empirical Legal Studies Society, at https://papers.ssrn.com/sol3/papers.cfm?abstract_id=2815665 (last accessed 28 May 2020)

Roux, Theunis and Fritz Siregar (2016) 'Trajectories of Curial Power: The Rise, Fall and Partial Rehabilitation of the Indonesian Constitutional Court' *Australian Journal of International Law* 16: 1–21

Roznai, Yaniv (2018a) 'Israel: A Crisis of Liberal Democracy?' in Mark Graber, Sandy Levinson, and Mark Tushnet (eds), *Constitutional Democracy in Crisis?* (Oxford UP) 355–75

—— (2018b) 'Constitutional Paternalism: The Israeli Supreme Court as Guardian of the Knesset' *Verfassung und Recht in Übersee* 51: 415–36

Saffron, Maria Paula (2007) 'Can Constitutional Courts be Counterhegemonic Powers Vis-à-vis Neoliberalism: The Case of the Colombian Constitutional Court' *Seattle Journal for Social Justice* 5: 533–68

Salacuse, Jeswald W. (2010) 'The Emerging Global Regime for Investment' *Harvard International Law Journal* 51: 427–74

Sallon, Hélène (2005) 'The Judicialization of Politics in Israel: Promoting Arab Collective Claims in the Judicial Arena' *Bulletin du Centre de recherche français à Jérusalem* 16: 287–300, at http://journals.openedition.org/bcrfj/259 (last accessed 29 May 2020)

Sanborn, Cynthia and Álvaro Peredes (2014) 'Country Study: Peru' *Americas Quarterly* (Spring) 55–60

Sands, Anna (2020) 'Does the Investment Treaty Regime Promote Good Governance? The Case of Mining in Santurbán, Colombia' *Investment Treaty News* 11(4): 14–16, at https://www.iisd.org/itn/en/2020/12/19/does-the-investment-treaty-regime-promote-good-governance-the-case-of-mining-in-santurban-colombia-anna-sands/ (last accessed 13 August 2022)

Sapir, Gideon (2018) *The Israeli Constitution: From Evolution to Revolution* (Oxford UP)

Sarigih, Bagus BT (2012) 'SBY Frets Over Int'l Arbitration' *The Jakarta Post* (29 June) 1

Sassen, Saskia (2002) *Territory, Authority, Rights: From Medieval to Global Assemblages* (Princeton UP)

Sattorova, Mavluda (2018) *The Impact of Investment Treaty Law on Host States: Enabling Good Governance?* (Hart)

Savitiri, Dewi Nurul (2019) 'Constitutional Preview and Review of International Treaties: France and Indonesia Compared' *Constitutional Review* 5: 39–68

Schacherer, Stefanie and Rhea Tamara Hoffman (2019) 'International Investment Law and Sustainable Development' in Markus Krajewski and Rhea Tamara Hoffman (eds), *Research Handbook on Foreign Direct Investment* (Edward Elgar) 563–618

Schepel, Harm (2019) 'A Parallel Universe: Advocate General Bot in Opinion 1/17' *European Law Blog* (7 February) at https://europeanlawblog.eu/2019/02/07/a-parallel-universe-advocate-general-bot-in-opinion-1-17/ (last accessed 11 March 2023)

Scheu, Julian (2022) 'Applicable Law and Interpretation' in Marc Bungenberg and August Reinisch (eds) *CETA Investment Law: Article-by-Article Commentary* (Hart/Beck/Nomos) 704–37

Scheuerman, William E. (1996) 'Introduction' in William E. Scheuerman (ed) *The Rule of Law Under Siege: Selected Essays of Franz L. Neumann and Otto Kircheimer* (University of California Press) 1–25

Schill, Stephan W. and Christian J. Tams (2022) 'International Investment Protection and Constitutional Law: Between Conflict and Complementarity' in Stephan W. Schill and Christian J. Tams (eds) *International Investment Protection and Constitutional Law* (Edward Elgar) 2–37

—— (eds) (2022) *International Investment Law and Constitutional Law* (Edward Elgar)

Schmitt, Carl (2004) [1932] *Legality and Legitimacy*, translated by Jeffrey Seitzer (Duke UP)

—— (2008) [1928], *Constitutional Theory*, translated by Jeffrey Seitzer (Duke UP)

Schnapper, Dominique (2010) *Une Sociologie au Conseil Constitutionnel* (Gallimard)

Schneiderman, David (1996) 'NAFTA's Takings Rule: American Constitutionalism Comes to Canada' *University of Toronto Law Journal* 46: 499–537

—— (2000) 'Constitutional Approaches to Privatization: An Inquiry into the Magnitude of Neo-Liberal Constitutionalism' *Law and Contemporary Problems* 63: 83–109

—— (2004) 'Affidavit of David Schneiderman' Ontario Superior Court of Justice, Court File No. 01-CV-208141 (17 September) at https://www.international.gc.ca/trade-agreements-accords-commerciaux/assets/pdfs/disp-diff/cupw-10.pdf (last accessed 16 October 2022)

—— (2008) *Constitutionalizing Economic Globalization: Investment Rules and Democracy's Promise* (Cambridge UP)

—— (2009) 'Promoting Equality, Black Economic Empowerment, and the Future of Investment Rules' *South African Journal on Human* Rights 25: 246–79

—— (2010a) 'A New Global Constitutional Order?' in Rosalind Dixon and Tom Ginsburg (eds) *Research Handbook on Comparative Constitutional Law* (Edward Elgar) 189–207

—— (2010b) 'Investing in Democracy? Political Process Review and International Investment Law' *University of Toronto Law Journal* 60: 909–40

—— (2010c) 'Judicial Politics and International Investment Arbitration: Seeking an Explanation for Conflicting Outcomes' *Northwestern Journal of International and Business Law* 30: 383–416

—— (2011) 'Legitimacy and Reflexivity in International Investment Arbitration: A New Self-Restraint?' *Journal of international Dispute Settlement* 2: 471–95

—— (2013a) *Resisting Economic Globalization: Critical Theory and International Investment Law* (Macmillan Palgrave)

—— (2013b) 'Power and the Production in Global Legal Pluralism: An International Political Economy Approach' in Amanda Perry-Kessaris (ed) *Socio-Legal Approaches to International Economic Law: Text, Context, Subtext* (Routledge) 98–117

—— (2014) 'The Global Regime of Investor Rights: A Return to the Standards of Civilized Justice?' *Transnational Legal Theory* 5: 60–80

—— (2015) *Red, White and Kind of Blue? The Conservatives and the Americanization of Canadian Constitutional Culture* (University of Toronto Press)

—— (2016a) 'Global Constitutionalism and International Economic Law: The Case of International Investment Law' *European Yearbook of International Economic Law* 7: 23–43

—— (2016b) 'The Paranoid Style of Investment Lawyers and Arbitrators: Investment Law Norm Entrepreneurs and their Critics' in Chin Leng Lim (ed) *Alternative Visions of International on Foreign Investment: Essays in Honour of M. Sornarajah* (Cambridge UP) 131–55

—— (2017) 'Listening to Investors (and Others): *Audi Alteram Partem* and the Future of International Investment Law' in Armand de Mestral (ed) *Second Thoughts: Investor-State Arbitration Between Developed Democracies* (Centre for International Governance Innovation) 131

—— (2017b) 'Investment Law's Unending Legitimacy Project' *Loyola University of Chicago Law Journal* 49: 229–69

—— (2018a) 'Unwritten Constitutional Principles in Canada: Genuine or Strategic?' in Rosalind Dixon and Adrienne Stone (eds) *The Invisible Constitution* (Cambridge UP) 517–40

—— (2018b) 'Against Constitutional Excess: Tocquevillian Reflections on International Investment Law' *University of Chicago Law Review* 85: 585–608

—— (2018c) '"Writing the Rules of the Global Economy": How America Has Defined the Contours of International Investment Law' *London Review of International Law* 6: 255–78

—— (2018d) 'North America Investment Law and Policy: 2017' in Lisa Sachs, Lise J. Johnson, and Jesse Coleman *Yearbook of International Investment Law and Policy* (Oxford UP) 289–304

—— (2020) 'Investment Arbitration as Constitutional Law: Constitutional Analogies, Linkages and Absences' in Thomas Schultz and Frederico Ortino (eds) *Oxford Handbook of International Arbitration* (Oxford UP)

—— (2022a) *Investment Law's Alibis: Colonialism, Imperialism, Debt and Development* (Cambridge UP)

—— (2022b) 'The Place of International Economic Law in Constitutional Interpretation' in Carlos Bernal, Sujit Choudhry, and Kate O'Regan (eds) *Research Handbook on Constitutional Interpretation* (Oxford UP)

—— (2022c) 'Hayek's Dream: International Investment Law and the Denigration of Politics' *Leiden Journal of International Law* 35: 743–59

—— (2022d) 'Local Resistance: At the Margins of Investment Law' *Globalizations* 19: 897–910

—— (2022e) 'Constitution' in Jaakko Husa, Madalena Narciso, Jan Smits, and Catherine Valcke (eds) *Elgar Encyclopedia of Comparative Law* (Elgar)

—— (2023a) 'International Economic Law in Constitutional Interpretation' in Carlos Bernal, Sujit Choudhry, and Kate O'Regan (eds) *Research Handbook on Constitutional Interpretation* (Oxford UP)

—— (2023b) 'National Treatments' in David Schneiderman and Gus Van Harten (eds) *Rethinking Investment Law: Perspectives and Prospects* (Oxford UP)

Scholtes, Julian (2021) 'Abusing Constitutional Identity' *German Law Journal* 22: 534–56

Schwarzenberger, Georg (1986) *International Law as Applied by Courts and Tribunals*, Vol. IV: International Judicial Law (Steven & Sons Limited)

Scott, James C. (1985) *Weapons of the Weak: Everyday Forms of Peasant Resistance* (Yale UP)

—— (1990) *Domination and the Arts of Resistance: Hidden Transcripts* (Yale UP)

Segal, Jeffrey A. and Harold J. Spaeth (1993) *The Supreme Court and the Attitudinal Model* (Cambridge UP)

Segal, Zeev (1995) 'Israel Ushers in a Constitutional Revolution: The Israeli Experience, the Canadian Impact' *Constitutional Forum* 2: 44–53

—— (1997) 'The Israeli Constitutional Revolution: The Canadian Impact in The Midst of a Formative Period' *Constitutional Forum* 8: 53–58

—— (2011) 'Judicial Activism Vis-à-Vis Judicial Restraint: An Israeli Viewpoint' *Tulsa Law Review* 47: 319–29

Segev, Joshua (2022) 'The Standing Doctrine: What Went Wrong?' in Aharon Barak, Barak Medina, and Yaniv Roznai (eds) *Oxford Handbook of the Israeli Constitution* (Oxford UP)

Shameh, David (2014) 'Natural Gas to Cost Israelis Double World Average, Report Says' *The Times of Israel* (19 December) at https://www.timesofisrael.com/natural-gas-to-cost-israelis-double-world-average-report-says/ (last accessed 11 December 2022)

Sharon, Avinoam (2024) 'Recent Developments in Israeli Law' *Versa: Opinions of the Supreme Court of Israel* at https://versa.cardozo.yu.edu/opinions/movement-quality-government-v-knesset (last accessed 27 January 2024)

Sharvit, Shai (2016) 'ISDS Through the Looking Glass: The Case of Israel' *Kluwer Arbitration Blog* (14 April) at http://kluwerarbitrationblog.com/2016/04/14/isds-through-the-looking-glass-the-case-of-israel/ (last accessed 26 April 2017)

Shea, Donald R. (1955) *The Calvo Clause: A Problem of Inter-American and International Law and Diplomacy* (University of Minnesota Press)

Shetreet, Shimon (1994) *Justice in Israel: A Study of the Israeli Judiciary* (Martinus Nijhoff)

Shetreet, Shimon and Walter Homolka (2017) *Jewish and Israeli Law—An Introduction* (de Gruyter)

Shinar, Adam (2018) 'Israel's External Constitution: friends, Enemies, and the Constitutional/Administrative Law Distinction' *Virginia Journal of International Law* 57: 735–68

Shiva, Vandana (1993) *Monocultures of the Mind: Perspectives on Biodiversity and Biotechnology* (Zed Books)

Scholtes, Julian (2023) *The Abuse of Constitutional Identity in the European Union* (Oxford UP)

Shrybman, Steven (2012) 'Legal Opinion From Steven Shrybman to Paul Moist re: Canada-European Union: Comprehensive Economic and Trade Agreement' (15 March) at https://goldblattpartners.com/wp-content/uploads/Opinion-on-Reservations-under-CETA.pdf (last accessed 6 February 2023)

Shrybman, Steven and Scott Sinclair (2001) 'Public Auto Insurance and Trade Treaties' CCPA Briefing Paper 5:1 (June) at www.policyalternatives/documents/National_Office_Pubs/breif5-1.pdf (last accessed 16 October 2022)

Sierra, Jimena (2021) 'Is the Arbitral Award in the *Eco Oro v Colombia* Dispute "Bad Law"?' *Afronomicslaw Blog* (11 November) at https://www.afronomicslaw.org/category/analysis/arbitral-award-eco-oro-v-colombia-dispute-bad-law (last accessed 11 August 2022)

—— (2022) 'The "*consultas populares*" in Colombia: Restrictions on Mechanisms for Citizen Participation in Foreign Extractive Projects from the Perspective of the Capitalocene' *Globalizations* 19: 865–75

Sierra, Jimena and Federico Suarez (2023) 'Right to Regulate' in David Schneiderman and Gus Van Harten (eds) *Rethinking Investment Law: Perspectives and Prospects* (Oxford UP)

Singer, Roni (2015) 'Deri Resigned "Regretfully" from the Ministry of Economy; The Government Approved Transferring Its Powers to the Prime Minister, *Calcalist* (11 November) at https://www.calcalist.co.il/local/articles/0,7340,L-3672339,00.html (last accessed 23 May 2020)

Siregar, Fritz Edward (2015) 'The Political Context of Judicial Review in Indonesia' *Indonesia Law Review* 2: 208–37

Sklair, Leslie (2002) *Globalization: Capitalism and its Alternatives*, 3rd edn (Oxford UP)

Slaughter, Anne-Marie (2003) 'A Global Community of Courts' *Harvard International Law Journal* 44:191–219

Slaughter, Anne-Marie (2004) *A New World Order* (Princeton UP)

Smith, Herbert Arthur (1923) *Federalism in North America: A Comparative Study of Institutions in the United States and Canada* (The Chipman Law Publishing Company)
Smith, Rogers M. (2008) 'Historical Institutionalism and the Study of Law' in Gregory A. Caldeira, R. Daniel Keleman, and Keith E Whittington (eds), *The Oxford Handbook of Law and Politics* (Oxford UP)
Somek, Alexander (2014) *The Cosmopolitan Constitution* (Oxford UP)
Sornorajah, M. (2010) *The International Law on Foreign Investment*, 3rd edn (Cambridge UP)
—— (2019) 'The Battle Continues: Rebuilding Empire Through State Contracts' in Jochen von Bernstorff and Philipp Dann (eds) *The Battle for International Law: South–North Perspectives on the Decolonization Era* (Oxford UP) 175–97
Sotonye, Frank (2014) 'Stabilisation Clauses and Sustainable Development in Developing Countries' unpublished PhD thesis (July), University of Nottingham at http://eprints.nottingham.ac.uk/14466/1/PhD_Thesis.pdf (last accessed 31 May 2020)
—— (2019) 'Stabilisation Clauses in Long-Term Investment Contracts in the Energy Sector in Africa' in Kate Miles (ed) *Research Handbook on Environment And Investment Law* (Edward Elgar) 340–63
Soward, F.H. (1958) 'External Affairs and Federalism' in Arthur R.M. Lower, Frank R. Scott et al., *Evolving Canadian Federalism* (Duke UP/Cambridge UP) 126–60
St. John, Taylor (2018) *The Rise of Investor-State Arbitration: Politics, Law and Unintended Consequences* (Oxford UP)
Stevens, Christopher (2007) 'Creating a Development-Friendly EU Trade Policy' in Andrew Mold (ed), *EU Development Policy in a Changing World* (Amsterdam UP) 221–36
Stokes, Susan C. (1999) 'What Do Policy Switches Tell Us About Democracy?' in Adam Przeworski, Susan C. Stokes, and Bernard Manin (eds) *Democracy, Accountability, and Representation* (Cambridge UP) 98–130
Stone Sweet, Alec (1991) *The Birth of Judicial Politics: The Constitutional Council in Comparative Perspective* (Oxford UP)
—— (2000) *Governing with Judges: Constitutional Politics in Europe* (Oxford UP)
Stopford, John and Susan Strange with John S. Henley (1991) *Rival States, Rival Firms: Competition for World Market Shares* (Cambridge UP)
Strange, Susan (1983) '*Cave! Hic Dragones*: A Critique of Regime Analysis' in Stephen D. Krasner (ed) *International Regimes* (Cornell UP) 337–54
—— (1988) *States and Markets*, 2nd edn (Pinter Publishers)
Streeck, Wolfgang (2017) *Buying Time: The Delayed Crisis of Democratic Capitalism*, 2nd edn (Verso)
Suarez Ricaurte, Frederico (2019) 'Judgment C-2525 of 2019 of the Constitutional Court of Colombia: Change of Precedent on the Control of BITs' *Investment Treaty News* 10: 4–8
Suez, Sociedad General de Aguas de Barcelona, S.A. and Vivendi Universal, S.A. v. Argentine Republic (2010), 'Decision on Liability' ICSID Case No. ARB/03/19 (30 July) at https://www.italaw.com/sites/default/files/case-documents/ita0826.pdf (last accessed 25 September 2022)
—— (2015) 'Award' ICSID Case No. ARB/03/19 (9 April) at https://www.italaw.com/sites/default/files/case-documents/italaw4365.pdf (last accessed 25 September 2022)
—— (2017) 'Decision on Annulment' ICSID Case No. ARB/03/19 (5 May) at https://www.italaw.com/sites/default/files/case-documents/italaw8783.pdf (last accessed 25 September 2022)
Svampa, Maristella (2015) 'Commodities Consensus: Neoextractivism and Enclosure of the Commons in Latin America' *The South Atlantic Quarterly* 114: 65–82
Tamayo-Álvarez, Rafael (2020) 'Constitutionality of the Colombia–France Bilateral Investment Treaty' *American Journal of International Law* 114: 471–8

Tan, Richard Ming Kirk (2004) 'Restrictions on the Foreign Ownership of Property: Indonesia and Singapore Compared' *Journal of Property Investment & Finance* 22: 101–11

Tañada v. Angara (1997) 338 Phil. 546 (S.Ct.) at https://elibrary.judiciary.gov.ph/thebookshelf/showdocs/1/34805 (last accessed 28 January 2024)

Taufik, Giri Ahmad (2020) 'The Interpretation of Article 33 of the Indonesian Constitution and its Impact on Independent Regulatory Agencies' *Australian Journal of Asian Law* 3: 1–20

Tecnicas Medioambientales TECMED S.A. v. Mexico (2003) Award, ICSID ARB(AF)/00/2 (29 May)

Teivainen, Teivo (2002) *Enter Economism, Exit Politics: Experts, Economic Policy and the Damage to Democracy* (Zed Books)

Teubner, Gunther (1997a) '"Global Bukowina": Legal Pluralism in the World Society' in Gunther Teubner (ed) *Global Law Without the State* (Dartmouth) 3–28

—— (1997b) 'Altera Pars Audiatur: Law in the Collision of Discourses' in Richard Rawlings (ed) *Law, Society and Economy: Centenary Essays for the London School of Economics, 1896–1995* (Oxford UP) 149–76

—— (2010) 'Constitutionalizing Polycontextuality' *Social and Legal Studies* 19: 210–29

—— (2015) 'Transnational Economic Constitutionalism in the Varieties of Capitalism' *The Italian Law Journal* 1: 219–48

Thomas, Christopher (2013) 'Affidavit of Christopher Thomas' Federal Court File No. T-153-13 (13 March) at http://www.italaw.com/sites/default/files/treaty-interpretations/italaw3231.pdf (last accessed 16 October 2022)

Thornhill, Chris (2016) *A Sociology of Transnational Constitutions: Social Foundations of the Post-National Legal Structure* (Cambridge UP)

—— (2021) *Democratic Crisis and Global Constitutional Law* (Cambridge UP)

Tiede, Lydia Brashear and Aldo Fernando Ponce (2011) 'Ruling Against the Executive in Amparo Cases: Evidence from the Peruvian Constitutional Tribunal' *Journal of Politics in Latin America* 3: 107–40

—— (2014) 'Evaluating Theories of Decision-Making on the Peruvian Constitutional Tribunal' *Journal of Politics in Latin America* 6: 139–64

Tienhaara, Kyla (2009) *The Expropriation of Environmental Governance* (Cambridge UP)

Titi, Aikaterini (2014) *The Right to Regulate in International Investment Law* (Nomos)

Titi, Catherine (2019) 'Opinion 1/17 and the Future of Investment Dispute Settlement: Implications for the Design of a Multilateral Investment Court' *Yearbook on International Investment Law & Policy* 514–53

—— (2020) 'Control constitucional y derecho internacional de inversiones a través de cuatro sentencias constitucionales en Colombia, Ecuador, y la Unión Europea' forthcoming in *Revista Latinoamericana de Derecho Internacional* (10 April) at ssrn.com/abstract=3569510 (last accessed 11 March 2023)

Trade Justice Network (2022) 'Stop the ratification of CETA! A joint statement by German and Canadian civil society groups' (20 August 2022) at http://tradejustice.ca/stop-the-ratification-of-ceta/ (last accessed 12 November 2022)

Tribe, Lawrence H. (2000) *American Constitutional Law*, Vol. 1, 3rd edn (Foundation Press)

Tucker, Todd (2020) 'North American Investment Law and Policy: Developments in 2019' Roosevelt Institute Working Paper (March) at https://rooseveltinstitute.org/wp-content/uploads/2020/07/RI_NorthAmericanInvestmentLawandPolicy_Working-Paper_202003.pdf (last accessed 12 October 2020)

Tully, James (1995) *Strange Multiplicity: Constitutionalism in an Age of Diversity* (Cambridge UP)

Tushnet, Mark (2009) *Weak Courts, Strong Rights: Judicial Review and Social Welfare Rights in Comparative Constitutional Law* (Princeton UP)
Tushnet, Mark V. (1999) 'The Possibilities of Comparative Constitutional Law' *The Yale Law Journal* 108: 1225
Ubilava, Ana (2020) 'Amicable Settlements in Investor-State Disputes: Empirical Analysis of Patterns and Perceived Problems' *Journal of World Trade and Investment* 21: 528–57
UNCITRAL (2017) 'Report of the Working Group III (Investor-State Dispute Settlement Reform) on the work of its 34th session (Vienna, 30 November–1 December 2017)' (19 December) A/CN.9/930/Rev.1 (UNCITRAL Working Group III Report, 34th Session)
—— (2019) 'Submission from the Governments of Chile, Israel and Japan' (15 March) A/CN.9/WG.III/WP.163 at https://undocs.org/en/A/CN.9/WG.III/WP.163 (last accessed 18 May 2020)
United Mizrahi Bank plc. v. Migdal Cooperative Village (1995) 49 (iv) P.D. 221 (all references are to the abridged English translation in *Israel Law Review* 31: 764-802; the full translation can be found at https://versa.cardozo.yu.edu/opinions/united-mizrahi-bank-v-migdal-cooperative-village) (last accessed 21 May 2020)
United Nations Conference on Trade and Development [UNCTAD] (2008) *International Investment Rule-Making: Stocktaking, Challenges and the Way Forward* (United Nations)
—— (2011) 'Best Practices in Investment for Development—How to Prevent and Manage Investor-State Disputes: Lessons from Peru' *Investment Advisory Series B* (Number 10) (United Nations)
—— (2015a) *World Investment Report 2015: Reforming International Investment Governance* (United Nations)
—— (2015b) *Investment Policy Framework for Sustainable Development* (United Nations)
—— (2016) *World Investment Report: Investor Nationality: Policy Challenges* (United Nations)
—— (2018) *World Investment Report 2018: Investment and New Industrial Policies* (United Nations)
—— (2019) *World Investment Report: Investor Nationality: Special Economic Zones* (United Nations)
—— (2022a) *World Investment Report: International Tax Reforms and Sustainable Development* (United Nations)
—— UNCTAD (2022b) 'Economic Restrictions in the West Bank Exact $50 Billion Toll Between 2000 and 2020' (22 November) at https://unctad.org/news/economic-restrictions-west-bank-exact-50-billion-toll-between-2000-and-2020 (last accessed 2 March 2023)
United States Trade Representative [USTR] (2015a) 'Fact Sheet: U.S. Investment Agreements' (n.d.) at https://ustr.gov/sites/default/files/The%20Facts%20on%20US%20Investment%20Agreements.pdf (last accessed 21 October 2022)
—— (2015b) 'Fact Sheet: Investor-State Dispute Settlement (ISDS)' (March) at https://ustr.gov/about-us/policy-offices/press-office/fact-sheets/2015/march/investor-state-dispute-settlement-isds (last visited 5 May 2017)
United States, Department of State (2019) '2019 Investment Climate Statements: Colombia' at https://www.state.gov/reports/2019-investment-climate-statements/colombia/ (last accessed 24 July 2020)
United States, International Trade Commission (2019) *U.S.–Mexico–Canada Trade Agreement: Likely Impact on the U.S. Economy and on Specific Industry Sectors* (April) Publication Number: 4889 at https://www.usitc.gov/publications/332/pub4889.pdf (last accessed 7 November 2022)

United Steelworkers v. American Manufacturing (1960) 363 US 564

Uprimny, Rodrigo (2004) 'The Constitutional Court and Control of Presidential Extraordinary Powers in Colombia' in Robert Gargarella, Siri Gloppen, and Elin Skaar (eds) *Democratization and the Judiciary: The Accountability Function of Courts in New Democracies* (Routledge) 46–69

—— (2015) 'The Recent Transformation of Constitutional Law in Latin America: Trends and Challenges' in César Rodriguez-Garavito (ed) *Law and Society in Latin America* (Routledge) 93–111

Uprimny, Rodrigo and Mauricio García-Villegas (2005) 'The Constitutional Court and Social Emancipation in Colombia' in Boaventura de Sousa Santos (ed) *Democratizing Democracy: Beyond the Liberal Democratic Canon* (Verso) 66–100

Urbaser SA v The Argentine Republic (2016) Award, ICSID Case No. ARB/07/26 (8 December)

Uribe Mallarino, Consuelo (2014) 'The Positioning of Economic Rationality in Colombia' *Bulletin of Latin American Research* 33: 46–59

Valderrama, Carlos José (2021) 'Investor-State Dispute Prevention: The Perspective of Peru' in Catherine Titi (ed) *Public Actors in International Investment Law* (European Yearbook of International Economic Law/Springer) 117–33

Van der Loo, Guillaume (2021) 'Legitimising the EU's Investment Court System but Raising the Bar for Compliance with EU Law' in Michael Hahn and Guillaume Van der Loo (eds) *Law and Practice of the Common Commercial Policy* (Brill) 98–127

van der Pas, Hilde and Riza Damanik (2014) 'The Case of *Newmont Mining vs Indonesia*' Indonesia for Global Justice Briefing (November) at https://www.tni.org/files/download/newmont-indonesia-case-4.pdf (last accessed 1 October 2022)

Van Harten, Gus (2007) *Investment Treaty Arbitration and Public Law* (Oxford UP)

—— (2008a) 'Investment Provisions in Economic Partnership Agreements' Commissioned Reports and Studies, Paper 130 at http://digitalcommons.osgoode.yorku.ca/reports/130 (last accessed 11 March 2023)

—— (2008b) 'Investment Treaty Arbitration and Its Policy Implications for Capital-Importing States' in Diego Sánchez-Ancochea, Kenneth C. Shadlen (eds) *The Political Economy of Hemispheric Integration* (Palgrave Macmillan) 83–111

—— (2013a) *Sovereign Choices and Sovereign Restraints: Judicial Restraint in Investment Treaty Arbitration* (Oxford UP)

—— (2013b) 'Affidavit of Gus Van Harten' Federal Court File No. T-153-13 (13 February) at http://www.italaw.com/sites/default/files/treaty-interpretations/italaw3214.pdf (last accessed 16 October 2022)

—— (2015) *Sold Down the Yangtze: Canada's Lopsided Investment Deal with China* (IIAP)

—— (2020) *The Trouble with Foreign Investor Protection* (Oxford UP)

Van Harten, Gus and Dayna Nadine Scott (2016) 'Investment Treaties and the Internal Vetting of Regulatory Proposals: A Case Study from Canada' *Journal of International Dispute Settlement* 7: 92–116

Van Harten, Gus, Jane Kelsey, and David Schneiderman (2019) 'Phase 2 of the UNCITRAL ISDS Review: Why "Other Matters" Really Matter' at https://digitalcommons.osgoode.yorku.ca/all_papers/328 (last accessed 23 July 2020)

Vandevelde, Kenneth J. (2010) *Bilateral Investment Treaties: History, Policy, and Interpretation* (Oxford UP)

—— (2017) *The First Bilateral Investment Treaties: U.S. Postwar Friendship, Commerce, and Navigation Treaties* (Oxford UP)

Vásquez, Piero (2013) 'La accidentada ruta constitucional de la jerarquía de los tratados en el derecho interno' *Themis* 63: 89–108

Vázquez, Carlos Manuel (1995) 'The Four Doctrines of Self-Executing Treaties.' *American Journal of International Law* 89: 695–723

Velásquez Ruiz, Marco Alberto (2016) 'The Colliding Vernaculars of Foreign Investment Protection and Transitional Justice in Colombia: The Challenge for the Law in a Global Context', PhD dissertation, Osgoode Hall Law School, York University (March) at https://yorkspace.library.yorku.ca/xmlui/bitstream/handle/10315/32676/Velasquez_Marco_2 016_PhD.pdf?sequence=2&isAllowed=y (last accessed 24 July 2020)

Venzke, Ingo and Philipp Günther (2022) 'International Investment Protection Made in Germany? On the Domestic and Foreign Policy Dynamics behind the First BITs' *European Journal of International Law* 33: 1183–1207

Verdier, Pierre-Hugues and Mila Versteeg (2018) 'International in National Legal Systems: An Empirical Investigation' in Anthea Roberts, Paul B. Stephan, Pierre-Hugues Verdier, and Mila Versteeg (eds) *Comparative International Law* (Oxford UP) 209–30

Vergara, Alberto and Aaron Watanabe (2016) 'Delegative Democracy Revisited: Peru Since Fujimoro' *Journal of Democracy* 27: 148–57

Vernon, Raymond (1971) *Sovereignty at Bay: The Multinational Spread of U.S. Enterprises* (Basic Books)

Villegas, Bernardo M. (1987) 'The 1986 Constitution and Democratic Ideology' in Florangel Rosario-Braid (ed), *Development Issues: Constitutional Response* (Manila: National Book Store) 171–8

Vogelman, Justice Uzi, Na' div Mordechay, Yaniv Roznai, and Tehilla Schwartz (2016) 'Developments in Constitutional Law: The Year 2016 in Review' at http://www.iconnectblog.com/2017/10/developments-in-israeli-constitutional-law-the-year-2016-in-review/ (last accessed 31 May 2020)

Von Bogdandy, Armin (2010) 'Founding Principles' in Armin Von Bogdandy and Jürgen Bast (eds) *Principles of European Constitutional Law*, 2nd rev edn (Hart/Beck) 11–54

Von Bogdandy, Armin and Ingo Venzke (2014) *In Whose Name? A Public Law Theory of Adjudication* (Oxford UP)

Vranes, Erich (2013) 'Constitutional Foundations of, and Limitations to, EU Integration in France' *European Public Law* 19: 525–54

Waelde, Thomas W. and George Ndi (1996) 'Stabilizing International Investment Commitments: International Law Versus Contract Interpretation' *Texas International Law Journal* 31: 215–67

Waldron Jeremy (2012) *The Rule of Law and the Measure of Property* (Cambridge UP)

Walker, Neil (2003) 'Postnational Constitutionalism and the Problem of Translation' in Joseph Weiler and Marlene Wind (eds) *European Constitutionalism Beyond the State* (Cambridge UP) 27–54

Weber, Max (1978) *Economy and Society: An Outline of Interpretive Sociology*, Gunther Roth and Claus Wittich (eds) (University of California Press)

—— (2010) 'The "Objectivity" of Knowledge in Social Science and Social Policy' in Hans Henrik Bruun and Sam Whimster (eds) *Max Weber: Complete Methodological Writings* (Routledge) 100–38

Weiler, Todd Grierson and Iain Laird (2008) 'Standards of Treatment' in Peter Muchlinski, Federico Ortino and Christoph Schreuer (eds) *The Oxford Handbook of International Investment Law* (Oxford UP) 260–302

Weill, Rivka (2012) 'Reconciling Parliamentary Sovereignty and Judicial Review: On the Theoretical and Historical Origins of the Israeli Legislative Override Power' *Hastings Constitutional Law Quarterly* 29: 457–512
—— (2020) 'The Strategic Common Law Court of Aharon Barak and its Aftermath: On Judicially-led Constitutional Revolutions and Democratic Backsliding' *Law & Ethics of Human Rights* 14: 227–72
Weiss, Wolfgang (2020) 'The CETA Investment Court and EU External Autonomy: Did Opinion 1/17 Broaden the EU's Room for Maneuver in External Relations?' *Hungarian Yearbook of International Law and European Law* 8: 15–39
Wells, Louis T. and Rafiq Ahemd (2007) *Making Foreign Investment Safe: Property Rights and National Sovereignty* (Oxford UP)
Witte, Inga (2018) 'Interactions Between International Investment Law: Promoting the Dialogue: A European Perspective on Judicial Cooperation and Deference' *Max Planck Yearbook of United Nations Law* 21: 468–575
Wolin, Sheldon S. (1989) 'Collective Identity and Constitutional Power' in Sheldon S. Wolin (ed) *The Presence of the Past: Essays on the State and the Constitution* (Johns Hopkins UP) 8–31
Wood, Gordon S. (2021) *Power and Liberty: Constitutionalism in the American Revolution* (Oxford UP)
World Bank (2017) 'Policy Note: What Drives Foreign Direct Investments in Indonesia?' (August) at https://openknowledge.worldbank.org/bitstream/handle/10986/30944/131402-WP-PUBLIC-2017-Cali-Hidayat-Briefing-on-FDI-in-Indonesia.pdf?sequence=1&isAllowed=y (last accessed 21 January 2023)
Xi, Gloria Loo Jing (2019) 'ASEAN and Janus-Faced Constitutionalism: The Indonesian Case' *International Journal of Constitutional Law* 17: 177–204
Yates, Julian S. and Karen Bakker (2014) 'Debating the "Post-Neoliberal Turn" in Latin America' *Progress in Human Geography* 38: 62–90
Yilmaz Vastardis, Anil (2020) 'Investment Treaty Arbitration: A Justice Bubble for the Privileged' in Thomas Schultz and Frederico Ortino (eds) *Oxford Handbook of International Arbitration* (Oxford UP) 617–40
—— (2023) 'Most Favored Nation Treatment' in David Schneiderman and Gus Van Harten (eds) *Rethinking Investment Law* (Oxford UP)
Young, Oran R. (1969) 'Interdependencies in World Politics' *International Journal* 24: 726–50
—— (1983) 'Regime Dynamics: The Rise and Fall of International Regimes' in Stephen D. Krasner (ed) *International Regimes* (Cornell UP) 93–113
Young, Oran R. (1983) 'Regime Dynamics: The Rise and Fall of International Regimes' in Stephen D. Krasner (ed) *International Regimes* (Cornell UP) 93–113
—— (1999) *Governance in World Affairs* (Cornell UP)
Zamir, Justice Yizhak (1996) 'The Legitimacy of Judicial Review' (unpublished on file with the author)
Zamir, Itzhak and Allen Zysblat (eds) (1996) *Public Law in Israel* (Oxford UP) 310–71
Ziv, Neta (2013) 'Constitutional Review of "Eligibility Conditions" in Social Rights Litigation' in Gideon Sapir, Daphne Barak-Erez, and Aharon Barak (eds) *Israeli Constitutional Law in the Making* (Hart) 349–67
Zuleta, Eduardo, María Camila Rincón (2019) 'Colombia's Constitutional Court Conditions Ratification of the Colombia-France BIT to the Interpretation of Several Provisions of the Treaty' *Kluwer Arbitration Blog* (4 July) at http://arbitrationblog.kluwerarbitration.com/2019/07/04/colombias-constitutional-court-conditions-ratification-of-the-colom

bia-france-bit-to-the-interpretation-of-several-provisions-of-the-treaty/?doing_wp_c
ron=1597935976.0785789489746093750000 (last accessed 20 August 2020)
Zuleta-Londoño, Alberto, Andrea Jamieson, Emilie Franklin, and Mandy Markar (2014) 'Colombia' in Stephen Jagusch and Epaminontas Triantfilou, *Investment Treaty Arbitration 2015* (Law Business Research) 17–21
Zuleeg, Manfred (2010) 'The Advantages of the European Constitution' in Armin Von Bogdandy and Jürgen Bast (eds) *Principles of European Constitutional Law*, 2nd rev edn (Hart/Beck) 763–86
Zürn, Michael (1993) 'Bringing the Second Image (Back) In: About the Domestic Sources of Regime Formation' in Volker Rittberger with Peter Mayer (eds) *Regime Theory and International Relations* (Oxford UP) 282–311

Index

For the benefit of digital users, indexed terms that span two pages (e.g., 52–53) may, on occasion, appear on only one of those pages.

Tables and figures are indicated by *t* and *f* following the page number

Aboriginal Peoples *see* Indigenous Peoples
Achmea B.V. v. The Slovak Republic 66–67, 141n.221
Ackerman, Bruce 41
Aguas Argentina 167
Akbar, Patrialis, Judge 153–54
Al'Afghani, Mohamad Mova 159
Allee, Todd 13
Alschner, Wolfgang 13, 85, 195
Amco Asia Corp. v. Indonesia 147
América Móvil S.A.B. de C.V. v. Republic of Colombia 131–32
Ankersmit, Laurens 68
apex courts (generally): in capital-exporting states 15–16, 187, 198
  in capital-importing states 187–88
  cooperation exhibited by 11
  democratic values and 187–88, 190–93
  dialogue with international law 7–9, 10–11, 11*f*, 190–98
  executive branch and 20
  independence of 14–15
  influence over international investment law 194–95
  judicial decision-making 9–10, 191–92
  jurisdiction of 19, 20
  regime maintenance and 6–7
  response to threat of shrinking constitutional space 3, 10–12, 11*f*, 15, 16, 20–21
  security of tenure in 14–15
  strategic behavior of 15–16
  see also individual courts
Argentina
  BG Group v. Argentina 48–49
  economic crisis 167–68, 169–70, 169n.38
  investment claims against 167
  Suez, Sociedad General de Aguas de Barcelona, S.A. and Vivendi Universal, S.A. v. Argentine 167–70
  Suez and Vivendi v. Argentina 167–70
  water tariff hikes 167, 169–70
Arroyo, Landa 97
ASEAN-China agreement 159–60

ASEAN Comprehensive Investment Agreement 150
Australia
  investment arbitration 2–3
Aymara Indigenous people 82–85

Baker v. Carr 46–47
Barak, Aharon, Justice 172–73, 174, 177–78
Batu Hijau gold and copper mine 147–48
Baxi, Upendra 8, 9, 14, 198–99
Bear Creek Mining v. Peru 82–86
Benvenisti, Eyal 7–8, 18–19, 171, 190–92
Bernal, Carlos, Judge 135–37, 138, 141
BG Group v. Argentina 48–49
Bickel, Alexander 191–92, 199–200
bilateral investment treaties (BITs) *see* individual country BITs
Breyer, Stephen, Justice 48–49
Broches, Aaron 12–13
Broude, Tomer 170–71
Brower, Charles N 51–52
Brown, Colin 1–2
Bungenberg, Marc 189
Bush, George W 43–44
Butt, Simon 151–52, 159

Cadilhac, Marie-Cécile 59–60, 61–62
Calvert, Julia 86–87, 106n.191
Calvo clause 91–92
Canada
  Aboriginal peoples 49–50
  Charter of Rights and Freedoms 177–78
  Clayton v. Canada 59, 71, 189n.13
  CUPW v. Canada 30–35
  Ethyl v. Canada 59n.64
  executive branch in 33–34
  FDI inflows 50
  federalism 28, 29
  in the First World War 28
  Hunt v. T&N PLC 29–30
  Hupacasath First Nation v. Canada 36–39
  international law and 49–50
  investment treaty commitments 29, 30

242 INDEX

Canada (*cont.*)
  investment treaty law and 19, 35, 39, 187
  Judicial Committee of the Privy Council 28
  Mikisew Cree First Nation v. Canada 38n.72
  Parliament, powers of 27, 27n.2
  tobacco industry regulation 35
  treaty negotiation 27–28
  see also Canada-China Foreign Investment Protection Agreement (FIPA); Canada-Peru Free Trade Agreement; Canada-EU Comprehensive Economic Trade Agreement (CETA); North American Free Trade Agreement (NAFTA); Colombia-Canada FTA; Quebec; Supreme Court of Canada
Canada-China Foreign Investment Protection Agreement (FIPA):
  critics of 38–39
  Hupacasath First Nation and 19, 30, 36–37, 38
Canada-EU Comprehensive Economic Trade Agreement (CETA): Bundestag ratification of 77
  climate change obligations 77
  committee system 65, 76–77
  democratic legitimacy of 75, 76, 77
  dispute resolution mechanism 63–64, 67–68, 70–71, 74–76
  equality principle in 61–62, 72–73, 75
  EU laws and 65, 67, 72
  fair and equitable treatment (FET) 77
  French *conseil constitutionnel* 54–62, 72
  French Constitution and 56–57, 58–60
  German Basic Law and 75–77
  German Constitutional Court and 62–65, 75–77
  indirect expropriation 77
  investment tribunals under 70–72, 74–75
  investor protections under 19–20, 63–64, 68, 69–70, 72, 72n.157
  Joint Interpretative Instrument of 57–58, 57–58n.51, 61–62, 69–70, 72
  as a mixed agreement 55, 64, 65
  as model 194
  negotiations of 28–29, 62
  non-discriminatory measures 68–69
  obstacles to adoption by European Parliament 57–58
  precautionary principle 58–59
  'right to regulate' clause 68–70, 74–76
Canada-Peru Free Trade Agreement
  annex on expropriation 84, 84n.31
  Bear Creek dispute 82–86
  exceptions clause 84–85, 85n.36

Canadian Supreme Court *see* Supreme Court of Canada
capital-exporting states
  defined 10n.88
  economic power of 12–14
  false universalization 196
  judicial responses in 12
  jurisprudence of 19
  preserving privileges 50
  reform of international treaties driven by 195–96
capital-importing states
  bargaining power of 186n.187
  constitutional jurisprudence in 20
  defined 10n.88
  judicial responses in 12, 23, 185–86
Castillo, Pedro 88
Cemento Sur 99
Cepeda-Espinosa, Manuel José 122
Charter Committee on Poverty Issues (CCPI) 33
chilling effect 35, 62, 68–69, 148, 183
  see also shrinking of policy space
Choi, Eun-bae 2–3
Chriki, David 170–71
Churchill Mining v. Indonesia 143–46
Clarkson, Stephen 31–32n.27
Clayton v. Canada 59, 71, 189n.13
Colombia
  América Móvil S.A.B. de C.V. v. Republic of Colombia 131–32
  bilateral investment treaties 115–16, 129t, 194
  constitutional order 117–21
  economic development 118
  Eco Oro Minerals Corp. v. Republic of Colombia 112–14, 132, 133, 133n.170
  executive branch 117
  foreign direct investment 115, 119–20
  Galway Gold Inc. v. Republic of Colombia 112–13, 132
  indigenous peoples 119, 132
  investment law and policy 115–17
  mining Agency 112
  mining concessions 112, 114
  National Agency for the Legal Defense of the State (ANDJE) 116
  National Council on Economic and Social Policy 115
  natural resources 115
  political regime 118, 124–25
  presidential emergency decrees 121–22
  protection of the páramo 112, 113–14
  reconciliation process 115
  Red Eagle v. Colombia 112, 131t, 132
  UNCITRAL treaty reform proposals 116–17
  violence in 117

INDEX 243

Colombia-Canada FTA 112, 113–14, 113n.21, 114n.29
Colombia-France BIT
  constitutionality of 21–22, 136–38, 194
  equality analysis 136–37, 140–41
  expropriation clause 140
  FET obligations 138
  investor-state dispute settlement clause 140–41
  language of 137–38
  MFN clause 139–40
  national treatment analysis of 138–39, 140n.213
  newly negotiated text of 142
  proportionality analysis of 136
  'reasonableness' test of 136
  see also Colombian Constitutional Court
Colombia-Israel BIT 110, 142
Colombian Constitution of 1886 121
Colombian Constitution of 1991:
  amendment to 3
  conflicting messages of 120–21
  on contractual rights 119–20
  on economic activity 119n.76, 123
  emergence of 115
  enforcement of 119
  generally 117–21
  neoliberal programme of 118–19
  provisions on fundamental rights 118, 123
  on social security 118–19
  on treaties 118
Colombian Constitutional Court
  América Móvil S.A.B. de C.V. v. Republic of Colombia ruling 131–32
  analysis of ISDS 140–41
  claims against health service providers 124
  Colombia-France BIT, review of (Judgement C-252/19) 110, 111, 134–42
  Colombia-UK BIT case 127–30
  Columbia-US FTA approval 130
  Colombia-UK BIT 194–95
  criticism of 123–24
  dialogical reasoning 110–11
  education cases 124
  executive branch and 124–26, 141–42
  Gran Colombia ruling (Judgment T-384A/14) 132
  on international investment agreements 127–30, 129t, 131t
  interpretation of basic rights 122–23
  interpretation of the Constitution 124–25
  jurisdiction of 121, 122, 125n.133
  judicial review process 134–35
  labour disputes 124
  neoliberal reforms 123
  proportionality analysis 136
  reasonableness' test of investment treaties 136
  record on investment treaties 126–34, 129t
  res judicata rulings 134, 135–36
  review of executive decrees 124–25, 126
  ruling in C-252/19 110, 111, 134–41, 194
  standard of scrutiny 135–36
  strategic behaviour of 124–25, 126
  Tobie Mining v. Republic of Colombia 132
  tutela decisions 123, 124, 124n.116, 126
  see also *Eco Oro Minerals Corp. v. Republic of Colombia*, Colombia-Israel BIT, Colombia-UK BIT, Colombia-US TPA
Colombia-UK BIT
  constitutional challenge of 21–22, 110, 115, 194–95
  expropriation clause 127, 128–30
  property rights clause 127–28
  question of constitutionality of 110–28, 127n.144
Colombia-US TPA 130, 131, 132
comparative constitutional law (generally) 1–2, 4–5, 20–21
  and style of scholarship 5–6, 20–21
Comprehensive and Progressive Agreement for Trans-Pacific Partnership (CPTPP) 86–87
  see also Trans-Pacific Partnership (TPP)
Conant, Lisa 18–19
conditional coexistence model 193–94, 195
constitutional courts see apex Courts and individual courts
constitutionality, block of 99, 123
constitutional identity 55, 55n.35
'Constitutionalism 3.0' 189
Constitutional Tribunal (Peru): crises in 95
  establishment of 95
  Executive Branch and 95–96, 98–99, 108–9
  Gramercy Funds Management LLC. v. The Republic of Peru 97–99, 108–9
  hard deference towards investment law's constraints 108–9
  incorporation of international law of indirect expropriation 97
  on labour protections 104–5
  on markets 95–96
  Peru-Chile FTA case 105–6
  Peru-China FTA case 107–8
  Peru-US FTA case 100–5
  on provision of life-saving treatment for HIV/AIDS 96–97
  on public sector collective bargaining 96
  on rights over indigenous lands 99–100
  on social justice 95–96
  tenure of justices in 95

244 INDEX

constitutions
 as compromises 1–2, 189–90, 193,
  198–99, 200
Convention on the Settlement of Investment
  Disputes Between States and Nationals of
  other States *see* International Convention
  on the Settlement of Investment Disputes
Cope, Kevin L 18–19
Correa Henao, Magdalena 124, 127, 134–35,
  136–37, 140–41
Cosigo Resources 115–16, 132
Court of Justice of the European Union (CJEU) 4–5
 Achmea B.V. v. The Slovak Republic 66–67,
  141n.221
 authority of 66
 CETA decision 19–20, 53–54, 67–68, 71–73, 74
 decision making style 60–61
 EU-Singapore FTA opinion 53, 55, 66
 on interpretive authority of tribunals 68
 jurisdiction of 66–67
 limited familiarity with international
  investment law 71
Cox, Robert W, 188
Crampton, Paul, Justice 37–39
Crawford, James 33–34, 35
Cruz, Eto, Judge 104–5
CUPW v. Canada 30–35
customary international law, defence of
  necessity 169n.37
Czech/Slovak Federative Republic-Netherlands
  investment treaty 66–67

Dargent, Eduardo 95
deference, hard 10, 11*f*, 19, 20, 21, 78, 82, 108–9
 vs. soft deference 10, 11*f*, 15, 21–22, 78,
  111, 135–36
 see also individual courts
defiance, hard 10–11, 11*f*
 vs. soft defiance 10, 11*f*, 14–15, 21–23, 111,
  135–36, 143, 157, 163, 185
 see also individual courts
Delek Group 178–80
Deri, Aryeh 180
Die Link parliamentary group 75–76
Downs, George W 7–8, 18–19, 190–92
Dressel, Björn 155
Dyevre, Arthur 59–60

Eckes, Christina 68
*Eco Oro Minerals Corp. v. Republic of
 Colombia* 111, 112–14, 132, 133, 133n.170

Ecuador
 constitutional review of treaties 11n.92,
  17n.132, 92n.95
Ecuadorian Constitutional Court 10–11, 194–95
Ely, J.H, 163
Equality, constitutional 55n.31, 56–57, 61–62,
  72–73, 75, 88–89, 96–97, 101–2, 104, 118,
  119–20, 127–30, 136–37, 140–41, 175–
  76, 194–95
Eslava, Luis 123–24, 134
Espinosa-Saldaña, Eloy, Judge 99–100
Ethyl v. Canada 59n.64
European Union
 arbitral mechanism 74
 bilateral investment treaties 66–67, 77
 Economic Partnership Agreements (EPAs) 52
 economic policies 52
 Environmental Charter of 2005, 58–59
 European Energy Charter Treaty (ECT) 51
 international agreements 53–54
 investment rules regime 51–52
 Lisbon Treaty 53
 portfolio investment, (non-direct foreign
  investment) 53, 66n.120
 proposal for multilateral investment court 2–3
 replacement of traditional ISDS 74
 Treaty on the Functioning of the European
  Union (TFEU) 53n.14, 66–67
 see also Canada-EU Comprehensive Economic
  Trade Agreement (CETA)
executive branch 16–17
 international law and 17–19
 Lockean character of 16–17
 see also individual courts

fair and equitable treatment (FET) 42, 43,
  59n.64, 65, 70–71, 77, 113, 114, 132, 133–34,
  138, 139–40, 147–48, 150, 158n.123, 160–
  61, 162n.148, 168–69
Fandiño-Bravo, Juan Camilo 196
Farkash-Hacohen, Orit 179–80
Fletcher, William A., Judge 47–48
France
 Constitution of 1946, 54, 56–57
 Constitution of 1958, 56–57, 56n.43
 Declaration of the Rights of Man and
  Citizen 56–57, 136–37
 Fundamental Principles Recognized
  by the Laws of the Republic
  (FPRLR) 54n.21, 56–57
 investment treaty negotiations 51–52

judicial decision-making model 60–61
principle of equality 56–57
see also French Constitutional Council
Freeport mining company 148
French Constitutional Council
  CETA decision 19–20, 56, 58–60, 61–62
  conclusion on the precautionary
    principle 59
  constitutional complaints submitted to 59–60
  decision-making process 59–61
  equality analysis in 56–57, 57n.49
  jurisdiction of 54, 55
  legal disputes brought before 53–54
  origins and transformation of 54
Friedmann, Wolfgang 157n.113
Fujimori, Alberto Kenya 88, 89, 90, 91n.90, 92, 95, 109

Galway Gold Inc. v. Republic of Colombia 112–13, 132
García, Alan Gabriel Ludwig 94
Garcia-Villegas, Mauricio 124
German Basic Law 62–63, 75–77
German Federal Constitutional Court
  CETA decision 19–20, 63–65, 76–77
  on European Central Bank directives 63
  First Abortion decision 62–63
  history of 62–63
  legal disputes brought before 53–54
  Maastricht decision 63
  preliminary injunction 64n.107
  Solange ruling 33
German Magistrates Association *(Deutscher Richterbund)* 2–3
German Social Democratic Party of Germany (SPD) 62
Germany
  investment treaty law 62
Gilo, David 180
Ginsburg, Tom 17
Golove, David 41
Gómez, Alvaro 125
Gómez-Segura, Victoria 120–21
Goudge, Stephen T., Justice 32–33
Gramercy Funds Management LLC. v. The Republic of Peru 97–99, 108–9
Gross, Aeyal M, 174

Haftel, Yoram Z, 170–71
Hailbronner, Michaela 62–63
Hanim, Lutfiyah 160–61

Hayut, Esther, Justice 182–83
Hendrianto, Stefanus 157
Hidayat, Arief 156
Hirschl, Ran 175–76
Hofnung, Menachem 176–77
Horowitz, Donald L, 154
Hunt v. T&N PLC 29–30
Hupacasath First Nation
  Canada-China FIPA and 36, 37, 38
Hupacasath First Nation v. Canada 36–39
Hutagalung, Ifran R, 161

ILO Convention 169, 85–86
India, apex courts 9–10
Indigenous Peoples 49–50, 82–84, 85–86, 88, 90–91, 91n.90, 94, 99–100, 119, 132
  see also Hupacasath First Nation, Aymara Indigenous People
indirect expropriation 43, 62, 68–69, 70, 77, 84–86, 84n.31, 97, 101–2, 105, 112–14, 113n.21, 127–30, 140–41, 147–48, 152–53, 162
Indonesia
  Amco Asia Corp. v. Indonesia 147
  Churchill Mining v. Indonesia 144–46
  coal mining 144
  constitutional regime 150–53, 162, 163
  democratic practice in 150–51, 163
  disguised privatization 159
  economic globalization and 152
  Electricity Law of 2009, 156, 157
  financial crisis 150–51
  foreign investments 149, 152–53
  free trade agreements 149–50
  investment treaty programme 147, 149–50, 162
  ISDS reform 146, 147, 148, 150, 162
  legislative ratification of treaties in 151
  mining rights disputes 143–44, 147–48
  Newmont v. Indonesia 147
  political party competition 154
  presidential ratification of treaties in 151–52, 162–63
  relationship between the executive and legislative branches 151
  settlement of investment disputes 148, 149
  shrinking policy space 161
  sovereignty of 158–59
  treaty law 159–60
  see also Indonesian Constitutional Court; Indonesia-Netherlands BIT; Indonesia-Singapore BIT

Indonesian Constitutional Court
    appointments to 154
    case statistics 155
    criticism of 159
    decision-making process 155–56
    democratic interests and 163–64
    election disputes and 155
    Electricity Law case 156, 157
    on obligations of state 157n.113
    origins of 153–54
    Investment Law case 158–59
    jurisdiction of 144–45, 153–56
    land rights ruling 158–59
    neoliberalism and 157–59
    NGOs and 155–56
    scandals in 153–54
    separation of powers cases 155
    'soft defiance' of 143, 157, 163
    strategic behaviour 155, 156
    support for 154
    Treaty Law of 2007, 22, 159–63
Indonesian Constitution of 1945:
        as anti-colonial 152
    objectives of 162
    on organization of national economy 152
    on property rights 152–53
    on rights of foreign investors 152–53
Indonesia-Netherlands BIT 147–48
Indonesian Treaty Law of 2007: constitutional challenge of 159–60, 161, 162–63
    consultation mechanism 160
    FET commitments 160–61, 162
Indonesia-Singapore BIT 150
Inoue, Tomoo 155
Inter-American Court of Human Rights 99
International Convention on the Settlement of Investment Disputes (ICSID) 12–13, 31n.23, 67n.128, 88, 128, 146, 148
international investment treaty law and arbitration (generally)
    constitutional authorization 17–18
    content analysis 13
    democratic values and 192–93
    dominant purpose of 199
    economic power and 12–14
    executive branches and 18
    investor protections 1–2, 168–69, 182–83
    judicial anxieties 2–3
    judicial responses 8–12
    national constitutional law channeled by 195–96
    'no greater rights' claim 43–44, 57–58, 136–37
    success rates 199n.88
    trade and investment 18
    umbrella clauses 166, 166n.10
    values promoted by 199–200
    see also investor-state dispute settlement, individual courts
International Labour Organization (ILO) 28, 85–86, 99n.146
International Monetary Fund (IMF) 159
international political economy (IPE) 6–7
investor-state dispute settlement (ISDS): access to 45–46, 189–90
    critics of 45
    defined 1
    as enforcement mechanism 43, 101–2
    EU legal order and 74
    as external check 189
    future of 23
    see also UNCITRAL Working Group III
Israel
    bargaining power 186
    Capital Investment Encouragement Law 171
    constitutional order 22–23, 171–74, 175–76
    debt relief ('Gal Law') for agricultural farms 172–73
    foreign direct investment 170, 171
    Gas Outline Plan 178–82, 183–84
    governing coalitions 175–76
    government commitments to private contracts 178–79
    import and export of capital 170
    international investment agreements 170–71
    international obligations 171
    investment law and policy 170–71
    Movement for Quality Government v. Prime Minister of Israel 178–85
    occupied territories 170
    oil and gas industry 22–23, 179–80, 184
    personal rights 172
    political culture 174, 175–76
    property rights 173
    tax policy 179
    treaty-making and ratification 171
    see also Israel-Cyprus BIT; Israel Basic Laws; Israel Knesset; Israeli High Court of Justice; Noble-Dalek deal
Israel, Basic Laws
    absence of socio-economic rights from 174
    'Basic Law: Israel as the Nation-State of the Jewish People,' 175
    enactment of 171–72, 175–76

INDEX 247

on evaluation of reasonableness of executive branch actions 185n.182
formation of (Harari Resolution) 172
'Basic Law: Freedom of Occupation,' 173, 177–78
provisions on rights and freedoms 172–73, 174, 175–76
on review of 'reasonableness' of executive action 178n.124
Israel-Cyprus BIT 183–84
Israeli High Court of Justice
  criticism of 177
  decision on non-kosher meat 177–78
  decline in confidence in 177–78
  exercise of judicial review 176–77
  human rights cases 176–77
  judicial appointments 175
  jurisdiction of 174, 175
  opinion in Israeli gas outline case (*Movement for Quality Government v. Prime Minister of Israel*) 178–85
  political matters and 174
  reasoning of 182
  primary arrangements 181, 181n.147
  remedial tactics of 175
  rulings on investment treaties 22–23, 166–67
  secondary arrangements 181
  soft defiance of 22–23, 166–67, 185–86
  standing rules 175, 176–77
  strategic behaviour 177
  success rate of petitions to 176–77
  support for 175–76, 177–78
  United Mizrahi Bank plc. v. Migdal Cooperative Village 171–73, 176–77
Israel, Knesset
  as constituent assembly 172
  Economics Committee 183–84
  legislative activities 171, 172, 175–76, 177–78, 180–82
  power of 182–83
  Sheshinski Committees 179
  see also Israel

Jailani, Abdulkadir 149, 161–62
Jay Treaty 40, 41–42
judicial behaviour 15–16
judicial branches
  decision-making in Global North and Global South 8–10, 12
  dialogue with international law 7–9, 10–11, 11*f*, 190–98

'hard' and 'soft' approaches 10–11, 11*f*
and economic globalization 7–8, 11, 12, 188–89
judicial modesty 9
strategic behaviour 7–8, 10, 15–16, 93–94, 124–25, 126, 155, 156, 177, 190–91

Kamphuis, Charis 90–91
Keene, Edward 13–14
Kelsey, Jane 3
Kennedy, Anthony, Justice 49
Kennedy, Duncan 8–9
Kirchner, Nestor 102n.165
Knop, Karen 5–6
Korean Constitutional Court 3

labour arbitration
  investment law as 48–49
La Forest, Gérard Vincent, Justice 29–30
Lajoie, Andree 31
Laksono, Fajar 156
Landau, Moshe 123–24, 177
Larik, Joris 61–62
Lasser, Mitchel de S.-O.-L'E, 60–61
Legum, Barton 41–42
Licht, Avi 183–84
Lighthizer, Robert 44–45
Lindsey, Tim 159
Locke, John 16–17
Lomé Convention 52
Lord, Bernard 35
Lumbantobing, John 148
Lurie, Guy 176–77

Made in the USA Foundation v. United States 46–48
Magnon, Xavier 61–62
Manger, Mark S, 13
Marbury v. Madison 46–47, 172–73
Margel, Keren Weinshall 176–77
Marshall, John, Chief Justice 46–47
Mater et Magistra (Papal Encyclical) 95–96
McGinnis, John O, 42
McLachlan, Campbell 17
Merhof, Katrin 124
Metalclad Corporation v. Mexico 34
Mexico-US-Canada Agreement (MUSCA) 45–46
Mikisew Cree First Nation v. Canada 38n.72
minimum standard of treatment (MST) 43
minoritarian identity rights 8
Mochtar, Akil, Justice 153–54
monist-dualist divide 17–18

248   INDEX

monoculture of the mind   200
Movassagh, Hooman   18–19
Movement for Quality Government v. Prime Minister of Israel   166–67, 178–85
Movsesian, Mark L   42
Muñoz, Prieto   193–96
Murillo-Castaño, Gabriel   120–21
Murphy, Walter F,   15

Nagle, Luz Estella   123–24
Nardi, Dominic J   155–56
Narváez, Marianella Leonor Ledesma, Judge   99–100
Ndi, George   165
Netanyahu, Benjamin   22–23, 178–79, 180, 184–85
Netherlands
  investment treaty negotiations   51–52
New Brunswick
  auto insurance scheme   29, 35
'new constitutionalism'   123–24, 124n.111
Newmont v. Indonesia   147
Nigeria
  Niger Delta Development Commission v. Nigeria Liquified Natural Gas Company   165–66
Noble-Dalek deal
  economic implications of   181–82
  Government commitment to   178–80
  High Court ruling on   181–84
  investigation of   180
  Knesset approval of   180–81
  Noble Energy   178–80
  secrecy surrounding   184–85
  see also Israel High Court of Justice, *Movement for Quality Government v. Prime Minister of Israel*
North American Free Trade Agreement (NAFTA):
  Charter of Rights and Freedoms and   31, 32–33
  constitutional challenge to   19, 31–33, 34–35, 47
  criticism of   44–45
  foreign investment protection regime   31–32n.27
  investor-state arbitration mechanism   32–33, 41–42
  renegotiations of   44–45, 46–47
  violations of the investment chapter   29
  see also Mexico-US-Canada Agreement
Nusa Tenggara Partnership BV (NTPBV)   147–48
Nwodo, Regina, Justice   165–66

Obama, Barack   43–44, 49

OECD (Multilateral Convention to Implement Tax Treaty Related Measures)   116–17
Ojeda, Gonzales, Judge   102, 104
Ontario
  auto insurance scheme   29

Peinhardt, Clint   13
Penn Central Transportation Co v. New York City   43
Pepall, Sarah, Justice   32
Peru
  apex court   82
  approval of treaties   90
  Bear Creek Mining v. Peru   82–86
  bilateral investment treaties   86–87
  border dispute with Chile   105
  business community   94–95
  constitutional order   88–92
  economic system   81, 82, 90, 91–92
  executive branch   21
  extractivism policy   81–82
  foreign investments   81–82, 97
  Gramercy Funds Management LLC. v. The Republic of Peru   97–99, 108–9
  indigenous communities   82, 90–91, 91n.90, 99
  inflation   88
  informal transportation sector   95–96
  investment law and policy   86–88
  majoritarian institutions   88–89
  mining industry   81, 82, 88, 97
  mining rights law   82–83, 83n.18
  police powers   84–85
  political crises   88
  promotion of free trade   104
  response to investment claims   83–84, 87, 88, 187
  Sistema de Coordinación Respuesta del Estado en Controversias Internacionales de Inversión (SICRECI)   87
  social unrest   82, 83–84, 88
  see also Peru-Chile FTA; Peru-China FTA; Peru-US FTA, Peruvian Constitutional Tribunal
Peru-Chile FTA
  Constitutional Tribunal's ruling on   105–6
Peru-China FTA
  Constitutional Tribunal's ruling on   107–8
Peru-US FTA
  Constitutional Tribunal's rulings on   101–5
Peru, constitution of 1979,   90–91, 95

Peru, constitution of 1993: on economic
   system 90, 91–92
  introduction of 89
  on protection of foreign investors 91–92
  on ratification of treaties 90
  references to social and economic
   rights 90, 91–92
  on rights of Indigenous Peoples 90–91
Peruvian Tribunal of Constitutional
   Guarantees 92, 95
Peruvian Constitutional Tribunal
  amparo cases 92–93, 96–97
  appointments to 92–93
  decision rule 95
  consultation with Indigenous Peoples 99–100
  executive branch relations 95–96
  investor protections 97
  jurisdiction of 92–93
  on social market economy 90
  Peru-US FTA (No. 1), ruling on 101–3
  Peru-US FTA (No. 2), ruling on 103–4
  Peru-US FTA (No. 3), ruling on 104–5
  Peru-Chile FTA, ruling on 105–6
  Peru-China FTA, ruling on 107–8
  statistics of cases reviewed by 93–94
  strategic behaviour 93–94
Philippines Constitution 3, 185
Philippine Supreme Court 3, 185
Planet Mining PLC 144
Ponce, Aldo Fernando 93
portfolio investment, (non-direct foreign
   investment) 53, 66n.120
  see also Court of Justice of the European
   Union (CJEU)
precautionary principle in treaties 58–59, 63–64,
   75, 76, 112, 113–14
  definition of 113n.26
  investment arbitration 59, 59n.64
problem-solving theory 188–89, 198
  vs. critical theory 188
Propst, Robert Bruce 46–47
PT Newmont Nusa Tenggara (PTNNT)
   147–48

Quebec
  legal proceedings 29
  participation in international affairs 28–29

Rapoport, Cécile 59–60, 61–62
Red Eagle v. Colombia 112, 131t, 132
regimes
  domination within 12–13, 18, 23

  formation and maintenance of 6–7
  protection of investors and 92, 199–200
regime collision 4n.26
Reich, Arie 179
Reinisch, August 189
Ridlatama group 144, 145–46
Riffel, Christian 72n.157
Ríos-Figueroa, Julio 92, 94
Robert-Cuendet, Sabrina 57–58
Roberts, John Glover, Justice 49
Rodriguez, Cesar 124
Rodriguez-Raga, Juan Carlos 126
Roux, Theunis 163–64
Rubinstein, Elyakim, Justice 181–83, 184

Safaat, Muchammad Ali 156
Samper, Ernesto 125
Sands, Philippe 85–86, 111, 114
Schill, Stephan W, 196
Schmitt, Carl 120–21
Schnapper, Dominique 60–61
Schwarzenberger, Georg 41–42
Scott, Dayna Nadine 35
Scott, James 14–15
  see also transcripts
separation of powers 16–17
Shamgar, Meir 172–73
Shany, Yuval 176–77
Shiva, Vandana 200
shrinking (diminution of) policy space 3, 4,
   10–11, 15, 16, 18, 20–21, 29, 62, 75–76,
   82, 101–2, 107, 108–9, 138–39, 159, 161,
   163, 167
  see also chilling effect
Siregar, Fritz 163–64
Skougaerskiy, Dmitriy 13, 195–96
Slovak Republic
  Achmea B.V. v. The Slovak Republic 66–67,
   141n.221
societal constitutionalism 196, 197
soft deference 10, 11f, 15, 21–22, 78,
   111, 135–36
  vs. hard deference 10, 11f, 19, 20, 21, 78,
   82, 108–9
  see also individual courts
soft defiance 10, 11f, 14–15, 21–23, 111, 135–36,
   143, 157, 163, 185–86
  vs. hard defiance 10–11, 11f
  see also individual courts
Sohlberg, Noam, Justice 181, 183, 185–86
Somek, Alexander 189
Sornarajah, M 31–32n.27, 33–34, 178–79

South Korea
  Constitutional Court 154–55
  opposition to ISDS 2–3
stabilization clauses in state contracts 165–66, 182–83
states *see* capital-exporting; capital-importing
Stover, David 184
Stratas, David W, 38–39
Sudarsono, Sudarsono 156
Suez, Sociedad General de Aguas de Barcelona, S.A. and Vivendi Universal, S.A. v. Argentine 167–70
Suharto, President of Indonesia 150–51, 154
Sukarno, President of Indonesia 150–51
Supreme Court of Canada
  equality analysis 73
  executive branch and 33–34n.42
  Hunt v. T&N PLC 29
  lack of constitutional courage 30
  reasoning of 19
  recognition of extra-provincial legal proceedings 29
systems theory 197–98
  see also regime collision; societal constitutionalism

Tamayo-Álvarez, Rafael 141–42
Tams, Christian J, 196
Taufik, Giri Ahmad 152
Tecnicas Medioambientales TECMED S.A. v. Mexico 191–92
Teubner, Gunther 197, 198
theory
  critical 188
  problem solving 188–89, 198
  see also systems theory
Third Restatement of the Foreign Relations Law of the United States 34–35
Thomas, Christopher 36–39
Tiede, Lydia Brashear 93
Tobie Mining 115–16, 132
Trade Promotion Authority Act of 2002, 43–44
Transatlantic Trade and Investment Partnership (TTIP) 43–44, 62, 196
transcripts
  public and private 14–15
  vs. hidden 14–16
  see also James Scott

Trans-Pacific Partnership (TPP) 43–44, 49
  see also Comprehensive and Progressive Agreement for Trans-Pacific Partnership
Trump, Donald 44, 44n.114
tutela cases 119, 124, 124n.116
  see also Colombian Constitutional Court

UNCITRAL Working Group III 116–17, 150, 170–71
United Kingdom
  bilateral investment treaty with Colombia 3, 127–30, 194–95
  investment treaty negotiations 51–52
  see also Colombia-UK BIT
United Mizrahi Bank plc. v. Migdal Cooperative Village 171–73, 176–77
United Nations Conference on Trade and Development (UNCTAD) 81–82, 87, 149–50
United Parcel Service (UPS) 30–31
  see also *CUPW v. Canada*
United States
  Articles of Confederation 39–40
  congressional-executive agreements 40–41, 46–48
  equal protection doctrine 43, 43n.107
  foreign investment policy 43–45, 50
  friendship, commerce and navigation (FCN) treaties 42
  Jay Treaty 41–42
  judicial engagement with investment law 46–48
  Made in the USA Foundation v. United States 46–48
  Trade Act of 1974 41
  Trade Promotion Authority Act of 2002 43–44
  treaty-making practice 39–41, 43
  United Steelworkers v. American Manufacturing 48–49
  see also United States-Korea Free Trade Agreement, United States Trade Representative
United States-Korea Free Trade Agreement (KORUS-FTA) 3
United States Supreme Court
  Baker v. Carr 46–47
  BG Group v. Argentina 48–29

Marbury v. Madison 46–47, 172–73
Penn Central Transportation Co v. New York City 43
United States Trade Representative (USTR) 43–45, 49
United Steelworkers v. American Manufacturing 48–49
Uprimny, Rodrigo 124–25
US constitutional law
  influence of 43–44, 196

Vandevelde, Kenneth J, 42
Van Harten, Gus 35, 36–37, 38–39, 192–93
Vastardis, Yilmaz 199
Vattenfall 62
Vélez, Luis Guillermo 116
Verdier, Pierre-Hugues 17–18
Vergara, Alberto 94–95

Versteeg, Mila 17–18
Vienna Convention on the Law of Treaties (VCLT) 16, 69–70, 76

Waelde, Thomas W 165
Wahid, Abdurrahman 153–54
Watanabe, Aaron 94–95
Weill, Rivka 172–73, 177
Weimar Constitution of 1919 120–21, 121n.86
Witte, Inga 196–97
World Trade Organization (WTO), also General Agreement on Tariffs and Trade (GATT) 3, 52, 63n.104, 69–70, 84–85, 97n.131

Yudhoyono, Susilo Bambang 143–44, 147–48, 149, 153–54

Zamir, Yitzhak, Justice 174
Zuleta-Londono, Alberto 115–16